Smith County, Tennessee

DEEDS

- Vol. 2 -

1835-1852

Compiled By:

Thomas E. Partlow

Southern Historical Press, Inc.
Greenville, South Carolina

Copyright © 1997
 By Southern Historical Press, Inc.

All rights reserved. No part of this publication may be reproduced, stored in a retrieval system or transmitted in nay form or by any means without the prior permission of the publisher.

Please Direct all Correspondence & Orders to:

**Southern Historical Press, Inc.
P.O. Box 1267
375 West Broad Street
Greenville, S.C. 29602-1267**

ISBN # 0-89308-383-6

Printed in the United States of America

This Book

is

Respectfully Dedicated

To

My Friends

JIMMY C. McCULLOUGH

&

PHYLLIS MASON McCULLOUGH

PREFACE

The earliest deeds in Smith County are located in the Register's Office at Carthage. These deed abstracts contain all pertinent genealogical information found in the Register's Office. If the place of residence is not given for the individual, then that person resided in Smith County.

Many of the records are difficult to read. If there are any doubts as to accuracy, it is suggested that the original records be checked. Copies of the originals can be obtained by writing to the State Library in Nashville. In so doing, it is necessary to quote the name of the book and page number desired.

Thomas E. Partlow
Lebanon, Tennessee

DEED BOOK N

Thomas Felton to John Hale 40 acres. 26 October 1835. (P. 1)

Moses Fite to Obadiah M. Garrison 103 acres. 25 April 1835. (Pp. 1-2)

Archibald O. Greer to David Goodall a tract of land that he received as an heir of Andrew Greer deceased. 10 November 1835. (P. 2)

Joseph Adamson to Sarah Mullinax a tract of land on Clear Fork. 16 May 1834. (P. 3)

Jonathan Griffith to David Griffith a tract of land on Helton's Creek. 15 January 1836. (Pp. 3-4)

Dan C. Finley to Henry H. Jones some livestock. 27 February 1836. (Pp. 4-5)

Lot Hazard to H. H. Jones, John Morris, Jacob K. Spooner James H. Jones, W. E. Jones, William A. Riley, Henry Spencer, D. A. Crenshaw, J. H. Hunt, C. M. Hazard, Thomas Black, Dan C. Dixon, A. J. Goodloe, John G. Park, G. B. McNeill, John H. Trigg, and Washington Meachum a tract of land in the town of Carthage. 2 March 1836. (Pp. 5-6)

Micajah Kettle to John S. Carter, trustee of Dicking Ward, some personal property. 27 February 1836. (Pp. 6-7)

David Perkins, Sr. to Allen Piper a tract of land formerly owned by Robert Bowman deceased. 14 December 1833. (Pp. 8-9)

William Cook to Davidson Draper and Robert C. Glover 150 acres. 21 February 1836. (P. 9)

Simon P. Hughes to Davidson Draper a tract of land on Indian Creek. 29 May 1828. (P. 10)

William Cook to Davidson Draper 30 acres. 10 March 1831. (P. 11)

George R. Dillard to Davidson Draper 25 acres. 8 January 1835. (Pp. 11-12)

Daniel Smith to William Draper a tract of land on Defeated Creek. 2 January 1836. (P. 12)

Alessander Dillard to Samuel Caplinger and Jesse Lancaster some livestock. 17 February 1836. (P. 13)

James Malone to Josiah Whitley a tract of land. 30 November 1835. (Pp. 13-14)

William Overstreet to Patrick Hubbard a tract of land on the south side of the Cumberland River. 13 March 1832. (Pp. 14-15)

Hardy Jones to Jesse Gray 57½ acres. 28 February 1834. (P. 15)

Jacob Fite to Nathan Evans 113 acres. 6 February 1836. (P. 16)

DEED BOOK N

Robert Williams to Nicholas Waggoner 30½ acres. 5 September 1835. (P. 17)

Tilmon Norris to William C. Towson a tract of land in the town of Rome. 183?. (P. 17)

Matthias Scudder to Dabney Lancaster. 21 March 1836. (P. 18)

James Beloat, Sr. to Stephen Roland a tract of land on Mulherin's Creek. 10 October 1835. (Pp. 18-19)

Josiah Marshall to John Rankin eight acres on Goose Creek. 30 January 1834. (Pp. 19-20)

William Floyd to James Eaton 100 acres. 1 November 1830. (Pp. 20-21)

Samuel Burdine to Wesley (Mates) one fourth of an acre. 3 November 1835. (P. 21)

Samuel Burdine to James Pope a tract of land. 28 January 1832. (Pp. 21-22)

David Robertson to Daniel Robertson a certain negro boy slave. 2 March 1834. (P. 22)

Jacob S. Johnson, administrator of John Johnson, to William C. Bransford a tract of land on Goose Creek. 16 October 1835. (P. 23)

George Hamilton to Thomas J. Hubbard a tract of land in the town of Rome. 7 January 1836. (P. 24)

Fielden Waldon to S. E. Belcher of Wilson County 69 acres on Brush Creek. 16 October 1835. (Pp. 24-25)

Mary Glenn and Patsy Tally of Sumner County to Cyrus W. Brevard a tract of land on Goose Creek. 27 January 1836. (Pp. 25-26)

Woodson Fitts to Daniel Wilkerson a tract of land on Bluff Creek. 23 November 1835. (Pp. 26-27)

J. W. Paty to Simon Jones 100 acres. 20 February 1836. (Pp. 27-28)

Henry B. McDonald to Thomas Walker his interest in a tract of land. 7 March 1835. (P. 28)

Randolph Murry to Daniel Glover a tract of land on Hurricane Creek. 12 January 1835. (Pp. 28-29)

Stephen Bridges to Allen J. Bridges 150 acres. 18 September 1827. (P. 29)

John Meaders to Marcus L. Donoho a tract of land. 2 November 1835. (Pp. 30-31)

John H. Wilbourn of Allen County, Kentucky to Benjamin Wilbourn his interest in the estate of Sarah Ligon. Said Sarah received a child's part of Arthur Heron's estate. 4 February 1836. (P. 31)

DEED BOOK N

William P. Lawrence, executor of L. Bigelow, to Abraham H. King a tract of land in the town of Carthage. 19 March 1836. (Pp. 32-33)

Thomas L. Knight to John Knight a tract of 70 acres. 20 September 1835. (P. 33)

Frederick Mitchell to John A. Debow a tract of land on Goose Creek. 5 January 1836. (P. 34)

Joel Dyer to Daniel Smith a tract of land on the Cumberland River. 8 February 1836. (P. 35)

William F. McDaniel to Thomas A. Lancaster some personal property. 20 February 1836. (P. 36)

Mary Grant to Elijah C. Davis a tract of land on Goose Creek. 1 December 1835. (Pp. 36-37)

Wilson T. Meader to Daniel L. Taylor, Reason Barrow, and Robert L. Taylor a tract of land on Goose Creek. 5 February 1836. (Pp. 37-38)

Thomas L. Hardy to William Uhls 70 acres on Goose Creek. 24 June 1835. (P. 39)

Joshua Morris to Fieldon Waldon a tract of land. 26 September 1835. (Pp. 39-40)

Lemuel Turney from Drury Spurlock a tract of land. 11 March 1836. (Pp. 40-41)

James Eaton to Isaac Jones 100 acres on Hickman's Creek. 21 December 1833. (Pp. 41-42)

Hezekiah Robertson to Jane Maggard a tract of land. 1836. (P. 42)

Nathan Evans to Peter Hays 121½ acres. 18 December 1832. (P. 43)

William Cleveland to Andrew Payne. 8 April 1836. (P. 44)

Jane Stephens to Hopkins Richardson five negroes. 26 March 1836. (Pp. 44-45)

William Williaz and Margaret Williaz of Jackson County to H. Richardson five negroes. 24 March 1836. (P. 45)

Uel Gregory to Jesse Hard a tract of land. 31 January 1835. (Pp. 45-46)

Peter Wynn to James Depres of Miami County, Ohio a tract of land. 9 October 1818. (Pp. 46-47)

William Alexander from Elijah Simms some livestock. 1 April 1836. (Pp. 47-48)

STATE OF TENNESSEE Grant. No. 3277. 110 acres to Elias Overall. 6 August 1811. (P. 49)

Administrator of George B. Pierce to Benjamin Pierce. 21 April 1836. (Pp. 49-50)

DEED BOOK N

Agreement between Jacob S. Yerger, administrator of George B. Pierce, and Benjamin Pierce, administrator and surviving partner of George Pierce deceased and executor of Elizabeth H. Pierce. 21 April 1836. (Pp. 51-52)

Benjamin Clardy to B. F. Morris a tract of land on Goose Creek. 12 November 1835. (P. 53)

John Tibbs of White County to Amzi C. Patterson of Cannon County a tract of land on the Caney Fork. 7 March 1836. (P. 54)

Endyman Taylor and Robert L. Taylor to Franklin B. Day a negro woman. 21 September 1835. (P. 55)

James Evans to John S. Vaughn a tract of land in the town of Liberty. 9 November 1835. (Pp. 55-56)

Elijah Hale to William Flowers, Sr. a tract of land on Fall Creek. 16 April 1836. (Pp. 56-57)

David Stanford to Milton Cary and his wife Phebe C. Cary a tract of land for the love and affection that the said David has for his sister in law, the said Phebe C. Cary. Children of the said Carys are Beverly Cary, Mary Jane Cary, and Ann Eliza Cary. 4 April 1836. (Pp. 57-58)

Isham Beasley to James Bradley a tract of land on the Cumberland River. 20 April 1836. (P. 59)

John H. Burford to James S. Murphree a tract of land. 15 January 1835. (Pp. 59-60)

James Rucks to Nelson Thornton a town lot in the town of Carthage. 22 April 1835. (P. 60)

Joseph Cartwright to Reuben Turner a tract of land on Peyton's Creek. 4 April 1836. (P. 61)

Elizabeth Pryor to Elihu Wood a negro woman. 21 August 1834. (P. 61)

John Hooker to Lewis Allison a tract of land on Mulherin's Creek. 5 May 1836. (P. 62)

William Escum to Dempsy Powel a tract of land. 6 March 1835. (Pp. 62-63)

Thomas Walker of Wilson County to John Hooker a tract of land on Brush Creek. 2 May 1836. (P. 63)

John Hooker to Isaac H. Davis a tract of land on Mulherin's Creek. 25 December 1835. (P. 64)

James Fagg of Sumner County to Jesse B. Kerby a tract of land on Barren River. 8 June 1835. (Pp. 64-65)

Isaac Moore to Ely Davis a tract of land on Brush Creek. 10 February 1834. (Pp. 65-66)

Drury Andrews to John McDonald 150 acres. 6 May 1829. (P. 66)

DEED BOOK N

James Walton and Timothy Walton to David Roland a tract of land on the Caney Fork. 13 May 1836. (P. 67)

Isaac Morris to John Luckey a tract of land on Hickman's Creek. 19 September 1835. (P. 68)

John B. Armstrong to Robert Hodges a tract of land. Said John B. is the husband of Nancy Armstrong. 1 December 1835. (P. 69)

Robert Hodges and wife Elizabeth and John Turner to John B. Armstrong and wife Nancy a tract of land. 1 December 1835. (Pp. 70-71)

John B. Armstrong and wife Nancy and Robert Hodges and wife Elizabeth to John Turner their interest in a tract of land on Round Lick Creek, it being a tract of land owned by Benjamin Turner. John Turner is the brother of Robert Turner. 1 December 1835. (Pp. 71-72)

John H. Trigg to John Stevens. 10 May 1836. (Pp. 73-74)

Hezekiah Sloan to C. Cliborn a tract of land. 28 December 1835. (P. 74)

David Jones to Thomas Reed a tract of land on Goose Creek. 12 May 1835. (P. 75)

Henry Lyon to Sullivan & Hall a tract of land in the town of Carthage. 6 June 1818. (P. 76)

The administrators of James Cook relinquish their claims to a tract of land. 1818. (P. 76)

Henry Lyon to Sullivan & Hall a tract of land. 6 June 1818. (Pp. 77-78)

E. C. Davis to B. S. Dalton a tract of land. 20 May 1836. (Pp. 78-79)

James Herrod, Mary Ann Lane, formerly Mary Ann Herrod, and David M. Lane of Obion County appoint Hopkins Richardson as their attorney in settling the estate of William Herrod. 17 May 1836. (P. 79)

David M. Lane and James Herrod to Hopkins Richardson their interest in some slaves. 18 May 1836. (Pp. 80-81)

Horace Oliver to O. B. Hubbard a tract of land. 3 June 1836. (P. 82)

Joshua Hadley to Patrick McEachern a tract of land on Hickman's Creek. 10 September 1814. (P. 83)

Joseph Butts to Joseph D. Lucas a tract of land. 7 June 1836. (Pp. 83-84)

Joseph D. Lucas to Thomas Jackson 25 acres. 8 June 1836. (Pp. 84-85)

William McClain to Marcellus Mitchell a negro man. 28 March 1836. (P. 85)

DEED BOOK N

Henry J. Murry to Lot Hazard. 4 June 1836. (Pp. 85-86)

Samuel P. Howard to John Cochran a tract of land. 4 June 1836. (Pp. 86-88)

Booker Dalton to E. C. F. Donoho a tract of land on Goose Creek. 1 March 1836. (Pp. 88-89)

Isaac Davis to John Grandstaff a tract of land on Brush Creek. 13 September 1834. (Pp. 89-90)

James Dobbins to Drury Andrews a tract of land on Peyton's Creek. 19 February 1830. (Pp. 90-91)

Rice M. Ballew to Thomas Phelps some personal property. 21 June 1836. (Pp. 91-92)

William Burk to John Ramsay a tract of land on the Caney Fork. 21 December 1835. (Pp. 92-93)

Zadock B. Thackston to William Young a gray mare. 2 January 1833. (Pp. 93-94)

Adam Ferguson of Marshall County, Mississippi to Patrick Ferguson a tract of land. 28 June 1836. (P. 94)

Samuel P. Howard to William Newbell a tract of land on Snow Creek. 5 July 1836. (P. 95)

Pleasant Chitwood to Samuel (Dewhit) several tracts of land. 4 June 1836. (Pp. 95-96)

John W. Mann to William D. Evans a tract of land on Snow Creek. 23 November 1835. (P. 96)

John Buckner to James Wootten a tract of land. 27 May 1836. (P. 97)

Thomas Baliff to James Wootten a tract of land. 25 June 1836. (P. 98)

Thomas Baliff to Joseph Wootten a tract of land. 4 June 1836. (Pp. 98-99)

Frederick Decker to James Wootten a tract of land. 25 June 1836. (Pp. 99-100)

William N. Mitchell from A. Worthy. 11 July 1836. (Pp. 100-101)

William Newbell to Jesse Meacham a tract of land on Snow Creek. 9 July 1836. (Pp. 101-102)

William Massey to Thomas Owens a tract of land on the Cumberland River. 28 July 1832. (P. 102)

John B. Uhls to John Wilson some personal property. 12 July 1836. (P. 103)

William Massey to Thomas Owens a tract of land. 28 July 183?. (Pp. 103-104)

William Patterson to Benjamin Parrott a tract of land.

DEED BOOK N

1836. (Pp. 104)

Creed Penn to John S. Page some personal property. 4 July 1836. (P. 105)

Claborn Wilson and Michal L. Uhls to Bartlett B. Uhls a tract of land. 20 July 1836. (P. 106)

Arthur L. Hogan of Franklin County, Alabama to Benjamin (Denny) a tract of land. 2 October 1835. (Pp. 106-107)

William Newby to James Gill a tract of land. 24 June 1835. (Pp. 107-108)

John Seay to Ervin Bell a tract of land on Round Lick Creek. 13 March 1835. (Pp. 108-109)

Frederick Decker to James Wootten 30 acres. 27 May 1836. (Pp. 109-110)

William Allen to E. Harrison a tract of land on Mulherin's Creek. 30 July 1836. (Pp. 110-111)

Thomas Bishop to Burton Allen some livestock. 2 August 1836. (Pp. 111-112)

Thomas Hickman to William Dale a tract of land. 16 April 1823. (Pp. 112-113)

William L. Martin and wife Sarah S., formerly Sarah S. Greer and one of the heirs of Andrew Green, a tract of land. 4 July 1836. (P. 113)

Henry Mark to Charles Mark 150 acres. 16 March 1829. (P. 114)

John Minton to William Hodges a crop of corn. 3 August 1836. (Pp. 114-115)

Stephen Johnson to William Dixon, David Bratton, and J. B. Short some livestock. 26 July 1836. (Pp. 115-116)

Benjamin Parrott to John G. Park some personal property. 1 August 1836. (P. 116)

John Gordon to William Bailey 80 acres. 13 July 1836. (P. 117)

Henry L. Day to Franklin B. Day a sorrel horse. 1 August 1836. (P. 117)

William Nichols to Marcellus Mitchell 41½ acres. 1 August 1836. (P. 118)

Henry L. Day to John Stafford and Franklin B. Day some livestock. 4 August 1836. (P. 119)

Lawrence Thompson bound to Bannaster W. Mading. 3 November 1827. (Pp. 119-120)

Zachariah Alues to Henry Williams a tract of land on Plunkett's Creek. 14 July 1836. (Pp. 120-121)

DEED BOOK N

Henry L. Day to Franklin B. Day a tract of land on Dixon's Lick Creek. 1 August 1836. (P. 121)

James Uhls to Robert L. Taylor a tract of land. 13 November 1835. (Pp. 121-122)

Thomas Mading to H. H. Johnson a crop of tobacco. 3 August 1836. (P. 122)

D. C. Moore and W. B. Moore transaction. 30 July 1836. (P. 123)

Archibald Thompson and his wife Elizabeth quit claim deed to Cyrus W. Brevard. 7 May 1836. (P. 124)

David Thomason to Pleasant Thomason a tract of land. 13 December 1834. (Pp. 124-125)

William S. Duncan and wife Nancy, John Lipscomb and wife Sarah to James Wadmore a tract of land. 13 June 1836. (Pp. 125-126)

Stephen Debow to Lawrence Thompson a tract of land on Dixon and Goose Creeks. 2 August 1836. (P. 127)

Vardaman Parker to Goolsberry Parker a gray mare. July 1836. (P. 128)

Sterling (   ) to John Lancaster a negro boy. 15 December 1834. (P. 128)

Henry Linville and wife Emily to William Linville. 15 August 1836. (Pp. 129-130)

William Stanley to Matthew Tunstall a crop of corn. 19 August 1836. (P. 130)

John Gwaltney and Godfrey Gregory to Wesley Harvey a tract of land. 20 August 1836. (P. 131)

Wilson Meaders to John Block a tract of land on Goose Creek. 8 June 1836. (Pp. 131-132)

Thomas Young married Sally Martin, daughter of William Martin, in 1817. Said William to his daughter and son in law several slaves. 23 August 1836. (P. 133)

William Alexander to James H. Vaughan a tract of land at Dixon's Spring. 15 January 1836. (P. 134)

Andrew G. Ford to Reason Barrow a tract of land on Goose Creek. 19 August 1836. (Pp. 134-135)

William Dillard and Alexander Dillard to William Petty 58 acres. 27 July 1831. (P. 135)

Young Morgan to William F. Gleaves a tract of land on Payton's Creek. 7 February 1832. (P. 136)

Andrew G. Ford to Robert Adams a tract of land on Goose Creek. 1 May 1810. (P. 137)

George Goad to Draper Huddleston. August 1836. (Pp. 137-138)

DEED BOOK N

Jacob K. Spooner to Andrew Payne and Francis H. Gordon. 24 August 1836. (Pp. 138-139)

Lindsey Mann to William Garner. 15 August 1836. (Pp. 139-140)

Reuben Johnson to James Yeargin a tract of land on Dismal Street. 10 January 1832. (Pp. 140-141)

Abner Lack to Samuel Caplinger a tract of land on Smith's Fork. 17 January 1833. (P. 141)

Daniel W. Mentlo to Alfred A. Brevard a tract of land on Goose Creek. 25 October 1833. (P. 142)

Randolph Murray to William Snider a crop of tobacco. 21 August 1836. (P. 143)

Martin Shoemake to William Snider a crop of tobacco. 23 August 1836. (Pp. 143-144)

Jacob Fowler to Alexander A. Short 130 acres on Goose Creek. 10 March 1834. (Pp. 144-145)

Jacob M. Shoemake, the son of Martin Shoemake, and Parker Shoemake, also the son of Martin Shoemake, transaction. 19 August 1836. (P. 145)

Edward Sweatt of Wilson County and Joseph Bradford and Samuel Walker to John Moore a tract of land on Mulherin's Creek. 8 April 1836. (P. 146)

James Green to Robert Allen, Jr. some personal property. 27 August 1836. (Pp. 146-147)

William Lynn to John Moore some livestock. 27 August 1836. (Pp. 147-148)

James W. Smith, executor of John Owen, to Drury Denton. 25 August 1836. (Pp. 148-149)

Samuel P. Howard to Frederick Uhls a tract of land on the Cumberland River. 23 August 1836. (P. 150)

Jacob Young to Sarah Wallis a tract of land on Rock Spring Creek. 29 June 1834. (P. 151)

Elijah Haynie to Thomas Weatherford 135 acres. 11 August 1836. (P. 152)

William Owen, executor of Benjamin Roe, to John Williams a tract of land. 14 May 1836. (Pp. 152-153)

Frederick Uhls to John Parker a tract of land. 5 October 1833. (Pp. 153-154)

Sheriff Samuel P. Howard to Swan Thompson. 27 August 1836. (P. 154)

William Linville to William B. Reece a tract of land on Goose Creek. 8 August 1833. (P. 155)

Reuben Johnson to Thomas Whaley a tract of land near the

DEED BOOK N

town of Liberty. 4 August 1829. (P. 156)

William Collie to John Parker 50 acres. 5 October 1833. (P. 157)

Jacob Young to Sarah Wallis 100 acres. 29 June 1834. (Pp. 158-159)

James Shelton to Elisha Walker 230 acres. 16 July 1836. (Pp. 159-160)

John A. Debow to Thomas Porter a tract on Dixon's Lick. 11 January 1836. (Pp. 160-161)

James Birchett to John L. Carter. 29 August 1836. (Pp. 161-162)

D. C. Ward, William B. Moore, and A. Moore to Mary Ann Elizabeth McCall a tract of land. 28 May 1836. (Pp. 162-163)

James McCormack, John McCormack, and Chaffin McCormack to James Young. 3 September 1836. (P. 163)

D. C. Ward and others to Joseph McCall a tract of land near the town of Rome. 28 May 1836. (P. 164)

D. C. Ward and others to John McCall a tract of land in the town of Rome. 28 May 1836. (Pp. 164-165)

D. C. Ward and others to David McCall one fourth of an acre. 28 May 1836. (Pp. 165-166)

Hiram H. Johnson to Humphrey and Samuel Smithwick a tract of land on Dixon's Creek. 20 April 1835. (Pp. 166-167)

Robert Bowman to Branch Nunley a tract of land on the Cumberland River. 6 September 1836. (Pp. 167-168)

Wilson Butts to John Stallings 100 acres. 8 January 1835. (P. 168)

Robert Craighead to William Snider a crop of tobacco. 9 September 1836. (P. 169)

Allen Piper to Elijah S. Banks 118 acres. 12 March 1836. (P. 170)

Robert Bowman and Joseph Bowman to Pauline Hester, Sarah Hester, John Hester, and James Hester a tract of land on Spring Creek. 9 June 1836. (P. 171)

Stephen Haynes to John Black a crop of tobacco. 27 August 1836. (P. 172)

John Bell to Gideon H. Bransford a crop of corn. 7 September 1836. (P. 173)

Samuel N. Robinson to Joel Holloman a crop of corn and tobacco. 9 September 1836. (P. 174)

Joseph Bowman to Branch Nunley ten acres. 1836. (P. 174)

DEED BOOK N

James Walton and Timothy Walton to Joseph H. Durham a tract of land on Snow Creek. 6 September 1836. (P. 175)

Isaac H. Davis from James F. Gains his interest in the dower which descended to Eliza M. Jenkins, the late widow of Joseph Jenkins. 1836. (Pp. 175-176)

Evan Williams to John Enose a tract of land. 18 July 1835. (P. 176)

Henry Hallum to Jefferson Thomas a tract of land. 12 September 1836. (P. 177)

Frances Adams to William Snider a tract of land on Defeated Creek. 8 September 1836. (Pp. 177-178)

Frederick Uhls to his son William a tract of land on the Cumberland River. 10 September 1836. (Pp. 178-179)

Samuel Hughes to William Snider a crop of tobacco. 13 September 1836. (P. 180)

Joel Holladay to William Snider a crop of tobacco. 12 September 1836. (Pp. 180-181)

John A. Hughes to William Snider a small filly. 20 August 1836. (Pp. 181-182)

Allen Holladay to William Snider a crop of tobacco. 12 September 1836. (P. 182)

James Fentress to David Dies 107 acres. 2 November 1835. (P. 183)

Roland Clark to Martin H. (   ) a crop of tobacco. 7 September 1836. (Pp. 183-184)

James Martin to John G. Martin a tract of land on the Cumberland. 16 April 1836. (P. 184)

Joel Towler to James Jones ten acres. 25 October 1833. (P. 185)

Raleigh Farley of Buckingham County, Virginia to his wife Mary Farley and William, John, Mary, and Emily Farley their children some negro slaves for love and affection. 1 August 1835. (P. 186)

Rufus Ledbetter to Joshua Goad 112 acres on the Cumberland River. 8 June 1836. (P. 187)

Archibald P. Furguson to Hugh Ferguson a tract of land. 16 October 1835. (P. 188)

Thomas Bradley to James A. Taylor 100 acres. 9 December 1835. (P. 189)

Larkin K. Austin to Samuel Thomason a crop of tobacco. 17 September 1836. (P. 190)

James Taylor to William Kyle 100 acres on Dixon's Creek. 16 September 1836. (Pp. 190-191)

DEED BOOK N

Richard Stone to William Wade some livestock. 15 August 1836. (P. 192)

John Stevens to H. B. McDonald a tract of land in the town of Carthage. 10 September 1836. (Pp. 192-193)

Wilson T. Meader to Alexander A. Short a tract of land in Meaderville. 5 February 1836. (P. 193)

William Young to Arris McCall a tract of land on Defeated Creek. 8 December 1835. (P. 194)

Simon P. Hughes to Horace Oliver a tract of land on the Cumberland River. 16 September 1836. (P. 195)

Wiatt W. Bailey to Sally Baker and her children, Mary Marinda, Louisa, and John a tract of 124 acres on Mulherin's Creek. 20 September 1836. (P. 196)

Jesse Johnson to Samuel Smithwick a crop of tobacco. 23 September 1836. (P. 196)

Michael Reaves to Jeremiah Gammon a crop of corn and tobacco. 19 September 1836. (P. 197)

Wilson Butts to W. W. ( ) a tract of land. 13 September 1836. (Pp. 197-198)

Benjamin Thomason to William L. T. ( ) a tract of land. 27 September 1836. (Pp. 198-199)

John P. Erwin and his wife Easter of McNairy County, Tennessee to William Brandon, Jr. 127½ acres. 22 November 1835. (Pp. 199-200)

Thomas Hale to George Waggoner a tract of land on Hogan's Creek. 18 September 1835. (P. 200)

Thomas Gibbs to William A. Corley a crop of tobacco. 9 October 1836. (P. 201)

George Sutton to Leroy Sutton 269 acres. 21 August 1836. (P. 202)

James Evetts indebtedness to Andrew Payne. 15 October 1835. (P. 203)

Thomas A. Frohock to E. Harrison a crop of tobacco. 30 September 1836. (Pp. 203-204)

Elijah Williams to Charles Richards a crop of tobacco. 8 October 1836. (P. 204)

Graves Thurman to Thomas S. Sneed a crop of tobacco. 11 October 1836. (P. 205)

Byrd Orange to Yearby Orange 37 acres. 24 November 1834. (P. 206)

William J. Bennett to William Lack a tract of land in the town of Lancaster. 7 October 1836. (Pp. 207-208)

Elizabeth Burnett to James S. Murphree eight acres. 19

DEED BOOK N

September 1834. (P. 208)

Matthew Harper to Alfred Harper 62 acres on Mulherin's Creek. 27 August 1836. (P. 209)

John Dickens to William Crosslin 65 acres. 8 December 1835. (P. 210)

D. C. Ward and others to William Johnson of Wilson County one fourth of an acre. 28 May 1836. (P. 211)

D. C. Ward and others to P. M. Wade one fourth of an acre. 28 May 1836. (P. 212)

William Dickens to William Crosslin 20 acres. 8 March 1836. (P. 213)

Robert Lock of Rutherford County to Isaac Wiseman a tract of land on Goose Creek. 20 February 1826. (P. 214)

Elijah Wheeler to William Thomas 170 acres. 18 June 1836. (P. 215)

Samuel P. Howard to Nepthali Durham a tract of land. 19 October 1836. (Pp. 216-217)

Lawson Stinson of Jennings' County, Indiana to Josiah Roark a tract of land on White Oak Creek. 11 December 1822. (Pp. 217-218)

Sterling Hylten to William J. Bennett a tract of land. 5 October 1836. (Pp. 218-219)

D. C. Ward and others to F. S. Harris of Wilson County a tract of land in the town of Rome. 28 May 1836. (Pp. 219-220)

Jane Maggard to William Crosslin a tract of land on Hurricane Creek. 8 March 1836. (Pp. 220-221)

John G. Martin to James Martin a tract of land on the Cumberland River. 1836. (Pp. 221-222)

John L. Sanders to Matthew Tunstall a crop of tobacco. 15 October 1836. (P. 222)

William Crosslin to Wright W. Crosslin a tract of land on Hurricane Creek. 15 March 1836. (P. 223)

Joseph Davenport to John Franklin and Henry Franklin 300 acres. 25 October 1836. (P. 224)

William S. Fairstair to W. R. Hallum some personal property. 26 October 1836. (P. 225)

Joseph L. Wilson and his wife Margaret of Wilson County to James Barnett a tract of land on Plunkett's Creek. Bounded: Samuel Barton. Other names signing the deed were James L. Wilson and Ewing Wilson. 25 November 1835. (P. 226)

Michael Uhls to John Drury a tract of land on Goose Creek. 7 September 1835. (P. 227)

DEED BOOK N

William Exum to John L. Powell 18 acres. 20 October 1832. (P. 228)

William Exum to John L. Powell a tract of land on the Caney Fork. 20 October 1832. (Pp. 228-230)

John J. Read to Philip T. Day a crop of tobacco. 31 October 1836. (P. 230)

James Griffin to Joseph Grisham a crop of tobacco. 2 August 1836. (P. 231)

Joel Dyer to O. B. Hubbard a negro girl. 28 October 1836. (Pp. 232-233)

William Gregory to Gabriel Dillard a crop of tobacco. 2 November 1836. (P. 233)

Drury Arvin to Carter Guthrey some personal property. 10 October 1836. (P. 234)

Henry L. Day to John Wilson and Philip T. Day a crop of tobacco. 19 September 1836. (P. 234)

Simon P. Hughes to J. R. Hazard a tract of land. 9 November 1836. (P. 235)

Romulus M. Sanders of Washington City, Jourdan M. Sanders of Warrenton, Virginia, and Ethelbert W. Sanders of Dallas County, Alabama to Henderson Haley a tract of land on the Cumberland. 10 January 1836. (P. 236)

Peter Herod, executor of Solomon Key, to David Canaday a tract of land. 13 December 1835. (Pp. 237-238)

John B. Uhls to John Wilson a sorrel mare. 14 November 1836. (P. 238)

George White to James B. Sanders a tract of land on Long Creek. 19 October 1836. (P. 239)

John Cliburn and Daniel Cliburn to William King a tract of 75 acres. 6 June 1836. (P. 240)

Charles McCullock to Josiah Baird and Joseph Holmes a tract of land on Hickman's Creek. 25 January 1836. (Pp. 241-242)

Isum Beasley to Matilda Metcalf a negro girl. 3 November 1836. (Pp. 242-243)

Frederick Uhls to Frederick T. Uhls, Jr. a crop of tobacco. 24 September 1836. (Pp. 243-244)

Wesley Harvey to Stephen D. Easley $55\frac{1}{2}$ acres. 17 October 1836. (Pp. 244-245)

Cyrus Goodner to William Snider a tract of land on Defeated Creek. 23 November 1836. (Pp. 245-246)

Joshua Tramel to John C. Duffee. 25 November 1836. (Pp. 246-247)

DEED BOOK N

William Uhls to Moses B. Freeman 70 acres on Goose Creek. 17 September 1836. (P. 248)

William F. Gloves to Alfred M. Winkler a tract of land on Peyton's Creek. 11 January 1836. (P. 249)

William Dixon to V. R. Lovelady 50 acres. 24 November 1836. (P. 250)

Henry C. Jones to Littleberry Hughes a negro woman. 28 September 1836. (Pp. 251-252)

Mitchell Childrop to Samuel B. Chandler. 1 December 1836. (Pp. 252-253)

John Sims to William Carter a crop of tobacco. 2 December 1836. (P. 254)

Wesley Harvey to David Davis a tract of 130½ acres. 30 August 1836. (Pp. 254-255)

Theodrick Ferrell to Matthew Nichols a crop of tobacco. 5 December 1836. (P. 255)

Thomas Roberts of Davidson County to James Norris a tract of land in the town of Rome. 1 November 1836. (P. 256)

Talifaro Hammock to John C. and Francis Duffy of Sumner County a crop of tobacco. 5 December 1836. (P. 257)

Lewis Turner to Samuel L. Turner a tract of land on Puncheon Camp Creek. 3 August 1836. (Pp. 257-258)

Lewis Turner to John L. Turner a tract of land. 3 December 1836. (Pp. 258-259)

Daniel Roark of Allen County, Kentucky to Frances Benson a tract of land on Puncheon Camp Creek. 1 June 1836. (Pp. 259-260)

Lewis Turner to John Lewis Turner a tract of land on Puncheon Camp Creek. 3 December 1836. (Pp. 260-261)

George Marricle to James Shelton a tract of land on Round Lick Creek. 21 November 1836. (Pp. 261-262)

David Stanford to Milton Cary and his wife Phebe C. and they children A. Cary, Mary Jane Cary, Ann Eliza Cary, and Sarah Elizabeth Cary a tract of land. 3 December 1836. (Pp. 262-264)

John Couch to M. and P. Duffy, and John C. and Frances Duffy some livestock. 10 December 1836. (Pp. 264-265)

George Reed to James Piper a crop of tobacco. 10 December 1836. (P. 265)

Micajah Cardwell to William Robinson. 1836. (P. 266)

James Young of Jackson County to William Thomas some slaves for love and affection. 12 August 1836. (P. 266)

James W. Gibson to Matthew J. Tunstal a crop of tobacco.

DEED BOOK N

13 December 1836. (Pp. 267-268)

David Rowland to Stephen Mann and Matthew Nichols a tract of land on Snow Creek. 30 September 1836. (P. 268)

Alfred Ewing to William Beck a tract of land on the Caney Fork. 8 March 1836. (P. 269)

William Allen to John H. Bedford a crop of corn. 6 December 1836. (P. 270)

Alfred Ewing to William Beck 22 acres. 8 March 1836. (P. 269)

Frances Abby to M. and P. Duffy a crop of tobacco. 10 December 1836. (P. 271)

Andrew McClelin to Benjamin Payne a tract of land on Defeated Creek. 15 December 1836. (Pp. 271-272)

John W. Redmon to Leroy E. Mitchell some personal property. 29 December 1836. (Pp. 272-273)

Daniel Y. Shines, George Lovick and wife Phebe of Lenoir County, North Carolina to Green Wright a tract of land on Dixon's Creek. 19 September 1835. (Pp. 273-274)

Sheriff Samuel P. Howard to Joseph Collier a tract of land in the town of Liberty. 23 December 1836. (P. 275)

H. H. Johnson to Jesse D. Carr 186 acres. 10 December 1836. (P. 276)

Jesse M. Armsted to John Cooper a negro man. 24 December 1836. (P. 277)

Neill McKinnis to William T. Cornwell a tract of land on Jenning's Creek. 5 December 1836. (Pp. 277-278)

Arthur S. Hogan appointed attorney for Amanda Walker, wife of W. E. Walker, Harriett Goodall, wife of Isaac Goodall, Sarah Winter, wife of Thack Winter, and William B. Hogan. Said parties are residents of Franklin County, Alabama. 6 September 1836. (Pp. 278-279)

Malinda Rowland to Malinda Hall her interest in 100 acres on Goose Creek. 20 November 1836. (P. 279)

Thomas J. Hubbard and William W. Seay to Wesley Motes a tract of land in the town of Rome. 19 August 1836. (P. 280)

James McConnell to John C. and Frances Duffy some livestock. 22 December 1836. (P. 281)

John O. and Jonas Paty to Nancy and Polly Paty our share of what we may receive at the death of our mother. 10 December 1836. (P. 281)

Benjamin R. Owen to William Allen a tract of land. 8 December 1836. (P. 282)

Josephus C. Cowen to Allen and Owen a tract of land. 8 December 1836. (P. 283)

DEED BOOK N

William Overstreet to Green and Sloan. 29 December 1836. (P. 284)

Reuben Sims to Thomas Phelps. 28 November 1836. (P. 285)

William Sullivan of Tipton County and B. B. Sullivan of Shelby County transaction. 11 January 1836. (Pp. 286-287)

Ellis Beasley to Roseta Culbreath, wife of John Culbreath, James M. Culbreath, Hezekiah Culbreath, Amanda E. Culbreath, and Nancy Ann Culbreath, children of the said John and Roseta Culbreath a tract of land. 3 November 1836. (Pp. 287-288)

James Rowland bound to George W. Scoggins. 30 October 1834. (Pp. 288-289)

Eliza Goss of Davidson County to Richard Williams a tract of land on Big Barren River. 20 January 1834. (Pp. 289-290)

Samuel Kearby to Austin Kearby a tract of land on Defeated Creek. 12 December 1836. (Pp. 290-291)

Hiram H. Johnson to Matthew J. Tunstall 131 acres. 6 January 1837. (Pp. 291-292)

John Gunn to Pleasant C. Meader a tract of land on Big Barren River. Said Gunn is a resident of Monroe County, Kentucky. 21 August 1834. (P. 293)

James Freeman to John C. and Frances Duffy. 6 January 1837. (P. 294)

Richard Freeman to John C. and Frances Duffy a crop of tobacco. 6 January 1837. (P. 295)

Branch Grigg to Peter Grigg 40 acres. 29 December 1836. (P. 295)

Charles Goodall of Sumner County to John A. Adams 50 acres. 7 April 1835. (P. 396)

Peter Grigg and Branch Grigg to Rhodeham G. Bryant a tract of land on Goose Creek. 28 April 1836. (P. 297)

Asa Earp to Carter Guthrey a crop of tobacco. 9 January 1837. (P. 298)

B. W. Mading to Benjamin F. Morris a tract of land on Goose Creek. 2 January 1837. (P. 298)

Leroy P. Adams to Hiram C. Adams 59 acres. 2 January 1837. (P. 299)

Charles Goodall and Peter Grigg to Branch Grigg a tract of land on Goose Creek. 7 April 1835. (Pp. 299-300)

Banister W. Mading to William A. Corley a crop of tobacco. December 1836. (Pp. 301-302)

DEED BOOK N

Joseph Arnold to William S. Carter a tract of land on Goose Creek. 30 December 1836. (P. 303)

B. W. Mading to Othaniel ( ) a tract of land on Dixon's Creek. 10 December 1836. (Pp. 303-304)

Lawrence Thompson to B. W. Mading a tract of land on Dixon's and Goose Creeks. 9 December 1836. (P. 304)

B. W. Mading to Benjamin F. Moore a tract of land on Goose Creek. 9 December 1836. (P. 305)

Abraham Tubbs to James Winfrey 120 acres on Smith's Fork. 10 January 1837. (Pp. 305-306)

Stephen Robinson to Israel Bates a tract of land on Smith's Fork. 3 October 1836. (Pp. 306-307)

James McKee to A. H. King 40 acres. 13 January 1837. (Pp. 307-308)

John R. Palmore to Daniel Smith. 16 January 1837. (P. 308)

Elijah Toney of Jackson County, Alabama to George Stevens a tract of land on the Cumberland River. 13 January 1837. (P. 309)

Elijah Toney to Timothy Walton, Jr. a tract of land on the Cumberland River. 13 January 1837. (Pp. 309-310)

John Culbreath to Henderson Haley a crop of tobacco. January 1837. (P. 310)

H. H. Johnson to Frances Duffy. 17 January 1837. (P. 311)

Craven Maddux of Jackson County to Thomas Maddux some personal property for the use of Elizabeth Maddux, wife of the said Craven and mother of the said Thomas. 18 January 1837. (P. 312)

Joseph Davenport to Samuel McClelin a tract of land on Buffalo Creek. 18 August 1836. (Pp. 312-313)

John Williams to John C. and Frances Duffy some personal property. 20 January 1837. (P. 313)

H. H. Johnson to Frances Duffy a crib of corn. 21 January 1837. (Pp. 314-315)

Matthew Tunstall from H. H. Johnson. 6 January 1837. (Pp. 315-316)

Thomas Leath to John C. and Frances Duffy a crop of tobacco. 21 January 1837. (P. 316)

Jesse Gray to Guilford Jones. 23 January 1837. (P. 317)

Jesse Gray to Benjamin Jones a tract of land on Hurricane Creek. 23 January 1837. (Pp. 317-318)

DEED BOOK N

Carter Guthrey to D. I. Lake. 1837. (P. 318)

Carter Guthrey to Lawrence Thompson a tract of land on Goose Creek. 23 January 1837. (Pp. 318-319)

Carter Guthrey to John Wilson and Philip T. Day a crop of tobacco. 23 January 1837. (Pp. 319-320)

James Wooten to Christopher Buckman a tract of land. 23 January 1837. (P. 320)

Josiah Marshall to Archibald McNeill a tract of land on Goose Creek. 24 December 1836. (P. 321)

Jesse Cornwell to James Andrews a crop of tobacco. 23 January 1837. (Pp. 321-322)

Jacob Uhls to John Wilson and Philip T. Day a crop of tobacco. 25 January 1837. (P. 322)

James Wooten to Henry Buckman a tract of land. 26 January 1837. (P. 323)

Samuel Johnson of Franklin County, North Carolina to William Ashley a tract of land on Hickman's Creek. 17 October 1836. (Pp. 323-324)

Thomas B. Day to John Johnson 50 acres. 30 January 1837. (Pp. 324-325)

Daniel Buie to Andrew Boston a crop of tobacco. 27 January 1837. (P. 325)

Benjamin Matthews to William Snider. 1 February 1837. (P. 326)

Samuel Furlong to John C. and Frances Duffy a crop of tobacco. 1 February 1837. (Pp. 326-327)

John Barton to John Wilson a crop of tobacco. 2 February 1837. (P. 327)

Hugh B. Barton to Alfred A. Brevard indebtedness. 1 February 1837. (P. 328)

Cyrus Goodner to Jacob Goodner some personal property. 3 February 1837. (P. 329)

J. B. Carditt to Blake B. Thaxton a tract of land on the Cumberland River. 2 February 1837. (P. 330)

Isham Beasley to his grandson Anthony Harrison Metcalf, son of Anthony H. and Matilda Metcalf of Madison County, Alabama, a negro girl. 6 February 1837. (P. 330)

Samuel Evetts to William Snider a crop of tobacco. 10 February 1837. (P. 331)

Drury Andrews to John Henderson a tract of land on Barren River. 11 February 1837. (Pp. 331-332)

Samuel Furlong to Emanuel Harris some mares. 13 February 1837. (Pp. 332-333)

DEED BOOK N

James G. Gordon enters into an agreement with his father John Gordon. 1 February 1830. (Pp. 333-334)

Eli Butts to Peter A. Wilkerson. 3 February 1837. (Pp. 334-335)

Samuel F. Patterson to George W. Reasonover a tract of land on Hickman's Creek. 21 August 1835. (P. 335)

Thomas Smith to John C. and F. Duffy some livestock. 4 February 1837. (P. 336)

Elizabeth Burnett to George W. Tate a tract of land on the Cumberland River. 18 July 1836. (Pp. 336-337)

Samuel Smithwick to Humphrey Smithwick a tract of land. 2 September 1836. (Pp. 337-338)

Mary Fitts to Blake B. Thaxton a tract of land. 22 September 1835. (Pp. 338-339)

Isham Beasley to Ellis Beasley a tract of land. 1837. (P. 339)

Thomas Snoddy to J. B. Carter a tract of land owned by James Sims who has departed this life. 1837. (P. 340)

Burton Underwood to Wesley Motes a tract of land in the town of Rome. 16 December 1836. (P. 341)

D. C. Ward to Will B. Moore a tract of land. 20 October 1836. (Pp. 341-342)

Samuel Burdine to Mary A. Roundtree a tract of land in the town of Rome. 3 January 1837. (Pp. 342-343)

William Allen to James Harrison a tract of land on Mulherin's Creek. 20 February 1837. (P. 343)

William Allen to James Harrison a tract of land on Mulherin's Creek. 7 February 1837. (P. 344)

Rachel Patterson, executrix of William Patterson of Lincoln County, Tennessee, appoints John C. Patterson of Lincoln County as her attorney. 1837. (Pp. 342-343)

William Allen to James Harrison a tract of land on Mulherin's Creek. 20 February 1837. (P. 343)

William Allen to James Harrison a tract of land on Mulherin's Creek. 7 February 1837. (P. 344)

Rachel Patterson appoints John C. Patterson as her attorney. 15 February 1837. (Pp. 344-345)

Samuel Burdine to Benjamin W. Burford a tract of land in the town of Rome. 12 July 1836. (P. 345)

D. C. Ward and others to Owen Pope a tract of land. 23 March 1836. (P. 346)

Samuel Burdine to heirs of Turner Roundtree a tract of land in the town of Rome. 3 January 1837. (P. 347)

DEED BOOK N

John Page to Thomas W. Page a tract of land on the south side of the Cumberland River. 5 January 1837. (Pp. 347-348)

Archabald Thompson to Lawrence Thompson his interest in his father's estate which he is to receive at the death of his mother. The said Archabald also mentions his sister's (Elizabeth) estate. 28 January 1837. (P. 348)

Sheriff Samuel P. Howard to Peter Fitch a tract of land. 17 February 1837. (Pp. 349-350)

Samuel Caplinger to Alfred M. Betty a tract of land on the Caney Fork. 1837. (P. 350)

Andrew Payne to Allen Piper a tract of land on Peyton's Creek. February 1837. (Pp. 351-352)

Joseph Davenport to Joseph Meador a tract of land. 3 December 1836. (P. 352)

Howel Hargis to Thomas Lovelady 50 acres. 18 July 1832. (Pp. 353-354)

John B. Hughes to Fielden Conditt $12\frac{1}{4}$ acres, it being a tract of land formerly belonging to John Hughes, Sr. 2 November 1836. (P. 354)

Thomas Lovelady to Thomas L. Hardie a tract of land on Goose Creek. 9 September 1836. (P. 355)

John F. Tally, James Tally, Benjamin Tally, William Jones and wife Mary, Leodosha Tally to Charles N. Tally their interest in a tract of land in Buckingham County, Virginia. 20 February 1837. (P. 356)

Isham Beasley to his grandson, Isham Beasley, Jr. a negro boy. 26 February 1830. (P. 357)

N. W. Watkins, Milton O'Bannun, G. H. Hall, and Manerva Hall, the legal representatives of Nancy Douglass, late Nancy Armstead, appoint Robert Douglass of Cape Guardian County, Missouri as their attorney. 6 February 1837. (P. 358)

William D. Turner to Zackinah Corder a girl slave. 4 January 1837. (P. 359)

Nathaniel Walker to Miles West a tract of land on the Caney Fork. 4 November 1836. (P. 360)

John Duncan to John Johnson a tract of land on Mulherin's and Hickman's Creeks. 15 March 1830. (P. 361)

Hiram Bruce to John Johnson a tract of land on Mulherin's Creek. 17 January 1837. (P. 362)

Thomas Wilburn to Evan S. Wilburn a tract of land on Dixon's Creek. 4 February 1837. (P. 363)

Phebe and James Asken to John Buckner 276 acres. 1837. (Pp. 363-364)

DEED BOOK H

Frederick N. Mitchell to Richard Brown a tract of land on Dixon's Creek. 15 January 1836. (Pp. 364-365)

Joseph F. Gifford to Dennis Hargis. 26 October 1833. (Pp. 365-366)

James Parker to Thomas Lovelady a tract of land on Goose Creek. 7 July 1832. (Pp. 366-367)

John Cooper to John Farmer a tract of land on the Caney Fork. 12 August 1833. (Pp. 367-368)

Wright W. Crosslin to William Crosslin a tract of land on Hurricane Creek. 13 February 1837. (Pp. 368-369)

Anderson Paschal and (Andrew) Paschal derived title to a tract of land as a result of the last will and testament of Samuel Paschal. 15 February 1837. (Pp. 369-370)

Albert and Elizabeth Burton to Wilson Walker our interest in the estate of William Walker. 20 May 1836. (P. 370)

William B. Dillon to Hugh H. Bradley $231\frac{1}{4}$ acres. 3 March 1837. (P. 371)

William Kelly to M. and F. Duffy a barn of wheet. 7 March 1837. (P. 372)

Willis Jones to Ruth Jones a tract of land on the Cumberland River. 10 February 1837. (Pp. 372-373)

Martha Douglass to William Shoemake a tract of land on the Cumberland River. 28 February 1837. (P. 373)

James Fentress and wife Cynthia to David Dies a tract of land on Dixon's Creek. 3 March 1837. (P. 374)

David Dies to George W. Walker a tract of land on Dixon's Creek. 4 March 1837. (P. 375)

Cyrus Goodner to Melton, Edward, and Brice M. Draper a tract of land on Defeated Creek. 28 February 1837. (P. 376)

William Patterson to John McGee a tract of land on the Caney Fork. 23 February 1837. (P. 377)

Martha Douglass to John Dickens a tract of land on the Cumberland River. 28 February 1837. (P. 378)

Nathan Stamps to Solomon Smalling a tract of land. 11 February 1837. (Pp. 378-380)

Mortimore Waters to Turner Lee Wilkerson 137 acres. 5 February 1837. (P. 380)

John Stafford to Caleb Carmon three negroes. 1837. (P. 381)

D. C. Ward and W. B. Moore to Armstead Moore a tract of land. 28 May 1836. (Pp. 381-382)

DEED BOOK H

Cyrus W. Brevard to Lot Hazard a tract of land in the town of Carthage. 25 March 1837. (P. 383)

William Patterson to William Bennett a tract of land. 11 October 1836. (Pp. 383-384)

Wesley Motes to Benjamin W. Burford a tract of land in the town of Rome. 16 December 1836. (P. 384)

Benjamin W. Burford to William Towson and Nathan Roberson a tract of land in the town of Rome. 16 December 1836. (P. 385)

Benjamin Piper to John Armstead a tract of land on Peyton's Creek. 22 October 1825. (P. 386)

Nathan Stamps and wife Mary to Solomon Smalling a tract of land on Peyton's Creek. 8 March 1837. (Pp. 387-388)

Jacob Lyday to Martin Freeman a tract of land near the Cumberland River. 20 November 1832. (Pp. 388-389)

W. B. Moore and A. Moore to D. C. Ward a tract of land. 20 October 1836. (P. 390)

J. B. Conditt and John Conditt to James Vaden a tract of land. 5 September 1836. (Pp. 390-391)

James Wammack to J. D. Gentry of Jackson County a small horse. 3 April 1837. (Pp. 391-392)

Vincent R. Lovelady to James Ellis 50 acres. 20 March 1837. (Pp. 392-393)

Dixon Ferguson to R. G. Brien and Elisha Steward a tract of land on Goose Creek. 14 March 1835. (Pp. 393-394)

George Dillard to Robert McHood a tract of land on the Caney Fork. 3 February. (Pp. 394-395)

Morris Robinson to John Robinson a tract of land on the Cumberland River. 8 April 1837. (Pp. 395-396)

Philomon C. Dill and William Dill to H. D. Marchbanks, Russell Marchbanks, and Thomas Marchbanks 50 acres. 28 September 1836. (Pp. 396-397)

William B. Perkins to James Chambers. 10 April 1837. (Pp. 397-398)

Samuel Slate, Sr. to Samuel Slate, Jr. 200 acres. 24 March 1837. (Pp. 398-399)

Decree of Chancery Court. Archibald Fulks, Charles Nolen, Rebecca Nolen, Christopher Beckman, Nancy Beckman, Francis Sampson, Letty Sampson, Anthony Helmontoller, Nancy Helmontoller versus Nancy Fulks, J. Fulks, and Martha Fulks. 22 March 1837. (Pp. 399-400)

George W. Reasonover to William Waters a tract of land in the 20th District. 17 March 1837. (Pp. 400-401)

DEED BOOK N

John Page and Cealia Page to Edwin Duncan 31 acres. 31 December 1836. (Pp. 401-402)

Edwin Duncan to John Page a tract of land. 5 December 1835. (Pp. 402-403)

Hiram E. Johnson to Wilson Martin some live stock. 18 April 1837. (Pp. 403-404)

Jane Johnson, widow of John Johnson, to her daughter Patsy Johnson a negro girl. Said Patsy and her daughter, Permelia, were especially kind to the said John who was in a helpless condition for several years. Also mentions grandson James (Whitson) and son John A. Johnson. 27 March 1837. (P. 405)

Elijah Hail to William Denny 100 acres. 3 August 1836. (P. 406)

John B. Dupriest to William Fiveash a tract of land. 1 October 1836. (Pp. 406-407)

Samuel Slate, Sr. to John Slate a tract of land on Salt Lick. 10 April 1837. (Pp. 407-408)

John Ballard to Sarah Evans a tract of land on Defeated Creek. 10 December 1836. (Pp. 408-409)

George W. Betty and Mary J. Betty to John Moss a tract of land on the Caney Fork. 13 May 1836. (Pp. 409-410)

George Betty of Floid County, Indiana, Polly Thaxton, Permelia Polly Betty of Smith County appoint Bernard Richardson as their attorney. 1 April 1836. (Pp. 410-411)

Bias Russell to John Ballard a tract of land. 10 December 1836. (P. 411)

Division of the lands of Sylvanus Stokes. Heirs: Thomas Stokes, William Stokes, and Jordan G. Stokes. 5 March 1831. (P. 412)

Henry Cornwell to Stephen Holland a tract of land on Goose Creek. 4 December 1832. (Pp. 413-414)

James L. Murphree to Ira Ledbetter a tract of land on the Cumberland River. 15 April 1837. (P. 414)

James Webb Smith, son of James D. Smith, to his grandson, James W. Smith, a slave in the possession of his son James D. Smith. 24 April 1837. (P. 415)

James W. Smith to his grand daughter Mary Smith, she being named after her grandmother Smith, daughter of my son James D. Smith a girl slave. 29 April 1837. (P. 416)

John Martin to William Snider a crop of tobacco. 27 April 1837. (P. 417)

Patrick Hubbard to Isham Beasley a tract of land on Vaden Branch. 26 April 1837. (P. 418)

DEED BOOK N

Abraham Tubb to William L. Tubb several slaves. 25 December 183?. (Pp. 419-420)

John B. Lewis of Jackson County to Margaret Dunlop a tract of land. 3 March 1837. (P. 420)

David K. Timberlake to Patrick Hubbard a tract of land on the Cumberland River. 21 March 1836. (P. 431)

An unhappy difference has taken place between Abraham Tubb and his wife Mary, she having filed for divorce. Said Abraham appoints James Tubb and John Lancaster as his agents in the matter. 21 February 1837. (Pp. 422-423)

Gideon Gifford to William Carlie a tract of land on Goose Creek. 25 July 1836. (P. 423)

John Hooker to John W. Paty a tract of land on Brush Creek. 8 October 1836. (P. 424)

Elijah C. Davis to Thomas B. Day a tract of land in the town of Meadorville. 28 April 1837. (Pp. 425-426)

John Conger to William Duncan a tract of land. 20 September 1836. (Pp. 426-427)

Jacob Uhls to James Anderson 150 acres. 3 May 1837. (P. 428)

James Bradley to John Page a negro girl. 26 April 1837. (P. 428)

Manson Young to H. B. Burton and A. J. Burton a gract of land on Goose Creek. 3 October 1836. (P. 429)

Lewis Adams to William Linville the interest I have in the estate of my father Allen Adams. 25 April 1837. (P. 430)

Henry Turner to William Games of Rutherford County a tract of land. 10 November 1834. (Pp. 430-431)

Ruth Jones to Edmund Rucks a tract of land on the Cumberland River. 10 February 1837. (Pp. 431-432)

Wiatt W. Bailey to Charles Allen a tract of land on Helton's Creek. 1 May 1830. (Pp. 432-433)

Isham Ellis to his grandson, James Ellis Beasley, son of Major A. Beasley a negro girl. 11 May 1837. (P. 433)

Samuel Furlong to Caleb Carman a bay mare. 1837. (P. 434)

Caleb Carman accepts the above trust. 15 May 1837. (P. 434)

Franklin B. Day to Charles McMurry a negro woman. 13 May 1837. (Pp. 434-435)

Franklin B. Day to Philip T. Day a tract of land on Dixon's Creek. 13 May 1837. (Pp. 435-436)

DEED BOOK N

Josiah Baird to Wilson Turner a tract of land on Hickman's Creek. 18 March 1837. (Pp. 436-437)

Jonathan Baker to Sinah Foster some livestock. 17 May 1837. (P. 437)

Joseph Holmes to Josiah Baird a tract of land. 18 March 1837. (Pp. 438-439)

Nepthali Durham to Joseph Haden a tract of land. 21 October 1836. (Pp. 439-440)

William D. Garrett to Hugh Bradley a negro woman. 26 May 1837. (P. 441)

William D. Garrett to Hugh Bradley. 26 May 1837. (Pp. 441-443)

James Evetts from Richard Haynes. 26 May 1837. (Pp. 443-444)

William F. McDaniel to William Games a tract of land on Wolf Creek. 30 May 1837. (Pp. 444-445)

William Cleveland to Joseph Gregory his interest in the estate of William Cleveland deceased. 22 May 1837. (P. 445)

James Pendarvis to Peter Haskel some livestock. 31 May 1837. (P. 446)

Thomas Overstreet to Leonard H. Cardwell. 17 May 1837. (P. 447)

John A. Newell to Young and Coker somelivestock. 1 June 1837. (Pp. 447-448)

James Evetts to Richard Haynes some livestock and personal property. 3 June 1837. (Pp. 448-449)

Thomas Palmer to Richard Haynes. 3 June 1837. (P. 449)

Charles Cole to A. A. Short and J. F. Cole 200 acres. 2 June 1837. (P. 450)

Braddock Beasley to Benjamin Piper a crop of tobacco. 5 June 1837. (P. 451)

Micajah Kittle to Thomas W. Wootten some livestock. 6 June 1837. (Pp. 451-452)

Silas Epperson to Anthony Epperson a tract of land on Long Creek. 1 March 1836. (Pp. 452-453)

Yearby Orange to Champion T. Thomas. 6 May 1837. (P. 453)

William Hutchison to Samuel Jones some livestock. 5 June 1837. (P. 454)

William Hall to William P. Hughes a tract of land on Mulherin's Creek. 5 June 1837. (P. 455)

DEED BOOK N

Leonard Jones to Silas C. Cornwell a tract of land on Defeated Creek. 31 December 1836. (P. 456)

Job Meader to Joel Meader 82½ acres. 12 January 1836. (P. 457)

Mary Morgan to Brice M. Draper a tract of land land to her by her husband Joseph Morgan deceased. 3 June 1837. (P. 458)

Samuel Lawrence of Sumner County to Anthony Epperson four acres. 15 April 1837. (P. 459)

Nathan Dillon to Essex Epperson and Polly Anderson, both of Sumner County a tract of land on Long Creek. 4 April 1837. (Pp. 460-461)

Richard Nichols of Robertson County to William Hutchison of Jackson County a tract of land. 2 January 1827. (Pp. 461-462)

Valentine H. Brown to Asa Johnson the interest I have in my father's estate. 9 June 1837. (Pp. 462-463)

James Garrison to Little B. Hughes 112 acres. 25 March 1837. (Pp. 463-464)

Hannah Dobbins to Daniel K. Witcher five negro slaves. 17 May 1837. (P. 464)

John B. Dupriest to William Owens a tract of land on the Cumberland River. 13 October 1836. (P. 465)

Mark Woodcock to Samuel Lawrence six acres. 10 April 1837. (P. 466)

Joseph Law to William Young 100 acres. 2 June 1837. (P. 467)

Neil McDuffee to John McDuffee 100 acres on Peyton's Creek. 13 June 1837. (P. 468)

William Roddy to Jacob Jones a tract of land. 6 March 1837. (Pp. 468-469)

William Carlie to Gideon Gifford a tract of land on Big Goose Creek. 25 July 1836. (P. 470)

Whereas by descent from George McGee, John McGee, Joseph C. McGee, Hiram McGee, George W. McGee, Nancy McGee, Elizabeth McGee, and Evelina McGee have title to a tract of land on the Caney Fork. 19 June 1837. (P. 471)

Leonard Jones to Silas C. Cornwell a tract of land on Defeated Creek. 10 May 1837. (P. 472)

Mark Woodcock to Lewis Hire 45 acres. 9 March 1837. (P. 473)

Josiah Moses to Joseph C. Dickens a tract of land on the Cumberland River. 19 December 1836. (P. 474)

John G. Burns to Rich.'d Bransford. 1837. (P. 475)

DEED BOOK N

John G. Burns to Richard R. Bransford and James W. Bransford a tract of land in the 7th District. 16 June 1837. (P. 476)

Samuel P. Howard to Major L. Sykes 100 acres. 17 June 1837. (Pp. 476-477)

Adam C. Perkins to Martin Miller a tract of land on Peyton's Creek about one mile above the David Perkins place. 17 June 1837. (Pp. 477-478)

Johnson Anderson to Caleb Read a tract of land on Peyton's Creek. 16 June 1837. (Pp. 479-480)

Martin H. Burris to Lemuel A. Hammock a bay mare and colt. 20 June 1837. (P. 481)

James Jones to James Anderson some livestock. 19 June 1837. (Pp. 481-482)

Michael Uhls to Dennis Hargis a tract of land on Goose Creek. 19 June 1837. (P. 482)

Dennis Hargis to Andrew Wallis a tract of land on Goose Creek. 12 June 1837. (Pp. 483-484)

Stephen Henry to David A. Crenshaw. 22 June 1837. (Pp. 484-485)

Horatio Cornick and his wife Elizabeth W. Cormick of Princess Anne County, Virginia to W. S. Betty a tract of land on the Caney Fork. 1837. (Pp. 485-487)

Moses Evetts to Richard Kemp a tract of land on the Cumberland River. 3 June 1837. (P. 487)

James A. Taylor of Maringo County, Alabama appoints Thomas Phelps as his attorney. 14 June 1837. (P. 488)

John Carter to Henry Martin a tract of land on Defeated Creek. 4 July 1837. (P. 489)

Isaac Moore to William D. Gowen a tract of land. 29 February 1836. (P. 490)

Thomas Jackson to Thomas W. Wooten. 27 June 1837. (Pp. 491-492)

Daniel McKiness, Sr. and Thomas McKiness his son, and Daniel McKiness, Jr. to Alexander Ferguson. 2 June 1837. (P. 492)

John W. Redman to L. E. Mitchell. 3 July 1837. (Pp. 493-494)

Thomas Phelps to Abraham C. Penn a tract of land east of Dixon's Creek. 18 June 1837. (P. 494)

Thomas D. Askin, William Askin, and John Payne to John Buckner 226 acres. 24 December 1836. (P. 495)

J. W. Smithage to Lindsey Mann. 1837. (P. 496)

DEED BOOK N

Sheriff Samuel P. Howard to John Hallum a tract of land. 26 September 1833. (P. 497)

Benjamin Franklin Dyer to Martin W. Sloan a tract of land in the town of Carthage. 30 September 1835. (P. 498)

Thomas Askin to John H. Newbell a tract of land. 22 June 1837. (Pp. 499-500)

Archery Robinson to James Malone a tract of land on Hickman's Creek. 7 November 1833. (Pp. 500-501)

Wamon Leftwick, administrator of James Rowland, to James Rowland. 4 July 1837. (Pp. 501-502)

Bartlett B. Uhls to Nicholas Waggoner a tract of land. 27 October 1836. (P. 503)

B. W. Mading to Abraham C. Penn a tract of land. 20 June 1837. (P. 504)

John Gwaltney and Godfrey Gregory to John Newbell 86 acres. 23 October 1835. (P. 505)

Jeremiah Reece to John Goodner a tract of 37 acres. 17 June 1828. (P. 506)

Richard Freeman and James Freeman, Sr. to M. and J. C. Duffy a tract of land. 5 July 1837. (P. 507)

Elijah Hail to Howel Rucks a tract of land. 17 April 1837. (Pp. 508-509)

Benjamin Arundell to Stephen Mann. 21 July 1837. (Pp. 509-510)

Andrew G. Ford to Charles Coker 220 acres. 24 July 1837. (Pp. 510-512)

John H. Gammon to Jeremiah Brauner 60 acres. 26 July 1837. (Pp. 512-513)

Hubard Wright to John Fleaman a tract of land on Goose Creek. 17 December 1836. (Pp. 513-514)

William S. Carter to John Fleaman a tract of land on Goose Creek. 29 March 1837. (Pp. 514-515)

Hubard Wright to John Fleaman a tract of land on Goose Creek. 17 December 1836. (P. 515)

Frances Kerby to John Bradley several items. August 1837. (Pp. 516-517)

F. N. Mitchell to Vaughan and Tunstall a tract of land on Dixon's Creek. 29 July 1837. (Pp. 517-518)

B. W. Mading to William A. Corley some livestock. 1 August 1837. (Pp. 518-519)

Robert Allen, Jr. to Charles Bolton. July 1837. (P. 520)

Jefferson Wallace to M. and P. Duffy. 1837. (Pp. 520-

DEED BOOK N

Thomas Phelps to Jacob Yerger. 7 August 1837. (Pp. 521-522)

William Robinson to James H. Green a tract of land on Snow Creek. 4 August 1837. (Pp. 522-523)

Thomas Phelps to David Burford 250 acres. 7 August 1837. (Pp. 523-524)

Stephen Stafford to William Willis 25 acres. 2 August 1837. (Pp. 524-525)

Malachi Shoulders to P. W. Cage a tract of land in the 4th District. 1 August 1837. (Pp. 525-527)

Stephen Pate, Booker Pate, and Beaman Graves, administrators of Hampton Pate, to Jubie E. Pate a tract of land in Smith and Jackson Counties. 1837. (P. 527)

James Mulherin of Davidson County to Benjamin Garrison 99 acres. 2 January 1824. (Pp. 528-529)

D. C. Ward and others to Regin Thompson a tract of land in the town of Rome. 15 October 1836. (P. 529)

James H. Vaden to Benjamin Rucks a tract of land on the Cumberland River. 9 August 1837. (Pp. 530-531)

John S. Brien and Henry B. McDonald to Samuel Graff of Cannon County a tract of land in the town of Alexandria. 7 August 1837. (Pp. 531-532)

Benjamin Piper to Henry Piper a tract of land on Peyton's Creek. 3 July 1834. (P. 532)

E. C. Davis to M. L. Donoho a tract of land on Big Goose Creek. 17 August 1837. (P. 533)

Obediah S. Richie to Lucy Richie a tract of land on Goose Creek. 8 August 1837. (P. 534)

William Summersett to John C. and Frances Duffy of Hartsville. 9 August 1837. (P. 535)

Henry L. Day to Solomon McMurry a crop of tobacco. 9 August 1837. (P. 536)

John McMurry to James McMurry. 11 August 1837. (P. 536)

Allen Cornwell to James Richardson 105½ acres. 4 August 1837. (Pp. 537-538)

Richard Brown to George W. Walker. 11 August 1837. (P. 538)

H. L. Donoho to John Holland a tract of land. 7 August 1837. (P. 539)

Joseph Wooten to James Wooten a tract of land on the Caney Fork. 12 August 1837. (P. 540)

Wilson Cage to James McMurry. 1837. (P. 541)

DEED BOOK N

Benjamin F. Morris to James Blackwell a tract of land on Goose Creek. 4 August 1837. (P. 542)

Isaac Wiseman and wife Peachy to E. C. F. Donoho a tract of land on Goose Creek. 15 February 1837. (P. 543)

Benjamin F. Morris to Hiram Dickens a tract of land. 7 August 1837. (P. 544)

Isaac Wiseman to Marquis L. Donoho a tract of land on Big Goose Creek. 8 August 1837. (P. 545)

William Wood to Matthew Pettress a tract of land on the Caney Fork. 18 January 1836. (P. 546)

Nathaniel Macon and wife Elizabeth, formerly Elizabeth Moore of Wilson County, to Mortimore Waters their interest in the estate of Thomas Moore. 7 August 1837. (Pp. 547-548)

John S. and Charles T. Jones, heirs of Charles Jones, to Thomas Sadler a tract of land. 8 December 1836. (Pp. 548-549)

Thomas Phelps to David Burford a negro girl. 19 August 1837. (Pp. 549-551)

Jonathan Pickett to George C. Gifford. 7 September 183?. (Pp. 551-552)

George Daugherty to Stephen Mann. 21 August 1837. (Pp. 552-553)

Ephraim Payton of Washington County, Kentucky to John Peyton of Sumner County 569 acres. 28 March 1812. (Pp. 553-554)

Joseph Grisham to John Lucky. 22 August 1837. 22 August 1837. (P. 555)

Tilmon Dixon to Grant Allen a tract of 640 acres. 24 November 1789. (P. 556)

William Hart certifies the above document. (P. 557)

H. B. McDonald to Charlott Clement 50 acres. 17 August 1837. (P. 558)

Samuel P. Howard & Andrew Pickett, administrators of Jonathan Pickett, to George C. Gifford a tract of land 21 August 1837. (Pp. 558-559)

Thomas B. Bishop to Campbell Crutchfield a tract of land on Hogan's Creek. 18 July 1837. (Pp. 560-561)

William Bailey to Francis H. Gordon a tract of land on Mulherin's Creek. 15 September 1836. (Pp. 561-562)

Isaac Wiseman from E. C. Davis a tract of land on Big Goose Creek. 13 November 1836. (P. 562)

George W. Lamb to Allen Cornwell 106½ acres. 8 June 1837. (Pp. 563-564)

DEED BOOK N

Evans S. Wilbourn to William S. Willis 33 acres. 19 July 1837. (P. 564)

Joseph Stept to George T. Wright 50 acres. July 1837. (Pp. 565-566)

Drury Andrews to Jesse B. Kearby 50 acres. 19 January 1837. (Pp. 566-567)

Banister W. Mading and Benjamin F. Morris to Lawrence Thompson 50 acres. 26 August 1837. (Pp. 567-568)

John Dawson to William Dawson a tract of land. 7 July 1837. (Pp. 568-569)

D. C. Ward and others to Thomas Owen 96 acres. 30 July 1836. (Pp. 569-570)

Wesley W. Jones to Thomas Huddleston 160 acres on Wartrace Creek. 31 August 1837. (Pp. 570-571)

William Askin and Thomas Askin to Issac Willeby a tract of land on Hickman's Creek. 24 December 1836. (Pp. 571-572)

John A. Debow to Solomon Debow a tract of land on Goose Creek. 5 January 1836. (Pp. 572-573)

John Black to Charles McMurry. 31 August 1837. (Pp. 573-574)

Samuel Thomason to Jabez Gifford a tract of land on Goose Creek. 4 August 1837. (Pp. 574-575)

Thomas Richardson to Joseph L. Carter 50 acres. 17 August 1837. (P. 576)

Division of the lands of Thomas Stokes. 1837. (Pp. 577-578)

Isaac Moore to Ezekiel Evans a tract of land. 26 November 1814. (P. 579)

William Foutch to Ezekiel Evans 72½ acres. 17 November 1823. (P. 580)

Elizabeth Robinson appoints her son James Robinson of Wilson County as her attorney. 1 September 1837. (P. 581)

Daniel Glover to Jeremiah Bush 140 acres. 1837. (P. 582)

W. W. Wade from William L. Fairstair and wife Nancy their interest in the estate of John Bradley, Sr. 4 September 1837. (Pp. 582-583)

William Williams to Lent Boulton some negro slaves. 7 September 1837. (P. 583)

William Williams to Lent Boulton his interest in the Carthage Hotel. 7 September 1837. (P. 584)

William Owens to Timothy Walton. 1837. (Pp. 584-585)

DEED BOOK N

Henry B. McDonald to Orville Green a tract of land in the town of Carthage. 11 September 1837. (P. 585)

John Hendrick to William McClard a tract of land on Goose Creek. 31 October 1832. (Pp. 586-587)

John Trousdale, Sr. to his two grand daughters, Martha S. Trousdale and Nancy Trousdale, daughters of his son John Trousdale, Jr., some livestock and one negro girl. 26 August 1837. (P. 587)

Sheriff Samuel P. Howard to James Young a tract of land. 31 August 1837. (Pp. 588-589)

James Paris to Wiatt Coleman a tract of land on Brush Creek. 30 December 1835. (P. 590)

James Bradley to Sharard Crostick a tract of land on the Cumberland River. 20 June 1837. (P. 591)

Josiah Rucks to Lewis Riggins a tract of land. 14 December 1832. (P. 592)

Eli Davis to Wiatt Coleman a tract of land. 21 July 1834. (P. 593)

John Morris to George M. B. Duncan some negro slaves. 8 September 1837. (Pp. 594-595)

Benjamin Rucks to Robert Holliday. 12 September 1837. (Pp. 595-596)

James H. Vaden to Robert Holliday a tract of land on the Cumberland River. 10 September 1839. (P. 596)

Sterling Whitlock to Benjamin Davis a tract of land on Hickman's Creek. 19 October 1835. (P. 597)

Henry Hallum to Ferdinand Thomas a tract of land on the Caney Fork. 18 August 1837. (P. 598)

Moses B. Freeman to Moses Ford and Henderson Toler. 15 September 1837. (P. 599)

Henry Hallum to Elizabeth Boze a tract of land granted to William and Henry Hallum. 18 September 1837. (P. 600)

Moses B. Freeman to Moses Ford and Henderson Toler. 1837. (P. 601)

Ferdinand P. Thomas to Elizabeth Boze 50 acres. 18 September 1837. (P. 602)

George C. Gifford to Moses B. Freeman a tract of land on Goose Creek. 14 September 1837. (P. 603)

Moses B. Freeman to Joseph L. Carter a crop of tobacco. September 1837. (P. 603)

Ellis Beasley to David Burford a tract of land on the Cumberland River. 29 June 1837. (P. 604)

Thomas Allison to Daniel Smith. 1837. (Pp. 604-605)

DEED BOOK N

Thomas B. Bishop to Campbell Crutchfield a tract of land. 18 July 1837. (Pp. 605-606)

Josiah Moses to Thomas Haley a tract of land on Payton's Creek. 12 September 1837. (Pp. 607-608)

William Bailiff of Alabama to Andrew Williams a tract of land on Walker's Creek. 16 August 1837. (P. 608)

Moses B. Freeman to Elijah Cannon a tract of land on Goose Creek. 15 September 1837. (P. 609)

Philip T. Day to John D. Day a tract of land on Dixon's Creek. 9 September 1837. (P. 610)

John Reeves to Taylor Whitley a tract of land on Ward's Creed. 14 June 1836. (P. 611)

DEED BOOK O

Alexander Ferguson to Lewis Turner a tract of land on Puncheon Camp Creek. 22 March 1831. (P. 1)

William Green to John Ballard 100 acres. 3 May 1837. (P. 2)

Romulus M. Sanders, Jourdan M. Sanders, and Ethelbert W. Sanders to Ellis Beasley a tract of land on the Cumberland River. 10 January 1836. (Pp. 3-4)

William Duncan to John Lancaster, Sr. a tract of land in the 22nd District. 21 September 1837. (Pp. 4-5)

Flemin W. Duncan, Sr. to Edwin Duncan a tract of land. Also to George A. Duncan of Wilson County. 1 June 1837. (Pp. 5-6)

Abraham H. King to Isaac Bradley a tract of land in the town of Carthage. 9 September 1837. (P. 6)

Ira L. Sulivant to Jordan Sulivant three acres. 26 July 1837. (P. 7)

William Askew and Thomas B. Askew to Benjamin Denny a tract of land on Hickman's Creek. 24 December 1836. (P. 8)

Adam C. Perkins to John Brame. 23 September 1837. (P. 9)

William Wootten to William Kerby. 25 September 1837. (P. 10)

David W. Burton of Lynchburg, Virginia to Green Wright a certain slave. 8 September 1837. (P. 11)

H. L. Donoho and his wife Patience to E. C. F. Donoho a tract of land. 8 February 1837. (Pp. 11-12)

A. L. Young and wife Patsy, William Cleveland and wife Alphema, T. L. Young, and Henry A. Young to Thomas Stafford a tract of land. 12 November 1836. (Pp. 13-14)

Nancy Corley to Edward Daugherty a negro man. 1837. (P. 14)

Mary Grant to Josiah Caruthers a tract of land on Goose Creek. 17 April 1837. (P. 15)

Randolph Murry and Charles Murry to Charles R. Blair a tract of land. 9 September 1835. (Pp. 16-17)

Nancy Corley to John Corley 40 acres. 9 January 1837. (P. 17)

Robert Lindsey of Jackson County and James Allison, executors of Joseph Allison, to John R. James a tract of land on Hickman's Creek. 18 February 1832. (P. 18)

Isaac A. Dale of Delaware to William Givan a tract of land willed to the said Isaac A. by his father Thomas Dale. 13 October 1821. (Pp. 19-20)

DEED BOOK O

James Freeman, Sr. and Richard Freeman to Frances Duffy a crop of tobacco. 25 September 1837. (P. 20)

Pleasant M. Walker to John McMurry. 26 September 1837. (Pp. 20-21)

Dennis Hargis to William Dixon a crop of tobacco. 25 September 1837. (Pp. 21-22)

Dennis Hargis to Lionel Hargis a tract of land on Goose Creek. 26 September 1837. (P. 22)

John A. Farmer to David Davis ten acres. 16 February 1837. (P. 23)

Samuel Paschal to Vincent R. Bradford a tract of land on Mulherin's Creek. 8 March 1837. (P. 24)

William Snead to Washington Glover a tract of land on Defeated Creek. 30 October 1835. (Pp. 24-25)

Simon P. Hughes to A. Ward a tract of land on Hickman's Creek. 22 September 1835. (Pp. 25-26)

Mary V. Grant to Isaac Wiseman a tract of land. 13 November 1836. (P. 26)

Henry Beasley to Ellis Beasley 144¼ acres. 3 July 1826. (P. 27)

William McKinney to Drury W. Denton 99 acres. 30 August 1837. (Pp. 27-28)

JOHN CARTER Will. Heirs: wife Charlotte; all my children. 18 March 1814. (P. 28)

Dicking Ward to Taylor Whitley a tract of land on Ward's Creek. 25 February 1825. (P. 29)

William Owens to Samuel High. 27 September 1837. (P. 30)

David Denton to H. G. Owens and Noles Purnell a tract of land. 7 September 1837. (P. 30)

Frances Adams to Israel McClelin. 2 October 1837. (P. 31)

James Adams to Abraham Adams a tract of land on Smith's Fork. 1 April 1832. (Pp. 32-33)

Chesley B. Thomas to James Jenkins 25 acres. 7 August 1837. (P. 33)

Thomas Walker to Green B. Lowe a tract of land on the Cumberland. 24 April 1837. (P. 34)

James G. Ford to John G. Park. 2 October 1837. (P. 35)

James G. Ford to John G. Park. 2 October 1837. (P. 36)

Turman Wheeler to William McCormick a tract of land. 25

DEED BOOK O

August 1836. (Pp. 36-37)

James C. Williams to Henry Law a tract of land on Defeated Creek. 28 October 1836. (Pp. 37-38)

Thomas Smith to M. and P. Duffy a crop of corn. 12 September 1837. (Pp. 38-39)

Andrew Payne to Joseph W. Allen two negroes. 4 October 1837. (Pp. 39-40)

James K. Hamilton to George Hamilton his interest in a tract of land in the town of Rome descended to him from his father, late of Wilson County. September 1837. (P. 40)

William Robertson to John G. Park some personal property. 1837. (Pp. 41-42)

Joseph and Thomas Morgan to Drury Cornwell a crop of tobacco. 7 October 1837. (Pp. 42-43)

William Stalcup to Thomas Allen a negro girl. 14 October 1837. (P. 43)

John Black to Thomas B. Day. 16 October 1837. (P. 44)

John Sloan to Matthew Anderson a tract of land. 24 February 1829. (Pp. 44-45)

Smith Gregory to Matthew Anderson a tract of land. 11 April 1820. (Pp. 45-46)

Matthew Anderson to James Piper a tract of land on Payton's Creek. 16 October 1837. (Pp. 46-47)

Jesse Meacham to Washington Meacham a tract of land on Snow Creek. 17 October 1836. (P. 48)

Andrew Payne to Alfred Davis a tract of land on Payton's Creek. 18 August 1837. (Pp. 49-50)

Henry Brawner to John Gammon 270 acres. 19 October 1837. (Pp. 50-51)

James Piper to Drury W. Denton. 19 October 1837. (P. 51)

Joseph Parker to Britton Richardson a tract of land on Dixon's and Peyton's Creeks. 17 October 1837. (Pp. 51-52)

Samuel Stephens to M. and P. Duffy a crop of corn. 7 October 1837. (Pp. 52-53)

Matthew Anderson to Thompson Mace a tract of land in Peyton's Creek. 20 October 1837. (Pp. 53-54)

Johnson Anderson to Matthew Anderson a tract of land. 20 October 1837. (Pp. 54-55)

Clabourn Hall to John Baker a tract of land on the Cumberland River. 1837. (Pp. 55-56)

DEED BOOK O

Robert L. Taylor to John Black. 21 October 1837. (Pp. 57-58)

Clabourn Matthews to Israel McClelin a crop of tobacco. 23 October 1837. (Pp. 58-59)

Bry Gregory to his daughter Suleny Dycus several items. 25 October 1837. (P. 60)

Joe W. Allen to Gideon Gifford. 25 October 1837. (P. 60)

John Wilson to William Burrow a tract of land on Goose Creek. 24 October 1837. (Pp. 61-62)

John Wilson to William Barrow 39 acres. 24 October 1837. (P. 62)

John Wilson to William Burrow a tract of land on the Cumberland River. (Pp. 63-64)

William Payne to David Burford 222 acres. 26 October 1837. (P. 65)

William Payne to David Burford. 1837. (Pp. 66-67)

Martin Miller to William Alexander. 26 October 1837. (P. 68)

Caleb Wilson to Archibald Parker a tract of land. 28 October 1837. (P. 69)

Hardy Williford to Lewis Stratton 71 acres. 7 October 1837. (Pp. 70-71)

Robert Beasley to William H. Beasley some personal property. 30 October 1837. (Pp. 71-72)

William Askew and Thomas B. Askew to John Denny, Sr. a tract of land on Hickman's Creek. 24 December 183?. (P. 73)

Joseph Law to Leonidas D. Hogg several items. 27 October 1837. (P. 74)

B. W. Mading to William A. Corley several items. 31 October 1837. (P. 75)

Henry Brawner to M. and P. Duffy a crop of tobacco. 28 October 1837. (P. 76)

Jacob Uhls to M. and P. Duffy a crop of tobacco. (P. 76)

Allen Adams appoints Nathaniel Adams as his attorney. 28 October 1837. (P. 77)

Allen Adams to his son Robert Adams five slaves. 25 August 1836. (Pp. 77-78)

Thomas J. Jones to William D. Turner a tract of land on the Cumberland River. 2 November 1837. (Pp. 78-79)

DEED BOOK O

William and George Creacy to M. and P. Duffy. 9 November 1837. (P. 79)

John Black to Thomas B. Day. 23 October 1837. (P. 80)

Pleasant M. Walker to James Clemmons 100 barrels of corn. 2 November 1837. (Pp. 80-81)

John Stafford to Thomas B. Day 40 barrels of corn. 8 November 1837. (Pp. 81-82)

John Stafford to Richard Uhls and David L. Taylor a tract of land on Goose Creek. 8 November 1837. (Pp. 82-83)

Robert L. Taylor to Jacob L. Johnson a tract of land on Goose Creek. 6 November 1837. (Pp. 83-84)

James B. Richardson to Elbert Holland 100 acres. 6 November 1837. (Pp. 85-86)

Elbert Holland to William Chamberlain 162 acres. 6 November 1837. (Pp. 86-88)

John Roark to Elijah Gammon a tract of land on Goose Creek. 8 November 1837. (Pp. 88-90)

Hardy Jones to Guilford Jones a tract of land on Mulherin's Creek. 1837. (P. 90)

Josiah Howell of Monroe County, Kentucky to Joel Simmons a tract of land on Goose Creek. 6 March 1837. (P. 91)

John Robinson and Allen Robinson to Winston High a tract of land where the said John now lives. 13 November 1837. (P. 92)

Charles McMurry to Archibald Parker a girl slave. 14 October 1837. (P. 92)

Howel H. Hargis to Young & Coker a tract of land on Goose Creek. 9 November 1837. (P. 93)

Hugh B. Burton to Manson Young 150 acres. 1 November 1836. (P. 94)

Thomas McClard to Taylor & Uhls several items. 8 November 1837. (P. 95)

Hugh B. Burton and A. J. Burton to John Black a tract of land. 6 April 1837. (Pp. 95-96)

Alanson Young to William Roark a tract of land on Goose Creek. 10 November 1835. (Pp. 96-97)

William Roark to _____ a tract of land. 14 November 1837. (Pp. 97-98)

George Stevens to Elijah Toney a tract of land. 9 November 1837. (P. 99)

Abraham Tubb to George Tary 141 acres. 1837. (Pp. 99-100)

DEED BOOK O

Stephen Garrett to Joseph L. Carter a tract of land on the Cumberland River. 18 October 1837. (P. 100)

Abner C. Perkins to Martin Miller. November 1837. (P. 101)

Thomas P. Short to Alexander A. Short several items. 16 November 1837. (P. 102)

Sally Baker from Elijah Saulman 16 acres. 16 February 1836. (P. 103)

Branch Grigg to R. G. Bryant 133 acres. 2 November 1837. (P. 104)

Joseph Arnold to William S. Carter a tract of land on Goose Creek. 31 March 1837. (P. 105)

Cyrus Watson to John Stafford, Sr. 20 November 1837. (Pp. 106-107)

Benjamin Matthews to Leonard H. Cardwell a crop of tobacco. 23 November 1837. (Pp. 107-108)

John Wilson to Archibald Parker 60 acres. 31 October 1837. (P. 108)

John Wilson to Archibald Parker a tract of land. 31 October 1837. (P. 108)

Andrew Hallum to James Boulton 100 acres. 29 November 1837. (Pp. 109-110)

Thomas Cartwright to John Slate 25 acres. 24 March 1837. (P. 110)

Asberry Cartwright to John Slate 25 acres. 1 March 1837. (P. 111)

William Rafferty to Edmond Teague 200 acres. 21 November 1837. (P. 112)

John Slate to Drury Holland 50 acres. 6 June 1837. (Pp. 113-114)

Alexander James to Frances Gordon a tract of land on Mulherin's Creek. 28 November 1837. (Pp. 114-115)

John Telford to John Muirhead. 7 August 1837. (P. 115)

Benjamin Jones to William Waters 127 acres. 4 December 1837. (Pp. 116-117)

Albert Burton to Jacob H. Burton a negro woman. 12 December 1835. (Pp. 117-118)

Clinton Hooks and wife to F. Duffy their interest in the estate of Joseph Summersett. 11 October 1837. (P. 118)

Robert Burton to B. E. Warren a tract of land on the Cumberland River. 24 November 1837. (P. 119)

DEED BOOK O

William Dickens and wife Caroline to John and Frances Duffy their interest in the estate of Joseph Summersett. 28 November 1837. (Pp. 119-120)

James Woodmore to his son Moses S. Woodmore 115 acres. 4 December 1837. (P. 120)

Nathan Hall to Palimore W. Cage several items. 6 December 1837. (P. 121)

Peter Thomason to George M. Carter a tract of land on Goose Creek. 22 November 1837. (P. 122)

James Read of Rutherford County to John Lucky ten acres. 14 February 1837. (P. 123)

Josiah Howell to Alfred A. Brevard a tract of land on Long Creek. 25 October 1837. (P. 124)

John Barton to Walker Wade a tract of land on Plunkett's Creek. Said land was granted to Samuel Barton on 7 December 1790. 4 September 1834. (P. 125)

John Goodner to Berry West a tract of land on the Cumberland River. 10 January 1836. (P. 126)

Nicholas Waggoner to William Slinkard a tract of land. 1 December 1837. (P. 127)

Bartlett James, Benjamin Moore, and Daniel James hold title to a tract of land. 21 October 1837. (Pp. 127-128)

Hardy Jones to Stephen Lyles a negro woman. 4 December 1837. (P. 128)

Henry H. Davis and his wife Perlina to David Mason a tract of land on Peyton's Creek. 2 December 1837. (P. 129)

Matthew Corley to his son William a tract of land on Plunkett's Creek. 1 December 1837. (P. 130)

Cyrus W. Brevard to James Wadmore eight acres. 3 December 1836. (Pp. 130-132)

Nathan Hall to P. W. Cage several items. 18 December 1837. (Pp. 132-133)

Samuel Smith to John C. And Frances Duffy several items. 9 December 1837. (P. 134)

Peter Grigg to Branch Grigg 40 acres. 12 December 1837. (P. 134)

Robert Frazer to Archibald Helms a tract of land. 21 January 1836. (P. 135)

Elom Russell to King Roberson a tract of land on Defeated Creek. 28 November 1837. (P. 136)

William Kyle to Chesley Bridgewater 100 acres. 15 December 1837. (Pp. 136-137)

DEED BOOK O

Drury Cornwell to Benjamin Payne five acres. 18 December 1837. (Pp. 137-138)

John Bridges and wife Milly of Green County, Illinois to Allen J. Bridges of the same county and state a tract of land on Barren River. 21 October 1837. (Pp. 138-139)

Abraham Eurlow, Justice of the Peace, certifies the signature of John Bridges and wife. (P. 139)

Emsley Wilson to Franklin Kearby a tract of land. 22 June 1837. (Pp. 139-140)

John Kirby to Drury Cornwell a tract of land on Defeated Creek. 28 December 1836. (Pp. 140-141)

John Parker to Drury Cornwell a tract of land on Defeated Creek. 16 February 1837. (P. 141)

William Burris of Wilson County to Larkin Payne a tract of land on Dixon's Creek. 16 December 1837. (Pp. 141-142)

Polly Woodson, Samuel Pugh, Carsey Pugh, Thomas Roberson, and A. Roberson to Tucker Woodson a tract of land in the State of Delaware given by Daniel James by will to Eth Sanders and her heirs. Said Edith Sanders is now Edith (Weeks) by marriage. 26 February 1820. (Pp. 142-144)

Tucker Woodson to Isaac Astin and wife Peggy of Cotaw County, Alabama 300 acres in Kent County, Delaware. Parties of the second part are legal heirs of Edith Sanders, since Edith (Weeks or Marks). 20 October 1819. (Pp. 144-145)

James Ray of Jackson County to John Carver, Jr. a tract of land on Wartrace Creek. 5 June 1837. (Pp. 145-146)

William R. Betty to Thomas A. Lancaster 1030 acres. 11 October 1837. (P. 146)

Martin H. Burrus to William T. Burrus 19 acres. 1 January 1836. (P. 147)

Thomas Harvey to David Jones. 1832. (P. 148)

Booker Dalton to John C. and F. Duffy several items. 19 December 1837. (P. 149)

Matthew M. Martin to Andrew Allison a negro woman. 24 November 1837. (P. 149)

Thomas Walker to Elijah Hale a tract of land. 7 November 1836. (P. 150)

Josiah Howell to William Chamberlain a tract of land on Goose Creek. 29 March 1831. (P. 151)

John Black and John Stafford to Bartlett B. Uhls one fourth of an acre. 22 September 1837. (P. 152)

John McNeely, Robert McNeely, Britton Neal and wife Elizabeth, Joseph Guthrie and wife Polly to Marshall B. Duncan a tract of land. 1829. (Pp. 153-154)

DEED BOOK O

William D. Garrett to Hugh H. Bradley a negro woman. 25 December 1837. (Pp. 154-155)

William Spears to Rowland W. Newby a tract of land on Round Lick Creek. 5 January 1837. (P. 156)

Barnet Lea, Jr. to Perigrine C. Garner. 26 December 1837. (P. 157)

Richard Chitwood to Samuel Dewhitt a tract of land on Salt Lick Creek. 24 September 1832. (Pp. 158-159)

Martin H. Burris to William T. Burris a tract of land on Dixon's Creek. Mentions "my father's old apple orchard." (P. 159)

Robert Glover to Davidson Draper 50 acres. 26 December 1837. (P. 160)

John Law, Jesse Law, William Law, Elizabeth Law, Nancy Law, Rebecca Law, Darkus Law, Damacis Law, and Henry Law, heirs of William Law deceased, to Drury Cornwell a tract of land. 5 December 1832. (Pp. 160-161)

Edmund Rucks and Howel T. Rucks transaction. 25 December 1837. (P. 161)

James Williams to Luke Ford a tract of land on Williams' Branch. December 1835. (P. 162)

Elijah Toney to Nelson Thornton a tract of land in the town of Carthage. 22 January 1833. (P. 163)

Robert Stratton of Cumberland County, Virginia, guardian for Lucy Jane Stratton, James Stratton, and Amanda Stratton, three of the orphan children of Peter Stratton, appoints Thomas J. Stratton of Smith County as their attorney. 2 March 1837. (Pp. 163-165)

Thomas Walker appoints Thomas J. Stratton as his attorney. 26 December 1837. (Pp. 165-166)

Alexander James to William B. Whitley. 11 December 1837. (Pp. 166-167)

Sheriff Samuel P. Howard to Andrew Allison a tract of 125 acres. 2 January 1838. (Pp. 167-168)

Andrew Allison to Alexander A. Short. 2 January 1838. (P. 169)

Joseph Meadow to Bennett Meadow a tract of land. 1 November 1837. (Pp. 169-170)

Jesse D. Carr to Thomas Dias 130 acres. 1837. (P. 170)

Andrew Payne to Thomas Taylor 203 acres. 28 March 1837. (P. 171)

Madison B. Alexander to Nel Winston and Murdock Stewart, a tract of land. 2 January 1838. (P. 172)

DEED BOOK O

Arthur S. Hogan to Timothy Walton 160 acres. 2 February 1837. (P. 173)

William Wilson to Clabourn Wilson a tract of land on the Caney Fork. 2 January 1838. (Pp. 173-174)

James Barnett to Samuel H. Wilson a tract of land on Plunkett's Creek. 30 October 1837. (Pp. 174-175)

David Burford to Thomas Dias 50 acres. 27 November 1837. (Pp. 175-176)

Alexander A. Short to Charles Coker a tract of land on Goose Creek. 19 December 1837. (P. 176)

John Wilson to David L. Taylor and Caleb Wilson a tract of land on Goose Creek. December 1837. (P. 177)

William Kearby to James Kearby a tract of land on Goose Creek. 21 November 1837. (P. 178)

Whereas by descent from Daniel Alexander deceased, Easther W. F., Robert Anderson, and William Alexander, we James D. Carr and Madison Alexander have title to a tract of land in the 8th District. 19 January 1837. (Pp. 179-180)

James C. Donoho to John C. Brevard. 8 January 1838. (Pp. 180-181)

James M. Donoho to Alfred A. Brevard a tract of land on Barren River. 8 January 1838. (Pp. 181-182)

Josiah Marshall to George Gifford eight acres. September 1837. (P. 182)

Thomas B. Askew to John H. Newbell a tract of land. 8 June 1837. (P. 183)

Thomas Dies to Frederick N. Mitchell 200 acres. 30 December 1837. (Pp. 183-184)

John Herrod to Guilford Jones. 1 January 1838. (P. 184)

Samuel H. Wilson to James Barnett a tract of land on Plunkett's Creek. 7 July 1836. (P. 185)

William Jones to Benjamin Jones a tract of land on Hickman's Creek. 10 March 1836. (P. 186)

John Black to Charles McMurry a town lot in the town of Meadowville. 24 August 1837. (Pp. 186-187)

Edmund Rucks to Tarlton Hughes 124 acres. 25 December 1837. (Pp. 187-188)

Patsy Cleveland, widow of William Cleveland, to Thomas Gregory her dower. 22 August 1836. (P. 188)

Esther Alexander, D. F. Alexander, and Robert Alexander to James D. Carr a tract of land. 19 September 1834. (P. 189)

DEED BOOK Q

John B. Cates to Hawkins Heflin a tract of land on Bolin's Branch. 28 December 1837. (Pp. 189-190)

Alfred Ewing to Daniel Dillard a tract of land on the Caney Fork. 25 August 1835. (Pp. 190-191)

Leonard Cardwell to Buckner A. Cardwell 100 acres. 12 January 1838. (P. 191)

Joseph Moses to Harvey H. Holland. 12 January 1838. (P. 192)

Ann S. Smith to Benjamin L. Douglass of Coffee County a negro woman. 13 January 1838. (P. 193)

Josiah Moses to Joseph Moses his interested in a tract of land granted to Isaac Johns. 12 January 1838. (Pp. 193-194)

George Thomason to James Brown a tract of land on Payton's Creek. 26 July 1832. (P. 194)

George Thomason to James Brown 150 acres. 14 December 1836. (P. 195)

Davis Gresham to Robert Bowman a tract of land on Spring Creek. 24 September 1832. (Pp. 196-197)

William Cassity to James D. McKinnis a tract of land. January 1838. (P. 197)

William Crosslin to James Thaxton a tract of land on the Cumberland River. 19 August 1836. (P. 198)

Josiah Moses to Green H. Sloan 81 acres. 19 January 1838. (P. 199)

Ira Meader to John H. Meader a tract of land on Goose Creek. Witness: Meredith Meader. 19 January 1838. (Pp. 199-200)

Thomas McClard to John Meader and Meredith Meader a tract of land on Goose Creek. 6 January 1838. (Pp. 200-201)

John H. Meader of Monroe County, Kentucky to John B. Johnston a tract of land on Goose Creek. 19 January 1838. (Pp. 201-202)

Jourdan McKenny to Clement McKenny a tract of 35 acres. 24 January 1838. (Pp. 202-203)

James Smith and William Hart to Lemuel Tilston nine and one half acres. 26 January 1838. (P. 203)

James Smith to William Hart five acres. 26 January 1838. (P. 204)

Madison B. Alexander to Daniel Kerby several items. 27 January 1838. (P. 205)

James D. Smith and William Hart to Lemuel Tilston nine acres. 26 January 1838. (P. 206)

DEED BOOK O

Edmund Teague to his son Raleigh Teague a tract of 200 acres. 29 January 1838. (P. 207)

Edmund Teague to his son Dabney Teague 200 acres. 29 January 1838. (P. 208)

Dabney Teague and Raleigh Teague agree to support their father Edmund Teague and his wife Mary Teague. 29 January 1838. (P. 209)

Washington Glover to John Snead 50 acres on Defeated Creek. 29 July 1836. (Pp. 209-210)

Abner A. Flippin to John G. Davenport several items. 31 December 1837. (P. 210)

Leonard Cardwell to Green H. Sloan a crop of tobacco. 12 January 1838. (P. 211)

John Barbee to John Litchford 61 acres. 29 August 1837. (P. 211)

Stephen Stafford to John Stafford 71 acres. 3 February 1838. (P. 212)

Franklin B. Day to Philip T. Day a tract of land in the 7th District. 5 February 1838. (P. 213)

Frederick N. Mitchell to Patsy Johnson a tract of land on Dixon's Creek. 16 January 1838. (P. 214)

Miles West to Robert West a tract of land on the Cumberland River. 23 November 1836. (Pp. 215-216)

Patsy Johnson to John A. Johnson a tract of land on Dixon's Creek for $300. 5 February 1838. (P. 216)

John Barbee to James Cunningham a tract of land on Roll's Creek. 28 August 1837. (P. 217)

Little B. Hughes to John Pigg eight and one fourth acres. 5 February 1838. (Pp. 217-218)

Solomon Smallin to David Philips a tract of land on Peyton's Creek. 11 February 1837. (P. 218)

Alfred Payne of Allen County, Kentucky to Henry M. Cook a tract of land. 28 September 1832. (Pp. 219-220)

William Pope to Joel Driver 100 acres. 12 August 1837. (P. 220)

Sheriff Samuel P. Howard to H. D. Marchbanks. 12 February 1838. (Pp. 221-222)

William Hutson of Jackson County to P. Hutson 20 acres. 7 June 1837. (Pp. 222-223)

James Hester to David G. Mason 94 acres. 17 February 1838. (Pp. 223-224)

Thomas Black to Meredith Meader. 18 January 1838. (P. 224)

DEED BOOK O

Sheriff Samuel P. Howard to Thomas Black a town lot. 18 January 1838. (P. 225)

Thomas Black to Meredith Meader a tract of land in the town of Maderville. 18 January 1838. (P. 226)

Isaac Wiseman to Gideon Gifford a tract of land on Goose Creek. 25 July 1836. (Pp. 226-227)

John S. Johnson to Jacob S. Johnson a tract of land on Goose Creek. 17 December 1837. (Pp. 227-228)

William Burrow to John S. Johnson 88 acres. 21 February 1838. (P. 228)

Clement McKinney to Wiley McKinney 32 acres. 22 February 1838. (P. 229)

William Burrow to John S. Johnson a tract of land on Goose Creek. 21 February 1838. (Pp. 230-231)

Valentine Presley to Jacob Null a tract of land. 1838. (P. 231)

Daniel F. Alexander of Lundes County, Mississippi appoints Madison B. Alexander as his attorney in settling the estate of Anderson Alexander. February 1838. (P. 232)

William Johnson and wife Martha of Franklin County, North Carolina to Samuel Johnson for love and affection 711 acres. 13 April 1831. (Pp. 233-234)

Samuel Johnson of Franklin County, North Carolina to William Ashley a tract of land on the Caney Fork. 1 March 1837. (Pp. 234-235)

A. C. Penn of Rutherford County to John O. Cosby a tract of land on Dixon's Creek. 30 January 1838. (Pp. 235-236)

John and Right Rigsby to John Hiett 25 acres. 21 December 1836. (P. 236)

William D. Turner to William Denny a tract of land in the 12th District. 23 February 1838. (P. 237)

James Wilson to Archibald Parker 15 acres. 18 January 1838. (P. 238)

Frances Coley to William Nickson a tract of land on Payton's Creek. 25 September 1837. (Pp. 238-239)

Joseph H. Durham to Clement McKinney a tract of land on Snow Creek. 5 March 1838. (P. 239)

Martin Freeman to Robert Bradley 100 acres. 6 November 1837. (P. 240)

William Ragland, Sr. to Christopher Simmons a tract of land on Long Creek. 15 February 1838. (P. 241)

Anthony Epperson to Annania Epperson 218 acres. 14 November 1837. (P. 242)

DEED BOOK O

Anthony Epperson to Peter Epperson a tract of land on Barren River. 20 November 1837. (P. 243)

Bryan Ward to Henry Ward a tract of land formerly owned by John Ward. 17 January 1829. (P. 244)

Benjamin F. Jones to William Denny 52 acres. 8 November 1837. (P. 245)

Archibald McNeill and wife Anny B. to Josiah Marshall a tract of land. 9 January 1837. (Pp. 245-246)

George Walton to Martin Binion a tract of land on Puncheon Camp Creek. 9 October 1830. (Pp. 246-247)

D. B. Donoho and wife Jane, Nathan Britton, and Richard Britton 100 acres. 7 October 1837. (Pp. 247-248)

David Tyree to Joseph Haden 100 acres. 24 July 1835. (Pp. 248-249)

Drury Anderson to Brantley Willman 18 acres. 16 October 1834. (P. 249)

John Stump and Nancy Stump, heirs of Nancy Douglass, late Nancy Armstead, appoint Robert Douglass as their attorney in settling the estate of her father, the late John Armstead. 1 July 1837. (P. 250)

John L. Dillard and wife Candis to Henry Ward the tract of land which the said Candis received from the estate of John Tate. 8 May 1837. (Pp. 251-252)

Drury Andrews to Brantley Willmore 50 acres. 16 October 1834. (P. 252)

Samuel Burdine to James Grissom a tract of land on the Cumberland River. 15 January 1838. (P. 253)

D. B. Donoho and others to R. G. Bryan 100 acres. 7 October 1837. (P. 254)

Elizabeth Sadler to her grandsons, John Sadler and Henry Sadler, a horse colt. 19 March 1838. (P. 255)

Edward Walton to Banister Meader a tract of land on Puncheon Camp Creek. 3 February 1838. (P. 256)

James Phillips to Israel McClelin a tract of land on Payton's Creek. 17 March 1838. (Pp. 257-258)

John Collum to Thomas A. Lancaster several items. 26 March 1838. (P. 258)

Alfred and Benjamin Pierce to William L. Alexander 569 acres. 29 March 1838. (Pp. 259-260)

Elijah Fouch from M. Fouch 139 acres. 6 March 1837. (P. 261)

STATE OF TENNESSEE Grant, No. 15140. Eight acres to Joel Simmons. 30 November 1820. (Pp. 261-262)

DEED BOOK O

STATE OF TENNESSEE Grant. No. 13168. Ten acres to Joel Simmons. 24 March 1819. (Pp. 262-263)

James Newby to Timan B. Flippin a tract of land on Rolls' Creek. 16 January 1838. (Pp. 263-264)

Sheriff Samuel P. Howard to Patrick Ferguson a tract of land. 11 April 1838. (Pp. 264-265)

Ezekiel Parkhurst to Elias Sloan and Samuel Winkler a tract of land on Peyton's Creek. 7 April 1836. (P. 266)

James Grissom to James Norris a tract of land. 30 June 1837. (Pp. 266-267)

James C. Williams to William Pistole and the other commissioners a tract of land for a meeting house and school house on Defeated Creek. 7 February 1838. (Pp. 267-268)

D. C. Ward to James Grissom a tract of land on the Cumberland River. 6 October 1835. (P. 269)

Samuel Winkler to Elias Sloan 175 acres. 28 February 1837. (Pp. 269-270)

John Smith to John A. Debow a tract of land on Goose Creek. 25 January 1811. (Pp. 270-272)

Abraham H. King to Samuel P. Howard a tract of land in the town of Carthage. 13 April 1838. (P. 272)

Charles Donoho to John Smith a tract of land on Goose Creek. 23 August 1808. (Pp. 273-274)

Romulus M. Sanders, Jourdan M. Sanders, and Ethelbert Sanders to John H. Burford a tract of land on the Cumberland River. 10 January 1836. (P. 274)

Ezekiel Parkhurst to Elias Sloan and Samuel Winkler a tract of land on Peyton's Creek. 7 April 1836. (P. 275)

William Robinson, Brooks Robinson to Patrick Hubbard 62½ acres. 6 March 1832. (Pp. 275-276)

Frances Parker to Alexander Pipkin a tract of land on the Cumberland River. 25 January 1836. (Pp. 276-277)

Elijah Toney of Jackson County, Alabama to Adam Ferguson a tract of land on the Cumberland River. 14 January 1837. (Pp. 277-278)

Guilford Jones to William Dennis 37 acres. 1838. (Pp. 278-279)

John Hudson to William Everett 78 acres. 2 April 1838. (P. 279)

John Hudson to John Enoch 50 acres. 19 January 1838. (Pp. 279-280)

John Duncan to Nancy Upton a tract of land on Hichman's Creek. 1 November 1837. (P. 280)

DEED BOOK O

John Wheeler to Isaac Mungle a tract of land on Goose Creek where Richard Britton deceased formerly lived. 15 October 1835. (P. 281)

Willis Jones to Robert Burton 33 acres. 24 January 1838. (Pp. 281-282)

Patrick Hamilton to George M. B. Duncan and others. 21 April 1838. (P. 282)

William Hutchinson to Thomas D. Hutchinson a tract of land on Barren River. 22 September 1837. (P. 283)

Edmund E. Cheatham to Samuel F. Patterson. 21 April 1838. (Pp. 283-284)

Robert Kinney to John Harper a tract of land. 12 January 1838. (Pp. 284-285)

Stephen Sypert to Henry B. McDonald a tract of land in the town of Carthage. April 1838. (P. 286)

James Walton to James High a tract of land on the Caney Fork. 21 March 1838. (Pp. 286-287)

James Gibson to Bennett Meader a tract of land on Barren River. 27 February 1837. (Pp. 287-288)

John Gann to Elijah Wilson a tract of 141 acres. 5 January 1838. (P. 288)

William Everett to William Martin, Jr. 78 acres. 16 April 1838. (Pp. 288-289)

William Owen to G. Owen 120 acres. 17 March 1838. (P. 289)

Joseph Watson appoints Charles J. Love as his attorney. 19 July 1837. (P. 290)

Andrew Hallum to William T. Williams a tract of land on the Caney Fork. 26 December 1837. (P. 291)

Josiah J. Caruthers to Marquis L. Donoho a tract of land. 30 January 1838. (Pp. 291-292)

William B. Dillon to William B. Hubbard. 23 April 1838. (Pp. 292-293)

Gunnery Wilbourn to Moses Loy a tract of land on Dixon's Creek. 2 September 1835. (P. 294)

Pamelia Penn to Charles McCullock a tract of land on Brush Creek. 14 November 1836. (P. 295)

Romulus M. Sanders and others to John M. Tunstall a tract of land on the Cumberland River. 10 January 1836. (P. 296)

Thomas Wilbourn to William S. Willis 85 acres. 16 April 1838. (P. 297)

Charles J. White to Wilson T. Meader 75 acres. 10 January 1838. (Pp. 297-298)

DEED BOOK O

Yearby Orange to John Gordon 37 acres. 28 April 1837. (Pp. 298-299)

George Stevens of Christian County, Kentucky appoints John Stevens as his attorney. 20 January 1838. (P. 299)

Isaac Morris to David T. Winfrey a tract of land on Brush Creek. 15 December 1834. (Pp. 299-300)

William Newby to Roland W. Newby a tract of land on Round Lick Creek. 4 April 1838. (P. 300)

Isaac Smith to Daniel T. Winfrey 142 acres. 28 July 1834. (P. 301)

James Sanders of Rutherford County to Joseph Acuff a tract of land on Long Creek. 5 May 1838. (Pp. 301-302)

Andrew J. Ford of McMinville to Obediah Hubbard a negro man now in the possession of Christopher Ford. April 1838. (Pp. 302-303)

William Lawrence to Isaac H. Davis 100 acres. 5 April 1838. (P. 303)

Jehu Meador to Elijah L. Richardson ten acres. 16 June 1833. (P. 304)

William Ashley to John A. Farmer seven acres. 29 October 1836. (P. 305)

Abraham Parker to Andrew Wallas a tract of land on Barren River. 9 July 1836. (Pp. 305-306)

Hickman Parker to Andrew Wallas a tract of land on the Cumberland River. 22 January 1836. (Pp. 306-307)

Joseph Woodcock to Samuel Law 45 acres. 21 October 1837. (Pp. 307-308)

Lewis Hire to John M. Cliburn a tract of land. 8 January 1838. (Pp. 308-309)

Samuel Lawrence to Joseph Woodcock $25\frac{1}{2}$ acres. 21 October 1837. (P. 309)

Lewis Jones to George W. Lamb a tract of land on Long Creek. 26 January 1838. (P. 310)

James H. Vaden to George M. B. Duncan a negro boy of dark color. 28 May 1838. (P. 311)

David Burford, Trustee of Smith County, to Frederick N. Mitchell. 20 March 1838. (Pp. 312-313)

Elijah Wheeler to Turman Wheeler 245 acres. 20 April 1838. (P. 313)

William Allen to Edwin Atwood a tract of land on Mulherin's Creek. 10 November 1837. (P. 314)

Benjamin J. Jones to Henry C. Jones 44 acres on Hickman's Creek. 1830. (P. 315)

DEED BOOK O

Andrew Allison to Timothy Walton a negro woman. 15 June 1838. (P. 315)

George Waggoner to Jacob Waggoner 25 acres. 15 June 1836. (P. 316)

Allen Cornwell to James M. Dill a tract of land. 23 June 1838. (Pp. 316-317)

Harriet Summersett to Jacob Towson the 130 acres she received at the death of her husband Joseph Summersett. 2 July 1838. (Pp. 318-319)

Peter Fitch to Cornelius Carver 50 acres. 5 September 1837. (P. 319)

William Carver to Joseph Carver 25 acres. 14 June 1837. (P. 320)

William W. Summersett to John C. and Frances Duffy his interest in the plantation of his father Joseph Summersett deceased. 5 July 1838. (P. 321)

Joseph Grisham to Christopher C. Penn a tract of land. 29 June 1838. (Pp. 321-322)

Isaac H. Davis to James Porter 107 acres. 13 September 1832. (Pp. 322-323)

Michael L. Uhls to Amzi Morgan a tract of land on Goose Creek. 16 October 1835. (P. 323)

John Drury to Amzi Morgan 26 acres. June 1837. (P. 324)

Amzi Morgan to James M. Chamberlain and Andrew Simmons a tract of land on Goose Creek. 16 July 1838. (Pp. 325-326)

Martin Burrus to William Tunstall several items. 23 July 1838. (P. 326)

Harriet Summersett to John C. and Frances Duffy four negroes. 21 July 1838. (P. 327)

Jacob Towson to Harriet Summersett his interest in the tract of land where Joseph Summersett lived. 21 July 1838. (Pp. 327-328)

Elbert G. Holland to Charles J. Bolton 63 acres. 21 July 1838. (Pp. 328-329)

William Parkhurst to Benjamin Tarver a tract of land. 28 July 1838. (P. 330)

David Parkhurst of Johnson County, Indiana to George Boston his interest in a tract of land on Peyton's Creek. 1838. (Pp. 330-331)

David Parkhurst to George Bolton 80 acres. 26 October 1836. (Pp. 331-332)

Rachel Wilkinson to George Boston five acres. 28 July 1838. (P. 332)

DEED BOOK O

William Duncan to Mary Pigg three tracts of land. 11 November 1837. (P. 333)

Isaac Moore of Bledsoe County, Tennessee to Isaac R. Moore of Dekalb County, Tennessee 120 acres. 10 July 1838. (P. 334)

Matthew Anderson to Peter A. Wilkinson 100 acres. 6 August 1838. (Pp. 335-336)

James B. and Elijah L. Richardson to Frances Duffy a crop of tobacco. 6 August 1838. (P. 336)

Matthew Anderson to George Sutton a negro slave. 3 August 1838. (P. 337)

Frances Adams to Shelby Hogg a crop of tobacco. 14 August 1838. (Pp. 337-338)

Chaffin McCormack and John McCormack to James E. Wheeler a crop of tobacco. 13 August 1838. (Pp. 338-339)

Thomas Cassity to William T. Cornwell a tract of land on Jennings' Creek. 13 December 1836. (Pp. 339-340)

Levi Gammon to John Shrum a tract of land on Big Barren River. 8 March 1834. (Pp. 340-341)

Price F. Martin to John C. Clardy of Christian County, Kentucky a negro girl. 20 August 1838. (P. 341)

John L. Sanders to Benjamin Pierce some personal property. 18 August 1838. (Pp. 341-342)

Thomas Leath to George M. Carter a crop of tobacco. 16 August 1838. (P. 342)

John T. Buckner to Joseph Gray 276 acres. 11 August 1838. (Pp. 242-243)

John Cooper to Joseph (Grief) a tract of land on the Caney Fork River. 28 December 1836. (P. 343)

Benjamin J. Vaden and James H. Vaden to Henry Goad a tract of land on the Cumberland River. 6 August 1838. (P. 344)

Henry Goad to Benjamin J. Vaden a tract of land on the Cumberland River. 6 August 1838. (Pp. 344-345)

James Sutton to John Luckey two tracts of land in the 22nd District. 17 August 1838. (Pp. 345-346)

Etheldred Warren to John E. Warren the land that he is entitled to as one of the heirs of John Warren deceased. 4 September 1837. (P. 346)

Thomas Phelps to John O. Cosby a negro girl or woman. 17 June 1838. (P. 347)

William Bratton to Charles J. Bratton a tract of land on Johns' Creek. 20 August 1838. (Pp. 347-348)

DEED BOOK O

Robert Worsham to William Taylor a crop of corn. 22 August 1838. (P. 348)

Anderson Bratton to Charles J. Bratton a tract of land on the Cumberland River. 20 August 1838. (P. 349)

E. L. Richardson to Joseph L. Carter and Joseph Gifford a tract of land. 13 December 1837. (Pp. 349-350)

Joshua M. Coffee to James Malone 334 acres. 19 November 1835. (P. 351)

Henry L. Day to Martin McMurry a tract of land. 23 August 1838. (Pp. 351-352)

Ellis Beasley to Mark Dyson 136 acres. 10 August 1838. (P. 352)

Solomon Debow and his wife Elizabeth, formerly Elizabeth Caruthers, daughter of Samuel Caruthers deceased, to John A. Debow a tract of land on Goose Creek. 19 September 1837. (Pp. 353-354)

Joseph Jones, Jr. to E. Kemp 93 acres. 4 August 1838. (P. 354)

Evan Williams to Archibald Fulks a tract of land on Mulherin's Creek. 14 December 1836. (P. 355)

Richard Kirby to Alsey Kemp 80 acres. 5 September 1836. (Pp. 355-356)

Avery Hester to Alsey Kemp 20 acres. 24 October 1836. (P. 356)

Thomas T. Hall to Thomas M. P. Hall his interest in a tract of land. 22 August 1838. (P. 357)

Thomas Cassity to Ensley Cassity 45 acres. 14 August 1834. (Pp. 357-358)

Isaac H. Davis to Martimore Waters 37 acres. 31 December 1836. (Pp. 358-359)

John A. Debow to Solomon Debow a tract of land on Goose Creek. 19 July 1838. (P. 359)

James L. Murphree to John Bridges of Wilson County a tract of land. 28 December 1836. (Pp. 359-360)

James C. Williams to John Parker 165 acres. 23 January 1838. (Pp. 360-361)

Eason Howell to Nathan Gays a tract of land on Big Barren River. 18 March 1837. (Pp. 361-362)

Pleasant Hall to Nathan Goss 80 acres. 29 April 1837. (P. 362)

John Brandon, Sr. to Nathan Goss a tract of land. 4 April 1838. (P. 363)

John Mitchell to John Reeves 90 acres. 1838. (Pp. 363-364)

DEED BOOK O

Walker Wade to John Reeves 121½ acres. 3 August 1836. (P. 364)

Andrew W. Wallis to Z. G. Goodall 125 acres. 18 April 1838. (P. 395)

Simon Jones to Thomas Belcher a bay mare. 21 May 1838. (P. 366)

Samuel Walker to William Hall a tract of land on Mulherin's Creek. 1 October 1836. (P. 367)

John Ballard to Auls Kemp 50 acres. 14 June 1837. (Pp. 367-368)

Abraham Snider to John Reeves. 29 August 1838. (P. 368)

William Burrow to Moses B. Freeman a tract of land on Goose Creek. 13 January 1837. (P. 369)

John Barton of Wilson County to Samuel Bell a tract of land granted to Samuel Barton by the State of North Carolina. July 1836. (Pp. 369-370)

Samuel Casey to Jonathan Dedman a tract of land on Walker's Creek. 14 October 1837. (P. 370)

Joseph Payne and John Payne, executors of William Payne, to Isaac N. Payne 66 acres. 2 June 1838. (P. 371)

James Malone to Phebe McCormick a tract of land on Helton's Creek. 4 July 1838. (Pp. 371-372)

Sheriff W. W. Bailey to Brien Tubb a tract of land. September 1838. (Pp. 372-373)

A. D. W. Williams to James Walton. 1 September 1838. (P. 374)

Benjamin Matthews to George Powell. 29 August 1838. (Pp. 374-375)

Samuel Hughes to Vincent Moreland a tract of land on Buffalo Creek. 31 September 1838. (Pp. 375-376)

Gabriel Hynes to Vincent Moreland. 31 August 1838. (P. 376)

Edmund Corley to Charles H. Tunstall a tract of land. 1 September 1838. (Pp. 376-377)

Isaac Willingham and wife Nancy of Graves County, Kentucky to William H. Jones a tract of land on the Caney Fork. 24 March 1837. (Pp. 377-378)

Robert E. Cleveland to William West. 3 September 1838. (P. 379)

John T. McClain to William McClain a negro girl. 27 March 1838. (P. 380)

Edmund Estate to David Goodall a crop of corn. 28 August 1838. (P. 380)

DEED BOOK O

Susan C. Marley agrees to put her dower in the possession of John F. Wilmot. 4 September 1837. (P. 381)

John Shelton to Stephen W. Malone 265 acres. 30 March 1838. (Pp. 381-382)

Archibald G. Sloan to Samuel T. Coker several negroes belonging to his father Archibald Sloan. 8 September 1838. (Pp. 382-383)

John Culbreath to Bossee Foley a crop of tobacco. 11 September 1838. (Pp. 383-384)

Alexander Dillehay to Abner Smith. 15 September 1838. (Pp. 384-385)

William Ashley to Jonathan W. Agee 75 acres. 3 September 1838. (P. 385)

Ezekiel Parkhurst to Elias Sloan and Samuel Winkler 200 acres. 21 October 1836. (P. 386)

William Ashley to Jonathan Agee 21 acres. 11 September 1838. (P. 387)

William Ashley to Ephraim Agee 191 acres. 8 September 1838. (Pp. 387-388)

Isaac Bradley to James R. Toney a town lot in the town of Carthage. 18 September 1838. (P. 388)

John Conger and Alexander Dillard to Mary Pigg one acre. 15 September 1836. (P. 389)

Dennis Hargis to M. and P. Duffy a crop of tobacco. 22 September 1838. (P. 390)

James Uhls to Joseph L. Carter a crop of tobacco. 24 September 1838. (P. 390)

Thomas D. Cardwell to Leonidas D. Hogg. 27 September 1838. (P. 391)

Jesse White to John Martin. 29 September 1838. (Pp. 391-392)

Susan Thompson to Charles Thompson. 1838. (Pp. 392-393)

Robert L. Taylor to Joseph L. Carter a crop of tobacco. 6 October 1838. (P. 393)

Stephen Early to John Early a tract of land. 1 August 1838. (Pp. 393-394)

Stephen Garrott and Josiah Garrott to Thomas D. Johnson a crop of tobacco. Said Garrotts live together on the place where James Philips lived. 6 October 1838. (P. 394)

James M. Ballew to John A. Sloan 25 acres. 3 October 1838. (Pp. 395-396)

Sheriff Samuel P. Howard to Andrew Pickett. 1837.

DEED BOOK O

(Pp. 396-397)

John Gwaltney and Godfrey Gregory to John Buckner 83 acres. 11 September 1838. (Pp. 397-398)

Lambert M. Cothron to Joseph L. Carter a crop of tobacco. 25 September 1838. (P. 398)

Mary Hammack to her son Leonard A. Hammack. 14 July 1838. (P. 399)

L. D. Hargis to Young & Coker several items. 9 October 1838. (P. 399)

Clibourn Matthews to Ezekiel West a crop of tobacco. 11 October 1838. (P. 400)

Beckman Nichols to Berrel Lay a tract of land. 10 March 1838. (Pp. 400-401)

David Robertson to Daniel Robertson a tract of land on Goose Creek. 15 October 1838. (P. 401)

Simon P. Hughes to Charles R. Blair 53 acres. 13 October 1838. (P. 402)

Simon P. Hughes to Patrick Hubbard 38 acres. 10 October 1838. (Pp. 402-403)

Simon P. Hughes to Michael Shoemake 59 acres. 13 October 1838. (Pp. 403-404)

Patrick Hubbard and Judas Hubbard, now Judas Shoemake and her husband Michael Shoemake, Frances Hubbard, now Frances Dillard and her husband Joseph Dillard, to John Maggart a tract of land on the Cumberland River. 8 October 1838. (P. 404)

William Harris and Robert Malone to their neighbors a tract of land for a place of worship and a school house. 9 June 1838. (P. 405)

Thomas Smith to M. and P. Duffy. 1838. (P. 405)

Bannister Meader to Bennet Meader a tract of land on Puncheon Camp Creek. 29 September 1838. (P. 406)

James Abel to Bennett Lay a tract of land on Goose Creek. 1 December 1834. (Pp. 406-407)

Jabez Burton to Andrew McClellin a tract of land. 26 September 1838. (Pp. 407-408)

Malachi Shoulders to G. W. (   ) a crop of tobacco. 2 November 1838. (Pp. 408-409)

William Shoemake, Jr. from William Shoemake, Sr. eleven head of hogs. 20 August 1838. (P. 409)

Woodson and Charlotte Palmer to Elijah Williams a tract of land adjoining the lands of Isaac Kitrell. 1838. (P. 410)

DEED BOOK O

Thomas D. Hutchinson of Jackson County and William Hutchinson to Jabez Burton a tract of land on Barren River. 1 November 1838. (P. 411)

Branch Grigg to R. G. Bryant 40 acres. 3 November 1838. (P. 412)

James Malone to Hezekiah Turner a tract of land on Hickman's Creek. 21 February 1838. (Pp. 412-413)

Thomas A. Lancaster to Frederick Decker 362 acres. 1838. (P. 413)

John Black to Young & Coker a tract of land on Goose Creek. 1 November 1838. (P. 414)

William Flowers to B. E. Warren a tract of land on Fall Creek. 5 November 1838. (Pp. 414-415)

R. G. Bryant to Nathaniel M. Adams 79 acres. 19 August 1837. (P. 415)

William Roark to Womack Parker 275 acres. 9 November 1838. (Pp. 416-417)

Asa Roark of Allen County, Kentucky to John Blankenship a tract of land on Puncheon Camp Creek. 20 August 1838. (P. 418)

Alexander Ferguson to Elijah Roark 15 acres. 2 November 1838. (Pp. 418-419)

Sion Cook of Allen County, Kentucky to A. Jent two tracts of land. 3 November 1838. (P. 419)

Sion Cook to A. Jent 106 acres. 3 November 1838. (P. 420)

Edmund P. Bryant to Brice Snider a tract of 129 acres. 6 October 1838. (Pp. 420-421)

Wilson T. Meader to Young & Coker a tract of land. 17 January 1836. (Pp. 421-422)

Green Wright to Gregory (   ) a tract of land. 31 October 1838. (Pp. 422-424)

Jesse Powell, John L. Powell, and Elijah Hylton to Thomas A. Lancaster 75 acres. 29 October 1838. (P. 424)

Barnet Blankenship to Jesse M. Blankenship a tract of land on Puncheon Camp Creek. 6 April 1838. (P. 425)

Allen Bryant to William Snider 50 acres. 5 November 1838. (Pp. 425-426)

John Haley to Godfrey Gregory 60 acres. 3 November 1838. (P. 426)

John A. Farmer to Godfrey Gregory a tract of land. 3 November 1838. (P. 427)

Jesse Meachum to Benjamin Arundell. 1838. (Pp. 427-428)

DEED BOOK O

Thomas Hunter to David Rowland a tract of land that he bought of Samuel Hill of North Carolina. 1 August 1838. (P. 428)

Charles Bolton of Shelby County, Tennessee to his daughters (Lousa), Estell, Cinderella, and Lucretia Bolton. 22 February 1838. (P. 428)

Thomas Sadler to Daniel Wilkerson 68 acres. 22 June 1838. (P. 429)

John G. Park to Thomas J. Black. 20 November 1838. (Pp. 429-430)

Josiah Howell of Kentucky to Burrell Harris a tract of land on Goose Creek. 14 September 1837. (Pp. 430-431)

Anthony Epperson to Ananias Epperson four and one fourth acres. 24 November 1838. (P. 431)

Joseph Mitchell to his sister Mary Mitchell some personal property. 10 November 1838. (P. 432)

Henry W. Glover to William Vaden some livestock. 1838. (P. 432)

Josiah Roark of Cole County, Missouri appoints Moses Carmel as his attorney. 10 February 1834. (P. 433)

Theoderick Ferrell to Burton G. Ferrell and Burchett F. Ferrell a tract of land on Snow Creek. 25 November 1838. (Pp. 433-434)

Moses Carman, attorney for Josiah Roark of Monroe County, Kentucky, to James Walker a tract of land. 29 November 1838. (Pp. 434-435)

Robert L. Caruthers to Daniel T. Lake 158 acres acres where Sally Caruthers now lives, she having a life estate. 1838. (Pp. 435-436)

Robert Hodges to Samuel Stoke 100 acres. 19 October 1838. (Pp. 436-437)

Robert Hodges to James Shelton a tract of land on Round Lick Creek. 19 October 1838. (P. 437)

Daniel K. Witcher to Gilbert B. Gibbs a tract of land that his father gave him. 1 November 1838. (P. 438)

Robert Hodges to John Turner a tract of land on Round Lick Creek. 19 October 1838. (P. 439)

John Knight to Thomas L. Knight, Ellis E. Knight, William M. Knight, Henry M. Knight, C. Y. Ramsey, Charlotte Smith, and Patsy West, heirs of the said John Knight a tract of 188 acres on Defeated Creek. 3 December 1838. (Pp. 439-440)

Wyatt W. Bailey, Sheriff, to William Ballenger. December 1838. (Pp. 441-442)

DEED BOOK O

Clabourn Wilson to James C. Sanders a tract of land on Bluff Creek. 18 November 1837. (P. 442)

Benjamin Turner from Robert Hodges a tract of land on Round Lick Creek. 19 October 1838. (P. 443)

Elijah Walker to Wilson Walker my interest in the estate of William Walker deceased. 14 May 1838. (P. 444)

Matthew Davis to Allen Matthews a tract of land on Defeated Creek. 2 July 1838. (P. 444)

John Knight to his seven sons and daughters eight slaves. 3 December 1838. (P. 445)

John Knight to his sons and daughters 25 head of horses. 3 December 1838. (Pp. 445-446)

William Bundy to his daughter Rebecca Bundy who had intermarried with Thomas Bundy a negro slave. 30 August 1838. (P. 446)

Anthony Hallmontoller to C. Nolen a tract of land. 8 December 1838. (P. 447)

Henry W. Glover to William Vaden. 8 December 1838. (P. 448)

Charles Nolen to Anthony Halmontoller a tract of land. 8 December 1838. (Pp. 448-449)

Isaac Willingham and wife Nancy of Graves County, Kentucky to Giles Williams their one fourth interest in a tract of land granted by the State of North Carolina to John Nichols. 27 July 1836. (Pp. 449-450)

Frances Adams to Andrew McClelin a crop of tobacco. 1838. (P. 450)

John Nichols, Kiziah Woodridge, and James H. Wilson of Williamson County, Tennessee to Giles Williams a tract of land on the Caney Fork River. 10 November 1838. (P. 451)

John Sloan to John Heath 100 acres. 20 November 1838. (P. 452)

Moses Eastes to Jacob Waggoner a negro girl. 5 December 1838. (P. 452)

Warren P. Cooker to Joseph L. Carter a tract of land that he drew of Johnson's estate. 17 December 1838. (P. 453)

Martin Armstrong of Surry County, North Carolina to L. Clark of Davidson County, Tennessee a tract of land. 7 December 1789. (Pp. 453-454)

Robert Thompson and Thomas Hickman of Davidson County to John Seay a tract of land. 16 December 18__. (Pp. 454-455)

Charles Bolton to Lent Bolton. 1835. (Pp. 455-456)

DEED BOOK O

James H. Wilson of Williamson County, Tennessee to Giles Williams a tract of land on the Caney Fork. 10 November 1838. (P. 456)

Charles Bolton to James Bolton 296 acres. 1 November 1838. (P. 457)

John Morris to John Brien several slaves. 1838. (Pp. 457-458)

Andrew McClelin to Samuel H. Wilson a tract of land on Buffalo Creek. 13 November 1838. (P. 458)

James W. Waugh to Hopewell Carman some livestock. 21 December 1838. (P. 459)

Holden W. Pruett and wife Elizabeth, James Hogan, and William Hogan of Franklin County, Alabama to Bartlett B. Uhls 425 acres. 7 December 1838. (Pp. 459-460)

Jesse Waldrong to Ezekiel W. Taylor 114 acres. 24 December 1838. (P. 461)

Sheriff Wiatt W. Bailey to Leonard H. Cardwell a tract of land. 21 December 1838. (Pp. 461-462)

Leonard H. Cardwell to Martin W. Sloan a tract of land. December 1838. (P. 463)

James Harrison to James Barrot a tract of land on Mulherin's Creek. 8 September 1838. (P. 464)

John R. Benson to James McMurry. 23 August 1838. (Pp. 465-466)

Benjamin J. Jones to William Nealey. 24 December 1838. (P. 466)

Aven Ward to Nancy Upton $34\frac{1}{4}$ acres. 10 August 1838. (Pp. 466-467)

William Martin to Thomas Highers a tract of land on Rawls' Creek. 20 December 1838. (P. 467)

William Martin to Elijah Wilson a tract of land on Rawls' Creek. 26 December 1838. (P. 468)

William Martin to Wilson Y. Martin a negro girl. 4 January 1837. (Pp. 468-469)

William T. Morehead of Lauderdale County, Tennessee to Marena O. Marley of Haywood County, Tennessee. 10 October 1838. (Pp. 469-470)

William B. Dillon to Nelson Thornton. 29 December 1838. (Pp. 470-471)

John B. Uhls to John L. Johnson some personal property. 22 December 1838. (P. 471)

Thomas L. Dillon from William Garrott some personal property. 4 January 1839. (Pp. 472-473)

DEED BOOK O

Jesse Smith and wife Mary of Scott County, Missouri to Stephen B. Lile a tract of land on Hickman's Creek. 1 May 183?. (Pp. 473-474)

Allen Holladay to George W. Hughes a tract of land on Buffalo Creek. 3 January 1839. (P. 475)

Gabriel Hines to Andrew McClelin. 5 January 1839. (P. 476)

Hugh L. Sloan to John L. Sloan his interest in the estate of Archibald Sloan deceased. 5 January 1839. (Pp. 476-477)

J. W. Smelledge to John Lucky nine acres. 7 January 1839. (Pp. 477-478)

Bartlett B. Uhls to Solomon Baker 131 acres. 22 December 1838. (P. 478)

Gregory Burns to Robert Green Wright a tract of land on Dixon's Creek. 2 November 1838. (Pp. 479-480)

James Harrison to James Barnet a tract of land on Mulherin's Creek. 8 September 1838. (P. 480)

James Pendarvis to Shelby C. Beasley a tract of land on Turkey Creek. 27 October 1838. (P. 481)

Joseph L. Carter and Joseph Gifford to John Holland a tract of land on Goose Creek. 21 November 1838. (Pp. 481-482)

Simon P. Hughes to Davidson Draper and Robert Glover a tract of land on Hurricane Creek. 1 December 1838. (P. 483)

Simon P. Hughes to Michael Shoemake a tract of land on the Cumberland River. 20 November 1838. (Pp. 483-484)

Ira L. Sullivan to Jourdan Sullivan a tract of land on Snow Creek. 1839. (Pp. 484-485)

C. J. Coker to Elijah Carman a tract of land on Goose Creek. 24 December 1838. (P. 485)

Andrew McClelin to Hugh McClelin a tract of land on Defeated Creek. 7 January 1839. (P. 486)

P. W. Cage to the heirs of Gabriel Dillard deceased 49 acres. 7 January 1839. (P. 487)

William Denny to Benjamin F. Jones and William D. Turner a tract of land in the 12th District. 3 January 1839. (Pp. 487-488)

John Parker to James C. Williams a tract of land on Defeated Creek. 23 January 1838. (Pp. 488-489)

Edmund Simmons to James C. Williams a tract of land on the Cumberland River. 28 October 1838. (P. 489)

Nathan N. Robinson to Littleton H. Carter and Robert Bowman a tract of land. 31 December 1838. (P. 490)

DEED BOOK O

Daniel T. Lake to Joseph F. Hibbitt a tract of land. 21 July 1838. (Pp. 490-491)

John Lucky to Philip Sadler 60 acres. 1 January 1839. (Pp. 491-492)

Peter Porter to John H. Newbell and Bartlett James, Jr. his part of a stallion. 26 November 1838. (P. 492)

Zedoc B. Roberts to William McClain 100 acres. 14 January 1839. (P. 493)

Elisha Worley to George H. Campbell 100 acres. 4 January 1839. (Pp. 493-494)

John Dawson to James Ragland 27½ acres. 26 March 1837. (P. 494)

John Barton of Wilson County to John Mitchell a tract of land granted to Samuel Barton by the State of North Carolina. 13 August 1838. (P. 495)

William Kyle to William Denny a negro girl. 5 January 1839. (P. 496)

Delilah Pugh and William Reaves enter into a marriage contract. 19 May 1835. (P. 496)

Augustus Robinson and Rachel Robinson of Mississippi to Nathaniel Terry a tract of land. 27 December 1838. (P. 497)

Augustus Robinson to Nathaniel Terry his interest in the estate of Stephen Robinson deceased. 27 December 1838. (P. 498)

Sarah W. Hallum, William H. Mason, and John L. Mason, heirs of John Mason of Montgomery County, Tennessee to John L. Hallum, husband of the said Sarah W. Hallum, a tract of land. 8 January 1839. (P. 499)

John L. D. Hallum of McCracken County, Kentucky and wife to John Stevens a tract of land in the town of Carthage. 19 January 1839. (P. 500)

Jackson F. Cole to Samuel F. Cole and William McClard some personal property. 20 January 1839. (P. 500)

Robert Harper to James Harper a tract of land on Jennings' Creek. 18 January 1839. (P. 501)

O. B. Hubbard to James R. Toney and Nelson Kyle. 17 January 1839. (Pp. 501-502)

Archibald Fulks to James Wooten a tract of land on Mulherin's Creek. 26 January 1839. (P. 502)

Thomas L. Hardy to George C. Gifford a tract of land on Goose Creek. 4 September 1838. (Pp. 503-504)

William Dillon to John W. Lauderdale of Sumner County several items. 31 January 1839. (Pp. 504-505)

DEED BOOK O

Samuel Read to Presley Askins some personal property. 31 January 1829. (Pp. 505-506)

Henry A. Young to Thomas Stafford some personal property. 1 February 1839. (P. 506)

DEED BOOK P

William C. Taylor to Thompson Mace his interest in the estate of his father, James Taylor, of Cumberland County, Virginia. Mentions that his mother is Mildred Taylor. 5 February 1839. (P. 1)

Abner C. Perkins to Martin Miller some personal property. 5 February 1839. (Pp. 1-2)

James Wamack to J. D. Gentry. 4 February 1839. (P. 2)

William B. Dillon to James R. Toney some personal property. 14 February 1839. (Pp. 3-4)

William B. Dillon to Nelson Thornton. 14 February 1839. (P. 4)

Asabel H. Durkee and his wife Mary E., formerly Mary E. Rogers, daughter of Warren Rogers of Maury County, Tennessee, appoints James Cunningham of Vermilion County, Illinois as their attorney in settingly the estate of the said Warren Rogers. 26 October 1838. (P. 5)

Benjamin Pearce and Alfred Pearce to William F. Andrews. 15 April 1839. (P. 6)

Jesse Fuller to Jonathan Fare a sorrel mare. 15 April 1839. (Pp. 6-7)

Champion T. Thomas to John Gordon some personal property. 25 February 1839. (P. 7)

Henry M. Carr and James R. Carr to James A. Scruggs some livestock. 7 March 1839. (P. 8)

George W. Reasonover to William Waters 40 acres. 17 March 1837. (Pp. 8-9)

Moses Eastes to Jonathan Bailey 206 acres. 4 April 1839. (Pp. 9-10)

David Thomason to J. L. Fare 70 acres. 30 March 1839. (Pp. 10-11)

Avin Ward to Benjamin R. Owen 200 acres. 25 February 1839. (Pp. 11-12)

James H. Vaden and Benjamin J. Vaden to Robert Holladay a tract of land. 26 September 1838. (P. 12)

James R. Kerr to Willis Coggin 100 acres. 21 February 1839. (P. 13)

Willis Coggin to Wade H. Wallace 100 acres. 21 February 1839. (Pp. 13-14)

William Parker to John Donoho a tract of land on Defeated Creek. 30 December 1837. (Pp. 14-15)

George White to George Cliburn a tract of land on Long Creek. 31 January 1839. (Pp. 15-16)

Sheriff W. W. Bailey to P. Vaughn. 20 December 1838. (Pp. 16-17)

DEED BOOK P

R. O. Maricle to James Shelton his interest in the estate of his father. Other heirs: George Maricle, Alfred Maricle. 4 February 1839. (P. 17)

David Bratton of Edminson County, Kentucky to William Burrow a tract of land on Goose Creek. December 1836. (Pp. 17-18)

Charles Marsh to William Marsh a tract of land on Big Barren River. 17 January 1835. (Pp. 18-19)

Philip Marsh to William Marsh 20 acres. 17 January 1835. (P. 19)

John Meador to Ira Meador 49 acres. 25 February 1839. (Pp. 19-20)

Article of agreement between Nathaniel Terry and James Eaton. 25 September 1830. (P. 20)

William D. Evans to Joseph H. Durham a tract of land. 8 January 1839. (Pp. 20-21)

Martin H. Burris to Lemuel A. Hammack his interest in the estate of his father Jacob Burris and his mother Susannah Burris. 16 March 1839. (P. 21)

William Allen to Abraham Caruthers a tract of land. 4 January 1839. (P. 22)

Moses Eastes to Solomon Caplinger three tracts of land in the town of Rome. 28 February 1839. (Pp. 22-23)

Robert Lindsey and James Elison, executors of Joseph Elison, to N. Durham 109 acres. 13 April 1839. (Pp. 23-24)

James Cunningham to William Flowers a tract of land on the Cumberland River. 11 May 1838. (P. 24)

William D. Gowan of Cannon County, Tennessee to Joshua Morris a tract of land. 22 January 1839. (Pp. 24-25)

Darcus Bohannon to John Dedman a tract of land on Hickman's Creek. 2 April 1836. (Pp. 25-26)

Henry Hall to David Hall and John Hall 77 acres. 22 January 1836. (P. 26)

Edward Glover to Thomas Bandy a tract of land on Long Creek. 2 May 1838. (P. 27)

Isaac Morris to Joshua Morris a tract of land. 7 December 1831. (Pp. 27-28)

Jabez Gifford to Joseph Gifford a tract of land on Goose Creek. 16 January 1839. (Pp. 28-29)

Jehu Meador to David Turner a tract of land. 25 February 1839. (Pp. 29-30)

Neill Patterson to Alfred M. Winkler 150 acres. 10 December 1837. (P. 30)

DEED BOOK P

Sampson Sloan to Christian Austin a tract of land on Peyton's Creek. 12 January 1837. (Pp. 30-31)

Vincent R. Bradford to Bleuford Oliver a tract of land on Mulherin's Creek. 30 March 1839. (P. 31)

Elijah Colbert of Allen County, Kentucky to James Jones, Jr. 62 acres. 30 June 1838. (P. 32)

Sheriff W. W. Bailey to John Stevens a tract of land. 1839. (Pp. 33-34)

John Stevens to David Hogg a tract of land. 1 March 1839. (Pp. 35-36)

William Flowers, Sr. to James Harrison a tract of land. 20 November 1838. (P. 36)

Samuel Burdine to John H. Flowers a tract of land in the town of Rome. 24 April 1839. (P. 37)

William Tubb to Isaac Bates a tract of land belonging to the estate of his father James Tubb. 21 August 1838. (Pp. 37-38)

This indenture between Ann Pillow, Greenwood Payne and Martha his wife of Davidson County, ( ) Payne, and Spencer Payne of Haywood County, Flower McGregor of Wilson County, Robert Boothe and his wife Manerva of Rutherford County, George W. Payne, son of George Payne deceased of Davidson County, and Mary, Manerva, (Eva), July, and Tennessee Payne, heirs of Esquire Payne deceased of Illinois to Robert Allen a tract of land on Turkey Creek. January 1839. (Pp. 38-39)

David L. Mitchell of Indiana to Smith Gregory a tract of land on Peyton's Creek. 22 October 1836. (Pp. 40-41)

Archibald Parker to George T. Wright. 20 April 1839. (P. 41)

Levi Garrison to John C. Tuck a tract of land. 12 February 1838. (P. 42)

James Cunningham of Illinois to Matthew Mooningham 92 acres. 15 April 1839. (P. 43)

Sarah Wallace to Wade H. Wallace 100 acres. 30 April 1836. (Pp. 43-44)

Excum Whitley to Daniel Wilkerson 25 acres. 16 January 1839. (Pp. 44-45)

John Duncan to Reuben Baird a tract of land. 17 December 1838. (Pp. 45-46)

Sheriff W. W. Bailey to Martin W. Sloan a tract of land. 1839. (Pp. 46-47)

Sarah Wallace to Wade H. Wallace a tract of land. 30 April 1836. (Pp. 47-48)

James Witcher to Francis Parker a tract of land on Big

DEED BOOK P

Barren River. 4 November 1835. (Pp. 48-49)

Thomas Jones to S. Burdine a tract of land on the Cumberland River. 22 December 1812. (Pp. 49-50)

Sheriff W. W. Bailey to William B. Taylor a tract of land. 1839. (Pp. 50-51)

The administrators of William Thompson to William Carter a tract of land on Big Goose Creek. 27 March 1836. (Pp. 51-52)

Andrew Goff of William County to Polly Hamilton, wife of John C. Hamilton, formerly Polly Turner, Berryman Turner, Nancy Turner, Betsy Turner, Robert Turner, Susannah Turner, and John Turner, heirs of Berryman Turner a tract of land on Round Lick Creek. 14 (   ) 1807. (Pp. 52-53)

John Mungle to Nathaniel W. Adams 30 acres on Goose Creek. 14 December 1838. (Pp. 53-54)

William Belcher to Thomas Belcher a tract of land. 25 April 1839. (P. 54)

Sheriff W. W. Bailey to Thomas Carman 117 acres. 1839. (Pp. 54-55)

William B. Pursley to Isaac Mungle a tract of land on Goose Creek. December 1836. (P. 56)

Jeremiah Smith to James Rollins a tract of land on Mulherin's Creek. 30 July 1838. (P. 57)

George White to Mary West a tract of land on Long Creek. 18 January 1839. (P. 58)

James Pendarvis to Henry Beasley a tract of land on Turkey Creek. 15 February 1839. (Pp. 58-59)

Woodson Fitts to William Strother a tract of land on the Caney Fork. 8 February 1839. (Pp. 59-60)

Robert Allen to his son Joseph W. Allen a tract of land in the town of Carthage. 4 May 1839. (P. 60)

William B. Rose to William D. Evans a tract of land on the Caney Fork. 4 October 1838. (P. 61)

David Pursley to William B. Pursley a tract of land. 27 September 1836. (Pp. 61-62)

David Bratton of Kentucky to William Burrow a tract of land. 22 March 1836. (Pp. 62-63)

Thomas Matthews, John Matthews, and Alexander Matthews of North Carolina and Tennessee to Christian Austin a tract of land on Peyton's Creek. 29 July 1836. (P. 64)

Robert L. Taylor to William Burrow a tract of land on Goose Creek. 1 June 1838. (Pp. 64-65)

David Pursley to Robert Pursley a tract of land. 6 February 1838. (Pp. 65-66)

DEED BOOK P

Hubbard Wright to William Burrow a tract of land on Goose Creek. 13 November 1835. (Pp. 66-67)

Wilson Cage to Gilbert Gibbs a tract of land. 18 February 1839. (P. 67)

Bartlett James, Sr. to Avin Ward a tract of land. 23 February 1839. (P. 68)

John McKinnis and Margaret McKinness 125 acres. 24 October 1838. (Pp. 68-69)

Andrew Wallis to Thomas Bray a tract of land on the Cumberland River. 12 June 1837. (Pp. 69-70)

Burrel Lay to Roda Redman a tract of land on Dixon's Creek. 6 November 1838. (P. 70)

A. M. Leatherwood to Presley Askins a tract of land. 14 May 1839. (P. 71)

George Thompson and James Shelton to Fleming Stubblefield a tract of land. 7 May 1838. (Pp. 71-72)

William R. Alexander to M. B. Alexander his interest in the estate of Daniel Alexander. 2 January 1835. (Pp. 72-73)

Isaac Mingle to Dickson Ferguson a tract of land. 12 June 1837. (Pp. 73-74)

James Wooten to Elihu Wood 60 acres. 20 January 1838. (P. 74)

David Pursley to H. L. and W. Y. Pursley 116 acres. 6 February 1838. (P. 75)

James Cunningham to William Flowers 92 acres. May 1838. (Pp. 75-76)

Samuel Tubb to Isaac Bates his interest in the estate of his father James Tubb. 22 December 1837. (P. 76)

John Ellis to William Burrow a tract of land on the Cumberland River. 8 December 1834. (P. 77)

Henry Jones to Samuel ( ) a tract of land. 29 September 1838. (Pp. 77-78)

James Pendarvis to Peter Hackett a tract of land. 4 April 1839. (P. 78)

Henry L. Day to Franklin B. Day a tract of land in the 7th District. 7 May 1839. (P. 79)

Booker L. Dalton to Josiah J. Caruthers a tract of land. 14 May 1839. (P. 79)

Rachel Patterson, executor of William Patterson, to Joseph Caruthers a tract of land. 1 October 1838. (P. 80)

Thomas A. Durham to Matthew Nichols. 21 May 1839. (P. 81)

DEED BOOK P

Stephen Mann to John Jared 286 acres. 6 October 1838. (Pp. 81-82)

Thomas A. Durham to Matthew Nichols 150 acres. 24 May 1839. (P. 82)

Andrew Clark to William P. Anderson and Overton B. Anderson a tract of land on Hurricane Creek. 15 February 1839. (Pp. 82-83)

Thomas A. Durham to Stephen Mann and Henry Mann a negro girl. 29 May 1839. (P. 83)

Isaac Wiseman and wife Peachy F. Wiseman, daughter of Josiah Wood and his widow Patience, to Josiah J. Caruthers a tract of land. 8 January 1839. (Pp. 83-84)

John Walton to James Young some negro slaves. 1 June 1839. (P. 84)

Josiah Howell and wife Sarah of Scott County, Missouri to Nathan Goss a negro woman. 17 May 1839. (P. 85)

Polly Vaughn, now the wife of Isaac Dillon, appoints Henry Rhodes of Sumner County as their attorney. 29 October 1838. (Pp. 85-86)

George Gifford to William C. Hargis a tract of land on Goose Creek. 28 January 1839. (Pp. 86-87)

John W. Mann to James C. Jones of Wilson County a negro woman. 29 May 1839. (P. 87)

Josiah Wildman of Allen County, Kentucky to Stephen Holland a tract of land. 13 April 1839. (Pp. 87-88)

John Crowder to John Adams a tract of land on Goose Creek. 17 November 1837. (Pp. 88-89)

Josiah Wildman to Rawley Crawford a tract of land on Goose Creek. 13 April 1839. (P. 89)

John Adams to John Gross a tract of land on Goose Creek. 10 October 1835. (P. 90)

Job Meador to Anderson Meador 100 acres. 7 June 1839. (Pp. 90-91)

John Drury to John Adams 125 acres. 26 September 1836. (Pp. 91-92)

George W. Walker to David Dies 15 acres. 13 April 1839. (Pp. 92-93)

Aaron L. Adams to John Adams a tract of land on Goose Creek. 30 March 1837. (Pp. 93-94)

Willis Allman to Daniel Allen 40 acres. 13 October 1829. (Pp. 94-95)

Elijah Banks and wife Jane to James Chambers their interest in the estate of her father John Chambers deceased. 29 January

DEED BOOK P

1838. (Pp. 95-96)

Jackson F. Cole to Samuel F. Cole some livestock. 1 July 1839. (P. 96)

Thomas Gregory to Lorenzo D. Cartwright a tract of land. 1 November 1837. (Pp. 96-97)

Simon P. Hughes to John Lawson a negro woman. 10 June 1831. (Pp. 97-98)

D. N. Estates and his wife Fanny, by statute of dower, to Edwin Atwood a tract of land. 24 September 1838. (P. 98)

William L. Wilburn to Edward A. White, L. W. White, and James H. Fisher, all of Wilson County, his interest in the estate left him by Arthur Herron of Virginia after the death of his grandmother, Sarah Liggin, who is now dead. 1 July 1839. (P. 99)

Arthur Isom and wife Eleanor D. of Hinds County, Mississippi to Leroy P. Adams a tract of land on Goose Creek. 1 January 1839. (Pp. 99-100)

Charles Chitwood from William Hudson 20 acres. 22 January 1839. (Pp. 100-101)

Daniel Chitwood to Pleasant Chitwood 75 acres. 4 February 1839. (Pp. 101-102)

James D. Smith of Jackson County to William Hart a tract of land in the town of Carthage. 10 July 1839. (Pp. 102-103)

Smith County to the heirs of Jonathan Pickett, to wit, Andrew G. Pickett, Edward B. Pickett, and Joseph G. Pickett. 1839. (Pp. 103-104)

Jesse Pipkin of Hardaman County, Tennessee to Thomas Dotson his interest in the estate of his father, Lewis Pipkin, Sr., and his mother Clemmy Pipkin. 22 July 1839. (P. 104)

Levi Roark of Allen County, Kentucky to Thomas Dotson his interest in the estate of his mother Clemmy Pipkin. 6 March 1834. (P. 105)

John Dotson to Abraham Parker a tract of land on Big Barren River. 26 March 1824. (Pp. 105-106)

Jehu Gunn of Monroe County, Kentucky to Thomas M. Wallis a tract of land on Barren River. 21 August 1834. (Pp. 106-107)

Thomas S. Richardson to Lewis Meador a tract of land on White Oak Creek. 20 January 1838. (P. 107)

Richard Williams to William Compton a tract of land on Barren River. 19 January 1835. (P. 108)

C. T. Thomas to John Gordon. 10 July 1839. (Pp. 108-109)

John Dotson to Phillip Marsh 15 acres. 1824. (Pp. 109-110)

DEED BOOK P

Nathan Goss to John Brandon 13½ acres. 4 April 1838. (P. 110)

William C. Wallis to John Harlin 140 acres. 18 August 1838. (P. 111)

Thomas M. Wallis to Rubin Garret 32 acres. 6 April 1835. (P. 112)

Peter Winn, Richard Winn, Richard S. Wilks and wife Martha, Joseph Townsend and wife Mary, Peter Stoval, John Sneed and wife Jane, J. Winn, and Willis H. Winn, all of Sumner County, to Francis G. Harwood a tract of land. 31 December 1821. (P. 113)

Nathan Goss to James Harlin 60 acres. 19 April 1839. (P. 114)

Alexander Pipkin, Isaac Pipkin, Robert Latimer, and Sena Pipkin, wife of the said Robert Latimer, to Thomas Dotson their interest in some slaves belonging to their mother Clemmy Pipkin. 28 July 1832. (Pp. 114-115)

John Springer to William C. Wallis a tract of 45 acres. 23 July 1838. (Pp. 115-116)

Isaac Pipkin to Jessy S. Creasey 70 acres. 20 July 1839. (P. 116)

Asa Roark to Ezekiel East a tract of land on White Oak Creek. 17 October 1828. (P. 117)

Benjamin C. Davis to John Pritchett a tract of land on Kitchen's Creek. 5 October 1836. (Pp. 117-118)

John Pritchett to William Sercy a tract of land on Kitchen's Creek. 8 May 1837. (Pp. 118-119)

John Knight deed of gift to Thomas L. Ellis, William Knight, Henry Knight, Caty Ramsey, Charlotte Smith, and Patsy West. 1 February 1839. (Pp. 119-121)

John Springer, Sr. to William C. Wallace a tract of land on Barren River. 23 July 1838. (P. 122)

John Johnson decree. Powell Hughes, William Hughes, Leonard Hughes, Littleberry Hughes, Leander Hughes, John Hughes, F. B. Hughes, Wade Hughes, Thomas Hughes, Isa Hughes, Sally Hughes, Nancy Hughes, Jesse Hughes, James Paris and wife Julia A., Littleberry Coleman and wife Philadelphia, James Paris and wife Gilla, Jacob Gill and wife Carolina, heirs of Leander Hughes and Jesse P. Hughes, Leander Hughes, Obadiah Hughes, Samuel Hughes, children of Gideliah Hughes deceased and grandchildren and heirs of Leander Hughes deceased. 1839. (Pp. 123-124)

Andrew Hesson to Peter A. Wilkinson a tract of land. 22 June 1839. (Pp. 124-125)

E. Payne of Benton Arkansas appoints William Payne as his attorney. 16 July 1839. (Pp. 125-126)

DEED BOOK P

Carter Guthery to George W. Walker. 3 August 1839. (P. 126)

John Farmer to Marcellus Mitchell 25 acres. 27 September 1838. (P. 127)

George W. Tate to James Barrett and George W. Stalcup 85 acres. 20 May 1839. (Pp. 127-128)

John W. Mann to Henry Mann a negro girl. 10 January 1839. (P. 128)

George Baker to Coleman Sampson 58 acres. 2 January 1838. (P. 129)

John M. Wilkinson to Peter A. Wilkinson his interest in a tract of land. 11 June 1839. (Pp. 129-130)

William Harvey to John Baughman 370 acres. 24 November 1838. (Pp. 130-131)

Sheriff W. W. Bailey to Robert Patterson a tract of land. 13 August 1839. (Pp. 131-132)

Eason Howell to Gronon Owen 100 acres. 1837. (Pp. 132-133)

Mathew S. Nichols to Henry B. McDonald his interest in the estate of his grandfather Jesse Nichols. 27 March 1839. (P. 133)

Henry L. Day to John McMurry a crop of tobacco. 14 August 1839. (Pp. 133-134)

Lovet Dias to George Walker a crop of tobacco. 10 August 1839. (Pp. 134-135)

James Uhles to Jacob S. Johnson a crop of tobacco. 19 August 1839. (P. 135)

James Williamson to Joseph Burk a tract of land on the Caney Fork. 15 November 1834. (P. 136)

Joseph Bush to William Wood a tract of land on the Caney Fork. 21 November 1836. (Pp. 136-137)

David Riddle to J. D. and G. Bond his interest in a negro boy. 2 February 1839. (P. 137)

Joseph Gifford to Joseph Vance a tract of land on Goose Creek. 18 July 1839. (Pp. 138-139)

Matthew Moore to Thomas A. Lancaster 60 acres. 25 July 1838. (P. 139)

Champion T. Thomas to Peter Porter a crop of tobacco. 21 August 1839. (P. 140)

William Roberson to Frederick Uhles, Jr. a crop of tobacco. 22 August 1839. (Pp. 140-141)

William G. M. Campbell, executor of Michael Campbell, to John Trousdale a tract of land. 1835. (Pp. 141-142)

DEED BOOK P

Isaac Hewitt to John Dickens a crop of tobacco. 21 August 1839. (P. 142)

Robert Craighead to John Y. Cornwell a crop of tobacco. 23 August 1839. (Pp. 142-143)

Lewis Harville and Jeremiah Dickens to John Dickens a crop of tobacco. 21 August 1839. (Pp. 143-144)

Martin Williamson to Young & Coker a crop of tobacco. 26 August 1839. (P. 144)

Joseph Bridges to T. A. Flippin. 19 December 1838. (P. 145)

James Nelson to Young & Coker a crop of tobacco. 23 August 1839. (Pp. 145-146)

Stephen Griffin to Frances Duffy a crop of tobacco. 26 August 1839. (P. 146)

John Culbreath to Will A. Herrod a crop of tobacco. 26 August 1839. (Pp. 146-147)

Alexander Dillard to Elisha Dillard 199½ acres. 7 February 1839. (Pp. 147-148)

James B. Morris to John Massie, William Massie, Asa Massie, Allen D. Massie, and Nancy Massie a tract of land on Mulherin's Creek. 1 November 1837. (Pp. 148-149)

Dennis Hargis to Francis Duffy a crop of tobacco. 26 August 1839. (P. 149)

Allen Hallady to William B. Young a crop of tobacco. 30 August 1839. (Pp. 149-150)

Joel Holladay to William B. Young a crop of tobacco. 30 August 1839. (Pp. 150-151)

John Piper to his granddaughter Rena Reed a featherbed and furniture. 2 September 1839. (P. 151)

John Piper to Hardy Calhoun a tract of 133 acres. 24 August 1839. (Pp. 151-152)

James B. Richardson to Francis Duffy a crop of tobacco. 4 September 1839. (P. 152)

Joseph Mitchell to John Reaves a crop of tobacco. 4 September 1839. (P. 153)

John Hallum to Hardy Calhoun 50 acres. 20 July 1839. (Pp. 153-154)

Elijah Adams to Ira Meador a tract of land on Goose Creek. 19 September 1837. (P. 154)

William Parkhurst to George Boston 250 acres. 2 September 1839. (Pp. 154-155)

Austin L. Harris to William C. Harris 50 acres. 31 August 1839. (Pp. 155-156)

DEED BOOK P

Nathan Dillon to Fountain Hanes a tract of land on Long Creek. 27 April 1836. (P. 156)

Jonah Wildman of Allen County, Kentucky to William C. Harris a tract of land in the 11th District. 20 March 1839. (P. 157)

Joseph Law to M. W. Sloan a crop of tobacco. 6 September 1839. (Pp. 157-158)

Jonah Wildman to Elijah Adams 50 acres. 30 March 1839. (Pp. 158-159)

Meredith H. Cliburn to James Jenkins a tract of land on Johns' Creek. 30 January 1836. (P. 159)

Thomas A. Lancaster to John Powell 60 acres. 18 October 1838. (P. 160)

John Adams to Joseph Arnold a tract of land on Goose Creek. 1 March 1827. (Pp. 160-161)

Jeremiah Dixon to Young & Coker a crop of tobacco. 6 September 1839. (P. 161)

Joseph Arnold and Daniel Arnold to Leroy P. Adams a tract of land on Goose Creek. 9 August 1839. (P. 162)

John A. Adams to William Snider 50 acres. September 1839. (P. 163)

Meredith H. Cliburn to James Jenkins a tract of land on Johns' Creek. 30 January 1836. (Pp. 163-164)

Francis Binion to Jonas Meador 87 acres. 17 December 1837. (P. 164)

Abner Shoulders to John McMurry a crop of tobacco. 10 September 1839. (Pp. 164-165)

Daniel Sullivan to Nathan Dillon 78 acres. 27 April 1836. (P. 165)

Charles Coker to James Young 220 acres. 10 August 1838. (P. 166)

Nathan Dillon to Christopher Meador a tract of land. 27 April 1836. (Pp. 166-167)

James C. Greenwood to Joseph Johnson a crop of tobacco. 10 September 1839. (P. 167)

James Harrison to John R. Eatherly of Wilson County a tract of land on Round Lick Creek. 5 September 1839. (P. 168)

Jesse Meachum to James Shoemake a tract of land. 13 September 1839. (Pp. 168-169)

James Shoemake to William Shoemake a crop of tobacco. 13 September 1839. (P. 169)

Moses Linville to Young & Coker a crop of tobacco. 1839. (Pp. 169-170)

DEED BOOK P

Elijah Adams to Fountain Harris and his wife Hannah, daughter of the said Elijah, a tract of land on Long Creek. 17 August 1835. (Pp. 170-171)

Talliferro Hammack to Wesley M. Adams 57 acres. 20 January 1838. (P. 171)

Nicholas Waggoner to John W. Estes 30½ acres. 15 February 1839. (P. 172)

John Russell, Jr. from John Russell, Sr. a tract of land on Defeated Creek. 2 June 1836. (Pp. 172-173)

Wilson Cage to Anthony (   ) 200 acres. 16 September 1839. (P. 173)

Jackson F. Cole to Samuel F. Cole a crop of tobacco. 16 September 1839. (P. 174)

Samuel Evitts to Henry B. Mooningham some personal property. 17 September 1839. (P. 174)

William Conger to Henry B. McDonald 50 acres. 14 September 1839. (P. 175)

John R. Palmer to Isham Kittrell a crop of tobacco. 16 September 1839. (Pp. 175-176)

Isaac Morgan and Alfred Morgan to Isham Kittrell a tract of land on Defeated Creek. 17 September 1839. (Pp. 176-177)

Jabez Gifford to John Gifford a crop of tobacco. 20 September 1839. (P. 177)

Anderson Cardwell to Sampson McClelin a crop of tobacco. 23 September 1839. (Pp. 177-178)

William McGee and Isaac McGee to Parks Chandler 40 acres. 23 September 1839. (Pp. 178-179)

John Bush to John Conger all the estate belonging to him and his late wife Mary. 24 September 1839. (P. 179)

Allen Smith to L. Carter a crop of tobacco. 25 September 1839. (P. 180)

Benjamin Burford to James R. Toney a tract of land in the town of Carthage. 7 September 1839. (Pp. 180-181)

A. Gibbs to John Hallum a crop of tobacco. 2 October 1839. (P. 181)

O. Cliburn to John White a tract of land. 4 October 1839. (Pp. 181-182)

Stephen Robinson to Bernard Richardson of Wilson County a tract of land on the Caney Fork. 13 September 1834. (Pp. 182-183)

Mary Zachary to her daughter Nancy P. McClanahan a certain negro slave. 21 September 1839. (Pp. 183-184)

DEED BOOK P

George Stubblefield to Archibald Parker a woman slave. 5 March 1839. (P. 184)

James C. Williams to Biaz Russell nine acres on Payton's Creek. 5 March 1839. (Pp. 184-185)

James C. Williams to John Ballard 11 acres. 5 March 1839. (P. 185)

William Carver to Hugh B. Robb. 10 October 1839. (P. 186)

James Harrison to Samuel Adamson a tract of land on the Cumberland River. 1839. (Pp. 186-187)

Asberry Cartwright to Thomas Cartwright 50 acres. 11 March 1839. (Pp. 187-188)

William Garner to Thomas A. Lancaster 100 acres. 14 January 1839. (Pp. 188-189)

Mathew Davis to Elijah W. Davis a tract of land on Defeated Creek. 2 July 1838. (Pp. 189-190)

Thomas Haley to Robert Haley two tracts of land on Payton's Creek. 12 October 1839. (Pp. 190-191)

Alexander Dillard to Robert Trawick 50 acres. 7 June 1839. (P. 191)

David McKinnis to Leroy Sutton a crop of tobacco. 30 August 1839. (Pp. 191-192)

Nathan Goss to Wiley Woodcock 300 acres. 7 October 1839. (Pp. 192-193)

John T. and William B. Stokes to Spencer Kelly a tract of land on Smith's Fork. 4 January 1836. ((P. 193)

Sarah Campbell to William M. Rice a tract of land on the Cumberland River. 22 November 1838. (P. 194)

George Sutton to John Russell 169 acres. 12 October 1839. (Pp. 194-195)

Leroy Sutton to John Russell 100 acres. 12 October 1839. (P. 195)

Edward Richardson to Stephen Griffin a tract of land. 18 October 1839. (P. 196)

Abner Perkins to Adam C. C. Perkins a crop of tobacco. 21 October 1839. (Pp. 196-197)

Lewis Kelly to Jeremiah Gammon 190 acres. 21 October 1839. (Pp. 197-198)

Daniel Buie to James M. Ballew a crop of tobacco. 24 October 1839. (Pp. 198-199)

Motes, Bains, & Company to Robert M. Boyers. 24 October 1839. (Pp. 199-200)

Giles Holt and wife Mary to Alexander Stubblefield 21 acres. 18 July 1839. (P. 201)

DEED BOOK P

Giles Holt and wife Mary to Moses Lipscomb 109 acres. Witness: Dauphin Holt. 5 October 1839. (Pp. 201-202)

William Gregory to High Person a crop of tobacco. 1839. (P. 203)

Daniel Huddleston to Edward B. Draper 50 acres. 15 March. (P. 203)

Jabez Burton to Jubal Burton his brother 70 acres. 10 July 1839. (P. 204)

Guilford Jones to John T. Winfree 145 acres. 28 October 1839. (Pp. 204-205)

Rowland Bright and wife Nancy to James W. Gipson a tract of land on the Cumberland River. 16 September 1839. (P. 205)

B. W. Burford to A. L. Bains some personal property. 18 November 1839. (P. 206)

B. W. Burford to James W. Gipson a tract of land in the town of Rome. 18 November 1839. (Pp. 206-207)

Joel Holleman to M. W. Sloan. 27 November 1839. (P. 207)

Warren Coker to George Sutton 200 acres. 14 June 1837. (P. 208)

George Sutton, executor of James Sutton, to James Sutton 65 acres. 22 July 1835. (Pp. 208-209)

George Sutton to Thompson Mace a girl slave. 15 November 1839. (P. 209)

James S. Kemp to John Y. Cornwell a crop of tobacco. 29 November 1839. (Pp. 209-210)

Gabriel Hinds to William B. Young a crop of tobacco. 29 November 1839. (Pp. 210-211)

Abner A. Flippin to John W. Paty some livestock. 2 December 1839. (Pp. 211-212)

John R. Benson to Thomas Gregory some personal property. 30 November 1839. (Pp. 212-213)

Charlotte Warren appoints George T. Wright as his attorney. 4 December 1839. (P. 213)

James B. Morris to Francis H. Gordon a tract of land on Mulherin's Creek. 9 February 1838. (P. 214)

Wilson Cage to Robert Kenny 357½ acres. 27 November 1839. (Pp. 215-216)

George W. Stalcup to William E. Chandler a tract of land on the Cumberland River. 25 November 1839. (Pp. 216-217)

Nicholas Waggoner to Samuel Baker 50 acres. 1839. (Pp. 217-218)

DEED BOOK P

Samuel Burdine to Ellis Beasley ten acres. 1 November 1839. (P. 218)

William C. Towson to Stephen M. Jones a town lot in the town of Rome. 1839. (Pp. 218-219)

Peter Foust of Blount County, Alabama to John Roe, Sr. a tract of land on Mulherin's Creek. 4 August 1823. (Pp. 219-220)

R. L. G. Hogg to John S. Cornwell some personal property. 7 December 1839. (Pp. 220-221)

A. A. Short to David Riddle a tract of land in the town of Meadorville. 19 October 1839. (Pp. 221-222)

Robert Bradley to Don C. Dixon a boy slave. 11 December 1839. (P. 222)

Wilson Boulton to William T. Williams a tract of land on the Caney Fork. 9 February 1839. (P. 223)

John Cliburn to J. C. Duffy a crop of tobacco. 9 November 1839. (Pp. 223-224)

Samuel McClenan to Roland W. Newby some personal property. 16 December 1839. (P. 224)

Armsted Moore to William Moore a negro boy. 30 March 1822. (P. 225)

A. A. Short to Young & Coker a town lot in the town of Meadorville. 19 October 1839. (P. 225)

David Goodall to N. M. Adams a tract of land on Goose Creek. 21 August 1836. (P. 226)

Armsted Moore to William Moore a tract of land. 31 January 1837. (P. 227)

Elijah Williams to Isham Kitrell a tract of land on the Cumberland River. 1 December 1839. (Pp. 227-228)

Mary Jovance to James W. Grissum her dower in the land of John Jovance. 15 October 1839. (P. 228)

William Beck to James McKinley a tract of land on the Caney Fork. 26 December 1837. (P. 229)

William B. Reece to John S. Johnson 53 acres. 19 April 1839. (P. 230)

John Claiborn and Daniel D. Claiborn to G. W. Terry a tract of land. 18 December 1839. (P. 231)

William McCormick and John N. Rhodes to Judy McCormick 68½ acres. 16 September 1839. (Pp. 231-232)

Rawley Crawford to Jonah Wildman 150 acres. 30 January 1839. (P. 232)

Thomas B. Durham to Jephtha Durham 100 acres. 24 December 1839. (Pp. 232-233)

DEED BOOK P

Thomas B. Durham to Jephtha Durham a tract of land. 24 December 1839. (Pp. 233-234)

Mary H. Wood to Sarah S. Caruthers a tract of land beginning at Patience Wood's dower. 17 December 1839. (Pp. 234-235)

William Hargis to Jackson W. Hargis a tract of land on White Oak Creek. 15 January 1839. (P. 235)

Joseph L. Carter to Price Carter 88 acres. 29 October 1839. (P. 236)

James Barnet to John B. Gullick and the other Commissioners of the Salem Cumberland Presbyterian Church a tract of land known as Barnet's Campground. 16 December 1839. (Pp. 236-237)

James Terry to Gideon Gifford 105 acres. 20 August 1839. (P. 237)

Nathaniel Kerby to Fleming Stubblefield a tract of land. 19 December 1839. (Pp. 237-238)

William Tubb, Asa Grisal and wife Franky, Benjamin Tubb, Elizabeth Tubb, and Jephtha Tubb to John H. Newbell 340 acres belonging to the estate of John Tubb. Other heirs: Labon Driver and wife Didama, John Tubb, George Tubb, Benson Tubb, and Malinda Askew, wife of Thomas Askew. December 1839. (Pp. 238-239)

Joseph L. Carter to Prier Carter a tract of land on Goose Creek. 29 October 1839. (P. 240)

James A. Gammon to Jackson W. Hargis a tract of land. 9 October 1839. (Pp. 240-241)

Isaac Pearce to John Reece a negro woman. 6 November 1839. (P. 241)

Joseph Moses to Thomas Carman a crop of tobacco. 6 January 1840. (Pp. 241-242)

Stephen Mann to Fielden Conduitte a tract of land on Snow Creek. 7 December 1839. (Pp. 242-243)

Elisha Walker to John G. Smith 230 acres. 9 December 1839. (P. 243)

Charles Thompson, trustee for Swan Thompson, to Harvey Hogg. 2 December 1839. (Pp. 243-244)

Peter Huff to Jacob Niell a tract of land on the Caney Fork. 24 November 1838. (Pp. 244-245)

Dennis Hargis to Francis Duffy a tract of land on Goose Creek. 10 January 1840. (P. 245)

John M. Dejarnette to James Barry a tract of land on Brush Creek. 23 March 1830. (P. 246)

Samuel Furlong to Wilson Y. Martin a crop of tobacco.

DEED BOOK P

20 January 1840. (Pp. 246-247)

　　Turner Wheeler to John Franklin and Henry Franklin 35 acres. 11 January 1840. (Pp. 247-248)

　　Marital agreement between Mary H. Wood and Archibald S. Parker. 14 December 1839. (P. 248)

　　Charles Bolton to Louisa, Estell, and Lucretia Bolton his daughters a tract of land. 22 February 1838. (P. 249)

　　William W. Jones to Joshua Sykes some personal property. 4 February 1840. (P. 250)

　　Matthew Nichols and his wife Polly to Robert Warren in the tract of land that John Warren died seized and possessed of. 12 August 1839. (P. 250)

　　Patrick Moore to George Whitlock a tract of land on Brush Creek. 30 July 1836. (P. 251)

　　Priscilla Warren appoints L. H. Cardwell as her attorney. 14 December 1839. (P. 252)

　　Daniel Smith and Jane Smith to Peter A. Wilkerson their interest in a tract of land. 31 January 1840. (Pp. 252-253)

　　Joseph Morgan to John Davis 14 acres. 4 November 1826. (P. 253)

　　Uel Gregory to John Gordon and Francis H. Gordon his interest in the estate of his mother Elizabeth Gregory. 4 January 1829. (P. 254)

　　Woodson Palmer and his wife Charlotte to Delila Davis his interest in the tract of land that Joseph Morgan died seized and possessed of. 24 August 1839. (Pp. 254-255)

　　John Stafford to Caleb Carman a negro girl. February 1840. (Pp. 255-256)

　　Powel Tuck to Abner Owen 120 acres. February 1840. (Pp. 256-257)

　　Allen G. Parker to Jesse B. Kerby 200 acres. 19 October 1839. (P. 257)

　　Elijah W. Davis to Allen Matthews a tract of land on Defeated Creek. 4 November 1839. (P. 258)

　　William McGinnis to Riley League a tract of 11 acres. 15 January 1840. (Pp. 258-259)

　　Elijah Carman to Moses B. Freeman. 1 June 1839. (Pp. 259-260)

　　William Ashley to Peter Porter 98 acres. 4 September 1838. (P. 260)

　　Peter Porter to Avin Ward 98 acres. 12 February 1840. (P. 261)

　　John Richardson to Andrew McClelon a tract of land on Buffalo Creek. 24 December 1839. (P. 262)

DEED BOOK P

William McCormack to Andrew McClelan a tract of land on Buffalo Creek. 1 January 1840. (Pp. 262-263)

Elizabeth Ferguhar, Elizabeth Gregory, and Godfrey Gregory to Pleasant Gold a negro boy. 9 October 1839. (P. 263)

Elizabeth Ferguhar to Pleasant Gold her interest in a percel of negroes. 1839. (P. 264)

John Garner and Thomas Garner to William Dillon several items. 22 February 1840. (Pp. 264-265)

Thomas Hickman appoints Eason Howell as his attorney. 25 February 1840. (P. 266)

Bry Gregory to Peter A. Wilkerson 25 acres. 12 February 1840. (P. 266)

Thomas Garner to P. W. Cage a tract of land. 24 February 1840. (P. 267)

The heirs of Randel Thompson of Maringo County, Alabama, to wit, Peter Williams, Matilda Williams, William Thompson, and Richard Thompson to Hezekiah Love 29 acres on the Caney Fork River. 7 January 1839. (P. 268)

John B. Gammon, Eli Gammon, Thomas Carman, Caleb Carman to Susannah Carman fifteen dollars a year for her support. 31 January 1840. (P. 269)

Yance Blackwell to James Brown a tract of land on Dixon's Creek. 16 January 1840. (Pp. 269-270)

Thomas Williams to Thomas Bandy a tract of land on Long Creek. 9 April 1831. (Pp. 270-271)

Samuel Burdine to John S. Rolls 98 acres. 11 March 1839. (Pp. 271-272)

John Gann, administrator of John Jovann, to Andrew W. Jovann 87 acres. 6 August 1838. (P. 272)

Samuel W. Horn to Leonard F. Hughes 44 acres. 14 March 1840. (P. 273)

James Eaton to William Bomar 94 acres. 20 November 1839. (Pp. 273-274)

Armsted Moore and William B. Moore to Razen Thompson a tract of land on the Cumberland River. 5 November 1839. (P. 275)

Jeremiah Whitlock to James Barry $34\frac{1}{2}$ acres. 4 October 1834. (P. 276)

William P. Hughes to Lewis Hall a negro woman. 6 March 1839. (P. 276)

Robert West to John Rees, Sr. a tract of land in the 2nd District. 3 March 1840. (P. 277)

William P. Hughes to Lewis Hall. 1839. (P. 277)

DEED BOOK P

Alfred R. Davis to Strother Settles a tract of land in the 3rd District. 1840. (Pp. 278-280)

Daniel Malone to John Trousdale 100 acres. 11 July 1838. (Pp. 280-281)

Joseph Grisham to William Smith a tract of land in the 22nd District. 30 May 1839. (P. 281)

A. Tubb to Isaac Bates his interest in a tract of land he is to receive at the death of James Tubb. 23 January 1840. (Pp. 281-282)

James D. Sloan and Hugh L. Sloan to John L. Sloan their interest in some slaves owned by Archibald Sloan deceased. John L. Sloan to John A. Sloan his interest in said slaves. 24 August 1839. (Pp. 282-283)

James Craig to Hiram Moses Craig his son a tract of land on Roll's Creek. 16 April 1840. (P. 283)

Articles of agreement between Alexander McCall and John Tate. 29 June 1829. (P. 284)

Joseph McCall to Mary Ann Elizabeth McCall his interest as one of the heirs of Alexander McCall. 14 April 1840. (Pp. 284-285)

Alexander Dillard to James A. Scruggs 300 acres. 1840. (Pp. 285-286)

William F. Brown to David McCall a negro slave. 6 March 1840. (P. 286)

Armsted Moore to John Suit a tract of land. 1840. (Pp. 286-287)

Larkin Corley to Mary Corley, Elizabeth Corley, Nancy Corley, and Elviry Corley, his lawful heirs, a certain negro woman. Nancy Corley, wife of the said Larkin, is to be trustee. 12 February 1829. (Pp. 287-288)

James W. Grissim to James L. Murphree a tract of land in the town of Rome. 30 March 1840. (P. 288)

Charles Thompson to William Ragland a negro woman. 21 December 1839. (P. 289)

James Harrison to B. T. Mottley two negro boys. 1 January 1838. (P. 289)

Joel Franklin to J. B. Short a young filly. 11 October 1839. (Pp. 289-290)

Josephus Cowen in his lifetime to William Allen a tract of land. 1840. (Pp. 290-291)

James Walton to Lot Hazard a tract of land in the town of Carthage. 23 April 1840. (P. 291)

Ruth Culwell to Ruth Love 50 acres. 8 January 1840. (Pp. 291-292)

DEED BOOK P

John Shepherd to William Ragland a negro man. 15 January 1838. (P. 292)

James Walton appoints Timothy Walton as his attorney. 23 April 1840. (Pp. 292-293)

Bry Gregory to William Parkhurst some property for the consideration of supporting him at his house during his natural life. 2 May 1840. (Pp. 293-294)

John Hearn to William Ragland a slave. 6 July 1839. (P. 294)

John Sloan to Jason R. Sloan his son the place where he now lives. 25 July 1834. (Pp. 294-295)

John Sloan to his son Josiah Sloan a tract of land. 10 March 1837. (P. 295)

Noel Goad to Samuel T. Coker 100 acres. 4 May 1840. (P. 296)

William Reaves to Stephen H. Douglas a tract of land on Ward's Creek. 16 December 1835. (Pp. 296-297)

John Sloan to his two sons, William and Archibald, 100 acres. 10 March 1837. (P. 297)

John Sloan to his daughter Mary a tract of land. 10 March 1837. (P. 298)

John Sloan to his daughter Elizabeth $91\frac{1}{4}$ acres. 10 March 1837. (Pp. 298-299)

Sheriff W. W. Bailey to H. B. McDonald a tract of land. 1840. (Pp. 299-300)

H. B. McDonald to Isaac Massey 130 acres. 14 May 1840. (P. 300)

Sheriff W. W. Bailey to M. Robinson a tract of land. 1840. (Pp. 300-301)

Sheriff W. W. Bailey to William Young a tract of land. 1840. (P. 302)

Eth Warren to Elijah Hylton a tract of land. 16 May 1840. (P. 303)

Samuel T. Coker and wife Margaret, heirs of Archibald Sloan, to John A. Sloan their interest in his estate. December 1838. (Pp. 303-304)

James D. Smith to H. B. McDonald a tract of $39\frac{1}{2}$ acres. 14 May 1840. (P. 305)

William Kyle to Palemon W. Cage a tract of land. 26 May 1840. (Pp. 305-307)

Catharine Ramsey to Margaret Dillehay 97 acres. June 1840. (P. 307)

Wiatt Bailey to James C. Sanders a woman slave. 4 February 1840. (Pp. 307-308)

DEED BOOK P

Stephen H. Douglass to Robert J. Douglass his power of attorney. 12 May 1840. (P. 308)

Deed of gift from John Knight to Catharine (Ramsey), Thomas Ed), William Knight, Henry Knight, Charlotte Smith, and Patsy West. 3 June 1840. (Pp. 308-309)

Charles J. White to John Street 45¼ acres. 18 May 1840. (P. 309)

Benjamin J. Jones to M. G. Ward a tract of land in the 20th District. 9 June 1840. (Pp. 309-310)

Godfrey Gregory to William R. Betty a certain stallion. 10 June 1840. (Pp. 310-311)

John Gwaltney to R. D. Allison some livestock. 10 June 1840. (P. 312)

Robert Warren to Leonard H. Cardwell a tract of land belonging to the estate of John Warren. 13 June 1840. (P. 313)

The heirs of William Walton divided. 10 June 1840. (Pp. 313-314)

B. B. Uhles to Thomas J. Black a negro girl. 15 June 1840. (P. 314)

A. S. Hogan to James and Timothy Walton. June 1840. (P. 315)

Kelly Asbury & Company to B. H. Rice. 16 June 1840. (Pp. 315-316)

Godfrey Gregory to Elizabeth Farguhar 50 acres. 17 June 1840. (Pp. 316-317)

James R. Toney to Clabourn Hall a tract of 33 acres. 1840. (P. 317)

Godfrey Gregory and John Gwaltney to John Buckner. 1840. (P. 318)

Godfrey Gregory and John Gwaltney to John Gwaltney, Jr. a tract of land. 8 August 1839. (Pp. 319-320)

C. T. Thomas to John Gordon some livestock. 20 June 1840. (P. 320)

Daniel Allen to Martha Douglass a tract of land. 22 August 1839. (Pp. 320-321)

John Gwaltney to John H. Newbell some livestock. 23 June 1840. (Pp. 321-322)

John F. Wilmot to Jonathan Moseley. 24 June 1840. (P. 322)

William Ashley to William Allen a tract of land. 29 June 1840. (Pp. 323-324)

James Lyon to John Burnett a tract of land. January 1840. (Pp. 324-325)

DEED BOOK P

M. W. Sloan to James R. Toney a tract of land on Smith's Fork. 29 June 1840. (P. 325)

Grogan Harper to William M. Gordon a tract of land. 15 June 1840. (Pp. 325-326)

Champion T. Thomas to Stephen D. Early a crop of tobacco. 7 July 1840. (P. 326)

Adam Stafford to Francis Duffy 36 acres. 6 July 1840. (P. 327)

Fielding Conditt to Lodwick Vaden 12½ acres. 6 July 1840. (Pp. 327-328)

Henry McWhorter to Thomas Bray of Monroe County, Kentucky a tract of land west of the Cumberland River. 20 April 1833. (P. 329)

The heirs of my grandfather, Daniel Hammack, to wit, Martin Hammack, Brice W. Hammack, William H. Hammack, James M. Hammack, Alexander A. Short and wife Sally, Joseph T. Hammack, and Lemuel A. Hammack relinquish to William L. Martin of Wilson County for my mother Patsey Young, formerly Patsy Hammack, 100 acres. My father, A. D. Young, did sell said land to Thomas Stafford. Therefore, I, Alonzo D. Young, convey to the said Thomas Stafford my interest. 16 October 1839. (P. 330)

Sheriff W. W. Bailey to Robert Nixon a tract of land. 16 June 1840. (P. 331)

Robert Nixon to Allen Piper 25 acres. 26 June 1840. (P. 332)

Matthew Petross to James A. Scruggs. 24 June 1840. (Pp. 332-333)

Samuel Anthony and Hannah Anthony of Madison County, Missouri appoint Josiah Anthony of Sumner County as their attorney in settling the estate of Susannah Britton, widow of Richard Britton. Said Hannah was the daughter of the said Richard Britton. 3 May 1839. (Pp. 333-334)

Gabriel Hines to John Y. Cornwell a bay filly. 16 July 1840. (Pp. 334-335)

Stephen D. Easley to William R. Betty. 16 July 1840. (P. 335)

George Read to Noel Read a crop of tobacco. 15 July 1840. (Pp. 335-336)

Bartlet James, Sr. to Bartlet James, Jr. 60 acres. 25 November 1835. (P. 337)

Bartlett James, Jr. to John H. Newbell a tract of land on Hickman's Creek. 20 July 1840. (Pp. 337-339)

James Thomas to John H. Newbell some livestock. 22 July 1840. (Pp. 339-340)

DEED BOOK P

Clerk & Master to Vincent R. Bradford a tract of land belonging to the heirs of William H. Chuck. 1840. (Pp. 340-341)

John Cochran to John J. Burnett and the other Trustees for the building of a Methodist Church in the town of Carthage. 15 July 1840. (Pp. 341-343)

John Gwaltney to Pleasant Gold of Wilson County 105 acres. 27 July 1840. (P. 344)

Jesse Hord of Washington County, Republic of Texas, appoints James Hord of Claibourn Parish, Louisiana as his attorney. 25 December 1830. (Pp. 344-345)

Mary Pigg to John Lancaster 400 acres. 30 September 1839. (P. 346)

B. B. Uhles to Samuel Oldham three slaves. 4 August 1840. (P. 347)

Timothy Walton, executor of John McGee, to Chesley Bridgewater a tract of land on Dixon's Creek. 4 August 1840. (Pp. 347-348)

John Luckey to William Coggin. 17 April 1840. (P. 348)

Elam Russell to Matthew Smith 129 acres. 18 January 1840. (P. 349)

Timothy Walton, executor of John McGee, to Mathew Ward a negro boy. 3 August 1840. (Pp. 349-350)

Philip Sadler to his heirs, Halbert C. and William C. Sadler a tract of land on the Caney Fork. 3 June 1840. (P. 350)

Charles McMurry to John A. Johnson two slaves. 6 August 1840. (Pp. 350-351)

David L. Taylor to B. T. Mottley a negro boy. 7 August 1840. (P. 351)

Thompson Mace to Mathew Anderson a girl slave. 10 August 1840. (P. 351)

Wilson Bolton to William T. Williams a tract of land on the Caney Fork. 27 June 1840. (P. 352)

Joseph McCall to James Murphree a tract of land in the town of Rome. January 1837. (Pp. 352-353)

Bartlett B. Uhles to James G. Parker a tract of land on Goose Creek. 16 July 1840. (Pp. 353-354)

Anney Butter to Jacob Null her interest in the estate of Michael Thornton. 11 August 1840. (P. 354)

James Shelton to Drury Clardy 138 acres. 20 June 1840. (Pp. 354-355)

James Shelton to Abraham Carmicle. 1840. (Pp. 355-356)

DEED BOOK P

William G. Wilson, Matilda G. Edmundson, J. K. Edmundson, and S. G. Wilson of Davidson County to Archibald McNeill part of the home tract of Andrew Greer deceased. 31 January 1840. (Pp. 356-357)

Wallace G. Wilson nominates John K. Edmundson as his attorney. 27 January 1840. (Pp. 357-358)

Thomas Malone to Jeremiah Coggin a tract of land on the Caney Fork. 24 November 1838. (P. 358)

Richard Kearly to James Sutton 12 acres. 16 September 1839. (P. 359)

James Cartwright to James Roach 320 acres on Defeated Creek. 5 June 1840. (Pp. 359-360)

Marshall B. Duncan to Josiah Caruthers two negro slaves. 20 August 1840. (P. 360)

Samuel Caplinger to Ira Ledbetter 65 acres. 14 October 1840. (Pp. 360-361)

Roland Clark to John H. Ligon a tract of land. 17 August 1840. (Pp. 361-362)

Newton Cannon to Joshua Hawkins. 17 July 1838. (Pp. 362-363)

Jeremiah Dickens and Lewis Harvel to Washington Meachum. 25 August 1840. (P. 363)

McCory Moore to Samuel Caplinger 73 acres. 24 September 1839. (P. 364)

W. W. Bailey to D. C. Hibbitts a negro woman. 10 August 1833. (Pp. 364-365)

Simon P. Hughes to D. C. Hibbitts a negro woman. 3 November 1831. (P. 365)

Stephen Haynes to Haley Young a tract of land on Defeated Creek. 27 August 1840. (Pp. 365-366)

Bartlett B. Uhles to Coleman Sampson a tract of land on Hogan's Creek. 2 April 1839. (Pp. 366-367)

Joseph Morgan to John Davis a tract of land. 4 November 1826. (P. 367)

B. J. Jones to S. F. Patterson 127 acres. 16 December 1839. (P. 368)

James L. Murphree to James W. Grissom a tract of land in the town of Rome. 20 March 1840. (Pp. 368-369)

Lindley M. Bransford, administrator of John Bransford, to William R. Betty a tract of land on Hickman's Creek. 23 April 1839. (P. 369)

John Goodner to Wiley Jones a tract of land on the Cumberland River. 1835. (P. 370)

DEED BOOK P

Patience Wood to her daughter Mary H. Wood a young mare. 29 January 1839. (Pp. 370-371)

Lovitt Dias to James Duffey. 29 August 1840. (Pp. 371-372)

Moses Linville to C. L. Shrum 25 acres. 7 August 1840. (Pp. 372-373)

James Cartwright to William Cartwright 50 acres. 5 June 1840. (P. 373)

Samuel D. Hughes to William T. Bennett a crop of tobacco. 27 August 1840. (Pp. 373-374)

James Cartwright to Richardson C. Cartwright a tract of land on Defeated Creek. 6 June 1840. (Pp. 374-375)

James Culbreath to Major A. Beasley a crop of tobacco. 1 September 1840. (Pp. 376-377)

Thomas Williams to B. M. Rains a crop of tobacco. 1 September 1840. (P. 377)

William McGee of Benton County, Tennessee to Joshua Hawkins a tract of land. 28 August 1840. (Pp. 377-378)

Vaughn & Tunstall to Albert Benton a tract of land on Dixon's Creek. 10 January 1838. (Pp. 378-379)

Nathaniel Britton to D. B. Donoho 96 acres. 4 March 1831. (Pp. 379-380)

Allen Holliday to John Richardson. August 1840. (Pp. 380-381)

Thomas Redman to James Duffy. 7 September 1840. (Pp. 381-382)

Henry L. Day to Thomas J. Noles. 5 September 1840. (P. 382)

Bird Read to Strother Settle. 7 September 1840. (P. 383)

Ann Sullivan to William Shoemake. 9 September 1840. (P. 384)

Thomas Carman and Joseph Moses to Joseph Dickens 117 acres. 12 September 1840. (Pp. 384-385)

Dennis Hargis to Francis Duffy a crop of tobacco. 8 August 1840. (P. 385)

Joseph Weaver to E. T. Corley a crop of tobacco. 28 August 1840. (P. 386)

William Gregory to Elijah Banks. 15 September 1840. (P. 387)

A. B. Newsom to Benjamin Piper a negro woman. 7 September 1840. (Pp. 387-388)

Mildred Maxey to B. T. Mottley a negro boy. 28 November

DEED BOOK P

1837. (P. 388)

John Mitchell to John Reeves 90 acres. 13 October 1839. (Pp. 388-389)

Richard G. Gifford to Nathan M. Adams a crop of tobacco. 17 September 1840. (Pp. 389-390)

Peter Grisham to James H. Brim a tract of land on Payton's Creek. 25 August 1840. (P. 390)

Britain B. Finley to Henry W. Wooldridge 54 acres. 27 June 1838. (P. 391)

Lambert M. Cothron to Charles Darnell 100 acres. 6 July 1840. (P. 392)

David Everet to John Cothran a tract of land on the Cumberland River. 1 January 1838. (Pp. 392-393)

Stephen H. Douglass to John Stallings a tract of land on Ward's Creek. 4 May 1840. (Pp. 393-394)

Levi Knotts of Jackson County to Drury Holland a tract of land on Defeated Creek. 4 August 1834. (Pp. 394-395)

Joseph Bishop to George Norris a tract of land on Rackoon Branch. 10 April 1838. (P. 395)

Robert W. Knight to James High 333 acres. 7 September 1840. (Pp. 395-396)

Richard McKinney and wife Ann, Jacob W. Roe, William E. Roe, Robert A. Roe, Emily H. Roe, Esther H. Roe, Mary L. Roe, and Sarah B. Roe, heirs of Benjamin Roe file a bill of complaint in Chancery Court. 1840. (Pp. 396-397)

Alexander A. Short to William M. Parker a tract of land on Goose Creek. 14 December 1839. (Pp. 397-398)

John Cooper to Joseph Goss a tract of land on the Caney Fork. 11 July 1840. (Pp. 398-399)

John Cooper to William Johns ten acres. 20 December 1839. (P. 399)

William Jones to John Cooper a tract of 17 acres. 11 July 1840. (P. 400)

Robert Denton to David Denton a tract of land on the Cumberland River. 24 September 1840. (Pp. 400-401)

W. W. Bailey to Lot Hazard. 25 September 1840. (Pp. 401-402)

Calvin W. Jackson and wife Jane B. to Zachariah Tolliver a tract of land belonging to the heirs of Andrew Greer. 28 September 1840. (P. 402)

Jane Durham, administratrix of N. Durham, to Mary A. Owen a woman slave. 29 August 1840. (P. 403)

James Wood to Obadiah B. Hubbard. 29 August 1839. (Pp. 403-404)

DEED BOOK P

Thomas L. Hardie to John D. Day a crop of tobacco. 1 September 1840. (P. 404)

Archibald Gibbs to David C. Saunders a crop of tobacco. 8 October 1840. (P. 405)

Clabourn Jones to Booker Pate a crop of tobacco. 6 October 1840. (P. 406)

Frederick J. Uhls to William Baker a crop of tobacco. 26 September 1840. (Pp. 406-407)

Braddock Beasley to L. Settle a crop of tobacco. 22 July 1840. (P. 407)

Ira L. Sullivan to C. C. Ford a crop of tobacco. 28 September 1840. (P. 408)

William Austin to his son Solomon some livestock. 6 May 1840. (Pp. 408-409)

Martin Williamson to Young & Coker a crop of tobacco. 13 October 1840. (Pp. 409-410)

Stephen Pate to Leonidas D. Hogg a tract of land. 6 August 1838. (P. 410)

Stephen Page to David Hogg a tract of land. 7 August 1838. (P. 411)

Joseph Brown to Eli McDuffy 100 acres. 24 September 1840. (Pp. 411-412)

Smith Gregory to Joseph Brown a tract of land on Payton's Creek. 5 March 1839. (Pp. 412-413)

John Hester to David G. Mason a tract of land. 9 October 1840. (P. 413)

Daniel Smith, administrator of Jesse West, to Margaret West 30 acres. 5 October 1840. (Pp. 413-414)

Samuel P. Howard to Leroy E. Mitchell two tracts of land in the town of Carthage. 29 September 1840. (P. 414)

Bry Gregory to William Parkhurst 115 acres. 27 April 1840. (Pp. 414-415)

Richard Fedlock to Custes W. York of Jackson County 100 acres. 12 October 1840. (P. 416)

William Smith to John F. Bransford. 17 October 1840. (Pp. 417-418)

Thomas B. Askew to John R. James. 20 October 1840. (P. 418)

Thomas B. Askew to Henry B. McDonald a town lot in the town of Carthage. 26 March 1840. (Pp. 418-419)

Allen Smith to Thomas Wilburn a crop of tobacco. 15 September 1840. (P. 419)

William Archer to Thomas Acock a negro woman. 1840. (Pp. 419-420)

DEED BOOK P

The heirs of Brazilla and Mary Taylor to Robert Harper 160 acres. 2 November 1840. (P. 421)

James Walton and Timothy Walton to Abraham Caruthers a tract of land on the Caney Fork. September 1840. (Pp. 421-422)

James M. Blackwell to Caleb Carman a negro boy. 7 April 1840. (P. 422)

William Andrews and John Andrews to Robert Cothran a tract of land on Goose Creek. 14 January 1834. (P. 423)

David Cochran to David Burford a tract of land in the 4th District. 10 September 1840. (Pp. 423-424)

John Moore to Gregory Moore a tract of land on Mulherin's Creek. 7 May 1840. (Pp. 424-425)

Archibald Parker to Drury A. Cothran 36 acres. 15 May 1840. (P. 425)

George Sutton to James M. Ballew five acres. 28 October 1840. (P. 426)

G. B. Parker and D. F. Galbreath to William Chamberlain a tract of land. 10 October 1840. (Pp. 426-427)

Joel Simmons to David F. Galbreath and Goolsberry Parker a tract of land. 16 March 1840. (Pp. 427-428)

Charles Thompson to James R. Toney. 15 October 1840. (Pp. 428-429)

Gideon Gifford to his son Gideon Gifford 50 acres. 8 August 1839. (P. 429)

Gideon Gifford to Barnett Gifford 50 acres. 8 August 1839. (P. 430)

Thomas J. Black to Nathaniel W. Parrott and James Boze 20 acres. 10 November 1840. (Pp. 430-431)

Hardy Willeford and his wife Nancy (who at the time of intermarriage was Nancy Taylor, widow of Joseph Taylor) to Archibald W. Overton a tract of land on the Cumberland River. 3 December 1836. (Pp. 431-432)

John Hawkins and wife Betsy to James W. Grissim a tract of land on Roll's Creek. 29 October 1840. (Pp. 432-433)

Thomas Owens to David C. Ward a tract of land. 13 August 1840. (Pp. 433-434)

Jabus Gifford to Alfred A. Brevard a crop of tobacco. 28 September 1840. (P. 434)

Etheldred Warren to John E. Warren a negro woman. 16 September 1840. (P. 434)

Major A. Beasley to William H. Grissim some personal property. 14 November 1840. (P. 435)

Archibald Fulks to Daniel Robinson a negro boy. 29

DEED BOOK P

October 1840. (P. 436)

Strother Settle to Allen Piper 100 acres. 18 November 1840. (Pp. 436-437)

Elijah Lester, Phillymon Beck, and John Hicks of Fayette County, Illinois to James Morris, Sr. a tract of land on Dixon's Creek. 18 November 1839. (P. 437)

Archibald Parker to Rhoda Redman, a free woman of color, his yellow man who she intermarried with some 16 to 18 years ago. 31 October 1840. (P. 438)

Rhoda Redman to John L. Gammon a tract of land on Goose Creek. 17 November 1840. (Pp. 438-439)

William Sloan to Martin W. Sloan his interest in the estate of his mother Agnes Sloan and Archibald Sloan. 20 November 1840. (Pp. 439-440)

Presley Askins to Little B. Coleman a tract of land on Mulherin's Creek. 26 May 1839. (Pp. 440-441)

H. H. Alsup to James M. Armstrong a man slave. 4 December 1840. (P. 441)

H. H. Alsup to G. M. Alsup a negro woman. 5 December 1840. (Pp. 441-442)

H. H. Alsup to S. J. Alsup a woman slave. 4 December 1840. (P. 442)

Robert Tate to William P. Beasley. 27 November 1840. (Pp. 442-443)

Elijah Oglesby to his two sons, Henry and Clifton A. Oglesby, 128 acres. 17 July 1839. (P. 443)

Rezen Thompson to David C. Ward a tract of land on the Cumberland River. 5 December 1840. (P. 444)

John Farmer to John A. Vanderpool a tract of land on the Caney Fork. December 1840. (Pp. 444-445)

Martin Whitten to Elisha Dillard a tract of land on the Caney Fork. 13 November 1840. (Pp. 445-446)

Elijah Toney and Samuel Burdine to John McCall one fourth of an acre. 5 December 1840. (Pp. 446-447)

George H. Shutt and his wife Hannah of Wilson County to John Payne a tract of land on the Cumberland River. 23 November 1840. (P. 447)

William Carter to Orville Green a tract of land on the Cumberland River. 12 September 1838. (P. 448)

Sheriff W. W. Bailey to James R. Toney. 1840. (Pp. 449-450)

James Tubb to Martin W. Sloan several slaves. 17 December 1839. (P. 450)

DEED BOOK P

Daniel Sullivan to Patrick Hubbard a tract of land. 16 December 1840. (P. 451)

Marriage agreement between John S. Turner of Jackson County and Nancy Coleman. 16 December 1840. (Pp. 451-452)

Sheriff W. W. Bailey to John Gann a tract of land. 17 December 1840. (P. 453)

Armstead Flippin and his wife Frances, heirs of Colonel Henry Dixon and wife Martha, being the same Colonel Henry Dixon who was a Lieutenant Colonel in the North Carolina Line, to Adam Ferguson. 10 August 1840. (Pp. 453-454)

William Sullivan to Samuel Caplinger a negro woman. 25 November 1830. (P. 455)

William Sullivan to Samuel Caplinger a negro woman. 13 September 1830. (P. 455)

Thomas A. Lancaster to Hiram H. Alsup a tract of land on the Caney Fork. 15 December 1838. (P. 456)

Hiram H. Alsup to Spencer Kelly a tract of land on the Caney Fork. 5 December 1840. (Pp. 456-457)

Robert Bradley to C. S. Bradley a negro man. 10 October 1840. (P. 457)

Jesse S. Lancaster to John Lancaster and Summers Decker. 21 December 1840. (P. 458)

John Haw to John J. Burnett his power of attorney. 17 September 1840. (P. 459)

William Sloan to Martin W. Sloan a crop of tobacco. 2 December 1840. (P. 460)

Archibald Sloan to William Sloan 50 acres. 7 December 1839. (Pp. 460-461)

Henry S. Moore to John Lamberson 91 acres. 1 August 1840. (P. 461)

John A. Chisom and wife Sarah to William Young. 7 September 1840. (P. 462)

William P. Ellis to James Ellis a tract of land on Goose Creek. 29 July 1837. (Pp. 462-463)

William Martin to William S. Martin of Wilson County a negro girl. 1840. (P. 463)

Elizabeth Williams, daughter of Colonel Henry Dixon and wife Martha, to Adam Ferguson. 1840. (P. 464)

James McKinley to Henry B. Clark. 15 August 1837. (P. 465)

Joel Meador to Christopher Simmons 82½ acres. 4 August 1840. (Pp. 465-466)

Pleasant Chitwood to Nathaniel Thurman 50 acres. 1839. (Pp. 466-467)

DEED BOOK P

Elbert G. Holland to Young & Coker a tract of land on Goose Creek. 24 December 1840. (Pp. 467-468)

Robert Alexander of Austin County, Republic of Texas appoints William R. Alexander of Mississippi as his attorney in setting the estate of Anderson Alexander. 18 August 1838. (Pp. 468-469)

John C. Tuck to Wesley W. Tucker 120 acres. 12 February 1839. (Pp. 469-470)

Abraham Caruthers to Stephen Mann 139 acres. 25 December 1840. (P. 470)

Abraham Caruthers to David K. Timberlake a tract of land on Snow Creek. 25 December 1840. (P. 471)

W. W. Bailey to Larkin Payne a negro boy. 29 December 1840. (P. 471)

Lemuel A. Hammack to Larkin Payne a tract of land on Dixon's Creek. 20 January 1840. (Pp. 471-472)

A. B. Newsom to John Payne a negro boy. 21 October 1840. (P. 473)

Stephen H. Douglas to William Horace Oliver a negro boy. 12 May 1840. (P. 473)

John Reeves to A. B. Newsom a negro boy. 30 November 1840. (P. 474)

Abraham Caruthers to John Timberlake a tract of land on Snow Creek. 25 December 1840. (P. 474)

James M. Nelson to his son Evan E. Nelson some livestock. 4 January 1841. (P. 475)

Peter Webster to Jonathan Dedmon some personal property. 4 January 1841. (P. 476)

David F. Winfrey to Samuel Pugh a tract of land on Brush Creek. 6 February 1835. (Pp. 476-477)

Robert Rowland to Elijah Miller a tract of land on Dixon's Creek. 23 November 1840. (Pp. 477-478)

Hannah M. Davis to John Dedmon a tract of land. 30 January 1840. (Pp. 478-479)

Henry Phelps to Joseph Cameron 33 acres. 23 November 1840. (P. 479)

Frances Coley to James Mathewson a tract of land on Payton's Creek. 1 February 1837. (P. 480)

Bartlett James, Jr. to R. D. Allison. 11 January 1841. (P. 481)

John Gwaltney, Sr. to Thomas Gwaltney a tract of land. 2 January 1840. (Pp. 481-482)

W. W. Bailey to Jonathan Bailey a tract of land. 13

DEED BOOK P

January 1841. (P. 483)

Joshua Morris to Edwin Atwood a tract of land on Brush Creek. 22 February 1840. (Pp. 483-484)

Joshua Morris to Isaac R. Morris 79 acres. 11 January 1841. (Pp. 484-485)

Joshua Morris to David F. Winfrey eight acres. 8 January 1835. (P. 485)

Adam F. Claiborne to Alexander Ferguson a horse. 15 January 1841. (P. 486)

Samuel H. Sloan to John A. Sloan his interest in a tract of land belonging to the estate of Archibald Sloan. 7 January 1841. (P. 487)

A. R. Davis to Allen Piper a tract of land. 16 January 1841. (Pp. 487-488)

A. Moore, Jr. to William Davis. 19 December 1840. (Pp. 488-489)

W. W. Bailey to William White. 20 January 1841. (Pp. 489-490)

Joseph W. Jeffres to Samuel Read some personal property. 26 January 1841. (Pp. 490-491)

David Hall to John Hall a tract of land on Brush Creek. 23 January 1841. (Pp. 491-492)

Little B. Hughes to John W. Hughes some livestock and personal property. 27 January 1841. (Pp. 492-493)

Little B. Hughes to William P. Hughes and John W. Hughes a tract of land on Mulherin's Creek. 27 January 1841. (Pp. 493-494)

James Walton to William C. Hubbard two negroes. 10 October 1840. (Pp. 494-495)

James Shelton to James Rucks, William Owen, O. B. Hubbard, David C. Hibbitts, Edmund Rucks, Benjamin Rucks, Warner F. Rucks, James R. Toney, John A. Toney, Elizabeth A. Toney, and Benjamin Rucks, trustee for the wife and children of William H. Jackson. 25 January 1841. (Pp. 495-496)

Frances Flippin, widow of Armstead B. Flippin and heir of Henry and Martha Dixon, to William E. Jones her power of attorney. 30 January 1841. (Pp. 497-498)

Tilman B. Flippin and Henry Flippin, administrators of Armstead B. Flippin, to William E. Jones their power of attorney. 1 February 1841. (Pp. 498-500)

W. W. Bailey to George W. Oldham a negro girl. 3 February 1841. (P. 500)

William Escum to Bennett Braswell 100 acres. 27 January 1841. (Pp. 500-501)

DEED BOOK P

William Massey to Loderick Vaden a tract of land. 18 January 1841. (Pp. 501-502)

John Henderson to Robert Fagg 100 acres. 18 August 1840. (P. 502)

Robert Fagg, William Roddy, Sally Roddy, Joseph Roddy, Emley Roddy, Eliza Dornwell, and Lidia Fagg to Robert Fagg a tract of land on Salt Lick Creek. 28 November 1837. (P. 503)

Henry Wakefield, Sr. to Henry Wakefield, Jr. 83 acres. 19 March 1840. (Pp. 503-504)

Jeremiah Willeford to William Willeford 60 acres. 27 October 1838. (P. 504)

William Willeford to Samuel Lankaster 60 acres. 10 November 1840. (P. 505)

Abraham Caruthers to Jesse Beasley 126 acres. 22 December 1840. (P. 505)

Solomon Debow to Robert Marshall a tract of land on Goose Creek. 7 August 1840. (P. 506)

Jordan Stokes of Wilson County to Joseph Dirickson 365 acres. 8 February 1840. (P. 506)

Joseph Dirickson to David S. Dirickson a tract of land on the Cumberland River. 10 February 1841. (P. 507)

Clement Mckinney to William F. Williams a tract of land on the Caney Fork. 7 September 1840. (P. 508)

Richard McConnell bound to Martin W. Sloan. 12 November 1840. (Pp. 508-509)

Jesse Fuller to Larkin Corley some personal property. 13 February 1841. (Pp. 509-510)

Powell Tuck to J. E. Reasonover some livestock. 13 February 1841. (P. 510)

Benjamin H. Price and Frances Pugh to Armstead Moore, Jr. a negro man. 18 February 1841. (Pp. 510-512)

James F. Kearley to Robert Rowland. 20 February 1841. (Pp. 512-513)

Willis Coggin to Robert L. Hughes 143 acres. 23 February 1841. (Pp. 513-514)

Meredith Hawkins to James M. Moles a crop of tobacco. 1 March 1841. (Pp. 514-515)

Nancy Uhls to her granddaughter Angeline Malviny Cole some personal property. 16 January 1841. (P. 515)

Josiah Davidson to Exum Whitley some personal property. 2 March 1841. (P. 516)

John W. Mann to Robert Warren a tract of land. 9 July 1840. (Pp. 516-517)

DEED BOOK P

Joseph Haden to Willis Dowell a tract of land. 22 March 1839. (P. 517)

James R. Toney to Charles Denney 64 acres. 4 January 1841. (P. 518)

Little B. Hughes to Henry C. Jones 47 acres. 15 February 1841. (P. 518)

William Dillard to Archibald Scruggs 50 acres. 19 March 1836. (P. 519)

John Congo to Malinda Congo. 31 October 1838. (P. 519)

Armstead Moore to Alexander Moore a negro boy. 11 January 1841. (P. 520)

Joseph Haden to Frances Dowell 158 acres. 22 March 1839. (P. 521)

Gabriel W. McWhorter of Monroe County, Kentucky to John New 50 acres. 2 March 1832. (Pp. 521-522)

James Adcock to William Dillard a tract of 154 acres. 31 October 1834. (Pp. 522-523)

N. Ward to Thomas Coleman a girl slave. 27 February 1841. (P. 523)

Andrew McClellin, Sampson McClellin, Martha McClellin, Beverly Graves and wife Judy to John Richardson a tract of land on Defeated Creek. 21 November 1840. (P. 524)

Jesse S. Lancaster to Thomas A. Lancaster 254 acres. 29 January 1841. (P. 525)

William W. Jones to Joshua Sykes some personal property. 6 March 1841. (P. 525)

Joseph Summersett to Frances Duffy the tract of land owned by his father Joseph Summersett at the time of his death. 9 March 1841. (P. 526)

Price Snider to William Robinson 282 acres. 5 March 1841. (P. 527)

Elisha Dillard to Daniel Dillard 199½ acres. 15 February 1841. (P. 527)

John E. Warren to Leonard H. Cardwell his interest in the estate of John Warren. 16 September 1840. (P. 528)

John Hardcastle to Jacob Ammonette. 20 March 1841. (P. 528)

David Cochran to James Bradley a tract of land. 16 March 1841. (P. 529)

David Cochran to David Burford 113¼ acres. 18 March 1841. (P. 529)

Resin Thompson to William M. Price 83 acres. 29 March

DEED BOOK P

1841. (P. 530)

James Arnold to Uriah White 50 acres. November 1839. (P. 531)

Benjamin Talley to Leroy P. Adams 100 acres. 13 March 1841. (P. 531)

Leroy P. Adams to John A. Adams 70¼ acres. 24 March 1841. (P. 532)

Articles of agreement between William Robinson and Loderick Vaden, administrator of Brooks Robinson. 1841. (P. 532)

Little B. Coleman, John J. Coleman, Sarah C. Coleman, Reuben Ragland, Delila Ragland, Thomas Williamson, Lidia Williamson, children and heirs of Jesse Coleman, to Nathan Ward 30 acres. 4 November 1840. (P. 533)

Nelly Coleman quit claim deed to Nathan Ward. 1840. (P. 534)

Robert Holladay to James A. King 131¼ acres. 8 April 1841. (P. 534)

John Parker to Elum Russell a tract of land on Defeated Creek. 3 April 1838. (P. 535)

Samuel Caplinger to James Bates. 12 April 1841. (P. 536)

R. L. W. Hogg to John J. Horton a negro woman. 15 April 1841. (P. 537)

Sheriff W. W. Bailey to Robert L. Caruthers 250 acres. 22 February 1841. (P. 537)

Godfrey Gregory to Henry B. McDonald a female slave. 17 April 1841. (P. 538)

Godfrey Gregory to John H. Newbell. 19 April 1841. (P. 538)

Robert McNeeley, John McNeeley, Brittan J. Neal, Joseph Guthrie, Elizabeth Neal, and Polly Guthrie to Marshall B. Duncan a tract of land that Robert McNeeley died seized and possessed of. 24 November 1829. (P. 539)

Isaac Mungle to Jesse Jones 100 acres. 30 September 1840. (P. 540)

Manson Young to Gideon Gifford, Sr. 40 acres. 3 August 1839. (P. 540)

Wilson Cage of Sumner County to Robert Rowland 181½ acres. 16 January 1840. (P. 541)

John Donoho to William Donoho 75 acres. 26 May 1840. (P. 541)

John Stubblefield to Archibald M. Debow 91¼ acres. 15 January 1841. (P. 542)

DEED BOOK P

James Terry to Fleming Stubblefield a tract of land on Goose Creek. 11 February 1841. (Pp. 542-543)

Higdon Robinson to Thomas A. Lancaster 184 acres. 24 February 1841. (P. 543)

James Young to Hiram C. Ford. 26 June 1839. (P. 544)

Joseph Campbell to Isaac Harlin a tract of land on Big Barren River. 30 March 1840. (P. 545)

Thomas Barnett to James Patterson 85 acres. 31 August 1839. (P. 546)

Giles Holt to Elisha O. Pursley a negro girl. 15 January 1841. (P. 546)

Levi Roark to Josiah Newman 180 acres. 24 October 1834. (P. 547)

William Roark to Manson Young a tract of land on Goose Creek. 20 July 1839. (P. 548)

Simeon Jones to Jordan Kilzer 100 acres. 18 February 1841. (P. 548)

Josiah J. Caruthers to Edmund Estes 40 acres. 11 February 1839. (P. 549)

Britton Holland to Robert Lancaster 20 March 1841. (P. 549)

William Snider to Julius Snider 50 acres. 30 March 1841. (P. 550)

John S. Johnson to John Burrow 25 acres. 25 January 1841. (P. 550)

John Burrow to John S. Johnson 70 acres. 9 February 1841. (P. 551)

Reubin Huggins to James Jenkins a boy slave. 2 October 1840. (P. 551)

Presley Askins to Stephen A. Farmer a tract of land on Mulherin's Creek. 26 May 1839. (P. 552)

Wilson Y. Martin to William Martin a negro girl. 2 January 1837. (P. 552)

Benjamin Orwell to Robin Hays 100 acres. 31 December 1840. (P. 553)

Henry W. Glover to Robert Holladay. 29 April 1841. (P. 554)

George Rowland appoints Jefferson Rowland as his attorney in settling the estate of David Rowland. 18 March 1841. (P. 554)

James Eaton to Cornelius Fisher a tract of 30 acres. 3 September 1831. (P. 555)

James Hall to John Merrett 200 acres. 16 March 1841. (P. 555)

DEED BOOK P

Ebenezer Wright and wife Olivia, James Beckwith and wife Rachael, and James G. Roulston to Orville Green a tract of land in the town of Carthage. 16 July 1840. (P. 556)

John M. Degernett to Lewis M. Gann. 18 May 1841. (P. 557)

Richard P. Hughes to Leonard F. Hughes a tract of land in the 17th District. 3 May 1841. (Pp. 557-558)

Valentine Presley to Benjamin Crowell 50 acres. 1839. (Pp. 558-559)

Ambrose Manion of Allen County, Kentucky to Calvin Cook a tract of 100 acres. 21 October 1831. (Pp. 559-560)

John Haggerty to Robert Allen. April 1841. Witness: Ogden Haggerty. (Pp. 560-561)

Hezekiah Blankenship to John Blankenship his interest in 42 acres he is to receive at the death of his mother Rhoda Blankenship. 5 October 1839. (P. 561)

Stephen H. Douglass to William Ballinger 40 acres. 9 November 1838. (P. 562)

P. M. Wade of Dekalb County, Tennessee to S. B. Chandler one fourth of an acre. 4 January 1840. (P. 562)

Mathew Petross to William Smith 80 acres. 19 August 1837. (P. 563)

Stephen Samson and Johnson Samson to John C. Sanders 25 acres. 9 March 1839. (P. 563)

Miles West to William D. Evans a tract of land on the Caney Fork River. 10 May 1841. (P. 564)

George W. Terry to James M. Winfrey 141 acres. 10 June 1841. (P. 565)

James Martin to Stephen W. Martin, trustee for Elizabeth Jane Dillon, granddaughter of the said James Martin, a trunk which she is to receive at the death of her mother Jane G. Dillon. Said trunk is on the property of William B. Dillon. 23 June 1841. (P. 566)

James Martin to Stephen W. Martin to his grandchildren, to wit, Elizabeth J. Dillon, James Dillon, and Thomas Dillon some personal property. 23 June 1841. (P. 566)

James McMurry to John McMurry a tract of land on Dixon's Creek. 5 January 1841. (P. 567)

Job Meador to Joel Meador 125 acres. 27 March 1839. (P. 567)

Sheriff W. W. Bailey to Lot Hazard. 1841. (P. 568)

John Cochran to David Tyree a tract of land on Mulherin's Creek. 23 January 1838. (P. 569)

Uriah White to John White 50 acres. 1841. (P. 570)

DEED BOOK P

Samuel S. Turner to Richard Bandy 105 acres. 28 March 1840. (P. 570)

Ira Meador to his son Jehu Meador 49 acres. 29 October 1839. (P. 571)

Joseph S. Acuff of Rutherford County to William F. Cliburn 50 acres. 25 July 1840. (Pp. 571-572)

Goolsberry Parker and Franklin Galbreath to Aaron S. Adams a tract of land on Goose Creek. 6 January 1841. (P. 572)

Henry McWhorter to John Robertson a tract of land on Big Barren River. 30 July 1840. (P. 573)

William P. Hughes to Stephen Garrett a tract of land on Goose Creek. 27 December 1838. (P. 574)

John Cliburn to Peter Epperson five acres. 12 June 1841. (P. 574)

Joseph Jenkins to James Jenkins 91 acres. 10 June 1841. (P. 575)

Samuel Lawrence to Fountain Hanes 45 acres. 12 June 1841. (P. 575)

David Turner to Jehu Meador 50 acres. 31 December 1839. (P. 576)

Joel Simmons to David F. Galbreath 150 acres. 15 May 1841. (P. 577)

Barnet Blankenship to his son David Blankenship a tract of land on Puncheon Camp Creek. 8 February 1841. (P. 577)

Ira Meador to Talleferro Hammack 37 acres. 12 June 1841. (P. 578)

Joel Simmons to George White 90 acres. 12 June 1841. (P. 578)

Austin L. Hanes to John White 130 acres. 12 June 1841. (P. 579)

Benjamin Piper to William D. Garrett 11 acres. 22 June 1841. (P. 579)

Uriah White to Tully Brickhouse a tract of land on Barren River. 28 March 1838. (P. 580)

DEED BOOK Q

Young & Coker to Howell H. Hargis 50 acres. 3 June 1840. (P. 1)

John Meador to Joel Meador his interest in 135 acres. 28 September 1839. (P. 1)

Talliferro Hammack to Austin S. Hanes 27 acres. 12 June 1841. (P. 2)

Austin S. Hanes to John White 75 acres. 12 June 1841. (P. 2)

Elizabeth Driver, Jesse Driver, Ezekiel East, Synthia East, Thomas Jent, and Elizabeth Jent, heirs of Dempsey Driver, to Joel Driver 100 acres. January 1831. (P. 3)

Calvin Cook to Joel Blankenship 100 acres. 12 June 1841. (P. 4)

Goolsberry Parker and D. F. Galbreath to Burrell Hanes 32 acres. 26 January 1841. (P. 4)

John A. Farmer to John H. Newbell. 15 July 1841. (P. 5)

Excum Epperson and Poley Anderson to Austin S. Hanes 45 acres. 16 November 1839. (P. 6)

Benjamin Piper to William D. Garrett a tract of land. 22 June 1841. (P. 6)

Isaac Pipkin to Samuel Pipkin 82½ acres. 1 February 1841. (P. 7)

David Tyree to Jefferson Roland a tract of land. 1841. (P. 7)

William B. Simon to Sinthia Philips 210 acres. 3 August 1840. (P. 8)

Daniel McKinnis to James D. McKinnis 25 acres. 13 April 1841. (P. 9)

William B. Taylor to William G. Simon and David C. Simon a tract of land. 5 July 1841. (P. 9)

Daniel McKinnis to Thomas McKinnis 79 acres. 13 April 1841. (P. 10)

Samuel T. Lancaster to Isaac Bates 171 acres. 20 February 1841. (P. 11)

Abraham Caruthers to Benjamin Arundel a tract of land on Snow Creek. 25 December 1840. (P. 11)

Benjamin Arundel 120 acres. 29 July 1841. (Pp. 11-12)

Edward B. Haynie to Thompson Mace a tract of land on Dixon's Creek. 28 October 1840. (Pp. 12-13)

Joseph Parker of Pike County, Illinois appoints Daniel Smith as his attorney in settling the estate of William Parker.

DEED BOOK Q

22 May 1841. (P. 13)

Reuben Branswell to Thomas W. Wooten. 2 August 1841. (P. 14)

Joseph Weaver to A. S. Baines eight acres. 6 August 1841. (P. 14)

John Lancaster to Frederick Decker a tract of land. 7 August 1840. (P. 15)

Abraham Perry to Reuben Braswell. 8 August 1841. (P. 15)

R. D. Allison to Henry Mann a tract of land on Hickman's Creek. 6 August 1841. (P. 16)

Zachariah Tolliver to John Lipscomb a tract of land on Goose Creek, it being lot number nine in the division of the lands of Andrew Greer and drawn by Jane B. Greer, now Jane B. Jackson, wife of Calvin Jackson. 30 July 1841. (P. 17)

Robert A. Massey to Isaac A. Massey. 16 July 1841. (P. 17)

Leroy P. Adams to James Reid a tract of land on Goose Creek. 14 June 1841. (P. 18)

William Petty to John Stokes 242 acres. 20 April 1841. (P. 19)

Joseph Dirickson to Jane Elvira, wife of Sylvester Harkreader, a tract of land on the Cumberland River. 5 July 1841. (P. 19)

Thomas W. Page to John B. Norris 100 acres. 9 August 1841. (P. 20)

Andrew McClellan to William Young 203 acres. 21 November 1840. (Pp. 20-21)

Isaac and Benjamin Pierce to Zachariah Corder a negro woman. 6 December 1839. (P. 21)

Coleman Sampson to William Ballinger 113 acres. 27 August 1838. (P. 21)

Richard E. Farley to Leroy H. Cage a crop of tobacco. 11 August 1841. (P. 22)

Henry Roark to Thomas Maddux several items. 10 August 1841. (P. 23)

William P. Hughes and John W. Hughes bound to Edward B. Tuck. 13 February 1841. (Pp. 23-24)

Archibald McNeill to John Lipscomb part of the home tract of Andrew Greer. 3 August 1840. (P. 24)

David Burford to Stephen W. Malone a tract of land on Dixon's Creek. 5 August 1841. (P. 25)

Henry S. Day to Philip T. Day. 1841. (P. 25)

DEED BOOK Q

Littleton H. Carter and Robert Bowman to William M. Price a town lot in the town of Rome. 4 March 1841. (P. 26)

John Gray Blount, Jr., by virtue of a power of attorney from his father, John Gray Blount, Sr., of Beaufort County, North Carolina, appoints Jesse Blackfan of Nashville as his attorney. 24 April 1820. (P. 26)

Sheriff W. W. Bailey to James Young. 17 August 1841. (P. 27)

John Gray Blount appoints his son John Gray Blount as his attorney. 1818. (P. 28)

Joseph Jones to John Donoho a crop of tobacco. 19 August 1841. (P. 29)

Silas C. Cornwell to William M. Knight 245 acres. 9 January 1840. (P. 29)

Avin Ward to John Ward and R. D. Allison. 1841. (P. 30)

R. D. Allison and John Ward to Peter Porter 98 acres. 19 August 1841. (P. 31)

Peter Porter to Frederick Jones 98 acres. 19 August 1841. (P. 32)

C. T. Thomas to John Ward. 18 August 1841. (Pp. 32-33)

Young & Coker to Elbert G. Holland a tract of land on Goose Creek. 11 July 1841. (Pp. 33-34)

Cyrus W. Brevard to Joseph S. Carter a tract of land on Goose Creek. 5 August 1841. (P. 34)

Elbert G. Holland to James Linsebaugh 100 acres. 10 July 1841. (P. 35)

John Fleman to Frances Duffy some livestock. 24 August 1841. (P. 36)

James B. Richardson to Frances Duffy a crop of tobacco. 18 August 1841. (P. 36)

William Wood to Martha Hogan, James Hogan, Bailey P. Hogan, Thomas J. Hogan, and Benjamin R. Hogan, the heirs of Anthony Hogan, 205 acres. 9 June 1841. (P. 37)

Alex Dillard to Martha Hogan and others. 9 June 1841. (Pp. 37-38)

Archibald Scruggs to Martha Hogan and others 12½ acres. 9 June 1841. (P. 38)

Clement Gillihan and William Gillihan to Martha Hogan and others 150 acres. 9 June 1841. (P. 39)

Jeremiah Moore to Israel McHill 50 acres. 27 August 1841. (Pp. 39-40)

DEED BOOK Q

John Conger to Alexander Dillard 800 acres. 7 August 1841. (P. 40)

John S. Sanders to John H. Burford a crop of tobacco. 30 August 1841. (P. 41)

G. B. Woodcock to John W. Atkinson 34 acres. 22 March 1839. (P. 42)

Ruth Jones to John McCall a negro girl. 20 November 1839. (P. 42)

Mary G. Wilson, Wallace Wilson, Sarah G. Wilson, heirs of Matilda Wilson, by their father George Wilson, to William L. Martin 320 acres. 1841. (P. 43)

John Culbreath to James Duffy. 1 September 1841. (Pp. 44-45)

Daniel Rawley to William B. Young a crop of tobacco. 10 September 1841. (P. 45)

Archibald Parker to Thomas Wilborn, Sr. 15 acres. 30 August 1841. (P. 46)

Hugh Campbell to James S. Campbell 78 acres. 8 September 1841. (P. 47)

Oscar Purnell to Samuel P. Williams a crop of tobacco. September 1841. (P. 47)

Hugh Campbell to George H. Campbell 78 acres. 8 September 1841. (P. 48)

Thomas Wilborn to John H. Ligon his interest in a negro belonging to the estate of Sarah Ligon. 22 August 1840. (P. 48)

Benjamin Crowell to Edward Anderson of Jackson County 100 acres. 7 July 1841. (P. 49)

John H. Gammon to Willis Ligon a crop of tobacco. 30 August 1841. (P. 49)

Sarah Perkins to Elijah Bomer 124 acres. 2 November 1840. (P. 50)

Yeatman Hicks to John Trousdale a crop of tobacco. 13 September 1841. (P. 50)

Sally Hubbard nominates David K. Timberlake a tract of land on the Cumberland River. 14 September 1841. (P. 51)

Thomas Williams to James Denton. 21 September 1841. (Pp. 52-53)

James, George, William, and Samuel Scoggins, the four last named being children of George W. Scoggins to Sarah Scoggins, wife of the said George W. a town lot. 20 September 1841. (Pp. 53-54)

Elizabeth Bolton appoints Amos Chapman as his attorney. 14 February 1840. (P. 54)

DEED BOOK Q

Ira S. Sullivan to C. C. Ford a crop of tobacco. 5 October 1841. (P. 55)

James N. Roy to Saban Driver a tract of land on Smith's Fork. 8 August 1841. (P. 55)

Samuel Stephens to Alexander Pipkin. 2 October 1841. (P. 56)

A. W. Gibbs to Isaac Lynch a crop of tobacco. 5 October 1841. (P. 56)

William H. Jones to William B. Young a crop of tobacco. 1 October 1841. (P. 57)

Frederick J. Uhls to Andrew J. Baker a tract of land on the Cumberland River. 5 October 1841. (P. 57)

Calvin Pope to Henry Sadler a tract of 50 acres. 4 October 1841. (P. 58)

William B. Stokes to John T. Stokes 300 acres. 4 January 1836. (P. 58)

William H. Jones to William B. Young a crop of tobacco. 1 October 1841. (P. 59)

Frederick J. Uhls to Andrew J. Baker a crop of tobacco. 5 October 1841. (P. 59)

Isaac Myres to William Corley and Larkin Corley, sons of Larkin Corley, a tract of land in the county of Dickson. 2 February 1829. (P. 60)

James Barrett to John Payne a negro boy. 4 October 1841. (P. 61)

James Green to C. C. Ford a crop of tobacco. 8 October 1841. (P. 61)

John T. Stokes to William W. Anderson a tract of land on Beasley's Bend. 9 August 1841. (P. 62)

John T. Stokes to Robert H. Cato 110 acres. August 1841. (P. 62)

Hopkins Richardson to Thompson Mace a negro man. 21 September 1841. (P. 62)

Abner A. Flippin to Lewis Hall. 2 October 1841. (P. 63)

Alfred Davis to Nelson Davis a tract of land on Peyton's Creek. 28 September 1831. (P. 63)

Alfred Davis to Nelson Davis 12 acres. 28 September 1831. (P. 64)

Harrison J. Ford to Hiram C. Ford a parcel of negroes. October 1841. (P. 64)

George Read to Alfred Smith. 18 October 1841. (P. 65)

Powell Tuck to William P. Hughes. 1841. (P. 65)

DEED BOOK Q

George W. Decker to C. C. Ford a crop of tobacco. 16 October 1841. (P. 66)

Thomas Carman to James Climer 100 acres. 30 October 1840. (P. 66)

Aram W. Sullivan to D. K. Timberlake and C. C. Ford a crop of tobacco. 20 October 1841. (P. 67)

Joseph Vandepool to John Trousdale a crop of tobacco. 25 August 1841. (P. 68)

John Buckner, Margaret Buckner, Malinda Tubb, Summers Decker, Richard B. Decker, Clarissa Lancaster, and John Lancaster to John Simpson 363 acres. 12 June 1841. (P. 68)

Winston Chandler to Aley Pipkin a crop of tobacco. 25 October 1841. (P. 69)

Francis Flippin, heir of Martha Dixon, widow of Col. Henry Dixon, appoints Adam Ferguson as her attorney. 28 April 1841. (Pp. 69-70)

Jacob M. Cleveland, one of fifteen heirs of William Cleveland, to Thomas Gregory, Jr. his interest in a tract of land. 27 October 1841. (P. 71)

James Mathewson and wife Mary to Thomas Gregory their interest in the estate of Charles Nixon. 30 October 1841. (P. 71)

Anthony M. Ballew to Lorenzo D. Bolton his interest in the estate of his father Leonard Ballew. 23 October 1841. (P. 72)

William Jones to Stephen Mann 150 acres. 1 November 1841. (Pp. 72-73)

Daniel Sullivan to Elizabeth and Thomas Hatchett, Sarah Rawlings, Mary and Isaac Hatchett a tract of land on Goose Creek. 18 September 1841. (P. 73)

Meredith Hawkins to A. S. Bains some livestock. 31 October 1841. (P. 74)

William Dawson, administrator of John Dawson, to John W. Brown a negro woman. 2 November 1841. (P. 74)

William Pulley to William Young a crop of tobacco. 21 September 1841. (P. 75)

William Jones to Joseph S. Carter two girl slaves. 1 November 1841. (P. 75)

Robert A. Tate to James W. Grissim a crop of tobacco. 1 November 1841. (P. 76)

John W. Bowen to R. G. Bryant a negro woman. 2 November 1841. (P. 76)

The heirs of Dempsey Driver to Thomas Jente a tract of

DEED BOOK Q

land. 26 January 1841. (P. 77)

Jesse Driver to Thomas Jent 95 acres. 14 June 1841. (P. 78)

Berry West to William West 50 acres. 12 February 1838. (P. 78)

Thomas Knight and wife Sarah H. to Daniel Huddleston their interest in the estate of Joanna Dillaha. 4 October 1837. (P. 79)

Wesley Motes to Edmund Harrison a tract of land in the town of Rome. 8 December 1840. (P. 79)

Britton M. Richardson and wife Mary to Josiah Sloan a tract of land on Peyton's Creek. 2 December 1840. (P. 80)

William Jones to Josiah Hallum 86 acres. 18 September 1841. (P. 81)

Dicken Ward to Thomas Wooten 216 acres. 15 September 1841. (P. 81)

Bird Debow to George Walker 230 acres. 7 June 1841. (P. 82)

Robert A. Taite to James W. Grissim 200 acres. 3 November 1841. (P. 82)

Jesse Meacham to C. C. Ford a crop of tobacco. 23 October 1841. (P. 83)

Richard Ervin to Elum A. Ervin. 11 November 1841. (P. 83)

Obediah Lack to David Prowell a crop of tobacco. 13 November 1841. (P. 84)

Wesley Motes to Thomas W. Page 200 acres. 13 November 1841. (Pp. 84-86)

William Wooten to John Trousdale a crop of tobacco. 15 November 1841. (P. 86)

A. S. Bains to Brice M. Baird a tract of land on Plunkett's Creek. 17 November 1841. (Pp. 86-87)

Mortimer Waters to Presley Askins several slaves. 24 July 1841. (Pp. 87-88)

Abraham G. Penn to Henry Mann several items. 27 November 1841. (P. 88)

The heirs of Benjamin Roe to Jacob W. Roe a tract of land. 1841. (Pp. 88-89)

John Lancaster loans to his mother, Rhoda Lancaster, a negro girl. 4 October 1841. (Pp. 89-90)

Chancery Court to Jordan McKinney. 1841. (Pp. 90-91)

Samuel Caplinger to Henry B. McDonald several slaves. 3 December 1841. (Pp. 91-92)

DEED BOOK Q

Henry Harper to William B. Young a crop of tobacco. 3 December 1841. (Pp. 92-93)

Allen Holliday to S. C. Cornwell and son and Sarah Williams a crop of tobacco. 30 November 1841. (P. 93)

John Collom and James Collom to C. C. Ford a crop of tobacco. 6 October 1841. (P. 94)

Summers Decker to John Lancaster a negro woman. 25 September 1841. (P. 94)

S. D. Hargis and J. B. S. Hargis to John H. Merryman a tract of land. 2 November 1841. (P. 95)

Armstead Moore to his daughter Frances B. Hardwick of Cadds Parish, Louisiana, William B. Moore, and Armstead Moore, Jr. a negro girl. 9 November 1841. (Pp. 95-96)

Jacob Lishy of York County, Pennsylvania appoints Louis C. Lishy of Nashville as his attorney. 24 April 1841. (Pp. 96-97)

Mary Andrews and Samuel Andrews to John Trousdale 50 acres. 27 November 1841. (Pp. 97-98)

William T. Cornwell to Thomas Harris 100 acres. 9 October 1835. (P. 98)

William T. Cornwell to John Adams 175 acres. 18 June 1839. (P. 99)

Thomas Carman to R. G. Bryant a negro boy. 6 December 1841. (P. 99)

Strother Settle to Alfred M. Winkler 20 acres. 2 November 1841. (Pp. 100-101)

Nancy Sloan to Peter Herod a tract of land she received from the estate of Archibald Sloan. 6 December 1841. (P. 101)

James White to John F. Pinckley 60 acres. 8 February 1841. (P. 102)

Edwin C. Grant to Moses Evetts a crop of tobacco. 10 December 1841. (P. 102)

R. G. Bryant to Prior Carter a tract of land on Goose Creek. 1 December 1841. (P. 103)

Hugh H. Bradley to Thomas Carman 231 acres. 2 November 1841. (P. 103)

Wilson Cage to John A. Sloan a tract of 176 acres. 6 December 1841. (P. 104)

John Stafford to Thomas and Caleb Carman, executors of Elijah Carman, a negro woman. 14 December 1841. (P. 104)

John Stafford to Thomas Carman a negro boy. 14 December 1841. (P. 105)

DEED BOOK Q

John McKinney and wife Martha of Davidson County to John Trousdale ten acres. 11 November 1841. (Pp. 105-106)

John A. Sloan and wife Elizabeth, Martin W. Sloan, John L. Miller and wife Sophia to Peter Herod 229 acres. 6 December 1841. (Pp. 106-107)

Samuel Lawrence to Robert Corten his power of attorney. 3 February 1841. (P. 107)

Thomas Allen to P. Anderson a negro boy. 26 November 1841. (P. 108)

Lydia Ray to Moses G. Ford and wife Susanah a negro man for love and affection. 24 August 1837. (P. 108)

Wesley Motes to Mason Walker two lots in the town of Rome. 1 November 1841. (P. 109)

John O. Cosby to William H. Cosby 50 acres. 20 November 1841. (P. 110)

Joshua Hawkins to Wesley and James M. Motes a tract of land on Rawl's Creek. 29 October 1840. (Pp. 110-111)

John Gregory to Thomas Gregory his interest in the estate of his father Major Gregory. 21 December 1841. (P. 111)

William Allen and William L. Alexander to Nancy Allen a negro man. 23 December 1841. (P. 112)

Josiah Newman of Monroe County, Kentucky to Mary, Samuel, and James Gunn, heirs of Lewis Gunn, a tract of land. 21 December 1841. (Pp. 112-113)

Thomas B. Jones to John Jones a tract of land on Goose Creek. 28 September 1841. (P. 113)

William C. Wallis to John F. Pinckley 40 acres. 1 February 1840. (P. 114)

Elisha Dillard to David Smith 100 acres. 2 April 1841. (P. 114)

John O. Cosby to his mother Elizabeth Cosby the negroes he received in the will of his father. 24 November 1841. (P. 115)

John Cooper to Thomas Taylor, administrator of Jesse M. Armstead, a negro man. 22 December 1841. (P. 115)

Elizabeth Cosby to her son John O. Cosby several negroes she received in the will of her husband Thomas W. Cosby. 24 November 1841. (P. 116)

John Reace to James B. Morris a man slave. 20 December 1841. (P. 116)

William W. McMann and wife Jane, Nancy Miller, Matilda Miller to William Jones 156 acres. 26 October 1841. (P. 117)

Miles West to J. B. Morris a woman slave. 13 December 1841. (P. 117)

DEED BOOK Q

William Kyle to William Dillon a negro woman. 30 November 1836. (P. 118)

John Wilson to William Wakefield 70 acres. 20 December 1841. (P. 119)

James Cook to Harris Cook 11 acres. 16 October 1841. (Pp. 119-120)

Wesley Harvey to Pleasant Roberts 150 acres. 9 August 1838. (P. 120)

Circuit Court to John Willis' heirs. Heirs: widow Ann, who is now married to Nathaniel Kirby; John Willis, John A. Willis, and Elizabeth Willis. 1841. (P. 121)

Pleasant Roberts to Daniel Robinson. 27 December 1841. (Pp. 121-122)

William McCormick to Israel McClelan 271 acres. 16 April 1841. (Pp. 122-123)

Chancery Court to George R. Dillard a tract of land belonging to the estate of James Wammack. 1841. (Pp. 123-124)

William C. Coleman to John Trousdale a crop of tobacco. 30 December 1841. (P. 124)

Joel Worley to James C. Williams 50 acres. 18 July 1840. (Pp. 124-125)

George R. Dillard to Isham Beasley 200 acres. 24 December 1841. (P. 125)

James Murphree to David McCall one half acre. 26 January 1841. (P. 126)

Jeremiah Coggin to David C. Hibbitts a negro man. 14 August 1833. (P. 126)

Stephen Mann to Warren Nichols and Joel M. Nichols one acre. 13 December 1841. (P. 127)

Elizabeth Broom to Elias Sloan ten acres. 24 October 1840. (P. 127)

William Broom to Elias Sloan 150 acres. 24 October 1840. (P. 128)

Henry M. Cook to Harris Cook 25 acres. 16 October 1841. (P. 129)

William Wilson to his daughter Lucy Whitley and her husband Josiah a negro girl. 17 November 1832. (P. 129)

Jeremiah Freeland to Robert Burton 40 acres. 12 October 1840. (P. 130)

Allen C. Winfree to Johnson Samson a crop of tobacco. 28 November 1841. (P. 130)

David Cochran to John Cochran several negroes. 8 January 1842. (Pp. 130-131)

DEED BOOK Q

John Stafford to Caleb Carman three negro girls. 7 January 1842. (P. 131)

Elijah Bomar to J. M. Mercer and Elbridge Mercer 30 acres. 23 November 1841. (P. 132)

Avin Ward to S. Ward several items. 13 January 1842. (Pp. 132-133)

John McGee, Mary McGee, Joseph C. McGee, Hyram McGee, Nancy McGee, Evaline McGee, George W. McGee, and Nathaniel W. Parrott and wife Elizabeth, heirs of George McGee, to John McGee a tract of land on the Caney Fork River. 1 January 1842. (Pp. 133-134)

Samuel Burdine to William Morgan, Sr. a town lot in the town of Rome. 29 December 1841. (P. 134)

James Kearley to Joseph S. Carter a man slave. 12 January 1842. (P. 135)

Chancery Court to William Hart a tract of land. 11 September 1841. (Pp. 135-137)

Jordan Kelzer to John A. Smart 100 acres. 19 June 1841. (P. 137)

Martha Moore, William Moore, Moses Springfield and wife Fanny, Nathaniel Macon and wife Elizabeth from John Moore a negro man. 28 July 1838. (P. 138)

Alfred Ewing to A. Ferguson 25 acres. 18 July 1836. (P. 138)

John Moore and others to Richard Butler 94 acres. 27 February 1841. (P. 139)

Alfred Wing to Lynus Ferguson a tract of land on the Caney Fork River. 8 November 1834. (Pp. 139-140)

John Moore and others to William Moore 93 acres. 26 February 1841. (P. 140)

Luke Ford to Stephen Petty a tract of land. 20 January 1842. (P. 141)

J. M. Conditt to Robert Allen a crop of tobacco. 25 January 1842. (P. 142)

Nathaniel W. Parrott bound to James Boose a tract of land. 22 January 1842. (P. 142)

Bartlett Patterson to George T. Wright several items. 25 January 1842. (P. 143)

William McDaniel and Gideon Smith to John Congo 25 acres. 12 January 1841. (P. 144)

Circuit Court to Richard P. Hughes a tract of land. 30 September 1841. (Pp. 144-146)

John Corley to Henry C. Jones a man slave. 2 February 1842. (P. 146)

DEED BOOK Q

Emily Lane, formerly Emily Settle, of Obion County, Tennessee appoints her husband, Granville Lane, as her attorney in settling the estate of George Wright. 7 December 1841. (P. 147)

Meredith Hawkins to T. P. Browning several items. 10 February 1842. (Pp. 147-148)

Bias Russell to John Ballard his interest in a tract of land. 17 March 1841. (P. 148)

John Gwaltney, Jr. to William R. Betty a negro woman. 14 February 1842. (P. 149)

N. B. Burdine to P. Anderson and Joseph Irby a negro boy. 27 January 1842. (P. 149)

W. W. Bailey to Moses Reeves a negro boy. 15 February 1842. (P. 150)

Joseph Thomas to John Ballad a tract of land on Peyton's Creek. 29 November 1841. (P. 150)

John Cochran to Samuel Bradley a negro girl. 6 January 1842. (P. 151)

N. B. Burdine to Thomas D. Price one half acre. 1 December 1841. (P. 151)

Thomas Weatherford to Hezekiah Taylor 133 acres. 14 August 1841. (P. 152)

Mathew Harper to Alfred Harper a crop of tobacco. 15 February 1842. (P. 152)

John Stafford to Thomas Carman three negro boys. 15 February 1842. (P. 153)

Lydia Ray to her grandson George M. Ray all of her negroes. 9 February 1842. (P. 153)

David Riddle to R. Barrow a tract of land. 11 June 1841. (P. 154)

Lewis Allison to Samuel Allison a tract of land belonging to Joseph Allison deceased. 31 November 1841. (P. 154)

Charles Boulton to Wilson Bolton a negro boy. 20 May 1840. (P. 155)

Jordan Stewart to James A. Scruggs several items. 28 January 1842. (P. 155)

Robert Hays to Robert Traywick 100 acres. 20 January 1842. (P. 156)

George W. Terry to Wilson T. Meador a negro girl. 27 December 1841. (P. 157)

Leroy B. Settle and wife Margery of Wilson County to William Thomas their interest in the estate of Andrew Greer. 30 March 1839. (P. 157)

DEED BOOK Q

Ephraim Talley to George W. Walker 135 acres. 19 February 1842. (P. 158)

Wilson Y. Walker, Damaris Walker, and Frances Walker to Ephraim Talley 135 acres. 20 January 1842. (P. 159)

C. T. Thomas to A. J. Wade. 23 February 1842. (P. 160)

James R. Kerr to William Petty a tract of land in the 22nd District. 24 February 1842. (Pp. 160-161)

W. W. Bailey to Johnson Beasley two negro boys. 26 February 1842. (P. 161)

Jeremiah Jamison and John McClarin appoint Joseph W. Allen as their attorney. 1 February 1842. (P. 162)

Samuel Caplinger to Isaac Bates, William Bates, and Thomas Bailiff four acres. 1 March 1842. (P. 163)

Samuel Caplinger and John Caplinger to John Hallum and Horace H. Patterson several slaves. 7 March 1842. (Pp. 163-164)

Hubbard Wright to Hiram C. Ford a tract of land on Goose Creek. 1 February 1840. (P. 164)

John H. Newbell versus the heirs of Mathew Harper. 1842. (P. 165)

David Goodall, Sr. to David L. Goodall, Jr. several negroes. 9 March 1842. (P. 165)

Circuit Court to William B. Moore a tract of land. 1842. (Pp. 166-168)

William B. Moore to Samuel Caplinger 600 acres. 16 March 1842. (P. 169)

Samuel Caplinger to Nicholas Smith of Wilson County 400 acres. 15 March 1842. (Pp. 169-170)

Robert Rowland to Chesley Bridgewater 131 acres. 9 February 1842. (P. 171)

David Denton to Robert Denton 90 acres. 19 March 1842. (Pp. 171-172)

Joseph Summerset to Frances Duffy five negroes left him by his father Joseph Summerset. 19 March 1842. (P. 172)

Elijah Toney of Jackson County to John A. Toney his interest in a town lot in the town of Carthage. 1 January 1842. (P. 173)

Elijah Toney to James R. Toney his son a deed of gift. 1 January 1842. (P. 174)

Byrd Orange to Thomas Belcher some livestock. 25 March 1842. (P. 175)

DEED BOOK Q

Elijah Toney to Benjamin Rucks a negro woman. 15 March 1842. (Pp. 175-176)

Edmond E. Cheatham to Zephaniah Orange some personal property. 28 March 1842. (P. 177)

Robert Braswell to H. L. Stephens and Hezekiah Love three tracts of land. 30 March 1842. (Pp. 177-178)

Allen Piper to Thomas Haley a tract of land on Peyton's Creek. 1 November 1841. (P. 179)

Walter Wever to A. L. Bains some livestock. 4 April 1842. (P. 179)

Elijah Creel to Thomas W. Page some livestock. 1 January 1842. (P. 180)

Edmond E. Cheatham to John R. James a white mare. 4 April 1842. (P. 180)

Nancy Dowell to John W. Paty a negro slave. 23 March 1842. (P. 181)

H. G. Flippin and J. B. Flippin, the heirs of A. B. Flippin, to Ezekiah Corder a woman slave. 1 February 1842. (P. 181)

Hezekiah Love to P. W. Presley a tract of land on Wolf Creek. 1 October 1839. (P. 182)

Hezekiah Love to P. W. Presley 30 acres. 5 September 1839. (P. 182)

Hezekiah Love to P. W. Presley 56 acres. 5 October 1839. (P. 183)

George Norris to Joseph Bishop a tract of land on Fall Creek. 10 April 1838. (P. 183)

Jesse Walton to David Taylor 100 acres. 6 April 1842. (P. 184)

George Gann and William Gann to James W. Grisham several items. 11 April 1842. (Pp. 184-185)

William Puryear and Benjamin Pierce to Stephen Malone four negro slaves. 13 April 1842. (Pp. 185-186)

Archibald McNeill to Josiah Marshall a tract of 12 acres. 1 April 1842. (P. 186)

Archibald McNeill to Josiah Marshall a tract of 114 acres. 15 April 1842. (P. 187)

Samuel Caplinger to Nicholas Smith 450 acres. 18 April 1842. (P. 188)

Richard Kemp to Isaac Kitrell 100 acres. 15 July 1837. (P. 189)

William J. Bennet to John G. Nollner a tract of land. 12 October 1841. (Pp. 189-190)

DEED BOOK Q

Archibald McNeill to Josiah Marshall 76 acres. 16 April 1842. (P. 190)

Richard P. Hughes to John J. Hughes 112 acres. 18 April 1842. (P. 191)

Godfrey Gregory to John Haley his part of the negroes owned by his mother Elizabeth Gregory. 9 October 1840. (P. 191)

Godfrey Gregory, William R. Betty, J. R. James, Hugh Moss, and Joseph Moss to Andrew McClelin of Jackson County a negro girl. 19 April 1842. (P. 192)

John Congo to Simon P. Hughes a negro girl. 5 April 1842. (P. 192)

William Petty to John T. Stokes 50 acres. 17 April 1841. (P. 193)

Charles and Nathaniel Williams to Peggy Mathews. 2 December 1841. (P. 193)

Williamson T. Hall to Tandy and P. D. Hall his portion of his father's estate, now in the possession of his mother. 19 April 1842. (P. 194)

Berryman Turner to John McCall a woman slave. 11 February 1842. (P. 194)

Benjamin J. Vaden from John T. Stokes 50 acres. 20 April 1842. (P. 195)

William L. Martin of Wilson County to Eli Gammon 320 acres. 24 January 1842. (P. 196)

Pierce Puryear to Azakiah Corder a negro girl. 24 December 1841. (P. 196)

William B. Moore, executor of Joseph Allison, to Lewis Allison 227 acres. 20 February 1837. (P. 197)

Solomon Caplinger to Jonathan Bailey three lots in the town of Rome. 4 April 1842. (P. 198)

E. A. Wright bound to William P. Hughes. 16 April 1842. (P. 198)

Richard Braswell to John Braswell 60 acres. 18 July 1841. (P. 199)

Joseph Gresham to John Trousdale 100 acres. 3 May 1841. (P. 199)

James W. Moss to Hugh Moss. 26 March 1842. (P. 200)

Frederick Uhls, Sr. to Richard Uhls 100 acres. 1 February 1837. (P. 200)

Thomas Highers to Henry Highers a tract of land on Roles' Creek. 14 April 1842. (P. 201)

Bartlett James, Jr. to Hugh Moss. 1842. (Pp. 201-202)

DEED BOOK Q

C. T. Thomas to John A. Farmer. 31 December 1841. (P. 202)

Joseph Gresham to Nelson F. Kyle 70 acres. 2 May 1842. (Pp. 203-204)

William P. Hughes to Frances Dowell a tract of land. 3 May 1842. (P. 205)

Stephen R. Samson and Mathew W. Morris to Jacob Baker several items. 4 May 1842. (Pp. 205-206)

Holbrook Nelson versus Archibald McNeill. 1842. (Pp. 206-207)

James B. Cooksey to William Finch some livestock. 1 May 1842. (P. 207)

Joseph Grisham to Robert W. Mann some livestock. 3 May 1842. (P. 208)

Mathew Mooningham to Jefferson Jones 22 acres. 14 May 1842. (Pp. 208-209)

W. H. Irwin to Isaac Willeby several slaves. 16 May 1842. (P. 210)

W. H. Irwin to David Hall some livestock. 16 May 1842. (P. 210)

James M. Mercer and Eldridge Mercer to John H. Newhouse a tract of land on Mulherin's Creek. 19 May 1842. (P. 210)

William Coffee to John Lamberson. 21 May 1842. (P. 211)

W. H. Jenkins to Willie Denny. 1834. (Pp. 211-212)

Buckner Cardwell to Abraham H. King a sorrel horse. 24 May 1842. (P. 212)

James M. Mercer to Willis McClanahan a crop of corn. 23 May 1842. (P. 213)

Lot Hazard and Tabitha D. Hazard to William Ragland a negro boy. 28 May 1842. (P. 213)

Anthony Apple to Madison D. Apple a bay mare. 31 May 1842. (P. 214)

Allen J. Bridges to Rolley Crofford a tract of land. 2 November 1828. (Pp. 214-215)

Milton Draper, Edward B. Draper, Brice M. Draper to Larkin and Henry M. Cornwell two acres. 13 January 1840. (P. 215)

Jacob W. Roe to William C. Roe and Robert A. Roe 104 acres. 18 May 1842. (Pp. 216-217)

N. C. Sanders versus F. B. Pierce. 1842. (P. 217)

Stephen M. Jones to John W. Sanders and George W. Martin a negro girl. 11 May 1842. (P. 217)

DEED BOOK Q

J. E. Patton to John Hyette a negro girl. January 1842. (P. 218)

John H. Newbell to John R. James 60 acres. 26 February 1842. (P. 218)

Daniel Smith to Allen Mathews ten acres. 25 November 1841. (P. 219)

Peter Craighead to Isaac Kitrell 42 acres. 7 May 1842. (P. 219)

Isaac Kitrell to Edwin Kitrell 100 acres. Witnesses: Daniel Smith and John F. Kitrell. 10 January 1842. (P. 220)

Bird Nichols to John Trousdale his interest in the land on which Lucy Nichols now lives. 1842. (P. 220)

Lot Hazard and Tabitha Hazard to Adam Ferguson several slaves. 7 June 1842. (P. 221)

John Lipscomb to Mosby Lipscomb a man slave. 7 January 1842. (Pp. 221-222)

E. Featherstone to R. P. Hall a boy slave. 8 June 1842. (P. 222)

Thomas R. Burnett to Isaac Tubb. 22 May 1821. (Pp. 222-224)

Charles McMurry to Solomon McMurry 185 acres. 11 June 1842. (P. 224)

Charles McMurry to James W. Bransford a negro woman. 10 June 1842. (Pp. 224-225)

John E. Patton to John Hiett a negro woman. 11 June 1842. (Pp. 225-226)

James M. Blackwell to Elizabeth Blackwell 60 acres. 11 May 1842. (P. 226)

Mar C. Hunt to William Rutherford and Robert Marshall his (her) interest in the estate of Margaret Rutherford. 19 January 1837. (P. 227)

John E. Patton to George W. Williams a negro boy. 11 June 1842. (P. 227)

Reece Wardrope to Allen Mathews a crop of corn and tobacco. 13 June 1842. (P. 228)

John Litchford to William Litchford 61 acres. 14 June 1842. (P. 228)

Charles McMurry to John D. Day 30 acres. 19 March 1842. (P. 229)

Sol McMurry to John B. Gammon a negro man. 15 June 1842. (P. 229)

Charles McMurry to Solomon McMurry. 1842. (P. 230)

DEED BOOK Q

Samuel D. McMurry to Solomon McMurry his interest in a parcel of negroes. 14 March 1842. (P. 230)

Solomon McMurry to William B. Wetherford 102½ acres. 19 May 1840. (P. 231)

William B. Wetherford to William Alexander and Richard Alexander a tract of land. 13 June. (Pp. 231-232)

John E. Patton to James R. Toney a negro man. 14 June 1842. (P. 232)

John H. Rodgers to John Hall a bay horse. 14 June 1842. (P. 233)

J. W. and J. E. Patton to John Hyett two negro girls. 11 June 1842. (P. 233)

Granville S. Pearce to Isaac and Alfred Pearce of Sumner County a tract of land formerly owned by Benjamin Pearce and George Pearce. Said Granville is a resident of Rutherford County. 1842. (P. 234)

Solomon McMurry to Henry L. Day several items. 17 June 1842. (P. 235)

Nathan Hall to James Bradley several items. 15 June 1842. (Pp. 236-237)

William B. Wetherford to Poleman W. Cage several items. 21 June 1842. (P. 237)

James Morris, Sr. to James Climer a tract of 85 acres. 4 May 1842. (P. 238)

Jeremiah Freeland to John P. Hughes a negro girl. 22 June 1842. (P. 238)

Jeremiah Freeland to Gideliah Hughes several items. 23 June 1842. (P. 239)

George Payne to Thomas Smithwick 50 acres. 8 August 1840. (P. 240)

Thomas Smithwick to George Boston 40 acres. 23 June 1842. (Pp. 240-241)

James Haynes to James A. Scruggs some livestock. 23 June 1842. (P. 241)

John Williams to Thomas W. Page 150 acres. 25 June 1842. (Pp. 242-244)

James M. Motes to John Williams 200 acres. 24 April 1842. (P. 244)

James H. Vaden to Samuel Hunter a negro man. 25 June 1842. (P. 245)

Hopkins Richardson to William C. Richardson and Britton M. Richardson 300 acres. 27 June 1842. (P. 245)

Hopkins Richardson to Josiah Richardson. 1842. (P. 245)

DEED BOOK Q

Gregory D. Burns to John H. Ligon a crop of tobacco. 27 June 1842. (P. 247)

Charles McMurry to James W. Bransford. June 1842. (Pp. 247-248)

Silas C. Cornwell to Isaiah Pyron 25 acres. 28 March 1842. (P. 249)

Hopkins Richardson to James Martin a negro girl. 6 November 1841. (P. 250)

Charles McMurry to James W. Bransford. 10 June 1842. (Pp. 250-251)

Thomas B. Durham, Jr. by his guardian Jephtha Durham versus Thomas B. Durham, Sr. and Jane Durham. 1842. (P. 251)

Leonard Ballew to William and Richard Alexander his interest in the estate of his father Leonard Ballew. 30 June 1842. (P. 252)

Samuel Brent to Zephaniah Orange a crop of tobacco. 2 July 1842. (Pp. 252-253)

Alexander R. Dillehay to Barnet T. Dillehay 64 acres. 4 July 1842. (P. 253)

Adam Stafford to Lawrence Thompson 62 acres. 28 November 1838. (P. 254)

Presley Askins to John Reeves a negro boy. 25 February 1842. (P. 254)

James D. Hammack to Lemuel A. Hammack his interest in the estate of Daniel Hammack that is now in the possession of Mary Hammack. 6 July 1842. (P. 255)

William D. Garrett to John Payne a tract of land on Peyton's Creek. 7 July 1842. (P. 255)

Turman Wheeler to James Wheeler a tract of land on the Cumberland River. 7 July 1842. (P. 256)

Henry Robinson to William Finch 73 acres. 3 October 1837. (P. 257)

William Finch to James Gill a tract of land. 7 July 1842. (Pp. 257-258)

Roland W. Newby to John Reeves a tract of land in the 18th District. 6 July 1842. (P. 258)

Micajah D. Cardwell to William Cardwell. 7 July 1842. (P. 259)

John Turner to Daniel Seay 225 acres. 9 August 1842. (P. 260)

Henry L. Day to Philip T. Day 38 acres. 11 July 1842. (Pp. 260-261)

James W. Bransford to Elizabeth Blackwell a woman slave.

DEED BOOK Q

8 July 1842. (P. 261)

Charles McMurry to Elizabeth Blackwell a negro boy. 12 July 1842. (P. 261)

John W. Hall to Neil Patterson a crop of tobacco. 14 July 1842. (P. 262)

John G. Richardson to John H. Newbell several items. 15 July 1842. (Pp. 262-263)

John J. Hibbitt to his two nieces, Phebe Ann Featherstone and Mary Featherstone, several items. 25 June 1842. (P. 263)

R. S. Wilbourn and Lucy Wilbourn to William S. Willis 35 acres. 17 January 1842. (P. 264)

Archibald Parker to William S. Willis 30 acres. 17 January 1842. (P. 265)

R. S. Wilbourn and Lucy Wilbourn to Thomas Wilbourn 257 acres. 5 February 1842. (Pp. 265-266)

Robert Hawkins to Ferdinand Ford 25 acres. 20 July 1842. (P. 266)

Ferdinand Ford to Stephen Petty a tract of land. 19 July 1842. (P. 267)

Samuel Caplinger to Andrew Caplinger 80 acres. 21 July 1842. (P. 268)

Johnson Sampson to Thomas Snoddy and William Strother. 21 July 1842. (P. 269)

Jehu Timberlake to Lente Boulton a tract of land. 22 July 1842. (P. 270)

William Searcy to John High a tract of land. 18 July 1842. (Pp. 270-271)

Gideon Gifford to B. T. Mottley four negroes. 18 October 1837. (P. 271)

George Jenkins to Peter A. Wilkerson several items. 27 July 1842. (P. 272)

William D. Nash to George Nash a crop of tobacco. 25 July 1842. (Pp. 272-273)

John G. Richardson to James Thomas a crop of tobacco. 28 July 1842. (P. 274)

John W. Hughes to John R. James a negro man. July 1842. (Pp. 274-275)

Stephen R. Samson and Mathew W. Morris to Jacob Baker a crop of tobacco. 1 August 1842. (P. 275)

Samuel Black to James Duffy. 1 August 1842. (P. 276)

John McMurry to William and Richard Alexander 138 acres. 28 July 1842. (P. 277)

DEED BOOK Q

Lewis Strador to Jemima Porter 71 acres. 8 November 1841. (Pp. 277-278)

Mark Dyson to John O. Pope a tract of land on Roll's Creek. 17 December 1839. (P. 278)

Thomas Carman to Robert Haley a tract of land on Payton's Creek. 16 November 1840. (P. 279)

Jehu Timberlake to Patrick Hubbard a tract of land on the Cumberland River. 29 July 1842. (P. 280)

James C. Williams to Ellis Kemp 114 acres. 6 July 1842. (P. 281)

Regen Thompson to Leroy H. Cage and David McCall a town lot in the town of Rome. 13 July 1842. (P. 282)

James Reynolds to Thomas Fisher, Jr. 40 acres. 30 July 1842. (P. 282)

J. T. Owens and H. G. Owens to Joseph J. Bridges 117 acres. 20 August 1841. (P. 283)

Thomas Bandy to Samuel Andrews 14 acres. 3 January 1842. (P. 283)

William Ashley to Hugh Moss 150 acres. 1 August 1842. (P. 284)

James Craig to Hiram M. Craig 27 acres. 1 August 1842. (P. 284)

Nicy Harris to Caleb Carman her dower in the estate of Emanuel Harris. 23 February 1842. (P. 285)

Bartlett Patterson to James W. Bransford. 30 July 1842. (Pp. 285-286)

John A. Sloan, Martin W. Sloan, and John Miller to Reuben Turner a tract of land belonging to Archibald Sloan, deceased. 1842. (Pp. 286-287)

Booker Wakefield to William J. Ballew a negro girl. 2 August 1842. (P. 287)

Elijah Miller to Chesley Bridgewater a tract of land on Dixon's Creek. 30 June 1842. (Pp. 287-288)

Booker Wakefield and wife Manerva to L. D. Ballew their interest in the estate of Leonard Ballew. 3 August 1842. (P. 288)

Frances H. Gordon to David C. Ward and John W. Newhouse 900 acres. 5 August 1842. (Pp. 289-291)

Henry L. Day to Wilson Y. Martin a crop of tobacco. 4 August 1842. (P. 291)

Edmund Estes to George C. Gifford 40 acres. 4 August 1842. (P. 292)

P. W. Cage to John C. Chambers a negro girl. 3 November 1841. (P. 292)

DEED BOOK Q

James Cawthon to John S. Page a woman slave. 27 December 1840. (P. 293)

John Culbreath to Thomas Tunstall a crop of tobacco. 15 June 1842. (P. 293)

William M. Armstead to Martha Armstead a negro woman. 8 August 1842. (P. 294)

John Stevens to James B. Morris a tract of land on Mulherin's Creek. 28 April 1842. (P. 294)

John Stevens to James B. Morris a man slave. November 1841. (P. 295)

John Trousdale to William McClain a negro man. 8 August 1842. (P. 295)

William P. Hughes to John Gordon a tract of land on Hickman's Creek. 9 August 1842. (Pp. 295-296)

Elisha Dillard to James Ballard 130 acres. 8 June 1842. (P. 297)

John Trousdale to John Cooper a negro boy. 5 April 1842. (P. 297)

C. C. Ford to Robert W. Mann a negro woman. August 1842. (Pp. 298-299)

Sheriff W. W. Bailey to Hampton W. Marley two negroes belonging to Lot Hazard. 10 August 1842. (P. 299)

John W. Hughes to Thomas Bridges a negro woman. 3 July 1842. (P. 299)

Charles McMurry to Thomas Tunstall. 25 July 1842. (P. 300)

William Ferrell bound to William D. Turner. 20 December 1838. (Pp. 300-301)

Thomas Snoddy to Campbell Crutchfield, Vincent R. Bradford, and John Moore 190 acres. 12 August 1842. (Pp. 301-302)

John P. Hughes to Creed Penn 26 acres. 11 August 1842. (P. 302)

William Flowers to Richard Williams a tract of land on Big Barren River. 27 September 1834. (P. 303)

William Owen to Stephen Stone 100 acres. 22 January 1841. (P. 304)

John Hazard, Sr. and John R. Hazard, Jr. to Thomas Bridges a tract of land on the Cumberland River. 9 February 1842. (Pp. 304-305)

Ezekiel Evans to James Garrison a tract of land on Hickman's Creek. 6 September 1837. (P. 305)

John W. Hughes and Virginia Hughes to Creed Penn 26 acres. 11 August 1842. (P. 306)

DEED BOOK Q

Jeremiah Freeland to John P. Hughes his interest in the dower of Agnes Penn, formerly Agnes Freeland. Said Agnes is the widow of James Freeland. 11 August 1842. (P. 306)

Sheriff W. W. Bailey to William Ragland a negro man. 12 August 1842. (P. 307)

Alexander Dillard to Henry B. McDonald 800 acres. 12 August 1842. (P. 307)

Solomon McMurry to Martin McMurry his interest in a tract of land left him by his father Charles McMurry. 12 August 1842. (P. 308)

Robert Bradley to Hugh H. Bradley a negro girl. 9 July 1842. (P. 308)

John W. Hughes to Samuel C. Bridgewater 149 acres. 13 August 1842. (P. 309)

John W. Hughes to Creed Penn a slave. 13 August 1842. (P. 309)

Lot Hazard to T. J. Lee a tract of land. 19 July 1842. (P. 310)

Lot Hazard & Simms Massey 300 acres. 27 July 1842. (P. 310)

Lot Hazard to Howell H. Bryant a tract of land. 27 July 1842. (P. 311)

Lot Hazard to Timothy Walton, Jr. a tract of land. 12 August 1842. ((Pp. 312-313)

John W. Hughes to John H. Newbell. 13 August 1842. (P. 313)

John Hooker to Henry C. Jones a woman slave. 13 August 1842. (Pp. 314-315)

Joel Gregory to Sampson McClelan 75 acres. 11 August 1842. (P. 316)

Thomas Snoddy to William Baker a tract of land on Mulherin's Creek. 13 August 1842. (Pp. 316-317)

Stephen Stafford to Cain Stafford a tract of land on Dixon's Creek. 13 October 1840. (Pp. 317-318)

Christopher Baughman to Henry Mann a tract of land in the 14th District. August 1842. (Pp. 318-319)

Pleasant Morris and James Morris, Jr. to Wilson Y. Martin a crop of tobacco. 15 August 1842. (P. 320)

Jefferson Jones to John Bridges several items. 15 August 1842. (Pp. 321-322)

Elijah A. Wright to William A. Lancaster a tract of land on Mulherin's Creek. 20 January 1842. (P. 322)

DEED BOOK Q

E. Featherstone to John J. Hibbitt 76 acres. 13 August 1842. (P. 323)

Mary Hammack to Elijah H. Hammack a negro boy. 27 October 1840. (P. 323)

E. Featherstone to John J. Hibbitt a crop of tobacco. 13 August 1842. (P. 324)

Thomas Clemmons to Sampson McClelan. 15 August 1842. (P. 324)

Charles and Nathaniel Williams to Luke Ford 50 acres. 25 February 1840. (P. 325)

Luke Ford to Samuel Ford 50 acres. 16 June 1842. (P. 326)

James C. Greenwood to Thomas Tunstall a crop of tobacco. 15 August 1842. (P. 327)

William Edens to Thomas Wilbourn a crop of tobacco. 16 August 1842. (Pp. 327-328)

John Lancaster, Sr. to Joel Coffee 1200 acres. 13 August 1842. (Pp. 328-329)

John Brim to William Alexander a tract of land on Peyton's Creek. 13 August 1842. (P. 329)

Bennet S. Johns to his father Elias Johns two negro women. 8 August 1842. (P. 330)

Moses Burns to Samuel A. Hammack a crop of tobacco. 11 August 1842. (P. 330)

William Roark to Thomas Matlock a crop of tobacco. 13 August 1842. (P. 331)

Elijah A. Wright to J. R. Smith some livestock. 16 August 1842. (Pp. 331-332)

John Cochran to Jacob Waggoner a tract of land on Hogan's Creek. 16 August 1842. (P. 332)

John Lancaster to John Noolner 100 acres. 13 August 1842. (P. 333)

James Gill to Daniel Seay a tract of land on Round Lick Creek. 16 October 1841. (P. 333)

Dabner M. League to Thomas A. Lancaster a tract of land on the Caney Fork. 6 June 1842. (P. 334)

John G. Noolner to William Lancaster two acres. 1 July 1842. (P. 335)

Stephen Robinson to Thomas Stokes a tract of land on Smith's Fork. 13 November 1838. (Pp. 335-336)

Barnard Richardson to Alexander Dillard. 18 February 1837. (Pp. 336-337)

John Trousdale to John R. James. 1842. (Pp. 337-338)

DEED BOOK Q

John Hooker to Henry C. Jones some livestock. 17 August 1842. (Pp. 338-339)

Sheriff W. W. Bailey to William P. Hughes several items. 17 August 1842. (P. 339)

John P. Hughes of Sumner County appoints William P. Hughes as his attorney. 17 August 1842. (P. 339)

Elmore D. Page to John Page a negro woman. 17 August 1842. (P. 340)

Daniel Rawley to William B. Young a crop of tobacco. 17 August 1842. (P. 340)

William J. Gregory to William B. Young a crop of tobacco. 7 August 1842. (P. 341)

Stephen Haynes to William B. Young a crop of tobacco. 17 August 1842. (Pp. 341-342)

Larkin Monday to William B. Young a crop of tobacco. 17 August 1842. (P. 342)

Alexander Dillehay to William B. Young a crop of tobacco. 18 August 1842. (P. 343)

Henry B. McDonald to John Beckwith a tract of 100 acres. 1842. (Pp. 343-344)

John Hooker to John W. Patey a negro slave. 18 April 1842. (P. 345)

Charles E. Williams and Nathaniel A. Williams of Crittenden County, Arkansas appoint William Petty as their attorney in settling the estate of Boaz Mathews. 20 December 1840. (P. 345)

Moses Linville to Fleming Saunders 110 acres. 14 October 1841. (P. 345)

John H. Gammon to Fleming Saunders 60 acres. 14 October 1841. (P. 346)

Yeatman Hicks to Henry Mann a crop of corn. 20 August 1842. (Pp. 346-347)

Pierce Puryear to Archibald M. Debow a negro girl. 4 August 1842. (P. 347)

Sheriff W. W. Bailey to Frances H. Gordon. 17 August 1842. (P. 347)

James D. Parker to Thomas Wilbourn. 22 August 1842. (P. 348)

William L. Alexander, Sr. and William L. Alexander, Jr., executors of Grant Allen, bound to Grant A. Bowen and John H. Bowen. 16 October 1841. (P. 348)

The heirs of Frances Parker to Jeremiah Gammon. 1842. (Pp. 349-350)

DEED BOOK Q

William Searcy to Duncan Johnson 56 acres. 13 July 1842. (P. 350)

Green B. Lowe to Hickerson Barksdale of Wilson County 388¼ acres. 21 December 1838. (P. 351)

John West to John Kemp a crop of tobacco. 23 August 1842. (Pp. 351-352)

Abraham C. Lee to Thomas Tunstall a crop of tobacco. 24 August 1842. (P. 352)

John Lancaster to Russell Marchbanks and Thomas C. Marchbanks 1200 acres. 24 August 1842. (Pp. 352-354)

James Cartwright to Oliver Cartwright 40 acres on Defeated Creek. 26 July 1841. (P. 354)

John Lancaster, Sr. to Joel Coffee a negro man. 24 August 1842. (P. 355)

Frances H. Gordon and his father from Uel S. Gregory some slaves belonging to the estate of Uriah Gregory deceased. 22 August 1842. (P. 356)

John A. Farmer to John R. James a house of tobacco. 27 August 1842. (P. 356)

Robert D. Allison to Henry Mann 250 acres. 6 August 1841. (Pp. 357-358)

Robert Bradley to Poleman W. Cage a negro woman. 29 August 1842. (P. 358)

Pierce Puryear to Golman Donoho a negro man. 27 August 1842. (P. 358)

Granville S. Pierce of Rutherford County to Alfred Pierce and Isaac Pierce of Sumner County a tract of land owned by Benjamin and George Pierce. 21 February 1838. (P. 359)

Isaac and Alfred Pierce to Franklin B. Pierce and Washington G. Pierce their interest in a tract of land. 20 February 1838. (P. 360)

Buckner S. Cardwell to Isaac Bradley. 19 August 1842. (P. 361)

John Smallen to William B. Young. 29 August 1842. (P. 362)

Henry Nichols to John W. Nichols a negro girl. 30 August 1842. (Pp. 362-363)

Jacob W. Roe and Richard McKinney trade some slaves belonging to the estate of Benjamin Roe. 1 September 1842. (P. 364)

John A. Lyon to James Trousdale several items. 2 September 1842. (P. 364)

DEED BOOK Q

Eli Shy to Gregory Moore and Washington Shy 164 acres. 5 August 1842. (P. 365)

O. B. Hubbard of Hinds County, Mississippi to Reuben Braswell a tract of land on Hogan's Creek. 7 December 1841. (P. 366)

Joseph Vanderpool to Isaac Massey a crop of tobacco. 5 September 1842. (P. 366)

Jacob White to Alex Henson a crop of tobacco. 5 September 1842. (P. 367)

Alben P. Cardwell to Benjamin H. Ward. 5 September 1842. (P. 367)

William C. Cole to Jonathan Parker a crop of tobacco. 2 September 1842. (P. 368)

John Rigsby to William B. Young a crop of tobacco. 3 September 1842. (P. 369)

Silas C. Cornwell to Miles West, Sr. a negro girl. 18 August 1842. (P. 369)

Varnel L. Cardwell to Benjamin H. Ward a crop of tobacco. 5 September 1842. (P. 370)

William Exum to Hezekiah Love a tract of land in the 23rd District. 19 May 1841. (P. 370)

John Gomer to George Walker a crop of tobacco. 5 September 1842. (P. 371)

John Simmons to James Climer a crop of tobacco. 3 September 1842. (P. 372)

James N. Roy to Yancy A. Malone a tract of land on Smith's Fork. 12 October 1840. (P. 372)

Rowland Clark to John H. Ligon a negro boy. 13 June 1842. (P. 373)

Alfred Harper to David Prowell 62 acres. 6 September 1842. (P. 373)

Thomas Claiborne to Archibald W. Overton. August 1842. (P. 374)

Pierce Puryear to Frances Duffy three negroes. 1842. (P. 375)

Elizabeth Gillham to Matilda Gillham for love and affection several items. 10 October 1836. (P. 375)

Elizabeth Gillham to Elenor Colmas Gillham some personal property for love and affection. 10 October 1836. (P. 376)

William Meadows to Samuel Williams a crop of tobacco. 9 September 1842. (P. 376)

John Gibbs to V. R. Thompson a crop of tobacco. 10 September 1842. (P. 377)

DEED BOOK Q

Charles Richards to Benjamin H. Ward a crop of tobacco. 10 September 1842. (P. 377)

John W. Mann to George Daugherty and Joseph Gresham a tract of land on Snow Creek. 23 July 1842. (P. 378)

Joseph Gresham and George Daugherty to Henry Goad a tract of land on Snow Creek. 12 September 1842. (P. 378)

Joseph Gresham to John Beckman. 15 September 1842. (P. 379)

Bedford L. Herring indebtedness to M. W. Sloan. 20 September 1842. (P. 379)

Joseph Moses to William Pendarvis. 19 September 1842. (P. 380)

John Trousdale to Richard Duke a negro boy. 21 September 1842. (P. 380)

Reece Wardrope to William B. Young a crop of tobacco. 22 September 1842. (P. 381)

William B. Taylor from James Earps a crop of tobacco. 22 September 1842. (P. 381)

Robert W. Mann to Micajah Duke a negro boy. 26 July 1842. (P. 382)

Alfred Ewing to Donelson Stewart a tract of land in the 22nd District. 16 September 1842. (P. 382)

Josiah Marshall to E. H. Greer of Vicksburg, Mississippi lot number eight in the division of the lands of Andrew Greer and allotted to Joseph A. Greer. 17 September 1842. (P. 383)

Charles E. Smith to Stephen W. Malone the land he received from the estate of his father William Smith in Franklin County, Tennessee. 26 September 1842. (P. 384)

Joseph Gresham to John Trousdale a tract of land on the Caney Fork. 16 September 1842. (P. 384)

Mathis Newell to Thomas Tunstall a crop of tobacco. 29 September 1842. (P. 385)

Davidson Draper to John F. Vance 120 acres. 23 September 1842. (P. 385)

Joseph Craig to James Craig his interest in the estate of John Craig, Sr. 26 August 1835. (P. 386)

Mark Dyson to Clabran Wilson 69 acres. 20 June 1840. (P. 386)

John Timberlake to Lent Boulton a crop of tobacco. 2 September 1842. (P. 387)

William T. Williams to Martin W. Sloan 382 acres. 23 September 1842. (P. 388)

DEED BOOK Q

James D. Gregory to Willis Oldham a crop of tobacco. 3 October 1842. (Pp. 388-389)

James Cothran to Joseph Bowman. 3 October 1842. (P. 389)

James Beckwith to Joseph Gresham a tract of land. 20 September 1842. (P. 390)

Joseph Jones, Sr. to Alfred M. Kemp 60 acres. 23 September 1842. (Pp. 390-391)

Thomas T. Armstrong, executor of John B. Armstrong, to Samuel Burdine a tract of land on Round Lick Creek. 5 August 1842. (P. 391)

H. C. Jones to William T. Cardwell a negro girl. 27 September 1842. (P. 392)

J. W. Paty to John Hooker a negro girl. 27 September 1842. (P. 392)

John Caplinger to William H. Swindell several items. 5 (   ) 1842. (P. 393)

Shelton Harper to William B. Young a crop of tobacco. 28 September 1842. (P. 393)

Daniel Rawley to William B. Young a bay horse. 28 September 1842. (P. 394)

William Brandon to Franklin Erwin a tract of land on Goose Creek. 14 June 1842. (P. 394)

James R. Debow to Sam C. Debow 158 acres. 28 June 1841. (P. 395)

Franklin Erwin and wife Nancy to Archibald Debow 15 acres. 12 July 1842. (P. 395)

H. C. Jones to Thomas and Sarah Hooker a negro woman. 28 September 1842. (P. 396)

William B. Kyle to Elijah Powel a surrel mare. 1842. (P. 396)

James H. McCabe to David Burford a negro man. 12 October 1842. (P. 397)

John A. Lyon to James Trousdale a crop of tobacco. 15 October 1842. (P. 397)

Abraham Caruthers to Thomas A. Durham 160 acres. 25 December 1840. (P. 398)

Edwin C. Grant to Wilson Y. Martin a crop of tobacco. 1842. (P. 398)

George Highers to Josiah Highers 50 acres. 13 October 1842. (P. 399)

George Highers to David Highers 78 acres. 13 October 1842. (P. 399)

DEED BOOK Q

Turman Wheeler to Joseph Jones, Sr. and Richard Jones 215 acres. 23 September 1842. (P. 400)

Henry M. Cornwell to Sampson McClelan a tract of land on Defeated Creek. 18 October 1842. (P. 400)

Wilson Cage to Samuel P. Howard a tract of land. 16 October 1841. (P. 401)

Sheriff W. W. Bailey to Andrew Allison. 19 October 1842. (Pp. 401-402)

Andrew Jackson of Davidson County and Jacob D. Donelson of Rutherford County, executors of William Donelson, to John Law a tract of land on Defeated Creek. 24 August 1842. (Pp. 402-403)

John D. Haynes to Jefferson Jones a parcel of negroes. 28 October 1842. (Pp. 403-404)

Allen P. Sims to Caleb Preston 149 acres. 29 October 1842. (P. 404)

A. P. Sims to Caleb Preston some livestock. 29 October 1842. (P. 405)

Thomas Carman and Caleb Carman, executors of Elijah Carman, to Moses B. Freeman 251 acres. 20 December 1841. (Pp. 405-406)

John Stafford to William B. Taylor and John B. Gammon of Macon County a tract of land on Dixon's Creek. 31 October 1842. (P. 406)

Decree in favor of Josiah Marshall. 1842. (P. 407)

Benjamin Denney to Jesse B. Andrews 236 acres. 3 November 1842. (P. 408)

David Tyree to James M. Williams a parcel of negroes. 18 September 1842. (P. 408)

William M. Payne to Benjamin Rucks some personal property. 8 November 1842. (P. 409)

Creed Penn to William Denney a woman slave. 17 August 1842. (P. 409)

Thomas A. Durham to Loderick Vaden, administrator of Asa Beasley, 80 acres. 7 November 1842. (P. 410)

Uria Pankey to Ellis Kemp 30 acres. 7 November 1842. (P. 410)

Alexander Dillard to Sarah Fields a tract of land. 20 September 1839. (Pp. 410-411)

J. J. Caruthers to his mother, Sally Caruthers, the land which he purchased from Patience Wood, widow of Josiah Wood. 27 October 1842. (P. 411)

Wesley Motes to John Mills of Sumner County two negroes. 5 November 1841. (P. 412)

DEED BOOK Q

Wesley Motes to John Mills a negro girl. 2 November 1841. (P. 412)

N. B. Burdine to James G. Mills of Sumner County three negroes. 14 January 1842. (P. 413)

Wesley Motes to John Mills of Sumner County a negro boy. 1 September 1841. (P. 413)

E. A. Wright to J. R. Smith 180 acres. 1 January 1842. (P. 414)

James G. Ford to Lent Boulton some personal property. 16 November 1842. (Pp. 414-415)

R. W. Mann to William B. Moore a negro girl. 7 November 1842. (P. 415)

Robert Bowman to David Canaday a boy slave. 1 October 1842. (P. 415)

John Law to Miles West 55 acres. 23 November 1842. (P. 416)

C. C. Ford to James R. Toney a negro woman. November 1842. (P. 416)

James R. Toney to C. C. Ford a negro woman. 21 November 1842. (P. 417)

C. C. Ford to R. W. Mann a negro woman. 21 November 1842. (P. 417)

Samuel Brown to Josiah Hallum two head of hogs. 24 November 1842. (P. 418)

Josiah Marshall to E. H. Greer of Vicksburgh, Mississippi a tract of land on Goose Creek. 17 September 1842. (P. 418)

Pamela Penn to Creed Penn a negro boy. 5 November 1842. (P. 419)

George W. Martin to P. F. Cornwell and others. 29 November 1842. (P. 419)

Frederick Uhls to David Burford. 12 July 1841. (P. 420)

David Burford to Rosetta Culbreath, wife of John Culbreath, a tract of land. 28 July 1842. (P. 420)

John Maggart to Washington Meacham a tract of 36½ acres. 26 January 1841. (P. 421)

Elijah A. Wright to Presley Boley a tract of land. 20 January 1842. (P. 422)

Reuben Braswell to Andrew J. Baker a woman slave. 5 December 1842. (P. 423)

Thomas Felton to William Oakley 150 acres. 6 March 1841. (P. 424)

DEED BOOK Q

James Boze to George Baker 20¼ acres. 5 December 1842. (P. 424)

John Russell to James C. Williams 182½ acres. 2 December 1842. (P. 425)

Nathan Ward to Miles West a boy slave. 14 October 1842. (P. 425)

Joseph C. Dickens to William Hastey a tract of land on the Cumberland River. 7 December 1841. (P. 426)

James Eaton to George W. Ahart 60 acres. 1842. (P. 426)

Hannah M. Davis to George Ahart 21 acres. 1841. (P. 427)

C. C. Ford to James R. Toney a crop of tobacco. 6 December 1842. (P. 427)

William Exum to William H. Jones 100 acres. 15 September 1841. (P. 428)

Powel Tuck to Charles C. Denney several items. 5 December 1842. (P. 428)

Alfred M. Winkler to James C. Williams 87 acres. 5 December 1842. (P. 429)

Jefferson Jones to William Denney a tract of land. 1 October 1842. (P. 430)

Elijah W. Hale to Mary A. Massey 52 acres. 19 September 1842. (P. 431)

Benjamin F. Jones to William Denney 30 acres. 31 January 1842. (P. 432)

Reuben Braswell to Albert H. Ross a tract of land on Hogan's Creek. 7 December 1842. (Pp. 432-433)

Thomas Gregory to Poleman W. Cage. 8 December 1842. (P. 433)

Joseph Gregory to Peter A. Wilkinson a tract of 165 acres. 8 December 1842. (P. 434)

Joseph Gregory to Peter A. Wilkinson. 12 December 1842. (P. 435)

Joseph Gregory to George Gregory his interest in the estate of William Cleveland. 12 December 1842. (P. 435)

Joseph Gregory to Nelson Brown 149 acres. 9 July 1841. (P. 436)

Nelson Brown to Joseph Gregory eight acres. 9 July 1841. (P. 436)

Thomas Gregory, Jr. to Joseph Gregory a tract of land on Peyton's Creek. 7 December 1842. (P. 437)

William McGinnis to William Hail his interest in the

DEED BOOK Q

estate of Pleasant Pryor. 18 July 1842. (P. 437)

John Payne to Willis Oldham a tract of land on Payton's Creek. 9 May 1836. (P. 438)

Jeremiah Coggin to William Hail 50 acres. 1 October 1842. (P. 438)

Elizabeth Moores to her son Henry L. Moores 90 acres. 29 July 1840. (P. 439)

Willis W. Oldham to George W. Royster a tract of land on Payton's Creek. 14 December 184?. (P. 439)

Willis W. Oldham to George W. Royster. 14 December 1842. (P. 440)

Joseph W. Allen to Jeremiah Jamison and John McClarin a tract of land in the town of Carthage. 12 February 1842. (P. 440)

Anthony Apple to Thomas D. Cassity a tract of 50 acres. 15 December 1842. (P. 441)

James M. Winfree to Jacob Amonette 25 acres. 21 February 1842. (P. 441)

Thomas Sadler to Joseph Allen several items. 15 December 1842. (P. 442)

W. E. Jones to Martin Whitten some personal property. 19 December 1842. (P. 442)

David Burford to E. B. Drake & Brothers a negro boy. 21 November 1842. (P. 443)

Christopher C. Ford to Robert N. Mann 82 acres. Mentions that Mary A. Ford is to have choice in the division of said land. 19 December 1842. (Pp. 443-444)

William Person to John B. Hughes a negro girl. 19 December 1842. (P. 444)

Henry L. Moores to J. R. Smith 48 acres. 24 November 1842. (P. 445)

Stephen Robinson to Samuel Allison some livestock. 17 December 1842. (P. 445)

Coleman S. Samson to James Boze 35 acres. 20 December 1842. (P. 446)

Elias Sloan bound to Jefferson Jenkins. 21 October 1837. (P. 446)

Thomas Bridges to William Harris a negro woman. 25 December 1842. (P. 447)

Samuel P. Maxwell to Jacob Neil a tract of land. 11 October 1842. (P. 447)

Archibald W. Overton to Elihu H. Greer a tract of land on Goose Creek. 9 December 1842. (P. 448)

DEED BOOK Q

Silas C. Cornwell to James Young a tract of land on Salt Lick Creek. 19 December 1842. (P. 449)

Nancy M. Armstrong to Martin W. Armstrong 155 acres. 19 December 1842. (Pp. 449-450)

John Gordon to John Stevens a tract of land. 8 January 1842. (Pp. 450-451)

John Stevens to James B. Moores 33½ acres. 28 April 1842. (Pp. 451-452)

Elizabeth Moores to Richard Hodges. 1842. (P. 452)

Elizabeth Moores to her son Henry L. Moores her interest in the estate of her husband William Moores deceased. 14 November 1842. (P. 452)

H. C. Jones to J. R. Smith a negro girl. 28 September 1842. (P. 453)

Elizabeth Boze to William Jones 150 acres. 20 October 1841. (P. 453)

Alexander Dillard bound to Anthony Hogan of Jackson County. 1842. (P. 454)

Sarah C. Robinson of Illinois to Elijah Hylton her interest in 205 acres. 9 December 1842. (P. 455)

William Haines to Stephen Petty a tract of land. 20 December 1842. (Pp. 455-456)

Henry L. Moores to John Johnson 85 acres. 14 November 1842. (P. 456)

William D. Turner bound to John Cempsey. 19 May 1838. (P. 457)

Jesse Hord to Hawkins Heflin 255 acres. 6 August 1840. (P. 457)

Joshua Sykes to Fielding Gray a bay mare. 23 December 1842. (P. 458)

W. L. Ford to Charles Boulton a negro man. 26 December 1842. (P. 458)

Jefferson Rowland to Marmaduke Mason 188 acres. 29 December 1842. (P. 459)

John L. Powell to Jefferson Rowland 60 acres. 4 June 1842. (P. 460)

Elijah Hylton to Jefferson Rowland 130 acres. 23 December 1842. (P. 460)

John Cochran to James C. Sanders 212½ acres. 6 October 1842. (P. 461)

Thomas A. Durham to Stephen Mann some personal property. 30 December 1842. (P. 461)

DEED BOOK Q

John Trousdale to Gideon C. Matlock 318 acres. 30 December 1842. (P. 462)

Archibald W. Overton and Josiah Marshall agreement. 10 August 1842. (Pp. 462-463)

Ann W. Archer of Amelia County, Virginia appoints John Walker of Todd County, Kentucky in settling the estate of her father William Archer of Smith County. 23 November 1842. (P. 463)

William A. Herrod to Jeremiah Jamison some slaves. 31 December 1842. (P. 464)

William Thomas to William Ragland a negro girl. 2 January 1843. (P. 464)

John Law to Drury Cornwell 12 acres. 31 December 1842. (P. 465)

George Maricle, A. D. Maricle, Organ Maricle, Alfred Maricle, and George Maricle, Jr. to James Shelton 25 acres belonging to the estate of their father. 2 January 1843. (P. 465)

Mathew Cowen of Putman County to his daughter Mariah Bockman. 4 January 1843. (Pp. 466-467)

John Law to William B. Young 55 acres. 8 January 1843. (P. 467)

John Law to Elizabeth Law, Nancy Law, Rebecca Law, and Damaris Law 20 acres. 9 January 1843. (P. 468)

Elizabeth Ivanson to John Williams 28½ acres. 6 May 1840. (P. 468)

John Williams to Thomas W. Page 153 acres. 12 January 1843. (P. 469-470)

William R. Hodges to Jesse S. McClain a negro boy. 6 January 1843. (P. 471)

William B. Vaughan to Pleasant Gold a tract of land belonging to the heirs of William Vaughan. 16 January 1843. (P. 471)

Martha Fulks to Edmund James a negro girl. 12 January 1843. (P. 472)

William Newbell to William P. Hughes some personal property. 20 January 1843. (Pp. 472-473)

John Merritt to John Johnson several items. 21 January 1843. (P. 474)

Jonathan Bailey to Johnson Bailey. 15 August 1842. (P. 475)

Joseph Law to Rufus Perry several items. 2 January 1843. (P. 475)

DEED BOOK Q

Ephraim Agee to Samuel Read 60 acres. 25 January 1843. (P. 476)

John G. Nollner to Ann Lisa Nollner. 25 February 1842. (P. 476)

Thomas Gregory to Presley George. 30 January 1843. (P. 477)

Bennett Johns to William L. Martin three head of horses. 30 January 1843. (P. 477)

Robert Bradley to James C. Bradley of Sumner County a negro boy called Andrew Jackson for love and affection. 3 September 1842. (P. 478)

John Law to William Young several items. 6 February 1843. (P. 478)

James G. Ford bound to Stephen Mann. 1843. (P. 479)

Jacob Fry to Nathan W. Philips 72 acres. 23 September 1842. (P. 479)

David Fry and Jacob Fry agreement. 8 September 1842. (P. 480)

Bartlett James, Sr. to John Buckner a negro girl. 5 January 1843. (P. 480)

Nancy Ellison to Talifero Turner a tract of land on Hickman's Creek. 20 February 1836. (P. 481)

James B. Moores to Leonard B. Fite a girl slave. 3 February 1843. (P. 481)

William Jones to Jefferson Rowland 200 acres. 20 December 1842. (P. 482)

J. P. Martin to George C. Gifford a negro boy. 12 May 1842. (P. 482)

John Williams to Edward Harrison 200 acres. 11 February 1843. (Pp. 483-484)

Mason Walker to Orville Green one half acre where I now live. 16 February 1843. (Pp. 484-485)

John J. Hughes to Henry C. Jones 68 acres. 28 January 1843. (P. 485)

Willis W. Oldham to Samuel Oldham a tract of land on Peyton's Creek. 25 February 1843. (P. 486)

James Craig, Jane Craig, John Craig, Joseph Craig, W. W. Harris and wife Rachel, Basil Davis and wife Hannah, William Vincent and wife Elizabeth, William L. Leath and wife Nancy, heirs of John Craig, Sr., to John Barbee a tract of land. 1843. (Pp. 486-487)

William Farley to William Ragland a negro boy. 24 January 1843. (P. 487)

DEED BOOK Q

Robert Traywick to John Ballard 50 acres. 14 February 1843. (P. 488)

James R. Toney to Charles McClarin two town lots in the town of Carthage. 23 December 1842. (P. 488)

Eli Shy to Andrew Shy and James W. Shy 164 acres. 7 March 1843. (P. 489)

Eli Shy to Andrew Shy and James W. Shy a negro man. 7 February 1843. (P. 489)

Mark Dyson to his son in law James Haynes a negro girl. 11 January 1843. (P. 490)

Washington Meachum to Judd Strother a tract of land on Hurricane Creek. 1 December 1842. (P. 490)

Joseph Gresham to Elinas Ferguson a tract of land on the Caney Fork. 1836. (P. 491)

Davidson Draper and Robert Glover to Judd Strother 42 acres. 1 December 1842. (P. 491)

John Morgan to Robert Simmons several items. 11 February 1843. (P. 492)

Sheriff W. W. Bailey to Thomas Carman a girl slave. 13 March 1843. (P. 492)

Delana Sims to Catherine Thomason 73 acres. 10 January 1842. (P. 493)

Catherine Thomason to her son George Thomason 73 acres. 13 March 1843. (P. 493)

George Thomason to Martin Whitten 73 acres. 13 March 1843. (P. 494)

Henry Perkins to Robert W. Knight. 15 March 1843. (P. 494)

James B. Moores to Robert Williams a tract of land in the town of Carthage. 15 March 1843. (P. 495)

John Trousdale to Burton G. Ferrell 100 acres on the Caney Fork River. 23 March 1843. (P. 495)

Johnson Samson to John J. Coleman 62 acres. 8 January 1841. (P. 496)

Charles McMurry to Elizabeth Blackwell several slaves. 27 March 1843. (P. 496)

Daniel Vaughan to Creed Penn. 1843. (P. 497)

G. C. Matlock to H. B. McDonald several items. 28 March 1843. (Pp. 498-499)

George Smith to Robert Smith and his mother Sylvey Smith and sister Winney Smith a tract of land. 24 March 1843. (Pp. 499-500)

DEED BOOK Q

Ferdinand Ford to Robert G. and Charles F. Burton 25 acres. 1 March 1843. (P. 500)

George Smith to Elijah Smith 150 acres. 2 March 1843. (P. 501)

Mathew Davis to Allen Crowell 200 acres. 30 April 1842. (P. 501)

Thomas Presley to David Smith 75 acres. 3 April 1843. (P. 502)

Archibald Scruggs to David Smith a tract of land in the 22nd District. 19 August 1837. (P. 502)

John McGinnis and Susannah McGinnis to Thomas Lancaster 50 acres. 14 January 1843. (P. 503)

John Congo to John Harris and Turner Harris 40 acres. 4 September 1841. (P. 503)

Taylor Whitley to Jabez Burton and Jubel Burton a tract of land on Barren River in Macon County. 1843. (P. 504)

James B. Moores to Nathan Ward a man slave. 11 April 1843. (P. 504)

Creed Penn to John M. Eastes a girl slave. 12 April 1843. (P. 504)

James B. Moores to Sam Fite. 12 April 1843. (P. 505)

James B. Moores to Adam Ferguson a tract of land on the Cumberland River. 13 April 1843. (Pp. 505-506)

James M. Blackwell to Elizabeth Blackwell two slaves belonging to the estate of his father John Blackwell. 14 April 1843. (P. 506)

Samuel P. Coleman and wife Ann of Harrison County, Republic of Texas, to James B. Moores the land they received as heirs of Samuel Massey. 17 January 1843. (P. 507)

Stephen Goad to William B. Young. 15 April 1843. (P. 508)

Silas C. Cornwell to Barnet Cornwell four acres. January 1843. (P. 508)

Edward Stewart to Benjamin Jones 50 acres. 14 April 1843. (P. 509)

Alfred Ewing to Edward Stewart 50 acres. 9 September 1835. (P. 509)

Thomas Jones to Elinas Ferguson a tract of land on the Caney Fork. 25 February 1836. (P. 510)

Joel Gregory to William C. Taylor 100 acres. 22 September 1842. (Pp. 510-511)

William C. Taylor to Wildridge Taylor a tract of land on Peyton's Creek. 22 September 1842. (P. 511)

DEED BOOK Q

Nathan E. and J. R. Hazard to John Hazard, Sr. a tract of land. 9 April 1842. (P. 512)

Elias Johns to his son Bennet Johns a negro slave. Said Bennet is in a delicate state of health with a large and helpless family to support. 29 August 1842. (P. 512)

Simon P. Hughes to William West. 19 April 1843. (P. 513)

Lorenzo D. Cartwright to Coleman D. Goad 100 acres. 22 August 1840. (P. 513)

Timothy Walton to Josiah R. Smith a negro girl. 21 April 1843. (P. 514)

Sheriff W. W. Bailey to N. C. Winston a negro boy. 2 March 1843. (P. 514)

Robert Braswell to Samuel P. Maxwell. 24 February 1843. (Pp. 514-515)

Elisha Dillard to David Haynes 50 acres. 18 February 1841. (P. 515)

Sheriff W. W. Bailey to Reason Barrow a tract of land. 1843. (P. 516)

Sheriff W. W. Bailey to Rowland W. Newby a tract of land. 1843. (Pp. 517-518)

Rowland W. Newby to John Caplinger 175 acres. 3 February 1843. (P. 518)

John Caplinger to David Cook 175 acres. 3 February 1843. (P. 519)

Sheriff W. W. Bailey to James Haynie. 16 August 1842. (P. 519)

Solomon Gwaltney, Ann Gwaltney, and Polly Parris, formerly Polly Gwaltney, to William W. Jones their interest in the land they are to receive at the death of Leodicy Sykes, formerly Leodicy Gwaltney, widow of Elias Gwaltney. 26 October 1840. (P. 520)

John W. Hughes to John R. James a negro man. July 1842. (Pp. 520-521)

S. C. Bridgewater to Gidaliad Hughes 149 acres. 29 April 1843. (P. 521)

James M. Eastes to William Neeley a sorrel mare. 6 May 1843. (Pp. 521-522)

William B. Campbell and wife Fanny Isabella to Benjamin R. Owen 250 acres. 23 September 1840. (Pp. 522-523)

Alfred Payne to Edward Upton. 6 May 1843. (P. 523)

Samuel Bailiff to John Newbell a negro girl. 9 May 1843. (Pp. 523-524)

DEED BOOK Q

Robert D. Hughes to Lent Boulton a tract of land. 12 May 1843. (Pp. 524-525)

John B. Burdine to Samuel Burdine a man slave. 15 May 1843. (P. 525)

Allen G. Wilson to John D. Bradley several items. 16 May 1843. (Pp. 525-526)

Benjamin Pierce to William Hart a negro girl. 19 May 1843. (Pp. 526-527)

Articles of agreement between John B. Pearson, Richmond, and William Pearson. 6 January 1842. (Pp. 527-528)

Joseph Rawlings to John B. Pearson some livestock. 20 May 1843. (Pp. 528-529)

John B. Pearson to his granddaughter Margret Elizabeth Rawlings, daughter of Joseph and Leonaila Rawlings, formerly Leonaila Pearson, a bay mare. 22 May 1843. (P. 529)

William Pope to Marmaduke Mason a crop of tobacco. 22 May 1843. (Pp. 529-530)

The administrators of William Waters to Samuel F. Patterson a tract of land. 1843. (Pp. 531-532)

Judith Hinton to James Duffy. 23 May 1843. (Pp. 532-533)

Samuel Burdine to William W. Seay a tract of land in the 13th District. 15 May 1843. (Pp. 533-534)

Samuel Burdine to William W. Seay and John H. Bradford a tract of land in the town of Rome. 24 April 1841. (Pp. 534-535)

Stephen R. Wills to George H. Campbell his interest in several slaves. 9 May 1843. (P. 535)

George H. Campbell to Stephen R. Wills 78 acres. 9 May 1843. (Pp. 535-536)

T. C. Gipson to F. L. Harris a man slave. 1 June 1843. (P. 536)

Joseph G. McPherson to James Bradley several items. 2 June 1843. (Pp. 536-537)

Elizabeth Bradley to William Massey several slaves. Mary Elizabeth Massey, daughter of the said William, is to control the slaves. 30 May 1843. (P. 538)

Alfred Harper and Mathew Harper to Thomas Cockerham 26 acres. 1 June 1841. (Pp. 538-539)

Abraham Britton of Jasper County, Missouri to Charles Goodall of Sumner County 44 acres belonging to the heirs of Richard Britton. 18 October 1842. (Pp. 539-540)

Joseph Thomas to Stephen Canada. 1840. (P. 540)

DEED BOOK Q

William Kearley to James Kearley several items. 6 June 1843. (P. 541)

Ephraim Pursley to Marshall Duncan 36 acres. 19 March 1842. (P. 542)

Lent Boulton to Simon F. Hughes a tract of land on the Caney Fork River. 8 June 1840. (Pp. 542-543)

Willis Coggins to R. D. Hughes 143 acres. 23 February 1841. (Pp. 543-544)

Simon P. Hughes to D. K. Timberlake 405 acres. 6 June 1843. (Pp. 544-547)

Lent Boulton to James Boulton 180 acres. 5 June 1843. (P. 547)

Lent Boulton to Charles Thompson 6 June 1843. (P. 548)

Lent Boulton to William Ragland a tract of 100 acres. 2 June 1843. (Pp. 548-549)

John Kerby to R. C. Dalton 119 acres. 13 June 1843. (P. 549)

Robert W. Mann to John Baker a negro woman. 27 April 1843. (P. 550)

Martin Miller to James Duffy a tract of land on Spring Creek. 19 June 1843. (Pp. 550-551)

Frederick N. Mitchell to Patsey Johnson 140 acres. 20 June 1843. (P. 552)

Patsey Johnson to Pamelia Clark 65 acres. 15 January 1843. (P. 552)

Martin McMurry to James W. Bransford. 3 March 1843. (P. 553)

Martha Douglas to J. W. Patey. 1843. (P. 553)

Alfred M. Kemp to Ellis Kemp. 7 June 1843. (P. 554)

Moses B. Freeman to Walter Freeman a tract of land on Goose Creek. 13 December 1840. (P. 554)

Martin McMurry to James McMurry a negro boy. 23 June 1843. (P. 555)

Thomas Litchford to William Litchford several items. 21 June 1843. (P. 556)

Samuel Hunter to Loderick Vaden a negro man. June 1842. (P. 556)

William Ragland to Henry B. Haynie a negro boy. 10 January 1843. (P. 557)

Martin McMurry to James McMurry his interest in the land belonging to his mother Jane McMurry. 28 June 1843. (P. 557)

DEED BOOK Q

Joseph B. Gregory to Peter A. Wilkinson 28 acres. 29 June 1843. (P. 558)

Charles Powel to William Martin several items. 30 June 1843. (P. 559)

George Walker to John Organ a negro woman. 1 October 1842. (P. 559)

William Thomas to Lucresy Kemp a negro girl. 15 June 1843. (P. 560)

Thomas W. Wootten to Orville Green three negro boys. 27 June 1843. (P. 560)

Lucy Evans, estranged wife of Abner Evans, to Henry Mann the negroes she received from the estate of her grandfather. 24 October 1842. (P. 561)

William Newby to James Gill a tract of land on Round Lick Creek. 2 March 1841. (P. 562)

Joseph M. Gray to his nephews and nieces, James S. Gray, Julia A. Gray, Joseph M. Gray, Fielding W. Gray, children of his brother Fielding Gray, several items. 24 May 1843. (P. 562)

William Finch and Celia Finch to James Gill a tract of land. 5 October 1837. (P. 563)

William Newby to William Hankins 129 acres. 24 May 1843. (P. 563)

Archibald Thompson to James Kerley, Sr. a tract of land on Goose Creek. 12 October 1837. (P. 564)

Stephen Stafford to Wilson Y. Martin 71 acres. 24 June 1843. (P. 565)

William Circy to Spearmon Robinson. 6 July 1843. (P. 566)

Martin McMurry to John A. Debow a boy slave. 15 July 1843. (P. 567)

John Kittle to Parks Chandler several items. 17 July 1843. (P. 567)

James Chambers, Richard Chambers, Joseph Payne, Lacy Payne, John Payne, and Eunice G. Payne to Elijah Banks their interest in a tract of land. 29 January 1838. (P. 568)

Sheriff W. W. Bailey to Isham Beasley a tract of land. 1843. (Pp. 569-570)

James R. Kerr to Charles R. Ford a crop of tobacco. 21 July 1843. (P. 571)

John L. Miller and wife Sophia to John A. Sloan their interest in some negroes they received from the estate of Archibald Sloan. 18 July 1840. (P. 571)

DEED BOOK Q

Abraham C. Ser to Othaiel Searls. 20 July 1843. (P. 572)

Samuel Read bound to Elias Dowell. 19 June 1840. (P. 572)

William Harper to Mathew Harper 347 acres, it being the land on which the late Mathew, Sr. resided. Said land is now in the possession of Sarah Harper, widow of the said Mathew, Sr. 26 July 1843. (P. 573)

John Culbreath to William Cunningham a crop of tobacco. 27 July 1843. (Pp. 573-574)

Elizabeth Moores to her son Henry L. Moores 53 acres belonging to the estate of her husband William Moores. 26 November 1842. (P. 574)

Henry L. Moores to Samuel Allison a tract of land. 3 June 1843. (P. 575)

Henry L. Moores to Lewis Allison 35 acres. 3 June 1843. (P. 575)

Alfred Read to Eli Gammon his interest in a tract of land which his wife Mary Read deceased received as an heir of William A. Burton. Other heirs: Albert G. Burton, Richard Erwin and wife Elizabeth Ann. 15 July 1843. (P. 576)

William Kirby to John Carver a tract of land. 3 August 1841. (Pp. 576-577)

Circuit Court to John Ballard a tract of land. 1842. (P. 577)

John B. Watts from John Fite of Dekalb County. 2 August 1843. (P. 577)

Jacob Hubbard, George W. Hubbard, William H. Hubbard, David C. Hubbard, and John W. Hubbard to Benjamin Vaden some personal property. 26 July 1843. (P. 578)

John Vaden to Baker & Bradford a crop of tobacco. 4 August 1843. (P. 579)

William Ragland to John B. Hughes a negro boy. 4 August 1843. (P. 579)

William Ragland to John B. Hughes a tract of land on Snow Creek. 3 August 1843. (P. 580)

Silas C. Cornwell to Thomas L. Draper of Jackson County a tract of land on Defeated Creek. 2 June 1840. (P. 581)

Benjamin Rucks to Howel T. Rucks a negro boy. August 1843. (P. 581)

Edwin Featherstone to Malina Marshall of Sumner County a negro girl. 5 June 1841. (P. 582)

Grant Bowin to Archibald M. Debow. 1843. (P. 582)

DEED BOOK Q

William Gregory and Littleberry Worsham to Joseph Bowman. 14 August 1843. (Pp. 582-583)

Martin McMurry to John A. Debow 125 acres. 11 August 1842. (P. 583)

Major L. Sykes to John McGee a crop of tobacco. 14 August 1843. (P. 584)

William Person to Cynthia Hogg a negro woman. 14 August 1843. (P. 584)

Sheriff W. W. Bailey to Hezekiah Love 160 acres. 15 August 1843. (Pp. 584-585)

Henry D. Kemp to Washington Glover a crop of tobacco. 16 August 1843. (P. 585)

Henry D. Kemp to Ellis Kemp a negro boy. 16 August 1843. (P. 586)

John A. Debow to G. Goodall a negro boy. 19 July 1843. (P. 586)

Mary Butts to her daughter Sally Butts a tract of land. 16 August 1843. (Pp. 586-587)

Henry D. Kemp to William West his interest in a tract of land belonging to his father Jenks Kemp. 17 August 1843. (P. 587)

Anthony Apple to Samuel Fitzpatrick a tract of 160 acres. 21 October 1839. (P. 588)

DEED BOOK R

Archibald W. Overton to Archibald McNeill. 9 December 1842. (P. 1)

William Taylor and George Read to Sampson McClelin a crop of tobacco. 21 August 1843. (P. 1)

James A. King to Samuel King a tract of land on Salt Lick Creek. 18 August 1843. (P. 2)

Berryman Turner to Azariah Corder a boy slave. 15 February 1843. (P. 2)

Francis Dowell to Thornton Christer a tract of land on Brush Creek. 20 February 1843. (P. 3)

Elizabeth Ballard appoints William M. Williams of Henry County, Tennessee as her attorney in receiving land from John Ballard. 4 August 1843. (P. 4)

William Eden to James McClanahan. 19 August 1843. (P. 5)

John Stafford to James McClanahan. 18 August 1843. (P. 6)

Samuel Burdine bound to Armstead Moore. 21 July 1843. (P. 7)

Samuel Burdine to William B. Moore a tract of land in the town of Rome. 4 July 1843. (P. 8)

Samuel Burdine to Thomas A. Flippin a slave. 15 May 1843. (P. 8)

Booker S. Dalton to Marcus Donoho a crop of tobacco. 17 August 1843. (P. 9)

John W. Hall to Sampson McClelin a crop of tobacco. 21 August 1843. (P. 9)

Cyrus W. Brevard to Alfred A. Brevard a tract of 48 acres. 4 September 1841. (P. 10)

Samuel Burdine to N. B. Burdine four acres. 21 August 1843. (Pp. 10-12)

B. J. Vaden to Benjamin Little a negro slave. 19 August 1843. (P. 13)

Bolen D. High to William Denney two negro boys. 15 August 1843. (P. 13)

William L. Alexander of Sumner County to Hugh Patterson 31 acres. 13 May 1814. (Pp. 13-14)

John Squires to Frederick Jones. 22 August 1843. (Pp. 14-15)

John Squires to Thomas J. Slaughter a tract of land on Mulherin's Creek. 26 January 1843. (P. 15)

Elizabeth Moores to Henry L. Moores a tract of land belonging to her husband William Moores deceased. 21 August 1843. (P. 16)

DEED BOOK R

Henry L. Moores to Stephen A. Farmer 14 acres. 21 August 1843. (P. 16)

Joseph Bridges to Ann Carpenter 117 acres. 23 August 1841. (P. 17)

John Russell to Thomas Dean 161 acres. 19 July 1842. (P. 17)

S. P. Hughes to Lent Boulton three negro men and one woman. 3 June 1843. (P. 18)

Jonas Turner and Reece Wardrup to Sampson McClelin. 23 August 1843. (P. 18)

Henry Robinson to Thomas Lancaster, Jr. some livestock. 24 August 1843. (Pp. 18-19)

Presley Askins to John D. Bradley some livestock. 24 August 1843. (P. 19)

James Shelton to Robert H., William B., and Vallirus B. Turner, heirs of William D. Turner, a tract of land. 15 April 1841. (P. 20)

Greenberry Madden and Mathis Newel to John C. McCabe a crop of tobacco. 22 August 1843. (P. 20)

David Evetts to Sampson McClelin a crop of tobacco. 25 August 1843. (P. 21)

Jehu Timberlake to William F. Allen a crop of tobacco. 24 August 1843. (P. 21)

Alfred Cornwell to Sampson McClelin a crop of tobacco. 23 August 1843. (P. 22)

Walter L. Ford to Henry Robinson a crop of tobacco. 25 August 1843. (P. 22)

Lucian B. Sullivan to James R. Toney a negro man. 26 August 1843. (P. 23)

James B. Moores to Robert Marley 22 acres. 28 August 1843. (P. 23)

Joseph F. Hibbitt to James J. Malone, Amzi Malone, and Robert C. Malone a tract of land on Goose Creek. 23 September 1840. (P. 24)

Robert W. Mann to John Beckman a negro woman. 28 February 1843. (P. 25)

John Beckman to Henry V. Nichols, John B. Nichols, James Trousdale, William C. Trousdale, and John Trousdale, trustees, one acre on the Caney Fork to build a place of worship. 28 August 1843. (P. 25)

Benjamin F. Jones to Thomas J. Munford a negro boy. 11 July 1843. (P. 26)

John Trousdale, administrator of Ellis Parker, to A. G. Penn 100 acres. 16 August 1843. (P. 26)

DEED BOOK R

Henry Mann to R. C. Caruthers a negro man. 29 August 1843. (P. 27)

John Trousdale to Burton G. Ferrell 15 acres. 30 August 1843. (P. 27)

Burton G. Ferrell to John Condett a tract of land on the Caney Fork. 30 August 1843. (Pp. 27-28)

Andrew Payne to Milton Haynie a crop of tobacco. 30 August 1843. (P. 28)

Joel Coffee to Brice M. Draper and Edward B. Draper three slaves. 30 August 1843. (P. 29)

Hezekiah Love to Henry B. McDonald 160 acres. 31 August 1843. (P. 29)

Archibald Gibbs to Charles Thompson a crop of tobacco. 1843. (P. 29)

John C. Parker to William L. Smith 65 acres. 31 August 1843. (P. 30)

William L. Smith to John M. Wilkerson 65 acres. 1 September 1843. (P. 31)

Elijah Toney to Benjamin Rucks a negro woman for the use and benefit of Elizabeth Cornwell, wife of Pleasant F. Cornwell and daughter of the said Elijah Toney. 1 September 1843. (Pp. 31-32)

Cyrus Watson to John C. McCabe a crop of tobacco. 1 September 1843. (P. 33)

Freeman Leath to John C. McCabe a crop of tobacco. 1 September 1843. (P. 33)

Sheriff W. W. Bailey to Timothy Walton a negro woman. 1 September 1843. (P. 34)

Jefferson Jones to Timothy Walton, Jr. a crop of tobacco. 4 September 1843. (P. 35)

Stephen R. Samson to Johnson Samson. 2 September 1843. (P. 36)

H. Nichols to Nelson F. Kyle 222 acres he is to receive at the death of Lucy Nichols. 6 September 1842. (Pp. 36-37)

Thomas L. Hardee to Joseph Carter a crop of tobacco. 5 September 1843. (P. 37)

B. J. Gregory to Timothy Walton a crop of tobacco. 7 September 1843. (P. 38)

Benjamin Rucks to Elijah Toney a negro woman for the benefit of Elizabeth Cornwell. Said Elijah is a resident of Jackson County, Alabama. 7 September 1843. (P. 39)

Benjamin Mathews to Timothy Walton, Sr. a crop of tobacco. 8 September 1843. (P. 40)

DEED BOOK R

Samuel Evetts to Frances Duffy a crop of tobacco. 8 September 1843. (P. 41)

Lewis Franklin of Putnam County to John Franklin his son several slaves. 6 September 1843. (P. 41)

Lewis Franklin to his son John Franklin some slaves for his trouble and care about maintaining his brother William Ray Franklin. 1843. (Pp. 41-42)

Timothy Walton to Thomas Tunstall a woman slave. 9 September 1843. (P. 42)

Thomas Tunstall to his sister Tabitha D. Hazard a negro woman. 9 September 1843. (P. 43)

William A. Herod to William Duvall the Jackson Inn which he purchased from John Hallum. 4 January 1843. (P. 43)

Joseph Moses and Thomas Overstreet to Rufus Perry a crop of tobacco. 12 September 1843. (P. 44)

C. T. Thomas and James A. Thomas to Samuel Allison a crop of tobacco. 9 September 1843. (P. 44)

Stephen Goad to Thomas J. Jones a crop of tobacco. 12 September 1843. (P. 45)

John Collom and J. H. Collom to James Boulton a crop of tobacco. 17 August 1843. (P. 45)

James R. Toney to William C. Trousdale some livestock. 13 September 1843. (P. 46)

Martin J. Everett to D. M. Bradford a crop of tobacco. 13 September 1843. (P. 46)

William Meadows to Evan J. Williamson. 14 September 1843. (P. 47)

Alfred Read to Eli Gammon. 15 September 1843. (P. 47)

John Smalling to William Young a tract of land on Peyton's Creek. 23 August 1843. (P. 48)

William B. Dillon to William F. Andrews of Sumner County a crop of tobacco. 15 September 1843. (P. 48)

Henry L. Day to John C. McCabe a crop of tobacco. 14 September 1843. (P. 49)

Samuel P. Howard, administrator of William Cunningham, and also one of the heirs, who was a major of the Virginia State Line, appoints William E. Jones as his attorney. 10 May 1843. (P. 50)

Richard G. Gifford to George C. Gifford a crop of tobacco. 8 September 1843. (P. 51)

Mathew Carter to Thomas J. Jones a crop of tobacco. 19 September 1843. (P. 51)

DEED BOOK R

John S. Sanders to P. Duffy a crop of tobacco. 21 August 1843. (P. 52)

John Jones to William B. Whitley a crop of tobacco. 21 September 1843. (P. 52)

William P. Hughes to W. W. Bailey a negro slave. 22 September 1843. (P. 53)

C. C. Ford to Robert W. Mann a crop of tobacco. 22 September 1843. (P. 53)

Thomas D. Cassity to David Apple some personal property. 23 September 1843. (P. 54)

James J. Malone to Robert Malone, Sr. his interest in 300 acres. 20 September 1843. (Pp. 54-55)

O. B. Hubbard of Hinds County, Mississippi to John J. Burnett a town lot in the town of Carthage. 22 September 1843. (P. 55)

Tilman Cannon to P. Duffy a crop of tobacco. 23 September 1844. (P. 56)

James B. Crowder of Mississippi to Abraham Caruthers a tract of land. 15 August 1840. (Pp. 56-57)

William Haynes to Oliver Apple 50 acres. 1843. (P. 57)

Martin Williamson to Thomas McClard of Macon County a crop of tobacco. 25 September 1843. (P. 58)

William Willis to William Cunningham a crop of tobacco. 27 September 1843. (Pp. 58-59)

A. M. Presley to William Baker a crop of tobacco. 28 September 1842. (P. 59)

N. Ward to Sterling Ward a negro man. 27 September 1843. (P. 59)

Richard P. Hughes to R. Dowell two barns of tobacco. 30 September 1843. (P. 60)

Lemuel A. Jones to William F. McAlister a crop of tobacco. 30 September 1843. (P. 60)

James Read to Thomas Williams. 2 October 1843. (P. 61)

Joseph Bridges to William F. McAlister two and one half acres. 2 October 1843. (P. 61)

Benjamin F. Jones, administrator of John D. Hanes, to Calvin Bruer a negro girl. 1843. (P. 62)

John R. James to Ira B. Cowen. 2 October 1843. (P. 62)

James W. Smith, executor of John Owen, to Jeremiah Jamison. 1843. (Pp. 62-63)

DEED BOOK R

Ely Turner to William B. Whitley. 3 October 1843. (P. 63)

W. W. Bailey to John H. Savage a negro boy. 26 September 1843. (P. 64)

John C. Knight to William Young a crop of tobacco. 5 August 1843. (P. 64)

Jehu Timberlake and wife Elizabeth, formerly Elizabeth Hubbard, to Lewis Franklin their interest in the estate of Thomas J. Hubbard or in the estates of John Hubbard and Sally Hubbard, the father and mother of the said Elizabeth. 1843. (Pp. 64-65)

Daniel Allen to William B. Whitley a crop of tobacco. 5 October 1843. (P. 66)

James Shoemake to Rufus Perry a crop of tobacco. 7 October 1843. (P. 66)

Obediah Woodson to William B. Whitley a crop of tobacco. 3 October 1843. (Pp. 66-67)

Leonard J. Cardwell to Isaac Bradley a crop of tobacco. 9 October 1843. (P. 67)

William Black to Joseph Bowman a slave. 10 October 1843. (P. 68)

Micajah Kittle to Pinkney McKee a crop of tobacco. 10 October 1843. (Pp. 68-69)

William H. Kitrel to William Roe a crop of tobacco. 12 October 1843. (P. 69)

John H. Newbell to Gedeliah Hughes a slave. 24 April 1843. (P. 70)

John T. Stokes to John L. Hindsley a tract of land on Smith's Fork. 15 March 1843. (P. 70)

John T. Stokes to John L. Hindsley 40 acres. 15 March 1843. (P. 71)

James B. Conditt of Putnam County to Benjamin Vaden. 16 October 1843. (Pp. 71-72)

William H. Kittle to Parks Chandler some livestock. 16 October 1843. (P. 72)

William Nash to James McClanahan a crop of tobacco. October 1843. (P. 73)

James F. Warf to Major A. Beasley. 16 October 1843. (P. 74)

Zadock B. Roberts and wife Jane to James Trousdale their interest in the land on which Polly Trousdale, widow of William Trousdale, now lives. 16 May 1842. (P. 75)

John Nichols and James H. Wilson to William H. Jones. 7 October 1843. (P. 76)

DEED BOOK R

Samuel Vaden of Putnam County to Loderick Vaden, Sr. his interest in the estate of Judd Strother. 25 October 1842. (P. 77)

Caleb Carman and wife Elizabeth, Thomas E. Harris, Patterson Harris, Fleming Harris, Jane Harris, Martha Harris, and Mary Harris, heirs of Emanuel Harris, to Caleb Carman a tract of land. 1843. (P. 77)

James Roberts to Lewis Franklin 40 acres. 16 January 1824. (P. 78)

Martha Fulks to J. D. Smith a man slave. 30 October 1843. (P. 78)

Herald D. Marchbanks of Putnam County to Thomas C. Marchbanks his interest in the estate of Judd Strother. 28 October 1843. (P. 79)

Chesley Ballew, Mary E. Ballew, James L. Ballew, and Martha A. Ballew, heirs of James M. Ballew, to Ann Ballew a tract of land. 2 November 1843. (P. 79)

A. J. Chapman, Frances Chapman, James Boulton, Wilson Boulton, Lent Boulton, and Charles Boulton to Martin W. Sloan their interest in the estate of Charles Boulton, Sr. of Shelby County. September 1842. (P. 80)

Andrew Allison to John L. Jones a tract of land. 21 October 1843. (P. 81)

Daniel Buie to James McClanahan a crop of tobacco. November 1843. (P. 81)

Uzzi Pankey to Orville Green a negro boy. 14 October 1843. (P. 82)

Benjamin Rucks to Edmund Rucks his interest in the estate of his father Josiah Rucks. Mentions that his mother is still living. 28 September 1843. (P. 82)

Silas C. Cornwell and P. F. Cornwell to Uzzi Pankey a negro man. 10 October 1843. (P. 83)

Elijah A. Wright to J. R. Smith a crop of corn. 6 November 1843. (P. 83)

James Reynolds to Clinton B. Reynolds 120 acres. 1 November 1843. (P. 84)

Joseph Adcock to Calvin Dalton a crop of tobacco. 11 November 1843. (P. 84)

Micajah Kittle to Parks Chandler. 13 November 1843. (P. 85)

Duke Skelton to Jeremiah Smith 54 acres. 7 October 1842. (P. 85)

Jeremiah Smith to William Garrett 54 acres. 29 October 1842. (P. 86)

DEED BOOK R

Elihu H. Greer of Warren County, Mississippi to Archibald McNeill a tract of land on Goose Creek. 16 October 1843. (Pp. 86-87)

Thomas B. Askew to Jacen White. 21 November 1843. (P. 88)

Frederick Jones to Ephraim Agee 98 acres. 20 November 1843. (P. 89)

Sarah Williams to Jeremiah Jamison 449 acres. 29 November 1843. (P. 90)

Malinda Hall to Marshall B. Duncan her interest in a tract of land formerly owned by her husband Williamson Hall deceased. 30 November 1843. (P. 91)

Jesse Jones to Marshall B. Duncan 100 acres. 19 March 1842. (P. 91)

JOHN COCHRAN Will. Hinds County, Mississippi. Heirs: brother David Cochran; sisters Judith Hinton, Elizabeth Black, and Mary Johnston; nieces Nancy McFearson and husband Joseph; nephews Oscar Johnston, James B. Sanders, Owel Johnston, Oliver Johnston, and Oscar Johnston. Executors: James C. Sanders and Oscar Johnston. 28 April 1843. (Pp. 92-94)

James Thackston to James M. Shepherd a tract of land on the Cumberland River. 28 November 1843. (P. 94)

Anne Sullivan to William Shoemake 39 acres. 10 September 1843. (P. 95)

Samuel Burdine to John Payne one fourth of an acre. 11 November 1843. (P. 95)

Ann Sullivan to Samuel Hunter and William Hunter 84 acres. 16 September 1843. (P. 96)

Thomas Belcher to John Johnson $39\frac{1}{4}$ acres. 15 June 1840. (P. 96)

William B. Allen, Archibald Allen to Allen and Jones. 4 February 1843. (P. 97)

Hopkins Richardson to Othiel Johnson a negro girl. 24 January 1842. (P. 97)

Ann Sullivan to Blake B. Thackston 36 acres. 16 September 1843. (P. 98)

Thomas J. Rodgers to Robert Armstrong some slaves. 6 December 1843. (P. 98)

Thomas J. Rodgers of Dekalb County, Alabama to James R. Toney and Martin W. Sloan several negroes. 7 December 1843. (P. 99)

William C. Hubbard appoints William Hart as his attorney. 9 December 1843. (P. 99)

DEED BOOK R

William C. Hubbard to Armstead Moore some slaves. 1843. (Pp. 99-100)

Stephen D. Burton to his cousin, Elizabeth Jane Apple, a girl slave. 4 December 1843. (P. 100)

B. Armstrong, J. W. Armstrong, and Nancy M. Armstrong to Nathan B. Burdine. 5 December 1843. (P. 101)

Thomas W. Page, administrator of William B. Turner, versus William Ferrell, Harriet T. Turner, Robert B. Turner, Valerious Turner, and William Turner, the said Harriet being the widow. 1843. (Pp. 101-102)

Alexander F. Gaston of North Carolina to William Gaston of Craven County, North Carolina. 28 February 1843. (Pp. 103-104)

William Hale to Nehemiah Dowell a tract of land on Mulherin's Creek. 27 November 1841. (P. 105)

John Law to Daniel Huddleston 70 acres. 13 December 1843. (P. 106)

William A. Lancaster to Nehemiah Dowell 83 acres. 1 September 1842. (P. 107)

Jerusha McCulloh to Robert Dowell 63 acres. 9 November 1843. (Pp. 107-108)

Spencer Kelly to William Lancaster 155 acres. 13 September 1843. (P. 108)

John Lancaster to Thomas A. Lancaster a town lot in the town of Lancaster. 13 December 1843. (P. 109)

Ira B. Cowan to William Lancaster a negro boy. 26 September 1843. (P. 109)

John Lancaster to Russell and T. C. Marchbanks a tract of land on Smith's Fork. 21 December 1843. (P. 110)

John Lancaster to Russell and T. C. Marchbanks $74\frac{1}{4}$ acres. 21 December 1843. (P. 110)

Sarah Williams to Robert Williams two negroes. 12 December 1843. (P. 111)

Robert Williams to John Baker two slaves. 22 December 1843. (P. 111)

David McCall and Mary A. E. McCall, administrators of Alexander McCall, to John V. Tate a tract of 40 acres. 8 April 1843. (Pp. 111-112)

John V. Tate to David McCall three tracts of land. 28 November 1843. (Pp. 112-113)

Robert Harper to John Harper 390 acres. 29 January 1842. (P. 113)

Thomas Harper to John Harper. 1844. (P. 114)

DEED BOOK R

Armstead Moore to William C. Hubbard a negro slave. 30 December 1843. (P. 114)

Ann W. Archer of Amelia County, Virginia appoints John Walker of Todd County, Kentucky in settling the estate of her father William Archer. 25 May 1843. (P. 115)

Charlotte Hawkins to John Ballard her dower. 12 July 1843. (P. 116)

Jefferson Rowland to Sarah Pamelia Ford, Nancy Haines Ford, and Martha J. Ford, infant daughters of James Gordon Ford and wife Martha some personal property. 25 December 1843. (P. 116)

Branch Marley to James Haynie two acres. 29 December 1843. (P. 117)

John Wilcott to John Trousdale a tract of land on the Caney Fork. 2 January 1843. (Pp. 117-118)

John B. Hughes to Miles West a negro man. 1 January 1844. (P. 118)

George Sutton and James Sutton, executors of James Sutton, to Richardson C. Cartwright a tract of land on Defeated Creek. 22 July 1835. (P. 119)

Tandy P. D. Hall to William C. Towson a woman slave. 26 December 1843. (P. 119)

Joseph Gresham to Nelson Kyle a tract of land. 2 May 1842. (Pp. 119-120)

M. W. Sloan to John A. Sloan his interest in the estate of Archibald Sloan. 3 January 1844. (P. 121)

J. R. Smith to F. H. Gordon. January 1844. (P. 121)

Joseph B. Gregory to Peter A. Wilkinson 28 acres. 4 January 1844. (Pp. 121-122)

J.B. Hughs to Loderick Vaden a negro boy. 30 December 1843. (P. 123)

Loderick Vaden to J. B. Hughes a negro boy. 30 December 1843. (P. 123)

William L. Ramsey to Edwin M. Hughes a negro girl. 3 January 1843. (P. 124)

William D. Garrett to William W. Cunningham a tract of land on Peyton's Creek. 5 January 1844. (Pp. 124-125)

Brice F. Martin to William Martin a negro slave. 8 December 1843. (P. 126)

William E. Jones to M. W. Sloan. 1 January 1844. (P. 127)

William C. Roe to John Pinchum a woman slave. 5 January 1844. (P. 127)

DEED BOOK R

Marina Moorehead and husband Henry G., Robert Marley, Newton Marley, Hampton Marley, Young Marley, Josiah Marley, and Malvina Marley, heirs of Adam Marley, to John Maggart. 1844. (Pp. 128-129)

Jacob Hubbard to John McClarin a tract of 112 acres. 9 January 1844. (Pp. 129-130)

Andrew G. Pickett, Edward B. Pickett, and Joseph G. Pickett, heirs of Jonathan Pickett and Mary V. Pickett, to Samuel P. Howard a tract of land. 1844. (Pp. 131-132)

Robert D. Allison, John R. James, and James Barrett to William McClain 145 acres. 15 January 1844. (P. 133)

Richard Hodges to John A. Toney two negro slaves. 16 January 1844. (P. 134)

John Walker to Richard Hodges a negro woman. 17 January 1844. (P. 134)

Samuel Fuston to Leroy E. Mitchell a tract of land. 8 January 1844. (P. 135)

Chancery Court to James R. Toney. 1844. (P. 136)

James C. Sanders to Coleman S. Samson 150 acres. 16 October 1841. (P. 137)

James C. Sanders to Coleman S. Samson 76 acres. September 1843. (P. 137)

B. Kyle to Frances Dowell 350 acres. 25 January 1844. (P. 138)

Jabez Burton to David A. Tyree 60 acres. 30 January 1844. (P. 139)

Barkley Kyle to N. Ward two negroes. 29 January 1844. (Pp. 139-140)

Samuel Paschal to Bluford Cliver a tract of land on Mulherin's Creek. 25 December 1841. (Pp. 140-141)

Willis Whitley to William B. Whitley 65 acres. 9 June 1840. (P. 141)

Marmaduke Mason to William B. Whitley four and one half acres. 12 July 1843. (P. 142)

William Slinkard to George Waggoner 97 acres. 7 August 1843. (Pp. 142-143)

Samuel Burdine to John McCall eight acres. 29 July 1843. (Pp. 143-144)

Thomas W. Wootten to E. P. Lowe a negro woman. 22 January 1844. (P. 144)

Ira B. Cowan to David Smith three negroes. 12 February 1844. (P. 145)

Elijah Moore and Harriet F., formerly Harriet F. Archer of Mississippi, appoint Gregory Moore as their attorney in

DEED BOOK R

settling the estate of William Archer. 28 September 1842. (Pp. 145-146)

Thomas W. Gibbs to John H. Bates a crop of tobacco. 31 January 1844. (P. 146)

Daniel Dillard, administrator of Elisha Dillard, to Thomas Harper a tract of land on the Caney Fork. 16 March 1832. (Pp. 147-148)

Isaac Mungle to his daughter Sarah Mungle a negro girl. 8 December 1843. (P. 148)

Alfred Pierce of Rutherford County to William Alford of the same county 700 acres. 14 February 1844. (Pp. 148-149)

Solomon Smallin to Timothy Walton, Sr. a crop of tobacco. 17 February 1844. (Pp. 149-150)

John B. Gammon, Rusia Gammon, formerly Rusia Carman, Eli Gammon, and Frances Gammon, formerly Frances Carman, heirs of Elijah Gammon, appoint Thomas Carman and Caleb Carman as their agents. 15 January 1844. (Pp. 150-152)

Alexander F. Gaston of North Carolina to William Gaston of North Carolina a tract of land. 13 September 1843. (Pp. 153-155)

Henry Mann to Joel Coffee some livestock. 26 February 1844. (Pp. 156-157)

Bartlett Kyle to Edward Upton several items. 10 February 1844. (P. 157)

John Squires to William Price 173 acres. 24 February 1844. (Pp. 158-159)

William Cartwright to William C. and Benjamin F. Brockett a tract of land. 22 February 1844. (Pp. 159-160)

Robert Bowman and Rachel Bowman of Graves County, Kentucky to Joseph Bowman a negro man. 10 February 1844. (P. 160)

Robert Bowman and Rachel Bowman to Henry Beasley a negro man. 5 March 1844. (P. 161)

William Dawson to James Boze a tract of land. 23 January 1844. (Pp. 161-162)

James Shelton to Drury Clarada a tract of 54 acres. 24 February 1844. (P. 162)

Martin McMurry to John A. Debow a boy slave. 12 October 1843. (P. 163)

Thomas W. Wootten to E. P. Lowe a negro boy. 23 January 1844. (P. 163)

John Kerby to William Cartwright a tract of land on Peyton's Creek. 25 January 1837. (Pp. 163-164)

DEED BOOK R

Neil Patterson to Alex Patterson 150 acres. 16 June 1842. (P. 164)

Sam A. Sloan bound to John Evans. 11 June 1836. (P. 165)

Sampson Sloan bound to John ( ). 11 June 1836. (P. 166)

Division of the lands of Thomas Parsons. Heirs: William Parsons, Thomas Parsons, and William P. Little. 1821. (Pp. 166-168)

Adam Ferguson is to receive the amount of Colonel Henry Dixon's pay in the Army during the American Revolution. 20 February 1838. (Pp. 168-169)

Thomas W. Page, administrator of William D. Turner, to John Campsey 104 acres. 10 July 1843. (P. 169)

Mary A. E. McCall to William M. Price one fourth of an acre. 12 December 1842. (P. 170)

Milton Haynie to Jordan Beasley three negroes. 8 March 1844. (Pp. 170-171)

Leighton Philips to Thomas Haley 90 acres. 27 December 1842. (P. 171)

Henry B. Clark to Joseph H. Durham three acres. 19 January 1844. (P. 172)

W. W. Bailey to William Little two negro girls. 21 March 1844. (P. 172)

Jordan Stewart to James A. Scruggs some livestock. 30 March 1844. (P. 173)

Riggs ( ) & Company versus Martin W. Sloan and others. 7 March 1844. (P. 174)

William B. Crank to James S. Dyer a girl slave. 12 September 1843. (P. 175)

Nelson F. Kyle to H. V. Nichols 130 acres. 5 September 1842. (P. 175)

Nelson F. Kyle to W. W. Bailey a lot of negroes. 1844. (P. 176)

William Hart to William B. Campbell a tract of 62 acres. 9 December 1843. (P. 177)

Drury Holland to William Kerby 25 acres. 20 August 1840. (P. 178)

Warren Nichols to Christopher C. Ford a tract of land. 1 April 1844. (P. 179)

Timothy Walton and Robert Allen agreement. 2 April 1844. (P. 180)

DEED BOOK R

Timothy Walton to William Cullom 120 acres. 2 April 1844. (P. 181)

Susannah Hazard to William Harrison a negro man. 25 March 1844. (P. 181)

Henry Mann to William R. D. Phipps a negro girl. 18 March 1844. (P. 182)

Isaac Mungle to his daughter Malinda Gifford a negro girl. 8 December 1843. (P. 182)

Thomas Climer to Philip McClanahan a tract of land on Goose Creek. 23 November 1843. (P. 183)

Philip McClanahan to Philip T. Day 57 acres. 28 November 1843. (P. 184)

G. C. Gifford to Edmund P. G. Gifford a negro boy. 9 April 1844. (P. 185)

Sarah J. Williams to John A. Toney two town lots. 1844. (P. 185)

Jonathan Agee to Jeremiah Agee and Daniel B. Agee 134 acres. 13 April 1844. (P. 186)

Jonathan Agee to William Agee 19½ acres. 12 April 1844. (P. 187)

Augustine Thorn to James Young of Jackson County two and one fourth acres. 28 December 1843. (Pp. 187-188)

Thomas Fisher to James Fisher for the maintainance of him Thomas Fisher, Sr. and Rebecca Fisher 50 acres. 12 September 1843. (P. 188)

David Apple to Jefferson Wood 20 acres. 12 December 1841. (P. 189)

Samuel Caplinger of Missouri to Stephen Hickman his interest in a tract of land. 10 August 1831. (P. 190)

Abraham Caruthers to Robert D. Bell 170 acres in Wilson County. 26 March 1844. (P. 191)

Sheriff W. W. Bailey to William J. Payne. 17 June 1842. (Pp. 192-193)

Rachel Hallum, W. V. R. Hallum, Josiah Hallum, and Rachel Hallum to Lawrence Sypert a man slave. 24 February 1844. (P. 193)

Duncan Johnson to William W. Searcy 56 acres. 1844. (P. 194)

William Hart to Henry W. Hart a tract of five acres. 16 April 1844. (P. 195)

M. W. Sloan to James W. Morgan of Lynchburg, Virginia five acres. 19 April 1843. (P. 196)

DEED BOOK R

Solomon Debow to Robert S. Mills two negro slaves. 14 March 1844. (P. 196)

John S. Carter to Jefferson Link a negro boy. 19 April 1844. (P. 197)

William J. Bomar to Ephraim Cheek 150 acres. 16 November 1840. (P. 197)

Martin W. Sloan to Adam Ferguson a tract of land in the town of Carthage. 25 April 1844. (P. 198)

Thomas Howard to Harriett Helmontoller 40 acres. 30 September 1840. (P. 199)

Benjamin Harper to D. M. Johnson a tract of 200 acres. 2 May 1844. (P. 200)

Thomas Williams to Drury Holland 232 acres. 8 March 1836. (Pp. 201-202)

The heirs of Benjamin Roe to John O. Pope a tract of land. 1844. (Pp. 202-203)

Mary White and Hiram White, minor heirs of Sam White to ( ) ( ). 1844. (Pp. 203-204)

Jefferson Jones to C. Rucks some livestock. 1844. (Pp. 204-205)

James W. Moss to William W. Jones. 21 May 1844. (P. 206)

John H. Bowen to Archibald Debow his interest in certain negroes. 17 February 1844. (P. 207)

James G. Ford and Wilson F. Kyle to Andrew G. Pickett the Roland tract on Snow Creek. 8 May 1843. (Pp. 207-208)

Milton Haynie to Patrick Hubbard a negro girl. 7 May 1844. (P. 208)

Stephen Stafford to Eli Gammon a tract of land on Dixon's Creek. 1 June 1844. (P. 209)

Mecan Ship to John Page three acres. 24 May 1844. (P. 210)

J. W. Smellage to Adison Askins 76 acres. 1844. (Pp. 210-211)

Mecan Ship to Joseph Bishop a tract of land in the 12th District. 25 May 1844. (P. 211)

John Mitchell to John Reeves a tract of land. 5 December 1839. (P. 212)

Tabitha Moore to Robert Moore of St. Frances County, Missouri a negro man for the benefit of Amanda Tabitha, Mary Frances Armstead, and John H. Moore, children of the said Robert. 6 June 1844. (P. 213)

John G. Smith to William A. Corley. 1844. (P. 213)

DEED BOOK R

Lewis Hall to Willis Dowell 100 acres. 1844. (P. 214)

Lewis Hall to Frances Dowell a negro woman. 21 June 1844. (P. 214)

James D. Sloan to John L. Sloan his interest in the estate of Archibald Sloan. 20 February 1839. (P. 215)

David McCall to Troylus Violet a tract of land in the town of Rome. 26 January 1844. (P. 216)

Widow Parthena Rose, Charles Tate and wife Eliza, Sally W. Rose, George W. Rose, William J. Rose, Nancy Rose, Ezekiel Rose, John W. Rose, and Pleasant Rose, heirs of William Rose, to Pleasant H. Rose a tract of land. 1844. (Pp. 216-217)

Rolly Organ and James Organ to Stephen M. Jones a tract of land in the town of Rome. 11 January 1844. (P. 218)

William Jones to Jefferson Rowland 150 acres. 22 June 1844. (P. 218)

William Litchford to John Litchford 61 acres. 1 July 1844. (P. 219)

John Litchford to John D. Bradley 61 acres. 1 July 1844. (P. 219)

Andrew G. Pickett bound to John H. Bedford. 1844. (P. 220)

George Rowland, Robert Rowland, Jefferson Rowland, William Clemmons and wife Sarah, Sarah Hallum, Priscilla Hallum, and Elizabeth Hallum, Alfred H. Foster and wife Nancy, James G. Ford and wife Martha, heirs of David Rowland to Jefferson Rowland. July 1844. (Pp. 220-221)

Sheriff John Bailey to Jordan Stokes. 15 January 1841. (Pp. 222-223)

Frances Lawson to his daughter Elizabeth Haley a negro girl. 26 June 1844. (P. 223)

William Austin to Solomon Austin 202 acres. 15 March 1844. (P. 224)

A. L. Bains and Meredith Hawkins to D. M. Denton 150 acres. 5 July 1838. (P. 225)

Joseph Gresham to John B. Nichols 90 acres. 10 March 1844. (P. 226)

Henry Goad to John B. Costello a tract of land on Snow Creek. 25 July 1844. (Pp. 226-227)

Jacob White and David Harris to Sam Coker a crop of tobacco. 20 July 1844. (P. 227)

William Flowers to Joel S. Flowers a tract of land. 17 July 1844. (P. 228)

William Flowers, Sr. to his son George C. Flowers a negro girl. 18 July 1844. (P. 228)

DEED BOOK R

William Flowers, Sr. to Lucy W. Allen 38 acres. 17 July 1844. (P. 229)

William Flowers, Sr. to his son Joel S. Flowers several slaves. 1 January 1844. (P. 229)

William Flowers to his daughter Lydia Hughes a negro woman. 18 July 1844. (P. 230)

William Flowers, Sr. to his daughter Lucy W. Allen a negro woman. 17 July 1844. (P. 230)

William Flowers, Sr. to his son William L. Flowers a negro girl. 18 July 1844. (P. 231)

William Flowers, Sr. to his son Rolfe K. Flowers a negro girl. 18 July 1844. (P. 231)

William Flowers, Sr. to his grandson John H. Flowers a negro child. 20 July 1844. (P. 231)

William Flowers to his grandson William A. McClanahan a negro girl. 18 July 1844. (P. 232)

William Flowers, Sr. to his daughter Drucilla McAlister a negro girl. 13 July 1844. (P. 232)

L. H. Cardwell to William Flowers a tract of land sold by the Sheriff. 1844. (Pp. 232-233)

M. W. Sloan to Buckner J. Cardwell a tract of land. 21 January 1841. (P. 233)

E. P. Gifford to G. C. Gifford a negro boy. 15 July 1844. (P. 233)

Henry Mann to Joel Coffee a tract of land on the Caney Fork. 24 July 1844. (Pp. 234-235)

William Thomas to Henry Kemp 100 acres. 24 July 1844. (P. 236)

John Vaden to Andrew G. Pickett and John D. Vaden his son some livestock. 27 July 1844. (P. 237)

Sheriff John Bailey to the Bank of Tennessee a tract of land. 31 July 1844. (Pp. 237-239)

William Hall to T. J. Furlong a crop of tobacco. 30 July 1844. (P. 239)

Jacob Hubbard to D. Hogg & Son and Benjamin J. Vaden some personal property. 3 August 1844. (P. 240)

Marriage contract between David Monroe and Jane Ligon. 15 August 1843. (P. 241)

Bartlett Kyle to Daniel Cardwell several items. 7 August 1844. (P. 242)

William Martin to William M. Young a negro boy. 31 July 1844. (P. 242)

DEED BOOK R

Mathew Morris to John Minton a tract of land on the Cumberland River. 4 July 1842. (Pp. 242-243)

Ellis B. Kemp to James Kerby 93 acres. 19 July 1844. (P. 244)

Spencer Glascock to James C. Williams a negro man. 11 June 1844. (P. 244)

Lemuel A. Hammack to George T. Wright 167 acres. 30 July 1844. (P. 245)

Robert West to Rufus Haynes 65 acres. 6 August 1844. (P. 246)

James McMurry to James H. Vaughan a boy slave. 25 October 1843. (P. 246)

Joseph M. Clark, administrator of John Thornton, to Jacob Null 12½ acres. 5 August 1844. (P. 247)

George H. Walker to James H. Vaughan a negro boy. 27 March 1843. (P. 247)

Robert West to Thomas Haynes 70 acres. 6 August 1844. (P. 248)

William Flowers, Sr. to George C. Flowers a negro boy. 23 July 1844. (P. 248)

Thomas L. Draper to James C. Williams five acres. 30 July 1844. (P. 249)

H. Love to John Marks a negro boy. 9 July 1844. (P. 249)

Booker Wakefield to Samson McClelin. 5 August 1844. (P. 250)

Stephen Goad to Benjamin Payne a crop of tobacco. 9 August 1844. (P. 250)

Cyrus Watson to C. D. Brooks a crop of tobacco. 9 August 1844. (P. 251)

George C. Gifford to Z. G. Goodall a boy slave. 18 November 1843. (P. 251)

Sheriff John Bailey to John Stevens a tract of 100 acres. 12 August 1844. (P. 252)

Rawleigh Stott to John S. Stott a tract of land on Peyton's Creek. 25 March 1844. (P. 253)

Henry L. Day to C. D. Brooks a crop of tobacco. 15 August 1844. (Pp. 253-254)

Joseph Gresham to Stephen Mann a crop of tobacco. 19 August 1844. (P. 254)

Davidson Draper and Robert J. Glover to Henry Goad 36 acres. 19 August 1844. (P. 255)

John J. Jones to Robert Marshall. 1844. (Pp. 255-256)

DEED BOOK R

Samuel Evetts to Mathew Tunstall a crop of tobacco. 24 August 1844. (P. 256)

Thomas Gregory to John Nickson a crop of tobacco. 10 August 1844. (P. 257)

William Robertson, Martha Robertson, Ann W. Archer, John Walker, and Prudence Walker, heirs of William Archer, to Elijah Moore their interest in 200 acres. 22 February 1844. (P. 258)

James S. Murphree to William Denny three acres. 6 July 1844. (P. 259)

Ann W. Archer, by her attorney John Walker of Todd County, Kentucky, to Gregory Moore a negro man. 26 August 1844. (P. 259)

William Robertson and others to John Walker their interest in the estate of William Archer. 26 August 1844. (P. 260)

Isham Beasley to Robert L. Caruthers a negro man. 27 July 1844. (P. 261)

John Shoulders to Thomas Gregory. 28 August 1844. (P. 261)

Nicholas Grandstaff to Lewis Pendleton 94½ acres. 28 January 1840. (P. 261)

Booker S. Dalton to P. Duffy a crop of tobacco. 19 August 1844. (P. 262)

Davidson Draper and Robert Glover to Jesse Moreland 96 acres. 14 August 1844. (P. 262)

Jesse Moreland to John Dickens 96 acres. 29 August 1844. (P. 263)

Lucretia Kemp to Adam Hall s slave girl. 26 October 1843. (P. 264)

Michael Shoemake to Benjamin Arundell and the other trustees of the Methodist Episcopal Church one acre on Hurricane Creek. 16 July 1844. (P. 264)

M. W. Sloan to David C. Oats several slaves. 30 August 1844. (P. 265)

M. W. Sloan to William Cullom a negro man. 30 August 1844. (P. 265)

Henry Hicks to Hardy Goss. 18 September 1844. (P. 266)

Joseph Moses to Oran J. Simmons a crop of tobacco. 2 September 1844. (P. 266)

Johnson Anderson to Charles D. Brooks a crop of tobacco. 2 September 1844. (P. 267)

DEED BOOK R

Jonas Turner to William Young a crop of tobacco. 27 August 1844. (P. 267)

Jeremiah Jamison to Henry Beasley a tract of land on Dry Creek. 8 August 1844. (P. 268)

Henry Beasley to Milton Brockett 91 acres. 30 July 1844. (Pp. 268-269)

Jefferson Jones to Thomas J. Stratton a crop of tobacco. 2 September 1844. (P. 269)

Thomas Gregory to William T. Bennett a crop of tobacco. 3 September 1844. (P. 270)

Robert Williams to Henry Beasley a negro boy. 2 September 1844. (P. 270)

James Cawthorn and wife Parthenia, Henderson Massey, Leroy Bradley and wife Rebecca, William Massey, and Mary E. Massey to Leroy Bradley 231 acres. 1844. (P. 271)

Robert Williams to Henry Beasley a negro woman and child. 2 September 1844. (P. 272)

Robert Williams to John McClarin three negro slaves. 4 September 1844. (Pp. 272-273)

Martin Williamson to L. A. Hammack a crop of tobacco. 4 September 1844. (P. 273)

William Gregory to Joseph Bowman a crop of tobacco. 21 August 1844. (Pp. 274-275)

Mathis Newell to N. M. Adams a crop of tobacco. 9 September 1844. (P. 275)

Alfred Read to Thomas J. Noles. 10 September 1844. (Pp. 275-276)

John Smallen to William Young a crop of tobacco. 28 August 1844. (P. 276)

Charles C. Murray of Livingston County, Kentucky to Charles R. Blair a tract of 25 acres. 3 April 1841. (P. 277)

Lucy Self to Hannah Hodges her interest in the estate of Willis Hodges. 7 September 1844. (P. 278)

B. Kyle to David Davis a negro girl. 12 September 1844. (P. 278)

Richardson Roberts to William J. Davis 56¼ acres. 12 September 1844. (P. 279)

C. C. Ford to Robert W. Mann a crop of tobacco. 12 September 1844. (P. 279)

Charles C. Murray of Livingston County, Kentucky to Patrick Hubbard 25 acres. 3 April 1841. (P. 280)

John G. Anderson to Sampson McClelin. 1844. (Pp. 280-281)

DEED BOOK R

David Evetts to Sampson McClelin a crop of tobacco. 13 September 1844. (P. 281)

Braddoc Beasley to John Nickson 40 acres. 17 September 1844. (P. 282)

Robert Williams to Jesse G. Frazer a tract of land in the town of Carthage. 18 September 1844. (P. 283)

John Bell to Thomas J. Noles. 17 September 1844. (P. 284)

Lawson Dickerson to Sampson McClelin a crop of tobacco. 17 September 1844. (P. 284)

James R. Toney versus Mitchell High. 29 September 1844. (P. 285)

John A. Toney to William Farley. 10 August 1844. (Pp. 285-286)

William B. Whitley, administrator of Exum Whitley, to William Strother 62½ acres. 5 June 1843. (P. 286)

Avin Ward to Nathan Ward some livestock. 1 October 1844. (P. 287)

Alfred H. Richardson and wife Nancy, formerly Nancy Cleveland, to Smith Gregory their interest in the estate of William Cleveland. 4 September 1844. (P. 288)

Archibald W. Overton to Thomas Tunstall and Charles Tunstall a tract of land on Lick Creek. 1 October 1844. (Pp. 288-289)

Elias Dowell to Robert Dowell a man slave. 30 March 1844. (P. 289)

James Shoemake to Rufus Perry a crop of tobacco. 1 October 1844. (P. 290)

Thomas Climer to Timothy Walton, Sr. a crop of tobacco. 5 October 1844. (P. 290)

Benjamin Arundell to Cynthia Hogg a tract of land. 1 October 1844. (P. 291)

John D. Harvell to Samuel Fitchpatrick 25 acres. 11 October 1844. (Pp. 291-292)

John Haley to Thomas A. Lancaster a man slave. 14 August 1844. (P. 292)

John T. Stokes to Thomas A. Lancaster a negro girl. 22 August 1844. (P. 292)

John Litchford and Thomas Litchford to William Litchford. 19 October 1844. (P. 293)

Thomas Ferrell to Burkett F. Ferrell 35 acres on Snow Creek. 19 October 1844. (P. 293)

Burton G. Ferrell to Burkett F. Ferrell 95 acres. 10 March 1843. (P. 294)

DEED BOOK R

John Corley to John H. Newbell several slaves. 19 October 1844. (Pp. 294-295)

William B. Moore appoints Orville Green and Armstead Moore as his attorneys. 7 October 1844. (P. 295)

William Hallum to Stephen Mann a tract of land on Snow Creek. 7 September 1843. (P. 296)

Matthew Anderson to Thomas D. Gregory 102½ acres. 30 October 1844. (P. 297)

Robert Williams to Samuel P. Howard a negro boy. 28 October 1844. (P. 297)

Archibald Sloan to Jason R. Sloan his interest in the estate of John Sloan which he is to receive at the death of Mary Sloan, widow of the said John. 4 November 1844. (P. 298)

Joseph B. Gregory to Peter Herod 28 acres. 14 October 1844. (Pp. 298-299)

Benjamin J. Vaden to Rufus Perry 83 acres. 6 November 1843. (P. 299)

George McAllister to his daughter Eveline L. Ewing 60 acres. 16 October 1844. (P. 300)

George McAllister to his son William F. McAllister 82 acres. 16 October 1844. (P. 300)

James W. Grissim to Isaac Payne a town lot in the town of Rome. 1844. (Pp. 300-301)

George W. Walker to David McCall a negro boy. 4 November 1844. (P. 301)

William F. Allen to his nephews James and Joseph Allen, sons of his brother Robert Allen, several items. 23 October 1844. (Pp. 301-302)

Henry B. Mooningham to John Bridges a bay mare. 16 November 1844. (P. 302)

William Fiveash to David Morris nine acres. 6 November 1841. (Pp. 302-303)

William D. Nash to Sampson McClenon a crop of tobacco. 22 November 1844. (P. 303)

William W. McMann and wife Jane, Nancy Miller, and Matilda Miller to William J. Jones 50 acres. 29 January 1842. (P. 304)

William W. McMann and others to William J. Jones. 1844. (Pp. 305-306)

Michael Shoemake to Benjamin Arundell 32 acres on Hurricane Creek, excluding one half acre for the campground. 25 November 1844. (P. 306)

William P. Hughes and John W. Hughes bound to Edward B.

DEED BOOK R

Tuck. 13 February 1841. (Pp. 306-307)

Edward B. Tuck to Philip H. Tuck. 21 November 1844. (Pp. 307-308)

John Holeman and Mary Holeman to Henry V. Nichols 50 acres. 26 November 1844. (P. 308)

James R. Toney to William Cullom 104 acres. 27 November 1844. (P. 309)

Robert S. Mills to Stephen M. Jones a negro woman. 3 August 1844. (P. 309)

John L. Cornwell to David Hogg. November 1844. (P. 310)

George W. Walker and Frances Kerby to F. N. Mitchell six acres. 6 May 1840. (Pp. 310-311)

William Duvall from James R. Toney and W. W. Bailey. 3 December 1844. (Pp. 311-312)

Brice M. Draper and Edward B. Draper to Garland Hester 50 acres. November 1844. (Pp. 312-313)

George Waggoner to Reuben Braswell a tract of land on Hogan's Creek. 8 February 1843. (P. 313)

Olive Dawson, William Snoddy, Manerva Snoddy, Catherine Samson, S. R. Samson, Eleanor Morris, and Matthew W. Morris to Jacob Waggoner a negro girl. 11 December 1844. (P. 314)

Eliza J. Payne to Isaac N. Payne a negro boy for love and affection. 11 December 1844. (P. 315)

John B. Hughes to James Timberlake, Sr. of Franklin County, North Carolina a tract of land on Snow Creek. 18 December 1844. (P. 315)

Blake B. Thackston to William Shoemake 23 acres. 10 December 1844. (P. 316)

Sheriff John Bailey to the Bank of Tennessee. 1844. (Pp. 316-318)

Sheriff John Bailey to the Bank of Tennessee. 1844. (Pp. 318-321)

N. Ward to John Bridges a negro woman and child. 20 June 1844. (P. 322)

Elijah Fulks to Nathan Ward a crop of tobacco. 31 December 1844. (Pp. 322-323)

Pleasant Roberts to Hawkins Heflin 50 acres. 26 August 1844. (P. 323)

William B. Kyle to Avin Ward some personal property. 30 December 1844. (Pp. 323-324)

H. V. Nichols to James R. Toney a negro girl. 30 December 1844. (P. 324)

DEED BOOK R

William P. Hughes to E. A. Wright 180 acres. 23 February 1841. (P. 325)

Martin W. Sloan to John T. Right 76 acres. 2 January 1845. (P. 325)

Timothy Walton to Gideon B. Wray a tract of land in the town of Carthage. 3 January 1845. (P. 326)

Sheriff John Bailey to the Bank of Tennessee. 1845. (Pp. 326-328)

Edward Lawrence to David T. Winfrey ten acres. 24 September 1844. (Pp. 328-329)

Fergus S. Harris to William M. Price a tract of land in the town of Rome. 20 December 1844. (P. 329)

John Turner to W. M. Price a tract of land on Round Lick Creek. 1845. (P. 329)

John Turner bound to W. M. Price. 1845. (P. 330)

William Meadows to Matthew Corley several items. 10 December 1844. (P. 331)

Wilson Boulton to Jefferson Jeffrey a tract of land on Mulherin's Creek. January 1845. (Pp. 331-332)

David Prowell to John Bailey 62 acres. 18 January 1845. (Pp. 331-332)

Yancy Blackwell to Gideon Gifford a negro boy. 15 January 1845. (P. 332)

R. G. L. Hays to A. L. Bains several items. 12 January 1845. (Pp. 333-334)

Elijah Carter to David Harris a negro boy. 24 January 1845. (P. 335)

Eli Gammon from William Read. 25 January 1845. (Pp. 335-336)

J. R. Tomkins and wife Mary to John Madding 175 acres. 14 January 1845. (P. 336)

William Parkhurst to George Boston 115 acres. January 1845. (Pp. 337-338)

George W. Catron to O. P. Catron. 1845. (Pp. 338-339)

Edwin Atwood to Lemuel Barnett a tract of land. 21 November 1842. (Pp. 339-340)

Liza Gillum to David Hunt a negro woman. 6 February 1845. (P. 340)

Josiah Marshall to Thomas Marshall a tract of land on Goose Creek. 26 October 1844. (P. 341)

David Burford to Richard R. Bransford a tract of land on Dixon's Creek. 4 October 1843. (P. 342)

DEED BOOK R

David Hunt to Liza Gillum. 6 February 1845. (P. 343)

John H. Cunningham of Williamson County, Illinois to Henry D. Carter of Wilson County 300 acres. 10 February 1845. (Pp. 343-344)

John H. Cunningham appoints Henry D. Carter as his attorney in settling the estate of James Cunningham. 10 February 1845. (P. 344)

Joseph Jones, Sr. and Richard Jones to Sampson McClenon a crop of tobacco. 17 February 1845. (Pp. 344-345)

William Lynch to W. V. R. Hallum some livestock. 19 February 1845. (Pp. 345-346)

David Cook to Andrew Allison 175 acres. 16 February 1845. (P. 346)

Robert L. Caruthers to John Harper. 20 April 1841. (P. 347)

Henry Beasley to Robert Allen 195 acres. 30 July 1841. (Pp. 347-348)

W. W. Bailey to Lot Hazard. 25 February 1845. (Pp. 348-349)

James Stevens to John Stevens. 23 September 1844. (P. 349)

John Stevens to Armstead Moore. 7 October 1844. (P. 350)

The heirs of Charles Cole to James G. Parker a tract of land. 1845. (Pp. 351-352)

John Gwaltney to Jesse McClain a tract of land. 7 August 1843. (P. 352)

Martha Mitchell, widow of F. N. Mitchell, relinquishment. 18 December 1844. (P. 353)

The administrator of D. C. Ward to John Hale. 3 February 1845. (P. 353)

Henry V. Nichols to John B. Nichols a tract of land on the Caney Fork. 7 March 1845. (Pp. 354-355)

Joseph Moses to Thomas Overstreet. 1845. (P. 355)

John P. Hughes to Thomas E. Harris a negro woman. 14 March 1845. (P. 356)

Jesse McClain to John A. Andrews 18 acres. 22 March 1844. (Pp. 356-357)

William Exum to John Powell, trustee for Sally Robinson 60 acres. 10 March 1845. (P. 357)

James Wallace from Samuel Ford 50 acres. 19 March 1845. (P. 358)

William B. Perkins to Samuel Chambers. 1845. (Pp.

DEED BOOK R

359-360)

Armstead Moore to William C. Hubbard a negro slave. 3 April 1845. (P. 360)

Edmund Rucks to William F. Hughes a man slave. 5 April 1845. (P. 361)

John Kelley to William Bates and Isaac Bates 50 acres. 27 January 1845. (Pp. 361-362)

James Bradley to Alfred M. Wilkner a tract of land on Dry Creek. 24 October 1844. (P. 362)

John Williams to Albert Arrington 28 acres. 6 April 1843. (P. 363)

William H. Dillard to William A. Corley a negro woman. 10 February 1845. (P. 363)

James G. Goad to Stephen Mann a tract of land on Snow Creek. 18 December 1843. (P. 363)

Elizabeth Blackwell to William H. Corley a negro woman. 17 January 1843. (Pp. 364-365)

Andrew G. Pickett to Jeremiah Jamison several slaves. 8 April 1845. (Pp. 365-366)

Rezen Thompson to J. B. Norris several items. 14 April 1845. (Pp. 366-367)

David Blew to Wilson Turner a tract of land on Hickman's Creek. 2 March 1832. (P. 367)

Henry Newby to Hampton T. Withrow 125 acres. 1 July 1836. (Pp. 368-369)

Hampton T. Withrow to Drury Holland 125 acres. 16 January 1838. (Pp. 369-370)

Andrew G. Pickett to Leroy E. Mitchell a slave. 21 April 1845. (P. 370)

John Gwaltney, Jr. to Zephaniah Orange 17 acres on Hickman's Creek. 12 February 1845. (P. 371)

Bartlett James, Sr. to Zephaniah Orange a tract of land. 20 November 1826. (Pp. 371-372)

John Stubblefield to Archibald M. Debow a tract of land. 14 March 1844. (Pp. 372-373)

Isaac Kitrell and Mildred Maxey marriage contract. 14 January 1845. (Pp. 373-374)

David Stanford to William J. Stanford a tract of land. 16 April 1845. (P. 375)

Abel Gregory to David Stanford. 31 December 1844. (P. 376)

William Flowers to Rolf K. Flowers. 1845. (P. 377)

DEED BOOK R

George Gregory to Smith Gregory his interest in the estate of William Cleveland. 5 December 1843. (Pp. 377-378)

John T. Hunter to Robert Hays a tract of land. 17 August 1844. (Pp. 378-379)

The Bank of Tennessee to H. G. Bennett 650 acres. 20 March 1845. (P. 379)

H. G. Bennett to William Allen and Robert D. Bell a negro man. 7 April 1845. (Pp. 379-380)

Samuel Caplinger to John S. Hinsley a tract of land on Smith's Fork. 18 March 1844. (P. 381)

Daniel Smith to Bias Russell two tracts of land. 23 December 1839. (Pp. 382-383)

William B. Taylor, coroner, to David Burford. 23 April 1845. (Pp. 383-384)

Rowland W. Newby to Jeremiah Smith a tract of land on Round Lick Creek. 8 January 1840. (P. 385)

William Strother to Adam Ferguson a negro man. 25 April 1845. (P. 386)

S. F. Patterson to Obediah Jenkins a tract of land. 10 April 1845. (Pp. 386-387)

Division of the lands of Nehemiah Dowell. Heirs: Frances Dowell, Presley Dowell, John Dowell, Elisha Dowell, Willis Dowell, Elias Dowell, Robert Dowell, Mary Harris, William Dowell, and James Dowell. 1844. (Pp. 388-390)

Anthony Halmantoller to Martha Fulks 23 acres. 12 February 1842. (Pp. 390-391)

Stephen Hickman to William Hickman. 1 May 1845. (P. 391)

Thomas H. Smith appoints Armstead G. Morris as his attorney to settle the estate of Larkin Smith. 5 March 1845. (P. 392)

William Pendarvis to Ramsey Vance a tract of land. 10 April 1845. (Pp. 392-393)

William Worley of Bedford County, Virginia appoints Joel S. Worley at his attorney. April 1845. (Pp. 393-394)

Josel S. Worley to Benjamin C. Davis the land that William Worley received as one of the heirs of Zachariah Worley. May 1845. (Pp. 394-395)

John B. Gullick to Jonathan H. Gullick a negro man. 12 May 1845. (Pp. 395-396)

Isham Beasley to David Burford a tract of land. 31 March 1845. (Pp. 397-398)

Burrell R. Land to William Robinson. 1845. (Pp. 398-399)

DEED BOOK R

N. B. Burdine to A. S. Bains some personal property. 19 May 1845. (P. 399)

Creed Penn to John S. Page 52 acres. 20 May 1845. (Pp. 500-501)

Meret House to Agnes House his interest in the land belonging to the wards of William House deceased. 8 February 1845. (P. 401)

John Conditt to B. J. Vaden. 23 May 1845. (P. 402)

Samuel R. Goss to Josiah Hallum a sorrell horse. 24 May 1845. (P. 403)

Andrew Shy and James W. Shy to Gregory Moore 25½ acres. 9 May 1845. (Pp. 403-404)

L. D. Grisham to Henry Piper some personal property. 1845. (Pp. 404-405)

Matthew Harper to M. W. Sloan the land that he received from the estate of his father Matthew Harper. 3 June 1845. (Pp. 405-406)

Thomas Marshall Certificate. 2 June 1845. (P. 406)

Joseph Bowman to Daniel Robison his interest in the estate of William Reaves. 9 May 1845. (P. 407)

Laura Gwaltney to Paul S. H. Walker his interest in the estate of Leodicia Sykes. 28 March 1845. (Pp. 407-408)

John Stevens to Leonard H. Cardwell a tract of land on the Cumberland River. 17 December 1844. (Pp. 408-409)

George L. Swan to James G. Swan some livestock. 18 June 1845. (Pp. 409-410)

Samuel B. Chambers to C. G. McClelin a negro woman. 18 June 1845. (P. 411)

William Tyree, David Tyree, Sarah Tyree, Elizabeth Tyree, and William Tyree to Isaac Bates a negro woman. 21 February 1820. (P. 411)

Sheriff John Bailey to Martin W. Sloan a tract of land. 1845. (Pp. 412-414)

Stephen Stafford to William W. Cunningham 72 acres. 30 June 1845. (Pp. 414-415)

Jacob Gray and William Gray to James M. Sitton, all residents of Lincoln County, Missouri the interest they have in the estate of Jacob Burrus. 4 January 1845. (Pp. 415-416)

Martin W. Sloan and others to John Ballard 50 acres. 30 June 1845. (P. 416)

James M. Sitton, Matilda Sitton, and George W. Gray of Missouri appoint William Sitton of Missouri as their attorney. 24 February 1845. (Pp. 417-418)

DEED BOOK R

Meret House to Matthew W. Morris a tract of land on Mulherin's Creek. 27 June 1845. (Pp. 418-419)

James M. Williams, Randolph Lewis and wife Lucretia to Robert Harper 125 acres. 23 January 1845. (Pp. 419-420)

Meret House to Agnes House a negro boy. 2 July 1845. (Pp. 420-421)

Elijah Moore and Harriet F. Moore to John W. Estes their interest in 200 acres. 30 December 1844. (P. 421)

John Walker and Prudence Walker his wife and Ann W. Archer to John W. Estes a tract of land. 1845. (Pp. 421-422)

Willis L. Reeves certification. 1845. (P. 422)

John Campsey to W. M. Price. 3 July 1845. (P. 423)

William Coffee, Joel Coffee, and Joshua Coffee to John Lamberson their interest in a tract of land in which Cynthia Coffee has a life estate. 1844. (P. 424)

John Lamberson to Joel Coffee a tract of land. 2 March 1844. (Pp. 424-425)

Samuel A. Armstead and John H. Armstead from Henry Mann a tract of land. 1845. (Pp. 425-426)

Jacob Belcher to Samuel Allison a tract of land on Mulherin's Creek. 1845. (Pp. 426-427)

Jefferson Rowland to Robert W. Knight 290 acres. 7 July 1845. (P. 427)

Samson Dickerson to Sampson McClelin. 7 July 1845. (P. 428)

Sheriff John Bailey to Milton Draper a tract of land. 1845. (Pp. 428-429)

Hugh B. Robb to Sampson McClelin a sorrel mare. 12 July 1845. (P. 430)

Ivy Bush to James M. Shepherd 87 acres. 3 July 1844. (P. 431)

George Read to George Nash a crop of tobacco. 24 July 1845. (P. 432)

John McGee to David Prowell a tract of land on Mulherin's Creek. 3 May 1839. (P. 433)

Elizabeth Gregory to Pleasant Gold a tract of land. July 1845. (Pp. 433-434)

William Moore to Josiah R. Smith and John W. Paty six acres. 4 April 1845. (P. 434)

DEED BOOK S

Sheriff John Bailey to William Alexander. June 1845. (Pp. 1-2)

Alexander W. Stimson to John Farmer a tract of land on the Caney Fork. 7 November 1840. (Pp. 2-3)

Richard Britton, guardian of Abraham and James Britton of Madison County, Missouri and legatees of Samuel Britton, appoint Josiah Anthony of Sumner County as his attorney. 13 March 1845. (P. 3)

Elijah Creal to George W. Catron a crop of tobacco. July 1845. (Pp. 4-5)

E. Irwin to Marshall B. Duncan a tract of land formerly belonging to William Hall. 9 May 1845. (P. 5)

Bartlett James to John R. James his interest in the estate of his father, Bartlett James, Sr. 4 August 1845. (P. 6)

Robert West to Miles F. West a tract of 35 acres. 25 July 1844. (Pp. 6-7)

James West to Miles F. West a tract of land on Defeated Creek. 25 July 1844. (P. 7)

Thomas Snoddy to Gregory Moore a crop of tobacco. 5 August 1845. (Pp. 8-9)

John C. Parker to Henry Morgan two tracts of land. December 1844. (P. 9)

Winney Martin, Anny Martin, and James Kerble agreement. 1 January 1845. (P. 10)

William Vaden and Elias Johns, executors of Benjamin Johns, to John Harper a tract of land. 14 August 1841. (Pp. 10-11)

Thomas Harper, Benjamin Harper, Rachel McGaffee, John McGuffee, Nevels H. Smith, and Rebecca Smith to John Harper 390 acres. 16 July 1841. (Pp. 11-12)

Andrew G. Pickett to John H. Bedford a tract of land in the town of Carthage. 11 August 1845. (Pp. 12-13)

Joseph Holmes of Montgomery County, Tennessee to Green W. Shaw a tract of land. 10 November 1841. (P. 13)

Joseph Holmes to Green W. Shaw 87 acres. 3 October 1842. (Pp. 13-14)

Green W. Shaw to Duncan Johnson 87 acres. 13 October 1844. (P. 14)

Gregory D. Burns to James McClanahan a crop of tobacco. 13 August 1845. (P. 15)

Abraham Lee to James McClanahan. 18 August 1845. (Pp. 15-16)

DEED BOOK S

Samuel Caplinger to Tanday W. Fitts 540 acres. 12 February 1842. (P. 16)

John G. Anderson to Sampson McClelin. 19 August 1845. (P. 17)

Samuel Cunningham to Enock Gann my interest in the estate of my father James Cunningham. 21 August 1845. (P. 17)

Michael Halmantoller to Allen Harvel 96 acres. 20 March 1845. (P. 18)

Jabez Burton to David A. Tyree 61 acres. 18 August 1845. (Pp. 18-19)

David A. Tyree to John Reeves 61 acres. 23 August 1845. (P. 19)

John Kittle to Thomas W. Page a crop of tobacco. 25 August 1845. (P. 20)

William Eden to William Arnett a crop of tobacco. 23 August 1845. (Pp. 20-21)

David Honeycut and Jesse White to William W. Cunningham a tract of land. 18 August 1845. (P. 21)

Daniel Seay to James Gill a tract of land in the 18th District. 25 August 1845. (P. 22)

Thomas Stafford to Gunnery Wilbourn a tract of land on Dixon's Creek. 9 March 1841. (Pp. 22-23)

John Stafford to James McClanahan. 25 August 1845. (P. 23)

Henry L. Day to James Climer a crop of tobacco. 29 August 1845. (P. 24)

Michael Shoemake to Henry Beasley a tract of land on Hurricane Creek. 2 March 1844. (Pp. 24-25)

William Gregory and Bethel Gregory to Joseph Bowman a crop of tobacco. 28 August 1845. (Pp. 25-26)

Cyrus Watson to William Stafford a crop of tobacco. 29 August 1845. (P. 26)

Presley Boley indebtedness to William Craighead. 30 August 1845. (Pp. 26-27)

Steven R. Wills to Edward R. Wills a tract of 158 acres. 30 August 1845. (Pp. 27-28)

Matthew Carter to Sampson McClelin a crop of tobacco. 29 August 1845. (P. 28)

Jordan Beasley to Milton Haynes a crop of tobacco. 1 September 1845. (Pp. 28-29)

James Uhles to Major A. Beasley a crop of tobacco. 1 September 1845. (P. 29)

DEED BOOK S

Thomas A. Frohauk to A. J. Baker a crop of tobacco. 25 August 1845. (P. 30)

Jabez Burton to Orville Green a crop of tobacco. 4 September 1845. (P. 31)

Henry D. Flippin to Sylvester H. Harkreder. 1845. (Pp. 31-32)

Alfred D. Smith to Thomas Gregory a crop of tobacco. 8 September 1845. (Pp. 32-33)

John Smallen to Thomas Gregory a crop of tobacco. 8 September 1845. (P. 33)

Isaac Mitchell to John Williams a crop of tobacco. 8 September 1845. (P. 33)

William Grant to Charles McMurry. 8 September 1845. (P. 34)

Swan Thompson to William E. Jones a town lot in the town of Carthage. 6 September 1845. (P. 35)

Obediah Woodson, Sr. and John J. Turner to Thomas Woodson a crop of tobacco. 29 August 1845. (P. 35)

Johnson Anderson to Sampson McClelin a crop of tobacco. 11 September 1845. (P. 36)

John Turner to William W. Harris 84½ acres. 25 August 1845. (Pp. 36-37)

Jesse Meacham, Sr. to G. W. Meacham. 17 September 1845. (P. 37)

The heirs of Benjamin Roe to James Rowland a tract of land. September 1845. (Pp. 37-38)

Alexander James to John Stewart his interest in the estate of his father Bartlett James, Sr. 20 September 1845. (P. 38)

Ezekiel Hale to Thomas W. Wootten a crop of tobacco. 23 September 1845. (Pp. 38-39)

Harris Gresham to William W. Cunningham a tract of land on Beasley's Bend. 22 September 1845. (Pp. 39-40)

James B. Conditt to Henry Strother a crop of tobacco. 22 September 1845. (P. 40)

Oliver Cartwright to Joel L. Worley a tract of land on Defeated Creek. 16 September 1845. (P. 41)

John Turner to James Norris a tract of land on Round Lick Creek. 25 August 1845. (Pp. 41-42)

Phillip H. Mitchell to James H. Vaughan a negro slave. 30 September 1845. (P. 42)

Archibald Lindsey and wife Rhoda to Summer Decker their interest in a tract of land. 1841. (Pp. 42-43)

DEED BOOK S

Philip H. Mitchell to James H. Vaughan a tract of land belonging to the estate of Frederick N. Mitchell. 30 September 1845. (Pp. 43-44)

Samuel Caplinger to Benjamin Hensley 50 acres. 21 March 1844. (P. 44)

Willis W. Oldham to Thomas Gregory a crop of tobacco. 1 October 1845. (P. 45)

William Hall to William Tillman a crop of tobacco. 9 October 1845. (P. 45)

Charles Featherstone to P. Duffy a crop of tobacco. 7 October 1845. (P. 46)

William Petty to his only son Stephen Petty 60 acres. 4 October 1845. (P. 46)

Loyd P. Coggin to Henry S. McDaniel 110 acres. 14 February 1845. (P. 47)

Green Wright to his daughter Eliza A. Carter, wife of William Carter, of DeSoto County, Mississippi a negro slave. 25 April 1845. (Pp. 47-48)

Green Wright to his daughter Mary A. Brooks, wife of Charles Brooks, a negro slave. 25 April 1845. (P. 48)

Reuben Hinton to James McClanahan. 17 October 1845. (Pp. 48-49)

Joseph W. Allen of New Orleans to William Farley a tract of land in the town of Carthage. 13 August 1845. (P. 49)

Gilbert Ashlock and wife Nancy to Lucy Self their interest in the estate of Willis Hodges. 20 October 1845. (Pp. 49-50)

William Hart to William B. Campbell a tract of land. 14 October 1845. (P. 50)

William Summerset to P. Duffy several items. 27 October 1845. (P. 51)

Leonard Lamberson of Cannon County to the heirs of Conrood Lamberson a tract of land on Smith's Fork. 17 March 1836. (Pp. 51-52)

John Conger to Joshua Conger a tract of land on the Caney Fork. 17 January 1842. (Pp. 52-53)

Armstead Moore to William Hart. 31 October 1845. (P. 53)

Thomas C. Marchbanks to William Young a negro slave. 30 January 1845. (Pp. 54-55)

Robert Marley to Lewis Franklin 35 acres. 3 November 1845. (P. 55)

Robert Marley to John Maggart. 1845. (Pp. 55-56)

DEED BOOK S

John Maggart to Robert Marley 181 acres. 3 November 1845. (P. 56)

James Philips to Clibourn Matthews 50 acres. 28 December 1844. (P. 57)

John B. Tinis and wife Ameliza to Marshall B. Duncan their interest in the estate of William Hall. 28 October 1845. (Pp. 57-58)

Isaac Mungle to Allen Mungle and his mother Nelly and his sister Sally 145 acres for love and affection. 3 August 1844. (Pp. 58-59)

James McMurry to Martin McMurry his interest in 300 acres. 1 November 1845. (P. 60)

Martin McMurry to Thomas Woodmore 100 acres. 9 December 1843. (Pp. 60-61)

Andrew G. Pickett to Jeremiah Jamison some slaves. 10 October 1845. (Pp. 61-62)

Branch Nunley, Boling D. High and wife Martha to Elizabeth Buckley a tract of land on Peyton's Creek. 6 July 1843. (Pp. 62-63)

Richard B. Hall to Thomas M. P. Hall his interest in the estate of William Hall and the dower of Malinda Hall. 7 November 1845. (P. 63)

Taylor Whitley to Jabez Burton. 17 November 1845. (P. 64)

Philip F. McClanahan to Bassil G. Carman a tract of land on Goose Creek. 18 November 1845. (Pp. 64-65)

A. S. Burns to Alfred Clark and Robert Pope 57 acres. 20 November 1845. (Pp. 65-66)

Alfred Clark and Robert Pope to B. M. Bains a crop of tobacco. 20 November 1845. (Pp. 66-67)

Luther Furlong to William Johnson a crop of tobacco. 27 November 1845. (P. 67)

Edward Featherstone to Thomas Marshall a crop of tobacco. 14 November 1845. (P. 68)

John Right to Henry B. McDonald. 3 November 1845. (Pp. 68-69)

William A. Herod to G. C. Matlock some personal property. 17 January 1843. (P. 69)

Drury D. Claraday to John H. Bedford 192 acres. 12 December 1845. (Pp. 69-70)

Division of the lands of William Hall. Heirs: Malinda Hall, California Dunkan and husband M. B., Larena Tillman and husband William, William T. Hall, Eleaster Ervin, Richard T. Hall, Ann E. Tiree and husband John, Susan Campbell, Thomas

DEED BOOK S

Hall, Malinda Rowland, Faleena Hall and husband T. P. D. 9 May 1845. (Pp. 71-72)

Allen C. Winfree to Benjamin Winfree one acre. 3 April 1845. (P. 73)

William Dillon to David G. Mason of Shelby County, Alabama a negro girl. 13 December 1845. (P. 73)

Thomas Carman to William Mason a negro boy. 16 December 1845. (P. 74)

Joseph W. Armstrong to John H. Bedford his interest in the estate of his father John B. Armstrong. 18 December 1845. (Pp. 74-75)

Josiah Marshall to B. R. Noles four acres. 24 November 1845. (P. 75)

Henry B. McDonald to Hawkins Heflin 40 acres. 19 February 1844. (Pp. 75-76)

Patterson Hannah and Edny Hannah to William P. Malone a negro woman. 17 November 1845. (P. 76)

William M. Cook of Roanoke County certification. 17 November 1845. (P. 77)

Thomas Bailiff to Hawkins Heflin 50 acres. 20 December 1844. (P. 77)

John Reeves to William Litchford 90 acres. 21 June 1844. (Pp. 77-78)

A. S. Bains to Calvin Pope 100 acres. 10 December 1845. (P. 78)

H. D. Flippin to Tilman B. Flippin two negroes. 17 December 1845. (P. 79)

Thomas Woodmore to Henry D. Day 100 acres. 22 November 1845. (P. 79)

Alexander Dillard to H. B. McDonald several slaves. 16 December 1845. (P. 80)

Robert D. Hughes of Wilson County to Andrew G. Pickett his interest in the estate of Thomas J. Hubbard. 18 December 1845. (P. 80)

James W. Stepp to Larkin Payne 126 acres. 17 December 1845. (P. 81)

Reuben Hays to John Enock a tract of land. 22 May 1845. (P. 82)

S. D. McMurry to James W. Stepp 126 acres. 18 December 1845. (Pp. 82-83)

Josiah Marshall to Thomas Carman four slaves. 22 September 1843. (P. 83)

Thomas Williams to G. W. Catron. 1845. (Pp. 83-84)

DEED BOOK S

Howel T. Rucks to Oscar S. Ewing 16 acres. 9 August 1845. (P. 84)

William P. Hughes and John W. Hughes to Edward B. Tuck 198 acres. 21 August 1845. (P. 85)

E. B. Pickett to William Denny a man slave. 2 January 1846. (P. 86)

D. M. Johnson to Benjamin Winfree some personal property. 31 December 1845. (Pp. 86-87)

Benjamin Pierce and Harriett T. Turner, husband and wife enter into a contract. 30 December 1845. (P. 87)

William W. Cunningham to John A. Sloan a tract of land. 5 January 1844. (Pp. 88-89)

John Lipscomb to Mosby Lipscomb a tract of land. 12 March 1845. (P. 89)

David Highers to George Highers 78 acres. 4 November 1845. (Pp. 89-90)

Josiah Highers to James Barnett a tract of land. 15 April 1845. (P. 90)

James Barnett to Josiah Highers a tract of land on Plunkett's Creek. 15 April 1843. (P. 91)

Lipscomb P. McMurry, Vincent McMurry, James G. McMurry, Thomas W. McMurry, Elizabeth McMurry, Sally McMurry, William McMurry, and Archibald D. McMurry, heirs of Samuel W. McMurry, to Lipscomb P. McMurry a tract of land. 5 January 1846. (Pp. 91-92)

Elijah Banks, Sr. to William B. Perkins a tract of land on the Cumberland River. 9 September 1836. (Pp. 92-93)

Martin W. Sloan and Samuel F. Coker to William B. Campbell and others a tract of land. 13 November 1845. (Pp. 93-94)

Abner A. Perkins to William B. Perkins 36 acres. 5 October 1836. (P. 94)

William B. Perkins to Thomas Carman a tract of land on the Cumberland River. 5 January 1846. (P. 95)

Henry Beasley to Milton Haynie a negro woman. 7 January 1846. (P. 95)

Henry Beasley to Ellis Beasley some slaves. 7 January 1846. (P. 96)

Milton Haynie to Thomas Carman some slaves. 7 January 1846. (P. 96)

Elizabeth Boze to her son Joseph C. McGee a boy slave. 17 January 1846. (Pp. 96-97)

Hiram McGee to William Parris 32 acres. 8 January 1846. (P. 97)

DEED BOOK S

Ellis Beasley to Henry Beasley 160 acres. 10 January 1846. (Pp. 97-98)

Tennessee Erwin to William Johnson a crop of tobacco. 23 January 1846. (P. 98)

Samuel T. Coker to C. J. Coker a negro boy. 13 September 1845. (P. 99)

John McKinnis to John Nickson a crop of tobacco. 26 January 1846. (P. 99)

Stephen R. Willis to Lemuel Loyd a negro woman. 26 January 1846. (P. 100)

Susan Perry and Warren Perry to Avery Hester a sorrel horse. 26 January 1846. (P. 100)

Gideon Gifford to Flemin Stubblefield a tract of land on Goose Creek. 27 January 1846. (P. 101)

Flemin Stubblefield to Eli Gammon two negro boys. 20 December 1844. (P. 101)

Flemin Stubblefield to Gideon Gifford a negro woman. 9 November 1845. (P. 102)

Archibald M. Debow and wife Nancy G. of Sumner County to Gideon Gifford 50 acres. 29 March 1843. (P. 102)

William L. Munday certification. 29 March 1843. (P. 103)

George W. Ahart to Jeremiah E. Reasonover 21 acres. 1844. (Pp. 103-104)

Henry V. Nichols to James Trousdale 180 acres. 30 January 1846. (P. 104)

William H. Morgan of Davidson County to Seay, Bedford, & Company a tract of land in the town of Rome. 20 December. (Pp. 104-105)

William H. Browning to Ebenezer M. Frazer. 10 January 1846. (P. 105)

James C. Williams to Anderson Williams 50 acres. 2 February 1846. (P. 106)

James M. Estes to Henry Dowdy several items. 6 February 1846. (Pp. 106-107)

John Powell to John H. Rodgers a tract of land on Mulherin's Creek. 10 September 1846. (P. 107)

John Powell to John H. Rodgers 65 acres. 10 September 1845. (P. 108)

Andrew G. Pickett to John McClaran. 1846. (Pp. 108-110)

Gideon B. Wray to William Duvall a tract of land in the town of Carthage. 16 February 1846. (P. 110)

W. M. Price to John S. Page. 1846. (P. 111)

DEED BOOK S

Yancy Blackwell to William Tunstall a negro woman. 26 December 1845. (Pp. 111-112)

Enock Gann to Robert Gann his interest in the estate of James Cunningham. 25 February 1846. (P. 112)

Edward C. Sweatt and wife Sarah A. and John H. Tuggle to Daniel Seay their interest in the estate of Thomas Tuggle. Other heirs are James (Champ) and wife Mary. 9 February 1846. (Pp. 112-113)

Will Young to John Richardson a negro boy. 2 March 1846. (P. 113)

William Martin to Colly Stepp a tract of land. 3 August 1829. (Pp. 113-114)

Joseph Robinson and John Robinson to Levi Squires. 12 March 1831. (Pp. 114-115)

William Martin to his son Wilson Y. Martin a tract of land on Dixon's Creek. 10 January 1846. (Pp. 115-116)

Willis Dowell to Frances Dowell 35 acres. 10 November 1844. (P. 116)

James Tubb, Manson Brien, John S. Brien to William and Thomas Washer 200 acres. 15 September 1842. (P. 117)

Malachi Shoulders to P. W. Cage 131 acres. 18 June 1842. (Pp. 117-118)

David G. Mason of Shelby County, Alabama to William Dillon 94½ acres. 11 December 1845. (Pp. 118-119)

David Prowell to George Baker a tract of land on Mulherin's Creek. 16 March 1846. (P. 119)

Alexander Dillard to M. Brockett a tract of land. 3 April 1846. (P. 120)

William Goad of Craven County, North Carolina to Jeremiah Coggin a tract of land on the Caney Fork. 9 December 1828. (Pp. 120-121)

Agnes Williams to James R. Jones 80 acres. 12 March 1846. (Pp. 121-122)

Matilda Prowell to Mathew Harper her interest in 347 acres she is to receive at the death of Mary Harper. 1846. (P. 122)

Peter Porter to William R. Betty his interest a jack belonging to James S. Porter. 2 April 1846. (Pp. 122-123)

John Bailey to W. W. Bailey 56 acres. 7 April 1846. (P. 123)

James Taylor to Sampson McClelin a negro boy. 7 April 1846. (P. 123)

John H. Bowen to William Hart two negroes. 27 April 1844. (P. 124)

DEED BOOK S

Elum A. Erwin to N. C. Winston a negro boy. 6 April 1846. (P. 124)

(Pages are misnumbered)

Mathew Petross to Robert Trawick 85 acres. 1 September 1840. (P. 225)

James Green to William Herring 50 acres. 3 September 1844. (P. 226)

James W. Morgan and wife Caroline of Lynchburg, Virginia to William B. Campbell a tract of land. November 1845. (Pp. 226-227)

David Prowell bound to James Tuggle. 31 December 1844. (P. 228)

Thomas Rutherford (Weatherford) to Clabourn Hall nine acres. 1 July 1841. (P. 229)

George W. Jones and Nancy Jones of Williamson County, Illinois to her children, to wit, Hiram T. White and Mary J. Furlong, both of Williamson County her interest in the estate of Samuel T. White. March 1846. (Pp. 229-230)

William Wilson to Willis Wilson a slave. 1846. (P. 230)

George Highers to Moses Craig a tract of land. 16 April 1846. (Pp. 230-231)

John Farmer to David K. Timberlake a tract of land on the Caney Fork. 16 April 1846. (Pp. 231-232)

Sheriff W. W. Bailey to Moses Reaves. April 1846. (Pp. 232-233)

Frances Dowell to Willis Dowell 30 acres. 4 November 1844. (P. 233)

Bartley Kyle to James Upton 15¼ acres. 2 September 1825. (P. 233)

Bartlett Kyle to John Moore a negro girl. 2 January 1838. (P. 234)

Bartley Kyle to John Moore a negro boy. 22 February 1836. (P. 234)

Ira B. Cowan to W. McClain a slave. 25 January 1846. (P. 235)

John Moore to William B. Whitley a boy slave. 20 April 1846. (P. 235)

Fielding Kitrell to B. S. Cardwell a woman slave. 19 September 1845. (P. 235)

Isham Kitrell to Elijah Haynie a slave. 1 February 1842. (P. 236)

James R. Toney to John Haley. 1846. (P. 236)

DEED BOOK S

James Trousdale to Polly A. Trousdale a tract of land. 22 April 1846. (P. 237)

William Stalcup, administrator of James Brown, to Charles S. Tate a negro girl. 30 January 1846. (Pp. 237-238)

James Rowland to William C. Roe a tract of land. 15 March 1846. (P. 238)

John H. Burford to John Bridges. 1 April 1843. (Pp. 238-239)

John Bridges to John H. Burford 92¼ acres. 12 January 1846. (P. 239)

William Vaden to Rufus Perry a tract of land on the Cumberland River. 6 November 1843. (P. 240)

Deana Reaves of Wilson County to William Reaves her dower. 31 January 1845. (Pp. 240-241)

Milton Apple to Thomas S. Elms several items. January 1846. (P. 241)

H. H. Carman to James B. Duffee a negro woman. 6 April 1846. (P. 242)

M. Y. Brockett to Ross Webb a negro boy. 4 April 1846. (P. 242)

Jacob Ammonette to James H. Ammonette a tract of land. August 1845. (Pp. 242-243)

Abraham Goad to James Bishop 120 acres. 20 August 1842. (P. 243)

Thomas T. Terry to ( ) ( ) his interest in the estate of Thomas Terry. 1844. (Pp. 243-244)

Neal Goad to Smith Gregory a tract of land. 1 January 1829. (Pp. 244-245)

Andrew G. Pickett to John B. Hughes and others 405 acres. 22 April 1846. (Pp. 245-246)

Andrew G. Pickett to Jeremiah Jamison his interest in a tract of land. 3 May 1846. (Pp. 246-247)

John Wilcut to Brite Mitchell a tract of land. 30 April 1845. (Pp. 248-249)

Howell T. Rucks and wife Darthula to William T. Williams a tract of land. 6 February 1845. (P. 249)

John J. Coleman to Edmond James 62 acres. 19 May 1846. (P. 250)

James Rollings to Obediah Jenkins a tract of land on Hickman's Creek. 27 August 1845. (P. 250)

Flemming Stubblefield to Archibald M. Debow a tract of land. 30 March 1846. (Pp. 251-252)

The administrators of John Tubb to John H. Ammonette a tract of land. 28 April 1846. (P. 252)

DEED BOOK S

Elijah Toney of Jackson County, Alabama to William Duvall his interest in a tract of land. 1846. (Pp. 252-253)

Bartlett James to John H. Newbell several items. June 1846. (P. 253)

William B. Whitley, administrator of Benjamin James, to John T. Winfrey a tract of land in the 15th District. 1 June 1846. (Pp. 253-254)

J. R. James to John Buckner 60 acres. 1 June 1846. (Pp. 254-255)

Ira B. Cowan to Young Marley. 5 June 1846. (P. 255)

John Beckman to Samuel T. Coker 292 acres. 1 June 1846. (P. 256)

Samuel P. Howard to Allen S. Watkins a tract of land in the town of Carthage. 15 May 1846. (P. 257)

Sheriff John Bailey to Frances Dowell. 1846. (P. 257)

W. C. Hubbard to Jacob Hubbard and George Hubbard his power of attorney in settling the estate of Sally Hubbard. 24 February 1846. (P. 257)

Thomas Smith to Armstead G. Harris his interest in the estate of Larkin Smith. 5 March 1845. (P. 258)

Sheriff John Bailey to Marmaduke Mason a tract of land. 10 June 1846. (Pp. 258-259)

Levi Squires to John Squires a tract of land on Mulherin's Creek. 2 December 1831. (Pp. 359-360)

James D. Bennett to M. P. Hall his interest in the estate of William Hall and the dower of Melinda Hall. 22 June 1846. (P. 260)

Polly Goad to John Johnson 90 acres. 18 April 1844. (Pp. 260-261)

Henry L. Moores to Joel Coffee a tract of land. 25 June 1846. (P. 261)

Lot Hazard to Timothy Walton a tract of land. 1846. (Pp. 261-262)

John Squires to Campbell Crutchfield a tract of land on Mulherin's Creek. 1 October 1845. (P. 262)

Elias Pearce to Sampson McClelin a tract of land. 2 July 1846. (Pp. 262-263)

Jason Winchester to Joseph B. Waymouth a negro woman. July 1846. (P. 263)

Organ, Alfred, and George Maricle, children of George Maricle, to James Shelton a tract of land. July 1846. (Pp. 263-264)

DEED BOOK S

C. E. Avrett to E. P. Law a negro girl. June 1846. (P. 264)

Joseph Moses to Thomas Carman. 6 July 1846. (P. 264)

Samuel Fitzpatrick to Joseph Mitchell 100 acres. 3 July 1846. (P. 265)

Lot Hazard to William E. Jones 320 acres. 29 July 1846. (P. 265)

Daniel T. Lake to Caleb Carman 19½ acres. 16 February 1846. (P. 266)

R. D. Allison and James Barnett to Little B. Coleman 100 acres. August 1845. (P. 266)

Frances Kerby to William Tunstall three negroes. November 1845. (P. 267)

William Dillon to Elizabeth Kyle a tract of land on the Cumberland River. 8 June 1846. (P. 267)

W. M. Price, executor of Mark Dyson, to John Payne. 9 June 1846. (P. 268)

Joseph D. Lucas to Timothy Hankins. 4 July 1846. (P. 268)

Robert Mitchell to Mary Ann Hickman several items for love and affection. 1846. (P. 268)

B. R. Owen to John D. Owen 259 acres. 1 July 1846. (P. 269)

Ruth Jones to her daughter Cary Haynes 16 acres. 16 July 1846. (P. 269)

Frederick Wyett to James Wyett a tract of 50 acres. 3 January 1846. (P. 270)

Milton Ford of Alabama to J. T. Stokes 40 acres. 1831. (P. 270)

Milton Ford to J. T. Stokes a tract of land. 24 December 1831. (P. 271)

James A. Young certification. 1846. (P. 272)

Milton Ford to J. T. Stokes a tract of land on Smith's Fork. 24 December 1831. (P. 272)

James A. Young certification. 1846. (P. 273)

Flemming Stubblefield to Richard Averett a negro girl. 29 October 1845. (P. 273)

Lot Hazard to John Maggart a negro woman. 16 November 1841. (P. 273)

William Shields to his daughter Malvina V. Hogg a negro boy. 24 March 1846. (P. 273)

Tilman B. Flippin to Johnson Underwood one fourth of an acre. May 1846. (P. 273)

DEED BOOK S

John O. Cosby to William Tunstall a tract of land. 12 July 1846. (Pp. 273-274)

Elam Russell to David Smith 75 acres. 31 March 1846. (P. 274)

James Shelton to Davidson Johnson a slave. 28 July 1846. (P. 275)

Abraham C. Lee to Thomas Tunstall a crop of tobacco. 28 July 1846. (P. 275)

James Uhles to Major A. Beasley a crop of tobacco. 30 July 1846. (Pp. 275-276)

Reuben Hayes to Thomas W. Page a tract of 50 acres. 9 October 1845. (P. 276)

Andrew Allison to George C. Allen the interest of his wife Rebecca in the estate of Robert Allen. 28 May 1846. (P. 277)

James G. Allen of New Orleans and Joseph W. Allen of New Orleans to G. C. Allen a tract of land belonging to Robert Allen deceased. 1846. (P. 277)

Alletha Allen to G. C. Allen her interest in the estate of her husband Robert Allen. 6 February 1846. (P. 278)

William H. Jones and wife Elizabeth, Frederick Starnes and wife Polly, D. C. (   ) and wife Nancy to T. D. Exum their interest in the estate of Joseph Exum. June 1846. (Pp. 278-279)

Thomas Palmer to Charles T. Coker a crop of tobacco. 4 August 1846. (P. 279)

James Shoulders to Hugh McKinney a tract of land. 4 May 1846. (Pp. 279-280)

George Bains, Elizabeth Bains, Edward Carter and wife Lavinia, Thomas Butler and wife Lydia, William Bains, Samuel Bains, Mary M. Bains, A. S. Bains, and B. M. Bains to B. M. Bains their interest in a tract of land. 20 January 1846. (Pp. 279-280)

Reuben Hays to Mathew H. Ward 120 acres. 3 August 1846. (Pp. 281-282)

John Minton to Charles Thompson 68 acres. 5 August 1846. (P. 282)

Burton G. Ferrell to David G. Shepherd a tract of land in the 16th District. 6 October 1845. (Pp. 282-283)

Orville Green and W. B. Moore, the former of Smith County and the latter of Missouri to James High a negro woman. 3 June 1846. (Pp. 283-284)

William Payne to William B. Young. 7 July 1846. (Pp. 284-285)

DEED BOOK S

Oscar F. Purnell to G. G. Dillard. 8 August 1846. (P. 285)

Henry S. Day to James Climer a crop of tobacco. 12 August 1846. (P. 286)

William T. Williams to William E. Jones a tract of land in the town of Carthage. August 1846. (Pp. 286-287)

Bethel J. Gregory to Adam C. Perkins a crop of tobacco. 16 August 1846. (P. 287)

John Bell to Thomas J. Noles. August 1846. (P. 288)

James M. Winfrey to D. H. Farmer one acre. January 1842. (P. 288)

Freeman Leath to William Kerby a crop of tobacco. 24 August 1846. (P. 289)

John Conditt to David L. Shepherd a tract of land on the Caney Fork. October 1845. (Pp. 289-290)

James Harper to Nathan Ward a tract of land. August 1846. (P. 290)

William Reese to John Stafford a crop of tobacco. 20 August 1846. (P. 291)

Lot Hazard bound to William T. Williams. 1846. (Pp. 291-292)

James M. Shepherd to Ezekiel West a tract of land on the Cumberland River. August 1846. (P. 292)

James Ballinger to James Barrott a crop of tobacco. 28 August 1846. (P. 293)

James Ballinger to Thomas Ballinger a tract of land on Mulherin's Creek. 25 August 1846. (Pp. 293-294)

James Ballinger to James Barnett several slaves. 27 August 1846. (Pp. 294-295)

James Ballinger, having the great misfortune to lose his companion, to his children James Barrott and wife Nancy, Thomas A. Frohock and wife Sarah A., Thomas Ballinger, Franklin, Meredith, and Grandchildren Harris B. and Elizabeth Frances, the children of his deceased son Peter Ballinger. 1846. (Pp. 295-296)

Thomas A. Frohock and wife Sarah A. to James Barrott several slaves. 27 August 1846. (Pp. 296-297)

Alfred Read to Thomas J. Knowles a crop of tobacco. August 1846. (Pp. 297-298)

Mason Walker to Johnson Underwood a tract of land in the town of Rome. 24 August 1846. (P. 298)

John O. Pope to Johnson Underwood. 1846. (P. 299)

William D. Nash to George Nash. 4 September 1846. (P. 300)

DEED BOOK S

Thomas J. Jones and others to William and Richard Alexander. 1846. (P. 301)

William R. Gregory to Drewry A. West a tract of land. 5 September 1846. (Pp. 302-303)

Richard Shoulders to Christian Boston a crop of tobacco. 26 July 1846. (P. 303)

Matthew Worley of Crittenden County, Kentucky to Leander Hughes 150 acres, formerly owned by Zachariah Worley deceased. 14 May 1846. (P. 304)

Rachael Bowman to Joseph Bowman a negro girl. 24 February 1846. (Pp. 304-305)

William Gregory to Adam C. Perkins a crop of tobacco. 5 September 1846. (P. 305)

James Clark to Warren Walker a crop of tobacco. 29 August 1846. (P. 306)

Thomas Williams to G. G. Dillard a crop of corn. 7 September 1846. (Pp. 306-307)

Isaac Kitrell to Edwin Kitrell a negro man. 13 August 1846. (P. 307)

Samuel Black to William W. Cunningham a crop of tobacco. 5 September 1846. (Pp. 307-308)

Braddock Beasley to Joel Gregory. 21 August 1846. (Pp. 308-309)

John McFall to Willie Denny a tract of land on Mulherin's Creek. 3 November 1847. (P. 309)

John Harley to James R. Toney a negro girl. September 1846. (P. 310)

Henry Beasley to Mary Hoppel, formerly Mary Tipton, of Alabama a negro girl. 1 October 1846. (P. 310)

Jackson Adams, Patsy Adams, Larkin Gyger, Nancy Gyger, all of Lawrence County, Indiana and heirs of Wilson Adams, to Moses Woodruff their power of attorney. 1846. (Pp. 310-312)

Joel Bates to V. R. Bradford. 1846. (Pp. 312-313)

William B. Crank to Samuel B. Tinsley his interest in the estate of his maternal grandfather Booker Parrish. 15 September 1846. (P. 313)

Stephen Stafford to William W. Cunningham a tract of land on Dixon's Creek. 9 September 1846. (P. 314)

John Shoulders to Milton Haynie. 29 August 1846. (P. 315)

James B. Conditt to Leonard H. Cardwell a crop of tobacco. 7 September 1846. (P. 315)

Edwin Whitmore to Allison G. Cummins of Jackson County

DEED BOOK S

his power of attorney. 10 October 1846. (P. 316)

Stephen Mann to Robert Warren a tract of land on the Caney Fork. 5 October 1846. (P. 316)

William Herrod to Charles S. Long 140 acres. 18 August 1846. (P. 317)

John Beckman to David H. Nichols 28 acres. 31 August 1846. (Pp. 317-318)

Walter A. Beasley to Henry Beasley a tract of land. 9 September 1846. (P. 318)

Isaac Bates to Thomas Bailiff a tract of land. 5 September 1846. (Pp. 318-319)

Robert Marshall to James Climire 25 acres. 27 November 1845. (P. 319)

Robert Burton to William Alexander a tract of 65 acres. 30 August 1846. (P. 320)

Leander Hughes to Benjamin C. Davis 150 acres. September 1846. (P. 321)

Isaac Bates to William Bates a tract of land on Smith's Fork. 5 September 1846. (Pp. 321-322)

Isaac Bates to James Bates his part of a tract of land. 5 September 1846. (P. 322)

John Moore to Samuel Allison a tract of land. 1846. (Pp. 322-324)

James R. Toney to Samuel M. Fite some town lots in the town of Carthage. 11 September 1846. (Pp. 324-325)

William Turner to Henry C. Burks 69½ acres. 12 September 1846. (P. 325)

Philip Draper to Andrew McClelin a negro girl. 6 August 1846. (P. 325)

George Apple to Charles R. (   ) a tract of land. 1846. (P. 326)

Roland W. Newby and Whaley Newby, executors of William Newby, to James Gill 36 acres. February 1846. (Pp. 326-327)

James Gill to David Palmer a tract of land on Round Lick Creek. September 1846. (P. 327)

Henry Morgan to David Evetts a tract of land. 29 September 1846. (Pp. 327-328)

Moses Reaves to S. Baker 130 acres. 19 August 1846. (P. 328)

Robert Warren to Robert W. Mann 200 acres. 30 September 1846. (P. 328)

Robert W. Mann to Joseph Cowan. 1846. (P. 329)

DEED BOOK S

John Gordon to William Collom 452 acres. 31 October 1846. (Pp. 329-330)

Robert Pope and Alfred Clark to H. H. Stallings a crop of tobacco. 20 September 1846. (P. 330)

Joseph Moses to Abraham King a crop of tobacco. 23 September 1846. (Pp. 330-331)

David Harris to Samuel Goss a crop of tobacco. October 1846. (P. 331)

Jonathan Bailey to W. W. Bailey. 1846. (P. 332)

Mathew Carter to John Davis a crop of tobacco. 26 September 1846. (Pp. 332-333)

Josiah Marshall to Thomas Woodmore 62 acres. 19 September 1846. (P. 333)

Mathew Nichols to Stephen Mann two acres. 29 September 1846. (P. 333)

John Hinsley to Thomas Bailiff 115 acres. 7 October 1846. (P. 334)

Martin Everett to V. R. Bradford a crop of tobacco. 9 October 1846. (Pp. 335-336)

William Parkhurst to Peter A. Wilkerson a crop of tobacco. 10 October 1846. (P. 336)

Hezekiah Taylor to Frances Baker 133 acres. 12 October 1846. (Pp. 336-337)

James Boston to Christian Boston. 25 September 1846. (P. 337)

Johnson Anderson to Sampson McClelin a crop of tobacco. 28 September 1846. (P. 338)

Alfred N. Robinson to William Robinson 380 acres. October 1846. (Pp. 338-339)

Allen Crowell to Allen Matthews 25 acres. 4 March 1845. (P. 339)

James Phillips to Drury A. West 68 acres. 14 November 1846. (P. 339)

A. P. Taylor to David Black. 16 November 1846. (P. 340)

Phillip Swan to Silas Dice several items. 14 November 1846. (P. 340)

Miles West to William Young 55 acres. July 1845. (P. 341)

James ( ) bound to Fielding Conditt. 7 November 1846. (Pp. 341-342)

The heirs of Reuben Turner, to wit, Pleasant Turner, Sarah Turner, Elizabeth Turner, and John Turner versus William B. Turner. 1846. (Pp. 342-343)

DEED BOOK S

John Stafford to Levi Noles. 1 October 1846. (P. 343)

Robert Dalton to John Kerby a tract of land. 20 October 1846. (Pp. 343-344)

Sollomon McMurry to John McMurry several items. 13 November 1846. (Pp. 344-345)

E. C. Averett to R. C. Dalton a negro woman. 11 November 1846. (P. 345)

Thomas C. Marchbanks to John Simpson 75 acres. 13 July 1846. (Pp. 345-346)

Joseph Gifford to C. P. G. Gifford three slaves. 22 August 1846. (Pp. 346-347)

Ann Sullivan to John Reynolds her dower given in a deed made by Thomas C. Marchbanks and wife Josephine and other heirs of William Sullivan. 6 April 1846. (Pp. 347-348)

Thomas C. Marchbanks and wife Josephine and others to John Reynolds 150 acres. Other names on deed: Mary A. Sullivan, Lucien B. Sullivan, Harris Sullivan, Harbert Sullivan, Editha Ann Sullivan, and June Sullivan. 6 April 1846. (Pp. 348-349)

D. C. Ward, W. B. Moore, and A. Moore to James Cunningham 17 acres. 9 July 1836. (P. 350)

Martin W. Sloan to Joel Driver a tract of land. 1846. (P. 451)

C. Pursley to ( ) ( ) a tract of land. 1846. (Pp. 451-452)

The heirs of Andrew W. Jovance to Thomas C. Grissom a tract of land. 1846. (P. 452)

Enoch Gann to John Litchford a crop of tobacco. 14 October 1846. (P. 353)

George Rowland and Martha Rowland of Carroll County, Arkansas to James Rowland their interest in 150 acres. 9 November 1846. (Pp. 353-354)

Warren Nichols and Joel Nichols to Stephen Mann one acre. 22 August 1846. (P. 354)

Moses Robinson of Mississippi to Arthur E. Reynolds a tract of land. November 1844. (Pp. 354-355)

Arthur E. Reynolds to Alexander H. Robinson a tract of land on Smith's Fork. 14 November 1846. (P. 356)

Isaac Massey to Margaret Anderson of Jackson County a tract of land on the Cumberland River. 9 October 1846. (Pp. 356-357)

William J. Payne to Thomas Carman a tract of land on Peyton's Creek. 13 March 1844. (P. 357)

DEED BOOK S

Nancy Upton and Lucy G. Gwaltney to John Buckner a tract of land. 27 October 1846. (Pp. 357-358)

Robert Smith to D. W. Smith a crop of tobacco. November 1846. (P. 358)

Theby Anderson to Isaac Massey her life estate. 1 January 1847. (Pp. 358-359)

W. W. Bailey to Lewis Ferguson a tract of land. 1 January 1847. (Pp. 359-360)

John Trousdale to W. W. Bailey 100 acres. 1 January 1847. (P. 360)

Allen Matthews to Allen Crowell 30 acres. 4 March 1845. (Pp. 360-361)

Frances Wood to Booker S. Dalton a tract of land. 8 October 1846. (P. 361)

Booker S. Dalton to Horace Lawson eight acres. 20 November 1846. (Pp. 361-362)

Mary Caruthers and others to Booker S. Dalton a tract of land. 25 September 1846. (P. 362)

James Philips to Allen Crowell a tract of four acres. 4 March 1845. (Pp. 362-363)

Elijah Creal to G. G. Dillard a crop of tobacco. 17 October 1846. (Pp. 363-364)

Samuel D. McC) to Drewry Cornwell two acres. 10 November 1846. (P. 364)

Braddoc Beasley to Mary Ann Beasley 40 acres. 15 January 1846. (Pp. 364-365)

William Young to Drewry Cornwell a tract of 55 acres. 12 November 1846. (P. 365)

D. K. Timberlake to Henry J. Pipkins. 12 October 1846. (P. 366)

Andrew G. Pickett to Young B. Jones a town lot in the town of Carthage. 10 October 1846. (Pp. 366-367)

Marmaduke to Jabez Burton a tract of land. 24 November 1846. (Pp. 367-368)

Stephen Newbell to Isaac H. Davis 120 acres. 30 December 1845. (P. 368)

Frances Dowell to Lewis Hall a negro woman. 5 September 1844. (P. 369)

Josiah Gold to Henderson Haley 160 acres. 7 November 1846. (Pp. 369-370)

Sampson McClelin to Joel Gregory 75 acres. 28 May 1845. (P. 370)

John Trousdale to W. W. Bailey. 1847. (Pp. 370-371)

DEED BOOK S

Nicy Harris to William P. Malone two negro children. 30 January 1845. (P. 371)

N. Ward to Willis Dowell a negro girl. 20 October 1846. (P. 371)

John Page to Allen Matthews a tract of land. 30 November 1846. (Pp. 371-372)

William Thomas to Henry D. Kemp 70 acres. 1 December 1846. (P. 372)

Joseph Winchester to Fedderick ( ) some livestock. 1846. (Pp. 372-373)

Isaac Lynch to J. H. Smith a crop of tobacco. 4 December 1846. (P. 373)

James Wright to Cresay Coaley 75 acres. 3 June 1829. (P. 374)

Larkin Payne to Washington Payne 126 acres. 15 January 1847. (Pp. 374-375)

Daniel Huddleston to White ( ) 70 acres. 19 August 1846. (Pp. 375-376)

William West to Avery Hester a tract of land. 29 September 1846. (Pp. 376-377)

Plessant Roberts to Joel Coffee a crop of tobacco. 9 December 1846. (P. 377)

Willis Dowell to Lewis Hall a tract of land. 5 September 1844. (Pp. 377-378)

Dunkin Johnson to Lewis Williams 85 acres. 1846. (P. 378)

Darthula C. Danby to Henry B. McDonald her interest in the estate of her uncle James B. Crowder. 21 December 1846. (P. 379)

Henry B. McDonald to Darthula C. Danby a town lot in the town of Carthage. 29 December 1846. (P. 379)

Meredith G. Ward to Stephen M. Jones a town lot in the town of Rome. 26 August 1846. (P. 380)

James Rison to David Hodges his interest in 107 acres he is to receive at the death of Mary Rison. 30 December 1846. (Pp. 380-381)

John H. Rodgers to John Hall 67 acres. 2 January 1847. (Pp. 381-382)

William C. Ligon to Thomas P. Ligon his interest in the estate of their father W. W. Ligon. 5 January 1847. (P. 382)

B. J. Vaden to Henry Clark 35 acres. January 1847. (Pp. 382-383)

DEED BOOK S

Henry B. Clark to B. J. Vaden 75 acres. 29 December 1846. (Pp. 383-384)

Mathew Corley deed of gift to Edmond Corley. 15 December 1846. (P. 384)

Alexander Robinson to Andrew Vantrease 325 acres. 4 January 1847. (Pp. 384-385)

John W. Mann to Henry B. Clark 177 acres. 1 August 1839. (Pp. 385-386)

Elizabeth Black, John A. Chism and wife Sarah, Charles Thompson and wife Margaret, Vincent Thompson and wife Harriet, Thomas J. Black, Polly Smith, and David Black, heirs of Robert Black to William Black a tract of land. 11 June 1839. (Pp. 386-387)

Daniel Alexander to William E. Jones a town lot in the town of Carthage. 28 January 1847. (P. 388)

Pleasant Gold to Daniel James a tract of land on Hickman's Creek. 26 November 1846. (Pp. 388-389)

Daniel James to Paul L. H. Walker a tract of land on Hickman's Creek. 26 January 1847. (Pp. 389-390)

John T. Right to Henry B. McDonald 26 acres. 23 January 1847. (Pp. 390-391)

William Baker to Daniel Wilkerson a tract of land on Mulherin's Creek. 28 January 1847. (P. 392)

Jacob White to Samuel T. Coker a crop of tobacco. 1847. (P. 393)

A. Scruggs to Martin Whitten a herd of cattle. 1846. (Pp. 393-394)

William B. Johnson to James Dortch. 1847. (P. 394)

Thomas Carman to George W. Read a tract of land on Peyton's Creek. 1846. (P. 395)

Oscar D. Johnson of Mississippi to David Burford a negro man. 30 October 184?. (P. 395)

George Hughes to David Burford a negro slave. 1847. (P. 396)

Hubbard Wright to Hiram C. Ford a tract of land. 1 February 1840. (Pp. 396-397)

John Shoulders and others to Thomas Gregory. 1 February 1845. (P. 397)

Roland Smith to Thomas Gregory a tract of land on Peyton's Creek. 4 October 1843. (Pp. 397-398)

Solomon Austin to Susan Austin his mother 200 acres. 5 February 1847. (P. 398)

Samuel Harrison to T. J. Hubbard. 1847. (P. 399)

DEED BOOK S

John P. Hughes and Gideliah Hughes to Nathan Ward 149 acres. 26 January 1847. (P. 400)

Samuel Burdine to Edmund Rucks a tract of land. 29 September 1846. (Pp. 400-401)

William B. Johnson of Montgomery County to George N. Williams. 19 August 1846. (P. 401)

William A. Cook and wife Amanda to William Young their interest in the estate of Judd Strother. 9 February 1847. (P. 402)

Orville Green to A. H. King a tract of land in the town of Carthage. 30 December 1846. (Pp. 402-403)

P. H. Harris to Caleb Carman a negro woman. 25 January 1847. (P. 403)

John Bridges, administrator of Parks Chandler, Alexander Kenney and wife Peggy, James Chandler, Eliza G. Chandler, Hugh L. Chandler, and William Chandler, heirs of the said Parks Chandler file suit. 1847. (Pp. 403-404)

David Wofford, administrator of Elijah Foutch, Mary W. Dannon, William Foutch, and David Foutch versus Martin Davis and wife Sarah, Elijah Wofford, John Foutch, Mary Wofford, M. Wofford, Bartlett Wofford, Jane Wofford, Samuel Wofford, M. C. Wofford. 1847. (Pp. 404-405)

William Stalcup to Marcus L. Donoho a tract of land on Goose Creek. 5 February 1847. (Pp. 405-406)

W. W. Bailey to William Stalcup 239 acres. 8 February 1847. (P. 406)

David Burford to John McGee a tract of land on the Caney Fork. 9 February 1847. (P. 407)

Sheriff John Bailey to William Denny. 1847. (Pp. 407-409)

Sheriff John Bailey to John Corley. 1847. (Pp. 409-410)

Cornelius Fisher to Charles Washer 50 acres. February 1847. (Pp. 410-411)

Allen Matthews to Elizabeth Matthews a tract of land. 17 February 1847. (P. 411)

Henry Tooley of Matches, Mississippi to Osbourn Jeffreys a tract of 487 acres. 17 March 1814. (P. 412)

William P. Malone to H. Harris a negro girl. 1 March 1847. (P. 413)

Phillip B. Smith to Edwin Atwood his interest in his father's estate. 1847. (Pp. 413-414)

Woodson Knight to Caleb Jackson some slaves. 10 March 1847. (P. 414)

DEED BOOK S

Tiloadson Knight to Leroy B. Settle three negroes. 10 March 1847. (P. 414)

John Rigsby to William B. Young some personal property. 16 February 1847. (P. 414)

John H. Rodgers to N. Philips 62 acres. 18 February 1847. (P. 415)

Joshua Pruet to Gilbert Davis a negro girl. 7 August 1845. (P. 415)

George W. Perry to Jackson Malone 160 acres. 5 August 1846. (P. 416)

William Fiveash to John Morris eight acres. 4 December 1841. (P. 416)

Robert Pope to William C. Roe 57 acres. 23 March 1847. (P. 417)

Stephen Barret to James Barret a tract of land on Mulherin's Creek. 3 March 1843. (Pp. 417-418)

George W. Ahart to Jeremiah E. Reasonover 60 acres. 17 December 1844. (Pp. 418-419)

James Turner to William Young some personal property. 1 March 1847. (P. 419)

W. B. Whitley from J. C. Sanders a tract of land. 1847. (Pp. 419-420)

Jane Webb, formerly Jane Whitley, to Levi Foutch her interest in the estate of her father Wiley Whitley. 4 September 1846. (P. 420)

William L. Alexander, Sr. of Fulton County, Kentucky and William L. Alexander, Jr. of Sumner County, executors of Grant Allen, to George T. Wright a tract of land. 8 August 1846. (P. 421)

Allen T. Sims to William Grandstaff 85 acres. 5 November 1846. (P. 422)

James Sims to Levi Foutch 50 acres. 20 November 1846. (Pp. 422-423)

Elizabeth Sims to Levi Foutch a tract of land. 20 November 1846. (P. 423)

W. W. Bailey to A. H. Ross a negro girl. 15 January 1847. (Pp. 423-424)

Eliel Elston and wife Martha to Ephraim Cheek a tract of land on Hickman's Creek. 12 August 1845. (P. 424)

J. R. James and others to Pleasant Gold. 1847. (Pp. 424-425)

B. W. Harris to Thomas B. Grissom. 1847. (Pp. 425-427)

Leroy H. Cage to John Simmons. 1847. (P. 427)

DEED BOOK S

Zephaniah Crange to Jeremiah Agee 75 acres. 1 October 1846. (P. 428)

Josephus Cowan to Cowan William Dawson and Sam Ellison a negro boy. 22 March 1847. (P. 428)

James W. Grissim to John Reeves a negro boy. February 1847. (P. 429)

Hugh Moss to Joseph G. Moss 77½ acres. 22 March 1847. (P. 429)

Johnson M. Braden and Thomas Braden to William Grandstaff 71 acres. 5 November 1846. (P. 430)

Richard Butler to William Floid 76 acres. 9 January 1847. (P. 431)

John T. Hinsley to Thomas Bailiff. 2 March 1847. (Pp. 431-432)

Sheriff John Bailey to John Williams a tract of land. 1847. (Pp. 432-433)

John Moore to D. (   ) a tract of land. 1847. (Pp. 433-434)

John Russell to Robert A. Russell 120 acres. 19 August 1846. (Pp. 434-435)

Sheriff John Bailey to F. Duffee a tract of land. 9 April 1847. (Pp. 435-436)

H. C. Burks to Nicholas Vantrease a tract of land. 29 March 1847. (Pp. 436-437)

John Minon to Edward W. Spears a tract of land contracted by his wife Louisiana in Virginia. 21 March 1844. (Pp. 437-438)

Thaxton Cartwright to Rachael Cartwright a head of horses. 5 April 1847. (P. 438)

R. A. Bridgewater to Samuel C. Bridgewater several slaves. 24 March 1847. (P. 439)

Bartlett James to John J. Hughes a slave. 22 March 1847. (P. 440)

E. P. Lowe, August H. Lowe, Hickerson Barksdale and wife Harriet agreement. 3 April 1847. (Pp. 440-441)

Andrew G. Pickett to Young B. Jones a negro girl. 3 May 1847. (P. 442)

Reuben (Kelly) to John Kelly a tract of land on Smith's Fork. 10 February 1844. (P. 442)

Hezekiah Taylor to John W. Taylor a tract of land. 22 March 1845. (P. 443)

Frances H. Gordon to J. B. Smith. 11 November 184?. (Pp. 443-444)

DEED BOOK S

Jeremiah Dickson to Alfred A. Brevard. 4 April 1847. (P. 444)

William Carlie to Jacob Towson a tract of land. October 1847. (P. 445)

L. B. Coleman to Joel Coffee a tract of land. 1847. (P. 446)

Lewis Harring to William Searcy a tract of land in the 17th District. May 1846. (P. 447)

Thomas A. Jones to James Alexander a negro woman. 19 December 1846. (P. 447)

Hickerson Barksdale and wife Harriet agreement. 21 April 1847. (Pp. 447-448)

Elizabeth Chambers, widow, Samuel Chambers, Benjamin F. Chambers, Mary Chambers, ( ) Carman and wife Aletha, Robert Hodges and wife June, heirs of William Chambers versus Elijah Banks and wife Jane. 1847. (Pp. 449-450)

Samuel Bell to Thomas Slaughter a tract of land. April 1847. (Pp. 450-451)

Milly Squires and Levi J. Squires to Samuel Bell a tract of 52 acres. 1847. (P. 451)

( ) Haynie to ( ) ( ). 1847. (P. 452)

Archibald Taylor to William J. Jones a tract of land belonging to the estate of John W. Taylor. June 1847. (P. 452)

Mary Parrott to Lucy Self. June 1847. (P. 453)

Fleming Stubblefield to John Stubblefield a negro girl. 1 October 1846. (P. 453)

Susanah Lindsey and Walker Hooker to Samuel B. Lindsey their interest in a slave. 29 June 1847. (P. 454)

Harrison Goodall and his wife Frances to Daniel Seay their interest in the estate of Thomas Tuggle. 3 July 1847. (Pp. 454-455)

David Burford to Charles McClarin a tract of land in the town of Carthage. 25 June 1847. (P. 455)

Robert Harper, Nancy Harper, Randolph Lewis, Lucrecy Lewis, James M. Williams, Burton Williams, Thomas P. Williams, Lucy Williams, descendants of Giles Williams, to George Mires 50 acres. December 1846. (Pp. 455-456)

James Malone to Isaiah White 100 acres. 16 July 1836. (Pp. 456-457)

Robert Harper and others to Thomas Malone two tracts of land. 28 July 1846. (P. 457)

Ross Webb to A. H. King a negro girl. 12 July 1847. (P. 458)

DEED BOOK S

W. W. Price to A. H. King a tract of land in the town of Carthage. July 1847. (P. 458)

William McEnturf appoints David Hodges as his attorney. 10 July 1847. (P. 459)

Lot Hazard to Thomas Jefferson Lea a tract of land. 15 July 1847. (P. 459)

Stephen Mann versus Mathew Nichols and others. 1847. (P. 460)

William L. Hughes to William Burford. 1847. (P. 461)

William B. Campbell to George E. Allen and Henry Dowdy a crop of tobacco. 16 July 1847. (Pp. 461-462)

The executors of Grant Allen to John H. Bowen. 1847. (Pp. 462-463)

Thomas Bailiff to William Bates his interest in a tract of land. 1847. (P. 464)

Thomas Bailiff to William Bates four acres. 22 July 1847. (P. 464)

H. B. McDonald versus Robert (   ). 1847. (P. 465)

Olive Dawson and Temperance (   ) to Elizabeth Cage a tract of land on Mulherin's Creek. 22 July 1846. (P. 466)

Johnson Bailey and W. W. Bailey to F. G. Baker a negro man. 15 July 1847. (P. 466)

Philip Swan to James W. Spain. 27 July 1847. (P. 467)

Andrew G. Pickett to Armstead Moore a tract of land in the town of Carthage. 12 February 1847. (P. 468)

Samuel Allison's decree. 1847. (Pp. 468-469)

Samuel Allison to N. G. Belcher a tract of land. 26 July 1847. (P. 470)

Abel (Gregory) to John Shoulders a tract of land. 31 August 18__. (Pp. 470-471)

Allen Mathews to Daniel Smith a tract of land. 25 November 1841. (P. 471)

Joshua Coffee to Jackson Wallis 100 acres. 21 August 1846. (P. 472)

John T. Evans, Marcellus Mitchell and wife Eliza Jane, and Nancy Allen Evans, heirs of Philip Evans, to the widow Dicy Evans their interest in a tract of land. 1847. (Pp. 472-473)

J. L. Ford to Asa Washer 30 acres. September 1846. (P. 473)

Alexander Dillard to Sarah Fields 78 acres. 7 March 1844. (P. 473)

DEED BOOK S

Alexander Dillard to Sarah Fields and grandchildren Mathew Fields and Rufus Fields a tract of 39 acres. 1847. (P. 474)

Robert Hays to Pleasant W. Presley 50 acres. 1847. (Pp. 474-475)

Alexander Robinson to John Robinson. 1846. (P. 475)

Alexander Robinson and Louisa Robinson to John Robinson a tract of 36 acres. 21 December 1846. (P. 476)

( ) Hazard to Alexander Dillard a tract of land on Snow Creek. 7 March 1844. (P. 476)

Stephen Canaday to Henry M. Knight 60 acres. 12 August 1847. (P. 477)

Henderson C. Overstreet to Sampson McClelin a crop of tobacco. 30 July 1847. (P. 477)

Abner Shoulders and Richard Shoulders to Sampson McClelin. 12 August 1847. (P. 478)

Nathan ( ) to John Johnson a tract of land. 4 June 1847. (Pp. 478-479)

Littleberry Coleman to William P. Hale a tract of land on Mulherin's Creek. 11 February 1847. (P. 479)

W. W. Bailey to John Trousdale 50 acres. 1847. (P. 480)

John Trousdale to Samuel Allison a tract of land in the 16th District. 17 August 1847. (Pp. 480-481)

John R. James to Thomas Durham a tract of land. 1847. (P. 481)

William Collom from Jeremiah Jamison a tract of land. 24 August 1847. (P. 482)

Daniel Huddleston to Richard Jones a tract of land. 1847. (P. 483)

Richard Jones to James Herrod a tract of land. 1847. (P. 483)

James Reynolds to John Fisher a tract of land. May 1847. (P. 484)

Richard Jones heirs to ( ) ( ). 1847. (Pp. 484-485)

John Rigsby to W. B. Young a crop of tobacco. August 1847. (P. 485)

W. W. Bailey to John Bailey a tract of land on Hurricane Creek. April 1847. (P. 486)

Henry L. Day to James ( ) a crop of tobacco. 1847. (Pp. 486-487)

Joel S. Flowers to John ( ). 1847. (P. 487)

DEED BOOK S

Stanford Mitchell to Bartley ( ) a tract of land. 2 October 1847. (P. 488)

Richard Duke to William Payne a negro boy. 24 December 1846. (P. 488)

William Payne to Sampson McClelin a tract of land. 1 September 1847. (P. 489)

David Burford to James C. Sanders a tract of land. August 1847. (Pp. 489-490)

Lewis Vance to William Winchester a tract of land. 23 May 1846. (Pp. 490-491)

Lewis Vance to Jason Winchester a tract of land. 1847. (P. 491)

William Winchester to Jason Winchester a tract of land. 1847. (P. 492)

John Stephens to John Mason a tract of land for love and affection. 31 September 1847. (P. 492)

John Beckman to ( ) Heflin a tract of land. 30 August 1847. (P. 493)

J. R. James to John Dedman two slaves. 19 February 1847. (P. 494)

Thaxton Cartwright to Daniel Huddleston. 1847. (P. 494)

Johnson Anderson to Daniel Huddleston. 1847. (P. 495)

Sheriff John Bailey to to ( ) ( ). 1847. (Pp. 495-496)

Sheriff John Bailey to Whaley Newby a tract of land. 1847. (P. 497)

Allen Matthews to ( ) ( ) a tract of land. 1847. (P. 498)

Alfred Reed to Stephen ( ) a tract of land. 1847. (P. 499)

John B. Hughes to Jeremiah Jamison a tract of land. 1847. (P. 500)

Richard Hallum and wife Mary to Sam Fite. Said Mary is formerly Mary Rowland. 24 September 1847. (P. 501)

J. B. Flippin to Caleb Carman a tract of land. 1847. (P. 501)

James Walton and Timothy Walton to C. C. Ford a tract of land. 1847. (P. 502)

Sheriff John Bailey to William Payne a tract of land. 1847. (Pp. 503-504)

Thomas B. Bridges to David Philips a tract of land. 19 January 1847. (P. 504)

DEED BOOK S

David Philips to William Payne a tract of land. 4 October 1847. (Pp. 504-505)

John Smalling to James Piper. 1847. (P. 505)

Alfred D. Smith to James Piper. 4 October 1847. (P. 505)

John Shoulders to James ( ). 4 October 1847. (P. 506)

John W. Ballard to ( ) ( ). 1847. (P. 506)

John Boston and others to Colvert Porter. July 1847. (P. 507)

H. D. Bennett to William Washburn a tract of land. 1847. (Pp. 507-508)

William Floid to John A. Moss a tract of land. 1847. (Pp. 508-509)

John Gordon to Mathew Harper his interest in a tract of land he is to receive at the death of Sarah Harper. 12 October 1847. (P. 509)

(Pages are misnumbered)

William Stanford to David Stanford a tract of land on Cage's Branch. 8 October 1847. (P. 600)

David K. Timberlake from William Lawrence a tract of land. 1847. (P. 600)

David K. Timberlake to Jesse Beasley a tract of land. 16 October 1847. (P. 601)

T. D. Price to N. B. Burdine. 23 September 1847. (P. 601)

Abel Hunt to Dowell & Patterson a tract of land on Hickman's Creek. 1847. (P. 602)

William Floyd to John A. Smart 76 acres. 20 September 1847. (Pp. 602-603)

L. Gifford to W. Tunstall. December 1846. (P. 603)

C. C. Ford to Stephen Mann a tract of land. 1847. (Pp. 603-604)

Samuel Dew to James Allen 53 acres. 12 August 1847. (P. 604)

Isaac R. Moore to James S. Reese a tract of land. 24 July 1847. (P. 605)

James Malone to Robert Dowell a tract of land. 19 July 1847. (Pp. 605-606)

James Malone to Isaac H. Moore a tract of land. 22 July 1847. (P. 606)

William Burford to John Highers a tract of land. 27 October 1847. (P. 607)

DEED BOOK S

William Moore to Jorden Kilzer 94 acres. 1847. (Pp. 607-608)

John A. Toney of Dallas County, Arkansas to Abram H. King a town lot in the town of Carthage. October 1847. (P. 608)

Enock Rollins to L. W. (   ) a tract of land. 25 August 1847. (Pp. 608-609)

Miles McKnight and wife to T. Dillehay their interest in the estate of Edmond Dillehay. October 1847. (P. 609)

Ann Sullivan to William Bates. 15 September 1847. (P. 610)

Richard Lamberson and Editha Lamberson appoint William Bates as their attorney. 1847. (Pp. 610-611)

Jesse Frazer to William E. Jones a tract of land. 1 November 1847. (Pp. 612-613)

Isaac Kitrell to Edwin Kitrell 72 acres. 1847. (P. 613)

Daniel Smith to Nicholas Vantrease a tract of land on Hickman's Creek. 27 January 1845. (P. 613)

David Burford to Thomas T. Stovall a tract of land. 15 May 1847. (P. 614)

William Farley to James C. Sanders a tract of land. October 1847. (P. 614)

John Hooker to William Hooker his interest in the estate of his father Thomas Hooker. 30 October 1847. (P. 615)

John H. Bedford to Andrew G. Pickett a tract of land. 5 October 1847. (P. 615)

Andrew G. Pickett to Jeremiah Jamison a tract of land. 3 November 1847. (P. 616)

Henry Mann to (   ) (   ) a crop of corn. 1847. (Pp. 616-617)

Robert W. Mann to Stephen Mann. 2 November 1847. (P. 617)

Joel Coffee to Lewis McPherson a tract of land on Hickman's Creek. 24 September 184?. (P. 618)

Daniel Agee to Jonathan Agee 54 acres. 1847. (P. 619)

The heirs of Drewry Holland to Matilda Holland, the widow, a tract of land. Mentions Alfred Pistole and wife Betsy, John Holland, James Holland, Emeline Holland, Richard Holland, William Holland, (   ) Holland, Stephen Holland, Milton Holland, Amelia Huddleston, James Huddleston, Sarah Huddleston, and Drewry Huddleston. 1847. (Pp. 620-621)

J. D. Sloan to P. W. Estes his interest in the estate of John Sloan. 24 November 1847. (Pp. 620-621)

DEED BOOK S

Manson Young to Green Wright 150 acres. 31 August 1843. (P. 622)

Green Wright to his daughter Amanda F. Parker a tract of land. 10 March 1847. (Pp. 622-623)

Green Wright to his daughter Martha Wood a tract of land. 20 March 1847. (P. 623)

Aron G. Linsley, Walker Hooker, and Lafayette Linsley appoint Susan Linsley as their attorney. 2 December 1847. (P. 624)

M. W. Sloan to William (   ) a tract of land. 22 November 1847. (P. 625)

Michael Shoemake to Charles R. Blare a tract of land on Hurricane Creek. 22 July 1847. (Pp. 625-626)

DEED BOOK T

Drewry A. West to Barnett Dillehay a tract of land. 12 November 1847. (P. 1)

Alfred Wammack to Charles Blair a tract of land. 1847. (Pp. 1-2)

Barnett Dillehay to ( ) ( ) a tract of land. 1847. (P. 2)

Edward B. Tuck to ( ) ( ) a tract of land. 1847. (P. 3)

Jeremiah Smith to ( ) ( ) a tract of land. 1847. (Pp. 3-4)

Illegible. (Pp. 4-5)

Henry Brooks to Benjamin F. Jones of Davidson County to William Denny a tract of land on the Cumberland River. 1847. (P. 6)

Lot Hazard to Orville Green 125 acres. 8 December 1847. (P. 7)

Nathan Ward to Mathew Harper a tract of land. 1 March 1847. (P. 7)

William Uhles to Richard Chambers a tract of land. 26 November 1847. (P. 8)

B. B. Uhls and Mary Ann Uhls to William Duvall a tract of land. January 1848. (Pp. 8-9)

Joel Gregory to Berry West a tract of land on the Cumberland River. 4 December 1846. (P. 9)

James C. Robertson of Claborn Parish, Louisiana appoints his wife Sarah Robertson as his attorney in settling the estate of David Robertson. 28 November 1847. (P. 10)

James Barnett to Martha Ward a tract of land for love and affection. 1847. (P. 11)

James Barnett to his daughter Nancy Hale, wife of John Hale, a tract of land on Plunkett's Creek. 28 November 1847. (Pp. 11-12)

James Barnett to his daughter Mary C. Williams, wife of (George) N. Williams a tract of land. 1847. (P. 12)

Ballinger heirs to Jeremiah Smith a tract of land. 1847. (Pp. 12-13)

Ellick ( ) to Hawkins Heflin a tract of land. 1847. (Pp. 13-14)

J. B. Gullick to Hawkins Heflin 50 acres. 25 June 1847. (Pp. 14-15)

Samuel Watson to Jacob F. Slone a tract of land. (Pp. 15-16)

Fleming Stubblefield to E. P. Gifford. (P. 17)

DEED BOOK T

Mary Sampson to Captain William ( ). April 1847. (P. 18)

Mary Simpson to Michael Halmantoller a tract of land. 20 February 1841. (Pp. 18-19)

Thomas Malone to ( ) ( ) a tract of land. 19 February 1848. (P. 20)

John Exum to Andrew Winchester a tract of 50 acres. (P. 20)

Jonathan Smith to Isaac Barton 50 acres. 10 November 1843. (P. 21)

John Braswell to Pleasant W. Presley a tract of land. 10 January 1845. (P. 22)

Henry Tuggle to H. B. Tuggle. 15 October 1846. (P. 23)

James R. James to Thomas Watson 25 acres. 10 January 1848. (P. 24)

James T. Allen and Lucy Ann Allen to Thomas Malone a tract of land on the Caney Fork. 1848. (Pp. 24-25)

Gideon B. Wray to James G. McDonald about an acre. 1848. (Pp. 25-26)

Josiah Baird to Benjamin F. Hughes a tract of land on Hickman's Creek. 1848. (P. 26)

Jonathan Bailey to John Stevens 160 acres. February 1848. (P. 27)

T. J. Cassity to Wesly Woolard 50 acres. June 1845. (P. 27)

Wesly Woolard to Blair & High 50 acres. 1848. (P. 28)

Paul H. Walker and Ann Gwaltney to James Newbell 50 acres. 29 January 1848. (Pp. 28-29)

David Burford to Burton Harris 20 acres. 1848. (P. 29)

James Newbell and Ann Gwaltney to Paul H. Walker. 1848. (P. 30)

James Gwaltney Newbell and Paul H. Walker to Ann Gwaltney 51 acres. 25 January 1848. (P. 30)

Moses Woodmore to James Woodmore a tract of 115 acres. 7 December 1847. (P. 31)

John H. Burford to Burton Harris a tract of land. 1848. (Pp. 31-32)

John Woodmore to his son Moses S. Woodmore 53 acres. 4 February 1848. (P. 32)

Andrew Draper to John ( ). 1848. (P. 33)

DEED BOOK T

James Woodmore to Moses S. Woodmore a tract of land. 1 December 1847. (P. 33)

John W. Mann to Stephen Mann a negro girl. 25 January 1842. (P. 34)

A. L. Taylor to William J. Davis for the benefit "of myself and my mother" a tract of land. 4 January 1848. (P. 34)

Cane Stafford to Jacob F. Slone a tract of land on Goose Creek. 5 June 1830. (Pp. 34-35)

Martha Boulton and Charles Boulton to James Taylor and his brother Joseph J. Taylor a tract of land. 4 November 1847. (P. 35)

The heirs of Robert Taylor versus A. W. Overton. March 1848. (Pp. 36-37)

J. J. Malone to Tapley B. Pyran the tract of land on which Joseph Summersett's widow now lives. 15 February 1848. (P. 37)

Robert Malone to William Phelson 300 acres. 14 February 1848. (Pp. 37-38)

James Malone and Amzi Malone to Tapley B. Pyran a tract of two and one half acres. 14 February 1848. (P. 38)

J. J. Malone to Tapley B. Pyran a tract of land. 15 February 1848. (P. 39)

Archibald Debow to Jacob Towson a tract of land. 11 February 1848. (P. 39)

Samuel P. Howard to L. B. Hughes a tract of land. 10 February 1848. (P. 40)

Daniel T. Lake to Gideon Gifford 20 acres. 12 February 1848. (Pp. 40-41)

John Dias to Charles H. Tunstall his interest in the estate of his father Thomas Dias. 19 February 1848. (P. 41)

Sarah Cunningham to Robert Gann her interest in 94 acres in which she has a life estate. 28 March 1848. (P. 42)

L. B. Hughes to James Johnson 47 acres. 15 February 1848. (Pp. 42-43)

Robert Marshall to William B. Rutherford 60 acres. 27 November 1845. (P. 43)

James Malone to John Washer 150 acres. 10 August 1847. (P. 44)

J. C. Douglas to Hickerson Barksdale 56 acres. 30 October 1848. (P. 45)

Ross Webb to William Young. 1848. (P. 45)

DEED BOOK T

Thomas Cockerham versus J. G. Cockerham, Franklin Cockerham, Frances Boulton, Thomas Boulton, Lent Boulton, Mary Boulton, Elizabeth Boulton, Andrew Belfor, Mary Belfor, and Henry Belfor, the heirs of Henry Cockerham. 1848. (P. 46)

Elizabeth Moores to Uriah Pugh a tract of land on Mulherin's Creek. 21 January 1848. (Pp. 46-47)

Henry B. McDonald to Adam Ferguson 11 acres. 15 January 1848. (P. 47)

Pleasant Gold to Dawson Gwaltney a tract of land on Hickman's Creek. 29 March 1848. (P. 48)

Ephraim Cooksey to Mason Walker a tract of land in the 12th District. July 1844. (P. 48)

Mason Walker to Benjamin Cooksey his interest in a tract of land which belonged to John Cooksey at his death and seventh part of said tract on which Gilly Cooksey lived at her death. 31 March 1848. (P. 49)

Selva Wood, one of the heirs of Elihu Wood, to Samuel L. Bailiff 28 acres. 29 August 1849. (P. 49)

Susannah Murry of Jackson County to Drucilla Johnson, a woman of color, a negro man slave named Dick. 29 January 1848. (P. 50)

Joel M. Clevelin to Henry W. Hart a tract of land. 3 April 1848. (Pp. 50-51)

Augustine Robinson and wife Rachel of Mississippi to Nathaniel Terry a tract of land. 29 December 1845. (Pp. 51-52)

D. C. Sanders to James C. Sanders three negroes. 15 February 1848. (P. 52)

William D. Hale to Bryan & Caruthers 100 acres. 21 April 1848. (P. 53)

James Barnett to Thomas W. Wooten 59 acres. 3 November 1847. (P. 54)

Marmaduke Mason to William B. Whitley a tract of land on Mulherin's Creek. 19 January 1848. (Pp. 54-55)

James C. Sanders to William B. Whitley a tract of land on the Caney Fork River. 8 February 1848. (P. 55)

Thomas Marshall to George C. Gifford 17½ acres. January 1846. (P. 56)

Lot Hazard to Hawkins Heflin 25 acres. 9 February 1848. (P. 56)

Philip B. Smith, Prudence Smith, Samuel Allison, Elijah M. Smith, Nancy Smith, Martin Smith, Elizabeth Allen, John Allen, Mary Allen, Martha Allen, Martha Smith (widow of H. M. Smith), Fountain Smith, heirs of Larkin Smith, to Kitchens

DEED BOOK T

and others a tract of land. 1848. (Pp. 57-58)

Sampson Wood, one of the legatees of Elisha Wood, to Samuel Bailiff 78 acres. 20 December 1847. (P. 58)

J. W. Armstrong to John McCall a tract of land. 15 February 1848. (Pp. 59-60)

John H. Bedford to Joseph W. Armstrong his interest in the estate of his father John B. Armstrong. 15 February 1848. (P. 60)

Mathew Harper to Matilda Prowell a tract of land. 1847. (Pp. 60-61)

James W. Bransford and Richard R. Bransford to Joseph Evetts 76 acres. September 1845. (P. 62)

D. C. Sanders to Sarah Gordon a negro boy. 5 May 1848. (P. 62)

Little B. Coleman to W. W. Washburn and H. S. Patterson 100 acres. 24 November 1847. (P. 62)

Levi Squires to Gregory Moore 24 acres. 10 March 1848. (P. 63)

Joseph Evetts to Moses Evetts six acres. 11 March 1848. (Pp. 63-64)

Thomas Snoddy to to the Commissioners of Smith County one acre. 1 August 1845. (P. 64)

Thomas A. Frohock to William Baker a gray mare. 6 April 1848. (P. 65)

William Gresham to Baxton Harris 55 acres. 18 April 1845. (Pp. 65-66)

Jeremiah Mankin appoints John L. Sloan as his attorney in settling the estate of Edward Settle. 17 March 1848. (P. 66)

James Kearley to Josiah Marshall, executor of Thomas Marshall, a tract of land. 23 August 1847. (Pp. 66-67)

George Campbell to Elijah Solomon 100 acres. 4 June 184?. (P. 67)

William Wood to William Bush a tract of land on the Caney Fork. 7 February 1837. (P. 68)

Daniel James to William Duvall a negro man. 1 May 1848. (P. 69)

Lot Hazard to Henry B. McDonald a tract of land in the town of Carthage. 9 February 1848. (P. 69)

John Gordon to George W. McGee 50 acres. 22 January 1848. (P. 70)

John H. Newbell to George W. Newbell and Edmond Newbell 264 acres. March 1844. (Pp. 70-71)

DEED BOOK T

David Hogg to L. D. Hogg a tract of land. 1848. (P. 71)

L. D. Hogg to David Hogg a tract of 47 acres. March 1848. (P. 72)

Stephen Sampson to his son Coleman S. Sampson, Stephen Sampson, and daughter Drucilla Ligon, and the heirs of his daughter Nancy Dawson, to wit, Henry, Stephen, Harriet, Isaac, James, and John Dawson a tract of land. 4 May 1848. (Pp. 72-73)

Elias Barbee versus Enock Gann. 1848. (Pp. 73-74)

Widow Nancy Highers versus Dixon Highers, M. Highers, David Highers, Judiah Highers, Nancy Highers, Tennessee Highers, and Mary Highers, the heirs of Josiah Highers. 1848. (P. 74-75)

Nancy Highers to David Palmer 70 acres. 12 May 1848. (P. 75)

H. B. McDonald to Joseph G. Pickett a tract of land. 19 May 1848. (P. 76)

H. B. McDonald to Samuel T. Coker 26 acres. 4 March 1848. (Pp. 76-77)

J. C. Sanders to Darthula Ann Sanders, wife of David C. Sanders, a negro boy for love and affection. 21 April 1848. (P. 78)

Patrick Hubbard to Adkin M. Timberlake a tract of land on the Cumberland River. 15 January 1848. (Pp. 78-79)

Thomas Phelps appoints James High as his attorney to receive the land bequeathed to his wife, Ann Phelps, as an heir of Chesley Bridgewater. 22 May 1848. (P. 79)

Nathan Ward to Eli and Mary Butts a tract of land. 26 May 1848. (P. 80)

A. H. Ross to Jessy Smith a negro girl. 17 December 1847. (P. 81)

John Minton to Jefferson C. Bowman some personal property. 1848. (P. 81)

Ann Gillespie, widow of William Gillespie, to James A. Gillespie and Rachael Gillespie her children her interest in the estate. 8 September 1847. (Pp. 81-82)

Samuel Allison to Guthridge L. Robinson a negro girl. 28 December 1847. (P. 82)

Articles of agreement between Charles E. Williams and Nathaniel A. Williams. 1848. (PP. 82-83)

Levi Squires to John Reeves 45 acres. 17 January 1848. (Pp. 83-84)

William B. Moore to Armstead Moore. 1844. (P. 84)

DEED BOOK T

Thompson Mace to his daughter Polly Cartwright a tract of land on Peyton's Creek. 3 April 1848. (P. 85)

Pleasant Gold to Jordan Stokes a negro boy. 19 March 1845. (P. 85)

Ezekiel Wyatt to Thomas A. Flippin a tract of land on the Caney Fork. 2 February 1839. (P. 86)

Benjamin B. Smith to William A. Smith a negro slave. 1 June 1848. (Pp. 86-87)

Jesse Moorland to William J. Bennett a tract of land. 19 February 1848. (P. 87)

W. T. Williams and wife Elizabeth to W. Bolton. 29 August 1842. (P. 88)

Reuben Hinton to P. W. Cage. 27 May 1843. (P. 88)

Isham Kitrell, Delila Davis, M., Maryann, and James C. Morgan, minor heirs of Joseph Morgan. 1848. (Pp. 88-89)

Valentine Presley to Jefferson Rowland seven acres. 31 January 1848. (Pp. 89-90)

Edward West, William West, Robert West, James West, Ezekiel West, Berry West, James Philips and wife C., Miles West, Drewry West, and Claiborn West, heirs of Miles West, to Harriet Dillehay a tract of land. November 1845. (P. 90)

George Baker to William P. Evans a tract of land on Hogan's Creek. 9 February 1848. (P. 91)

Squire Woods to B. Johnson a tract of 70 acres. 26 June 1848. (Pp. 91-92)

Squire Woods to William Ballard 50 acres. 26 June 1848. (P. 92)

Tapley B. Pyron to Charles Pyron a tract of two and one half acres. 27 June 1848. (P. 93)

Mitchel M. Crowell to Even A. Crowell. 12 May 1848. (Pp. 93-94)

The executors of William Martin, to William Sloan 270 acres. 1 March 1848. (P. 94)

Tapley B. Pyron to J. J. Malone his interest in the land on which the widow of Joseph Summersett now lives. 1 February 1848. (P. 95)

Archibald Vanhorn Allen to James High 192 acres. 14 July 1848. (P. 96)

The administrator of Edward Bradley to James S. Bradley a tract of land. 4 July 1848. (Pp. 96-97)

Thomas Bridges to Thomas Arington 40 acres. 6 May 1848. (P. 97)

DEED BOOK T

James C. Sanders and William Strother to John Smart a tract of land on the Caney Fork. 17 February 1848. (P. 98)

Wilson Y. Martin to Ashley Standfield 300 acres. 21 October 1847. (P. 99)

A. P. Cardwell to B. S. Cardwell three negroes. 9 July 1848. 1848. (P. 99)

William Massey and wife Judith, formerly Judith Bradley of Montgomery County, to Charles Bradley their interest in the estate of George Bradley. 5 May 1848. (P. 100)

Paschal Roberts to Landon Burton. July 1848. (P. 101)

William Martin to George T. Wright a tract of land on Dixon's Creek. 23 May 1840. (P. 101)

Pascal Roberts to Robert Barton a tract of land. 14 July 1848. (P. 102)

William Hail to Jesse Hale 150 acres. 15 July 1848. (P. 103)

James McCulloc to his daughter Ferebee C. Crutcher, wife of James A. Crutcher, a negro woman. 1848. (Pp. 103-104)

Spearman Robinson and William Robinson to Edwin Kitrell 138 acres. 31 December 1847. (Pp. 104-105)

Sarah A. Kerby appoints James A. Winn as his attorney. 31 July 1848. (Pp. 105-106)

R. C. Wright, executor of George Wright, to W. A. Garrett a tract of land. 1 December 1847. (Pp. 106-107)

Gideon Gifford to E. P. G. Gifford. 13 September 1846. (P. 108)

Gideon Gifford to E. P. G. Gifford a tract of land in the 8th District. 6 March 1848. (Pp. 108-109)

William Garrot to Jeremiah Smith a tract of land on Mulherin's Creek. 22 June 1848. (Pp. 109-110)

Robert Warren to Hansford Boulton 91 acres. 2 December 2 December 1848. (P. 110)

Robert Dowell to Jesse T. Hollis 65 acres. 28 December 1847. (Pp. 110-111)

William Strother to James M. Milton 120 acres. 14 August 1846. (Pp. 111-112)

Jordan McKinney to John J. Barnett 35½ acres. March 1842. (P. 112)

Nathaniel Terry to Thomas Simpson his interest in the estate of Mary Simpson. 22 January 1848. (P. 112)

William Gillihan to Joseph Bush 30 acres. 17 March

DEED BOOK T

1848. (P. 113)

William Lancaster to William Ballard a tract of land on the Caney Fork. 5 December 1842. (Pp. 113-114)

John Reece to Sampson McClelin 100 acres. 26 May 1848. (P. 114)

M. L. Hughes to James S. Dyer. 31 July 1848. (P. 115)

Jesse Pope to John H. Bates 81 acres. 1 August 1848. (P. 115)

Calvin Pope, administrator of Silas Pope, versus Widow Nicey Pope, Jesse Pope, James H. Pope, Thomas Williams and wife Patsy, John Pope, Sewellen Pope, Elizabeth Pope, and Theoderick Pope. 1848. (P. 116)

Ellis B. Kemp, Henry Kemp, Beverly S. Kemp, Telitha Hogg, Larkin Kemp, and Henry H. Kemp versus Sampson D. Kemp, Harriet M. Kemp, Ruth E. Kemp, Lorey S. Kemp, Leonidas Kemp, and W. W. Kemp, heirs of Jenks Kemp. 1848. (Pp. 117-118)

Barnett Cornwell to William Draper a tract of land on Defeated Creek. 17 May 1848. (P. 118)

Jesse Pope to Elizabeth Pope 80 acres. 2 May 1848. (P. 119)

Van H. Allen to Joseph W. Allen one acre. 16 August 1848. (Pp. 119-120)

Armstead Moore to I. N. Jordan a tract of land in the town of Carthage. December 1847. (P. 120)

John Stubblefield to James D. Bennett 180 acres. 15 July 1848. (P. 121)

Hugh Moss and John Easley to Nancy Upton 128 acres. 6 February 1847. (Pp. 121-122)

William P. Evins to Thomas W. Wooten a tract of land on Hogan's Creek. 22 May 1848. (Pp. 122-123)

Isaac A. Bias to H. B. Haynie four negroes. 5 August 1848. (P. 123)

Ezariah Corder of Wilson County to William Ross a tract of land on the Cumberland River. 5 August 1848. (Pp. 123-124)

Marcellus Mitchell to Robert Mitchell 41 acres. 1847. (Pp. 124-125)

Margaret Compton to John Barbee her interest in the estate of Joseph Barbee, Sr. of Fauquier County, Virginia. 26 August 1848. (P. 125)

Joseph Barbee to John Barbee his interest in the estate of Joseph Barbee, Sr. 26 March 184?. (P. 125)

John Squires, James W. Denton, Thomas Slaughter, and

DEED BOOK T

Levi Squires, and Frederick Jones, heirs of Levi Squires. 1848. (P. 126)

Robert Donelson and wife Susan of New York appoint James W. Smith as their attorney. 19 October 1847. (P. 127)

Allen Watkins to James B. Moores a tract of land. 31 May 1848. (P. 127)

William Denny to William Stark a woman slave. 9 March 1848. (P. 128)

John Bailey to Henry D. Goss a tract of land on the Caney Fork. 14 August 1848. (P. 128)

John Bailey to Charles Patey a tract of land on the Caney Fork. 14 August 1848. (P. 129)

James R. Dickerson to Stephen R. Sampson a crop of tobacco. August 1848. (P. 129)

Barnett T. Dillehay to Beverly S. Kemp 142 acres. 20 August 1848. (P. 130)

Lot Hazard to Orville Green a tract of land on Snow Creek. 1848. (Pp. 130-131)

Bartlett James and others to John Stuart a tract of land. 1848. (Pp. 131-132)

Warren Nichols to Stephen Mann, Benjamin Arundell and the other Trustees of the Methodist Church on Snow Creek a tract of land. 1848. (P. 132)

Cynthia Hogg to David K. Timberlake a tract of land on Snow Creek. 26 August 1848. (P. 133)

Thomas J. Stratton to William F. McAlister a tract of land on the Cumberland River. 24 August 1847. (Pp. 133-134)

Willis Coggin to the heirs of Wade H. Wallace 50 acres. 30 September 1840. (P. 134)

Abraham Caruthers to William Dickins a tract of land on Hurricane Creek. 17 August 1848. (P. 135)

Patrick Hubbard to Dickerson Dickens 13 acres. 3 August 1848. (Pp. 135-136)

N. B. Burdine and Samuel Burdine to Hickerson Barksdale one half of an acre. 7 September 1847. (Pp. 136-137)

Susan Clark to Holloman and Clark a tract of land. 4 September 1848. (P. 137)

Susan Clark to Samuel H. McDonald her interest in the estate of Andrew Clark. 4 September 1848. (P. 138)

Samuel T. Coker to Henry B. McDonald a tract of land. 6 September 1848. (Pp. 138-140)

John T. Carter and wife Jane, formerly Jane Gregory,

DEED BOOK T

heirs of Uriah Gregory of Mecklenburg County, Virginia appoint George Ferrel of Williamson County, Illinois as their attorney. 18 August 1848. (P. 141)

George Ferrell appoints Pleasant Gold as his attorney. 8 September 1848. (P. 142)

Thornton Christie to Josiah Baird a tract of land. 30 August 1848. (Pp. 142-143)

Thornton Christie to Josiah Baird, Jr. and J. H. Baird a tract of land on Brush Creek. 13 August 1848. (Pp. 143-144)

John Franklin, Henry Franklin, Mary Ann Franklin, Garrett Sadler and wife Jane to Sally Franklin, Sr. and Louis Franklin a tract of land for love and affection. 11 September 1848. (Pp. 144-145)

Ellis B. Kemp to Fielding Kitrell a tract of land in the 5th District. 4 September 1848. (Pp. 146-147)

John H. Rodgers to Edwin Atwood a tract of land on Mulherin's Creek. 15 September 1848. (P. 147)

John H. Rodgers to Edwin Atwood a tract of land. 15 September 1848. (P. 148)

John B. Gullick to William B. Whitley a boy slave. 15 August 1848. (P. 148)

John H. Bates, H. D. Flippin, and R. D. Flippin to M. B. Kitrell a man slave. 24 September 1848. (P. 149)

Thomas A. Frohock to Thomas Ballinger a crop of tobacco. 19 September 1848. (P. 149)

Elijah Breeden and wife Lucinda, James Preston and wife Isabella, heirs of Tucker Woodson, to Frances Dowell a tract of land. 19 September 1848. (P. 150)

Henry Bailey to Frances Dowell a tract of land in the 20th District. 22 September 1848. (P. 151)

William Lynch to Josiah Hallum. 23 September 1848. (P. 151)

Sheriff John Bailey to J. G. Frazer. 20 September 1845. (P. 152)

J. G. Frazer to Donalson Stuart 60 acres. 27 September 1845. (P. 153)

Joel Bates to John Bates a crop of tobacco. 25 September 1848. (P. 153)

John D. Goss to Josiah Hallum. 27 September 1848. (P. 154)

B. S. Cardwell to Andrew G. Pickett a negro girl. 6 September 1848. (P. 154)

David Harris to Rufus Perry. 1848. (P. 155)

DEED BOOK T

Tucker Woodson to Benjamin F. Hughes and Jesse A. Hughes. 26 November 1845. (P. 156)

John Hopkins to Rufus Perry a crop of tobacco. 15 March 1848. (P. 158)

John Holly to David Davis several slaves. 22 September 1848. (P. 158)

William T. Bennett to Martha Flowers a tract of land. 30 September 1848. (P. 159)

Jeremiah Rollins to John R. Smith a tract of land. 6 October 1848. (Pp. 159-160)

John R. Rollins to his two daughters Elizabeth Atwood and Mary Ann Rollins 129 acres. 5 October 1848. (P. 160)

Benjamin F. Hughes and Jesse A. Hughes to Stephen H. Right. 3 October 1848. (P. 161)

Benjamin F. Hughes and Jesse A. Hughes to William P. Right and Stephen H. Right 140 acres. 3 October 1848. (Pp. 161-162)

Jacob White to Rufus Perry a crop of tobacco. 7 October 1848. (P. 162)

Grogan Harper and James Harper to Mathew Harper their interest in the estate of Mathew Harper. 7 October 1848. (Pp. 162-163)

Alexander B. Dillehay and Margaret Dillehay to Catherine Ramsey a tract of land. 7 October 1848. (P. 163)

Elizabeth W. Sloan, wife of Martin W. Sloan, to James W. Dickens a negro woman. 12 October 1848. (P. 164)

Dallison Stuart to Elisha Dillard a tract of land on the Caney Fork. 11 October 1848. (P. 165)

W. W. Bailey to William Young a negro boy. 8 October 1845. (P. 165)

Rawlings Stott to George W. Royster a tract of land on Peyton's Creek. 27 September 1848. (P. 166)

Rizen Thompson to Joel Allgood. 18 December 1846. (P. 167)

Spearman Robinson and Edwin Kitrell and wife Catherine to William Robinson 246 acres. 16 October 1848. (Pp. 167-168)

John A. Sloan appoints David Burford as his attorney. October 1848. (P. 168)

Samuel McClelin to Judith McCormack a tract of land on Buffalo Creek. 1 January 1840. (P. 169)

N. B. Pillow to ( ) Jamison a negro boy. 3 November 1848. (P. 169)

Abraham McCormack to Mary Woodcock a tract of land on

DEED BOOK T

Buffalo Creek. 6 November 1845. (P. 170)

John R. Sadler to Mathew Harper a tract of land. March 1848. (P. 171)

Rachael Bowman to her grandson James Bowman, the son of Joseph Bowman, a negro boy child. 4 November 1848. (Pp. 172-173)

Edwin Kitrell to Ellis E. Knight 138 acres. 6 October 1848. (P. 173)

Patrick Hubbard to John Maggart 30 acres. 31 October 1848. (P. 174)

James Norris to Josiah W. Hanson a tract of land. 30 September 1847. (Pp. 174-175)

James Boze to William B. Whitley a tract of land in the 17th District. 19 January 1846. (P. 175)

William B. Whitley to Marmaduke Mason a tract of land. 19 January 1848. (P. 176)

Bartlett James to John H. Newbell a tract of land. 21 October 1848. (Pp. 176-177)

William Lawrence and Frances Lawrence to Jesse T. Hollis a tract of land. 7 October 1848. (Pp. 177-178)

Samuel R. Goss to D. C. Sanders a crop of corn. 1848. (P. 178)

Henry Mann to John B. Gullick a negro woman. 23 August 1848. (P. 179)

John B. Gullick to Hawkins Heflin a negro woman. 10 November 1848. (P. 179)

Peter A. Wilkerson and Daniel A. Wilkerson to George Boston a tract of land. 1848. (P. 180)

Martin W. Sloan to George Allen a bay horse. 7 November 1848. (Pp. 180-181)

Martin W. Sloan to John McDougall 91 acres. 1848. (Pp. 181-182)

George Mires to Moses Craig a tract of land on Roll's Creek. 20 November 1848. (Pp. 182-183)

H. M. Craig to Samuel P. Williams a tract of land on Roll's Creek. 12 September 1848. (P. 183)

Sheriff John Bailey to Gideon Hughes a tract of land. 1848. (P. 184)

Neal McDuffee to M. Duffy a crop of tobacco. 21 November 1848. (P. 185)

Martin W. Sloan to William Robinson one acre. 20 November 1848. (Pp. 185-186)

Jesse Pope to Hizia Pope 25 acres. 1848. (P. 186)

DEED BOOK T

Fleming Stubblefield to Joseph L. Carter a slave. 1 January 1848. (P. 187)

John Moore to Samuel F. Patton a negro girl. 27 November 1848. (Pp. 187-188)

Isaac Kitrell to his son William Kitrell a negro boy. 9 January 1848. (P. 188)

Leonard D. Ballow to Lorenzo D. Ballow his interest in the estate of Leonard Ballow. 13 November 1848. (P. 189)

Brice M. Taylor to James W. Taylor his interest in the estate of his mother Tabitha Taylor, widow of Thomas Taylor. 21 November 1848. (Pp. 189-190)

B. R. Owen to Frances Dowell a tract of land. 25 November 1848. (P. 190)

James Grandstaff to Thomas Kitchen a tract of land on Brush Creek. 21 October 1848. (P. 191)

Thomas Kitchen to James Allen a tract of land on Brush Creek. 20 October 1847. (Pp. 191-192)

James W. Draper to John Wallace his interest in the estate of his grandparents James and Mary Wallace. 6 November 1848. (P. 192)

John Caley to David Malone a negro man. 28 August 1847. (P. 193)

John C. Brevard of Wilson County to Robert Wallace a tract of land on Goose Creek. 4 May 1831. (P. 193)

David Palmer to George F. Carpenter 170 acres. 1848. (Pp. 194-195)

Isham Beasley to William H. Beasley. 7 December 1848. (P. 195)

William Mason to John Mason his interest in the estate of Wyle Mason, his father. 16 November 1848. (P. 196)

William Garrett to Edwin (   ) a tract of land. 28 November 1848. (P. 197)

Stephen Ellison and wife Nancy to Mathew (   ) their power of attorney. 6 September 1848. (P. 198)

Mathew Worley and wife Huldah appoint ( ) ( ) as their attorney in settling the estate of Amos Ellison. November 1848. (P. 199)

Mathew Worley and wife Huldah and Stephen Ellison of Illinois to Harrison (   ). 1848. (P. 200)

Jefferson Jeffreys to John L. Arundell 50 acres. 11 December 1848. (P. 200)

William L. Martin to Charles Coker a tract of land. 4 September 1848. (P. 201)

DEED BOOK T

Edward ( ) to George Whitlock. 1848. (P. 202)

Stephen Goad to Joshua Goad a tract of land. December 1848. (P. 203)

John T. Hensley to Thomas Fisher 297 acres. October 1847. (Pp. 203-204)

John T. Hensley to Thomas Fisher a tract of land. October 1847. (P. 204)

Sheriff John Bridges to James A. Richardson a tract of land. 1848. (Pp. 204-206)

Isaac A. Parker and wife Sarah, Jane Parker, Samuel Moss, Samuel ( ) and wife Polly, William P. Moss, Daniel Apple and wife Alisha to John A. Moss their interest in a tract of land. 14 December 1848. (Pp. 206-207)

Bazzle Harmon to William Stalcup, Jr. a negro boy. 16 December 1848. (Pp. 207-208)

Hiram C. Cooksey to Benjamin Cooksey. 23 September 1848. (P. 208)

James Holland and wife Nancy of Effingham County, Illinois to Benjamin Cooksey their interest in the estate of Lilley Cooksey. 23 September 1848. (P. 209)

Mason Walker and wife Elizabeth to Benjamin Cooksey their interest in the land on which Gilly Cooksey now lives. 8 October 1848. (P. 210)

Benjamin Cooksey to E. P. Haley 15 acres. 6 December 1848. (Pp. 210-211)

Jesse Cunningham to Robert Gann his interest in the estate of James Cunningham. 28 December 1848. (P. 211)

S. B. Pyran and Charles T. Pyran appoint Tapley B. Pyran as their attorney in settling the estate of David Pyran. 1 January 1849. (P. 212)

Alethia Allen to Robert A. Lapley a tract of land. 1848. (Pp. 212-213)

Archibald Scruggs to Martin Whitten. 1848. (P. 214)

Eason B. Clark to Samuel B. McDonald his interest in several slaves. 7 September 1848. (Pp. 214-215)

Amanda Clark to Samuel B. McDonald in the slaves belonging to her father Andrew Clark. 11 August 1848. (P. 215)

James C. Sanders to William Dawson 120 acres. 1 September 1848. (Pp. 215-216)

William Bransford, Richard H. Bransford, James W. Bransford, Daniel Glen and wife Mary, Martin McMurry and wife Ann, Lindsley M. Bransford, Mary C. Bransford, Nancy Bransford, James Barnett and wife Mary, Charles McMurry, John M. McMurry, Sally McMurry, James McMurry, and Fountain McMurry, heirs of John Bransford. 1848. (Pp. 216-217)

DEED BOOK T

Stockard W. Coffee to Robert Hodges a tract of land. 1849. (P. 218)

Silas C. Cornwell, administrator of Edward Carver, bill of complaint against John Carver. 1849. (Pp. 218-219)

Addison Askins to Joannah Crowder 81½ acres. 4 March 1848. (Pp. 219-220)

Thomas G. Alvis to John S. Davis 86 acres. 20 January 1849. (P. 220)

B. S. Cardwell to Josiah Reece 324 acres. November 1848. (P. 221)

Henry Mann to Wilson Boulton 104 acres. 26 September 1848. (P. 222)

(Manerva) Durham to Wilson Boulton 50 acres on the Caney Fork. 20 October 1848. (P. 222)

Samuel Allison to Wilson Boulton 50 acres. 28 November 1848. (P. 223)

Mrs. Alethea Allen to Robert A. Lapley of Davidson County a tract of land. November 1848. (Pp. 223-224)

John Reece, Sr. to William Reece 50 acres. 5 October 1848. (Pp. 224-225)

Robert Douglas to Horace Oliver 60 acres. 4 January 1849. (P. 225)

Mary Risen to Felix G. Mann 97 acres. 6 January 1849. (P. 226)

James Tate of Illinois appoints Mathew Lynch as his attorney in settling the estate of his father John Tate. 9 January 1849. (Pp. 226-227)

Ashley Standfield to James H. Vaughan a boy slave. 9 February 1849. (P. 227)

(Page 228 is missing)

Ashley Standfield to Wright and Alexander a tract of land. February 1849. (P. 229)

Ashley Standfield to Wilson Y. Martin a tract of land. 10 February 1849. (P. 229)

E. P. Lowe to Hickerson Barksdale 100 acres. 1 January 1849. (P. 230)

John H. Davis to Ellis B. Kemp 130 acres. 3 February 1849. (P. 231)

Meredith G. Ward to Ellis Beasley 64 acres. 26 August 1846. (P. 232)

James Tate of Illinois to William Tate 254 acres. 16 February 1849. (Pp. 232-233)

John W. Daugherty to John Johnson a negro slave. 8

DEED BOOK T

February 1849. (P. 233)

Allen Piper to James Haynie a tract of land on Peyton's Creek. 15 January 1849. (Pp. 234-235)

James Haynie to James Chambers a tract of land. 16 January 1848. (Pp. 235-236)

James H. McKnight appoints William H. Slaughter as his attorney. Said McKnight is a resident of Texas. March 1849. (P. 236)

David Lynch and Sarah Lynch to William ( ) their interest in the estate of Mary Lynch. 1 February 1849. (P. 237)

Article of a contract between Sarah Pankey, widow of Uzzi Pankey, and her children. 1849. (Pp. 237-238)

D. C. Sanders to Henry Hart a tract of land. 10 February 1849. (P. 238)

B. S. Cardwell to L. H. Cardwell. 21 February 1849. (P. 239)

John James and William James of Arkansas appoint Philip Sadler as their attorney. 1849. (Pp. 239-240)

William C. Norris, William W. Reeves and wife Eliza, Josiah Stevenson and wife Delia, and Nancy Norris, widow of James Norris, to A. R. Creal ten acres. 4 November 1848. (Pp. 240-241)

Joel S. Flowers to Rolfe K. Flowers a lot of negroes. 1 March 1849. (P. 242)

Wilson Boulton to James Boulton a negro slave. 11 September 1840. (P. 242)

John Baker, administrator of John (Baker), Sr. versus Morgan W. Baker, Emily ( ), James ( ), C. Baker, William Haynie and wife Nancy, James Hart and wife Patsy, Thomas Weatherford and wife Matilda, Thomas M. Baker, John G. Davenport and wife Sally, Andrew J. Pendleton and wife Louisa, and James Baker. 1849. (Pp. 242-244)

David ( ) to ( ) ( ) a tract of land. 1849. (P. 244)

James Wolf to James ( ) a tract of 29½ acres. 25 November 1848. (P. 245)

Nancy Norris and others to William C. Norris a quarter of an acre. 22 December 1848. (P. 246)

Nancy Norris and others to Ellis Beasley a tract of land. 22 December 1848. (P. 247)

David Palmer to Warner Lambeth 125 acres. 28 December 1848. (P. 248)

Martin Whitten to James A. Scruggs 75 acres. 26 February 1849. (P. 249)

DEED BOOK T

Samuel P. Howard to the Trustees of the Carthage Female Academy a tract of land. 20 February 1849. (P. 250)

The trustee of Swan Thompson to John Cochran. 1849. (Pp. 250-251)

William D. Hail and Eliza J. Hail to Sterling Hale their interest in 91 acres belonging to the estate of John A. Moore. March 1849. (P. 252)

Richard James to William T. Bennett 115 acres. 5 March 1849. (Pp. 252-253)

Thomas Dies to L. A. ( ) his interest in his father's estate. 21 January 1849. (P. 253)

Stephen A. Farmer to George F. Flippin two tracts of land. 23 November 1848. (P. 254)

S. F. Heflin to H. W. Hart a tract of land on the Caney Fork. 1 March 1849. (Pp. 254-255)

E. S. Ewing to James W. Stephenson a woman slave. 30 January 1849. (P. 255)

E. Harrison to Alfred Catron one half acre. 2 March 1849. (P. 256)

Stephen Allison to James B. Moores a tract of land on Brush Creek. 26 February 1849. (Pp. 256-257)

Mathew Worley and Huldah his wife of Kentucky appoint James ( ) as their attorney. 20 January 1849. (Pp. 257-258)

Sarah Pankey to John H. Davis two negro slaves. 27 January 1849. (Pp. 259-260)

Solomon Williams and wife Mahulda of Mississippi to Mathew Harper their interest in the estate of Mathew Harper. 27 January 1849. (Pp. 260-261)

Robert Marley to James B. Moores a tract of land. 7 March 1849. (P. 261)

Sheriff John Bridges to William Farley a tract of land. 3 March 1849. (Pp. 262-263)

Abraham H. King from F. E. Mitchell four and one fourth acres. 15 December 1847. (Pp. 263-264)

Leroy E. Mitchell to Armstead Moore a tract of land. 9 December 1847. (Pp. 264-265)

Samuel P. Howard to Abram H. King three slaves. 19 March 1849. (P. 266)

Leroy E. Mitchell to William V. R. Hallum. 17 March 1849. (Pp. 266-267)

Samuel P. Howard & Leroy E. Mitchell to Jesse G. Frazier a stock of goods. 17 March 1849. (Pp. 267-268)

DEED BOOK T

Samuel P. Howard to Jesse G. Frazier a tract of land in the town of Carthage. 19 March 1849. (P. 269)

Samuel P. Howard to Oliver Haley two town lots. 3 February 1849. (P. 270)

Oliver Haley to John McClarin two town lots. 3 February 1849. (Pp. 271-272)

Thomas Woodson to D. Fry a tract of land. 20 March 1849. (P. 272)

William Duvall to Jeremiah Jamison and others a tract of land. 22 November 1847. (Pp. 272-273)

Nathan Ward to Samuel C. Bridgewater 160 acres. 22 January 1849. (P. 273)

William (   ) to F. G. Baker 160 acres. 20 March 1849. (P. 274)

Susan Moss and Thomas Moss to George W. Walker a negro woman. 9 December 1848. (P. 274)

Willis Cornwell of Jackson County to James Young a tract of land on Salt Lick Creek. 3 January 1849. (P. 275)

James W. Cage to Wright and Alexander his interest in the estate of his father Pleneon W. Cage. 26 March 1849. (P. 276)

Wilson Bolton to John Bailey two negroes. 22 February 1849. (P. 276)

Robert Whitten to David Smith. 26 March 1849. (P. 277)

William Robinson and M. W. Sloan to Timothy H. Williams a tract of land. 27 March 1849. (Pp. 277-278)

Pleasant Gold to Ephraim Cheek a tract of land on Hickman's Creek. 28 March 1849. (Pp. 278-279)

Thompson Mace to Thomas Gregory 16 acres. 3 March 1849. (Pp. 279-280)

John N. Tucker, Jesse C. Tucker to B. C. Davis their interest in the estate of Zachariah Worley. 29 March 1849. (P. 280)

William E. Jones to Samuel M. Fite a house and lot. 8 September 1848. (Pp. 280-281)

Pleasant Roberts to John B. Gullick a tract of land. 1849. (P. 281)

William Clifton to I. H. Cowan. 2 April 1849. (P. 282)

John J. Burnett to Armstead Moore five acres of wood land. 3 April 1849. (P. 282)

Stephen Austin to Benjamin Denny a tract of land. 21 October 1841. (P. 283)

DEED BOOK T

M. W. Exum to D. Exum his interest in the estate of Joseph Exum. 13 October 1848. (Pp. 283-284)

George Gann and William Gann to Edmund Wilson 55 acres. 15 January 1846. (P. 284)

Henry D. Wilson to Robert Gann 74 acres. 3 April 1849. (P. 285)

A. H. King to B. (   ) a slave. 1 November 1847. (P. 286)

Thomas Lancaster to James A. Richardson a negro woman. 14 April 1849. (P. 286)

Pleasant Rose and Sary Rose of Illinois appoint Richard Hubbard as their attorney in settling the estate of John Hubbard and Sally Hubbard. March 1849. (Pp. 286-287)

Thomas Ballenger to Benjamin Ballenger 200 acres. 12 April 1849. (Pp. 287-288)

Miles F. West, Drewry A. West, Clabourn W. West, Paul Clay, and Marthy Clay to Ridley R. West their interest in 209 acres. 20 October 1848. (P. 289)

William Robinson to Leonard Cardwell a tract of land. 30 March 1849. (Pp. 290-291)

Luther Cheek, Tilman Flippin and Araminta Flippin his wife to John Stevens a tract of land. 9 April 1849. (P. 292)

L. J. Squires to Mathew H. Ward a tract of land on Plunkett's Creek. 9 March 1849. (Pp. 292-293)

James A. Richardson to Thomas Lancaster 200 acres. 16 April 1849. (P. 293)

Wilson Boulton to Richard Bigs a tract of land. 17 April 1849. (P. 294)

J. J. Burnett to William Young a negro boy. 10 April 1849. (P. 294)

Jacob Towson to E. P. Gifford nine acres. 9 February 1848. (P. 295)

Robert Marley to William A. Hall a tract of land on the Cumberland River. 10 December 1846. (Pp. 295-296)

John Stubblefield to Moses Lawson a tract of land. 1849. (Pp. 296-297)

William Jackson to H. C. Sanders a tract of land. 23 April 1849. (P. 297)

Samuel P. Howard to John Dowdy a tract of land in the town of Rome. April 1849. (P. 298)

J. B. Hughes to his daughter Nancy Newsom who has intermarried with John N. (   ) a tract of land. 24 April 1849. (P. 298)

DEED BOOK T

Lot Hazard to Orville Green a tract of land. 29 March 1849. (P. 299)

Sheriff John Bridges to Jackey Ann (   ) a tract of land. 16 October 1848. (Pp. 299-300)

Mathew Exum and wife Jackey Ann, late Jackey Ann Underwood, to Manson Bryan, John S. Bryan, and John H. Savage a tract of land. 21 April 1849. (Pp. 300-301)

John Hailey to David C. Sanders a tract of land. 28 April 1849. (P. 302)

John Timberlake to Armstrong W. Allen a tract of land. 30 April 1849. (P. 303)

Jeremiah Reasonover to William Oakley 81 acres. 25 January 1849. (P. 304)

Sally Pankey, widow of Uzzi Pankey, Stephen Goad and wife Susannah, John Kemp and wife Judith, Joseph Jones and wife Sally, Ellis Kemp and wife Elizabeth, William Kemp and wife Molly, Henry W. Clenden and wife Aletha, William D. Cowley and wife Lucy, Alvan Cardwell and wife Pamelia versus Elisa Pankey. 1849. (Pp. 304-307)

Stephen Goad to Isham Goad 114 acres. 13 December 1848. (P. 308)

John N. Jaden to Nathaniel W. Williams and Leonidas Spraggins a tract of land. 5 July 1848. (P. 308)

Nathaniel W. Williams appoints Leonidas Spraggins as his attorney. 25 October 1848. (P. 309)

George W. Royster to Alben Smith 65 acres. 1849. (Pp. 310-311)

John Jared to Robert Warren 165 acres. 31 January 1849. (Pp. 311-312)

Thomas Ballenger, James Ballenger, and Benjamin Ballenger to James Barrett a tract of land on Mulherin's Creek. 12 May 1849. (Pp. 312-313)

William Duvall to James Piper a negro girl. 14 May 1849. (P. 313)

James A. Richardson, administrator and only heir of Bernard Richardson, to Martha J. Hogan, James E. Hogan, Bailey P. Hogan, Thomas B. Hogan, and Benjamin R. Hogan, the heirs of Anthony Hogan 285 acres. 7 May 1849. (Pp. 314-315)

Nathan Ward versus John W. Bowen, Elizabeth Moores and William B. Morris. 1849. (Pp. 315-316)

James A. Richardson to William Dillard 50 acres. 6 May 1849. (P. 317)

James Boston to Christopher Heston a tract of land. 17 May 1849. (P. 318)

DEED BOOK T

James Bradley, administrator of P. W. Cage to John ( ). 1849. (Pp. 318-319)

Henry B. Clark to Hannah Carlisle, formerly Hannah Allen and wife of Wesley Carlisle, and her children. 29 September 1847. (Pp. 319-320)

Archibald V. Allen to Allen Piper 125 acres. 18 January 1849. (P. 320)

Henry Morgan to James M. Taylor 103 acres. 14 August 1847. (P. 321)

Joel Algood, executor of Charles Ledbetter, to John H. Bates a tract of land. 6 January 1849. (Pp. 321-322)

James W. Blackwell to Alfred Winkler a girl slave. 10 February 1849. (P. 322)

Thomas W. Wooten to John Bradley a tract of land on Hogan's Creek. 5 July 1848. (P. 323)

Richard Chambers to his daughter Rebecca McKee a tract of land on the Cumberland River. 17 May 1849. (Pp. 323-324)

Richard Chambers to his daughter Emerelda Banks some negro slaves. May 1849. (P. 324)

William Duvall to Thomas Minton 115 acres. 8 June 1849. (P. 325)

Thomas Malone to Jeremiah Coggins a tract of land on the Caney Fork. 25 April 1848. (Pp. 325-326)

James Johnson to John Johnson a negro boy. 5 February 1848. (P. 326)

William R. Betty to John Haley a tract of land. 1848. (Pp. 326-327)

Thomas Gwaltney to John Haley a tract of 112 acres. 6 July 1848. (P. 327)

Thomas Gwaltney to J. N. Daugherty a tract of land on Hickman's Creek. 2 June 1849. (P. 328)

William Robinson to ( ) ( ). July 1849. (Pp. 328-329)

Elizabeth Cornwell and husband Pleasant versus Elijah Toney. 1849. (Pp. 329-331)

Mathew Harper to David P. Hodges a tract of land. 5 June 1849. (P. 331)

David Cochran to John Cochran 552 acres. 8 January 184?. (P. 332)

Thomas Clark and Emily Clark appoint David P. Hodges as their attorney. 9 February 1846. (P. 332)

Stewart Doss to Andrew J. Vantrease a tract of land. 18 August 1842. (P. 333)

DEED BOOK T

B. S. Cardwell to William ( ). July 1849. (P. 334)

William Duvall to Allen Piper a tract of land on the Caney Fork. 2 July 1849. (P. 334)

Zebulon McDonald to Samuel G. Slaughter a crop of tobacco. 5 July 1849. (P. 335)

Elizabeth Moores to S. C. Bridgewater her interest in the estate of William Moores. 3 July 1849. (P. 336)

George R. Nash to James Curlee 50 acres. 15 August 1848. (P. 337)

Evin R. Saterfield to G. G. (Killard) some personal property. 9 July 1849. (Pp. 337-338)

Thomas Williams to A. M. Ward. 16 July 1849. (Pp. 338-339)

Stephen Goad and Susan Goad to Ellis B. Kemp their interest in the estate of Uzzi Pankey. 9 March 1849. (Pp. 339-340)

Stephen M. Jones to John H. Bates a negro woman. 2 January 1849. (P. 340)

H. F. Beasley to Hardy Calhoun a crop of tobacco. 25 July 1849. (Pp. 340-341)

William Bates to Lucien B. Sullivan his interest the land he purchased from Richard and Editha Lamberson who were heirs of Horace N. Sullivan. 24 November 1847. (P. 341)

Jonathan Bailey to Hardy Calhoun a negro girl. 14 December 1848. (Pp. 341-342)

D. W. Thomas to Nathaniel Parrot a tract of two acres. June 1849. (P. 342)

Jacob Null to Valentine Presley 150 acres. 4 May 1849. (P. 343)

Valentine Presley to Joseph Mitchell 350 acres. 1849. (P. 344)

John Trousdale to Wilson Bolton a tract of land on the Caney Fork. January 1849. (P. 345)

Christopher C. Penn to Henry Mann 105 acres. 30 July 1849. (Pp. 345-346)

Thomas Haley to William B. Smith and James Smith 90 acres. 1 May 1849. (P. 346)

John H. Bates to William W. Bell. 8 January 1849. (P. 347)

Edward A. Corley and William O. Corley to Alfred Catron a tract of land in the town of Rome. 27 July 1849. (P. 347)

White Mires to Ellis B. Kemp. 1849. (P. 348)

DEED BOOK T

John McMurry to S. T. Harris a negro woman. 3 July 1849. (P. 349)

James C. Williams to James Kerley 182½ acres. 16 October 1849. (Pp. 349-350)

William H. Tucker to Benjamin C. Davis 140 acres. 1 May 1849. (P. 350)

Uriah Pugh to Samuel Pugh a tract of 26 acres. 28 March 1849. (P. 351)

David Fry to George Whitlock a tract of land on Brush Creek. 31 December 1845. (P. 352)

Austin Kerby to William Kerby a tract of land. 19 September 1841. (P. 353)

Allen Crowell to Miles F. West 54 acres. 30 July 1849. (Pp. 353-354)

Green Wright to Jonathan Parker 550 acres. 13 November 1845. (Pp. 354-355)

Joseph Dillard to Rufus Perry a crop of tobacco. 3 July 1849. (P. 355)

Daniel Buie to Joel Gregory a crop of tobacco. 31 July 1849. (P. 356)

Joanna Crowder to Jeremiah Coggin 81 acres. 29 July 1849. (Pp. 336-337)

Thomas A. Frohock to Campbell Crutchfield a crop of tobacco. 2 August 1849. (Pp. 357-358)

Samuel Hunter, Henry Hunter, R. R. Lawrence, Thomas G. Plummer and wife Alia M. to John Gordon a tract of land. July 1849. (Pp. 358-359)

George W. Glover and wife Charlotte, Maderson ( ) and wife Rachel, John Harvel and wife Martha, Rebecca Dickens, Bryant Dickens, Milton Bruce and wife Mary, Lewis Harvel and wife Alsey, John Sadler and wife Fanny, all heirs of Jeremiah Dickens. 1849. (Pp. 360-361)

William C. Richardson to Britton M. Richardson 160 acres. 1849. (Pp. 361-362)

Adam Stafford to Yancy F. Clardy a tract of land. 20 February 1849. (P. 362)

Instance Baugh to John W. Bowen. 2 August 1849. (P. 363)

Henry Rutland to William Floid some livestock. 24 August 1849. (Pp. 364-365)

Thomas A. Lancaster to Jefferson Rowland four acres. August 1849. (P. 365)

Samuel Burdine to Martin W. McCall a tract of land in the town of Rome. 7 April 1849. (P. 366)

DEED BOOK T

Hiram Moses Craig to T. B. Flippin a tract of land on Roll's Creek. 12 April 1849. (Pp. 366-367)

Moses Bellah to Henry Traywell a tract of land on the Caney Fork. 3 September 1846. (Pp. 367-368)

Ellis B. Kemp to William Kemp ten acres. 6 August 1849. (P. 368)

Samuel Lancaster to Harrison ( ) 34 acres. 11 August 1849. (Pp. 368-369)

Mathew Worley and wife Huldah and Stephen Ellison to Samuel Lancaster 189 acres. 11 August 1849. (Pp. 369-370)

John J. Burnett to James G. McDonald a tract of land. 14 August 1849. (Pp. 370-371)

John J. Burnett to B. S. Cardwell 29 acres. 14 August 1849. (Pp. 372-373)

B. B. Sullivan to William Bates and David Malone a tract of land belonging to the heirs of Horace Sullivan. Bounded: Anne Sullivan. 28 July 1849. (P. 373)

Lucian B. Sullivan to Robert H. Sullivan a tract of land belonging to the heirs of Horace Sullivan. 17 August 1849. (P. 374)

John J. Burnett to John Bridges a tract of land. 21 August 1849. (Pp. 374-375)

Sampson McClelin to William M. Knight a tract of 23 acres. 6 September 1849. (P. 376)

John Powell appoints Edward ( ) as his attorney. 18 August 1849. (P. 377)

William M. Payne to Rufus Perry a crop of tobacco. 23 August 1849. (P. 377)

Leonard H. Cardwell to William Robinson a tract of land. 27 August 1849. (P. 378)

Joel Gregory and Henry Jenkins to William Oldham a tract of land. 28 August 1849. (Pp. 378-379)

John Bates to William Snoddy a crop of tobacco. 29 August 1849. (P. 379)

Joel Bates to Stephen Barrett a crop of tobacco. 1849. (P. 380)

John Kelly to Samuel F. Vaden a crop of tobacco. 19 September 1849. (Pp. 380-381)

William D. Sullivan of Washington County, Arkansas appoint Lucian B. Sullivan of Dekalb County, Tennessee in settling the estate of Horace Sullivan. 16 July 1849. (Pp. 381-382)

Allen P. Cardwell to Francis B. Newsom a crop of tobacco. 22 August 1849. (Pp. 382-383)

DEED BOOK T

Martha Jane Tuggle, one of the heirs of Thomas Tuggle, to Daniel Seay her interest in 87 acres. 6 July 1849. (P. 383)

Robert A. Holliday to D&C West a crop of tobacco. September 1849. (P. 383)

Jesse Martin to Drewry A. West a crop of tobacco. September 1849. (P. 384)

J. Everett to Frances Dowell a man slave. 2 February 1848. (P. 384)

B. S. Cardwell to Henry Dowdy a negro boy. 5 September 1849. (P. 384)

Thomas Malone to Isaac Jones a tract of land. 21 August 1849. (P. 385)

Hugh Patterson and wife Cynthia versus Isaac Tinsley and wife Charlotte, William ( ) and wife Sally, Charles Howell and wife Sophia, Samuel Murry, and Harriet Murray. 1849. (Pp. 386-388)

Lot Hazard to James Ballard 17 acres. September 1849. (P. 388)

William McDonald to William McDonald a tract of land. 27 July 1848. (P. 389)

William Young to Elijah W. Crowell 97 acres. 3 September 1849. (Pp. 389-390)

Thomas Malone to Isaac Jones 14 acres. 4 September 1849. (P. 390)

Edwin R. Mathews to Rufus Perry a crop of tobacco. 11 September 1849. (P. 391)

William Young to W. D. Smart a negro woman. 6 July 1847. (P. 391)

William Young to C. B. Reynolds a negro slave. 1849. (P. 391)

James S. Kemp to William McClelin 98 acres. 3 September 1849. (P. 392)

Daniel Jones to Leonard Hughes a tract of land on Hickman's Creek. 19 December 1842. (Pp. 392-393)

Abel W. Williams to H. S. Crain a negro boy. 1849. (P. 393)

Daniel Smith to William Baugh ten acres. 8 March 1848. (P. 394)

John Timberlake to Rufus Perry a crop of tobacco. 5 September 1849. (P. 394)

Mathew Harper to Samuel Allison some personal property. 3 September 1849. (P. 395)

James King to William B. Williams. 1849. (Pp. 395-396)

DEED BOOK T

John Anderson to Sampson McClelin a crop of tobacco. 13 September 1849. (Pp. 396-397)

John Simpson and Effey Simpson to John Mayson their interest in the estate of William Wiley Mason. 19 February 1849. (P. 397)

William Lynch to Henry Perkins a crop of tobacco. 17 September 1849. (Pp. 397-398)

John H. Davis to ( ) Young a woman slave. 18 September 1849. (P. 398)

E. R. Wills and W. W. Wills to Bethel Dedman a boy slave. 29 August 1849. (Pp. 398-399)

Thomas R. Barnett to Harrison Bennett a tract of land on Hickman's Creek. 12 September 1849. (P. 399)

John Rowland to James Rowland seven negroes. 7 March 1848. (P. 400)

George Stephens of Todd County, Kentucky to Archibald W. Overton a tract of land in the town of Carthage. 24 September 1848. (P. 400)

L. E. Mitchell to ( ) ( ). 22 September 1849. (Pp. 400-401)

The Bank of Tennessee to David Smith. 20 September 1849. (P. 401)

D. K. Timberlake to John Armstead a tract of land. 6 September 1849. (P. 402)

John Reece, Sr. to Robert West a tract of land on Defeated Creek. 10 May 1847. (Pp. 402-403)

Stephen Mann to Littleberry (Fanner) a tract of land. 15 September 1849. (Pp. 404-405)

Jesse Pope to Dowdy a crop of tobacco. 27 September 1849. (P. 405)

Sheriff John Bridges to John J. Burnett a negro boy. 5 October 1849. (P. 404)

Dawson B. Harris and Eveline Denny marriage contract. 1849. (P. 404)

Louis Pendleton, George Wood, and James Berry agreement. 25 September 1849. (Pp. 405-406)

Nathan Ward to Jefferson (Bowman) 150 acres. 23 May 1848. (P. 406)

William Exum to John Powell 60 acres. 16 April 1849. (P. 407)

Linton Hale to John McGinnis 100 acres. 20 January 1849)

James M. Herrod to William J. Payne. 1849. (P. 408)

DEED BOOK T

Stewart Montgomery to David McCall a tract of land on Round Lick Creek. 20 June 1849. (P. 409)

Gideon Gifford of Sumner County to Samuel Andrews 20½ acres. 1849. (Pp. 409-410)

James Glasgow to his children, to wit, James, Rebecca, and John Glasgow the tract of land on which I now live. 10 August 1849. (Pp. 410-411)

Ala Dillard to William Dillard a tract of land on Smith's Fork. 4 October 1849. (P. 411)

John Dedman, Sr. to John Dedman, Jr. 50 acres. 15 November 1842. (P. 412)

William Moore to Edward R. Willis a tract of land in the 20th District. 11 August 1849. (Pp. 412-413)

John Harris and Joseph H. Harris to Rufus ( ) a crop of tobacco. 9 October 1849. (P. 413)

William Jones to William Duvall a crop of tobacco. 12 October 1849. (P. 413)

Jacob White to Rufus Perry a crop of tobacco. 13 October 1849. (P. 414)

Adam Ferguson to James Harvey a negro girl. 22 October 1849. (P. 414)

Franklin ( ) to Rufus Perry a crop of tobacco. 6 September 1849. (P. 415)

William Duvall to Charles Duvall 200 acres. 20 October 1849. (P. 415)

James C. Sanders to Vincent Thompson 108 acres. 23 October 1849. (P. 416)

B. S. Cardwell to Leonard H. Cardwell several slaves. 1849. (Pp. 416-418)

Jefferson E. Bowman to Elijah Ball 150 acres. 27 October 1849. (P. 419)

B. S. Cardwell to Asa Kemp. 24 October 1849. (P. 420)

John H. Bates to John B. Norris five acres. 26 October 1849. (P. 420)

Britton M. Richardson to John Anderson 169 acres. 25 May 1849. (P. 421)

John Hopkins to Robert Warren a crop of tobacco. 5 November 1849. (Pp. 421-422)

Alexander Jones to Higgs W. Thomas a tract of land. 24 November 1837. (P. 422)

Henry Strother nominates Abel J. Sullivan as his attorney. 10 March 1848. (P. 423)

John A. Sloan to William Bransford. 1849. (P. 423)

DEED BOOK T

John Hughes to Rufus Perry 209 acres. 6 November 1849. (P. 424)

John Shoulders to D&C West a crop of tobacco. 10 November 1849. (P. 424)

William D. Garrett to John Payne a tract of land on Peyton's Creek. 19 October 1842. (P. 425)

The heirs of James B. Crowder to Abraham Caruthers a tract of land. August 1849. (Pp. 425-426)

William B. Taylor to Daniel Smith. 1849. (P. 427)

W. D. Smart to C. B. Reynolds a negro woman. 4 August 1847. (P. 428)

William Duvall to Josiah Hallum a crop of corn. 13 November 1849. (P. 428)

William Hart versus I. D. Goodall and others. 1849. (P. 429)

Andrew McClelin to Allen Holladay a tract of land on Buffalo Creek. January 1846. (P. 430)

James Armstead to Alexander McKinnis 25 acres. 14 November 18__. (P. 431)

Samuel High to Armstead Moore a tract of land. 27 November 1849. (Pp. 431-432)

Thomas W. Page to William Litchford a tract of land on Plunkett's Creek. 20 November 1847. (P. 432)

George F. Carpenter to Warren Lambeth of Smith County a tract of land on Round Lick Creek. 13 March 1848. (P. 433)

William Vaden to William Strother a tract of land. 14 February 1848. (Pp. 433-434)

Harvey D. Wilson to William Litchford a tract of land on Plunkett's Creek. 20 November 1849. (P. 434)

William J. Payne to James P. Garrett a tract of land on Peyton's Creek. 28 August 1849. (P. 435)

Stephen W. Martin to Nathaniel W. Cage a tract of land on the Cumberland River. 1 November 1849. (Pp. 435-436)

Pleasant Parris to ( ) Baird a tract of 72 acres. 2 January 1849. (436)

Britton M. Richardson to William C. Richardson 220 acres. 1 March 1848. (P. 437)

Samuel Fitzpatrick agrees to support his mother Sarah Fitzpatrick. 7 September 1849. (Pp. 437-438)

Thomas Williams to Benjamin Williams 250 acres. 1849. (P. 438)

Josiah Baird, Sr. to Josiah Baird, Jr. 1849. (P. 439)

DEED BOOK T

John H. Davis to William Young a negro girl. 29 November 1849. (P. 439)

Matilda Prowell to Stockard W. Coffee her interest in the estate of Mathew Harper. 24 November 1849. (P. 440)

William Thomas to Oliver F. Young a negro slave. 24 November 1849. (P. 440)

Sheriff John Bridges to Colbert Porter a tract of land. 29 November 1849. (P. 441)

Sheriff John Bridges to Mary Woodcock a tract of land. 29 November 1849. (P. 442)

W. W. Reeves and Eliza Reeves to William C. Norris 150 acres. 1848. (P. 443)

John H. Bedford and Elizabeth A. Bedford to William W. Seay 214 acres. 1 December 1849. (P. 444)

Obediah Woodson to David Fry 132 acres. 30 November 1849. (P. 445)

Daniel Smith to William Arnett $37\frac{1}{2}$ acres. 1 December 1849. (Pp. 445-446)

Levi Foutch to John Jones 50 acres. 1849. (P. 446)

James Jones to John Jones 20 acres. 24 January 1849. (P. 447)

Eveline Toney to Daniel Rolley. 1849. (Pp. 447-448)

John J. Hughes to Charles L. Pig 68 acres. 21 December 1848. (P. 448)

Samuel Pugh to Matilda Prowell a tract of land on Mulherin's Creek. 7 November 1849. (P. 449)

Anthony Holland to Benjamin Payne 16 acres. 7 February 1849. (Pp. 449-450)

Moses Lawson to Edmond Harrison 146 acres. 16 November 1849. (P. 450)

William D. Hale and wife Eliza J. and her son John P. Burford to William E. Jones three negroes. 14 December 1849. (P. 451)

David Palmer to George F. Carpenter a tract of land. 4 December 1849. (Pp. 451-452)

Frances H. Gordon to David Palmer a tract of land. 4 December 1849. (P. 452)

Woodson Hubbard appoints David K. Timberlake as his attorney in settling the estate of Thomas J. Hubbard. 14 December 1849. (P. 453)

Sarah Pankey to John H. Davis a tract of land for taking care of her. 29 January 1849. (Pp. 453-454)

Thomas D. Cage to Wright & Alexander. 1849. (Pp. 454-455)

DEED BOOK T

James Young of Jackson County to Augustine S. (Thorn) two and one fourth acres. 26 November 1849. (P. 455)

Augustine S. Thorn to James Ray 50 acres. 20 October 1849. (P. 456)

John L. Dillard and Helen Dillard to Henry B. McDonald a tract of land. 15 May 1848. (P. 457)

Henry B. McDonald to William B. Campbell and others a town lot in the town of Carthage. 30 June 1849. (P. 458)

( ) ( ) to Caleb Carman 59 acres. 15 December 1849. (P. 459)

William Reece to John Reece, Sr. 50 acres. 1 December 1849. (P. 459)

George C. Allen to William E. Jones a negro woman. 26 September 1849. (P. 460)

Patsy Cleveland to S. Settle one acre. 12 November 1835. (P. 460)

James McMurry to Richard Bransford $100\frac{1}{2}$ acres. 18 December 1849. (P. 461)

John Corley to Thomas Driver and John H. Ammonett a tract of land. 25 December 1849. (Pp. 461-462)

Elizabeth L. Banks, Ermehilda Banks, Charles F. McKee and wife Rebecca, heirs of John C. Chambers, received the slaves of their brother, the said John C. Chambers. 1849. (Pp. 462-463)

W. H. Allen to Young Marley some slaves. 5 January 1850. (P. 463)

Nancy Cunningham to Robert Gann her interest in the estate of James Cunningham. 1 January 1850. (P. 464)

William D. Hale and Eliza J. Hale to Samuel Allison a tract of land on Mulherin's Creek. 1 January 1850. (Pp. 464-465)

Robert Allen, Sr. to Jacob Roberts a tract of land. 7 February 1842. (P. 465)

Joseph W. Stevenson, Delia A. Stevenson, and William C. Norris, heirs of James Norris, to William C. Norris a tract of land. 9 July 1848. (P. 466)

Henry B. McDonald to William E. Jones a tract of land in the town of Carthage. 27 August 1849. (P. 467)

Samuel Bell to William Litchford 260 acres. 22 February 1849. (Pp. 467-468)

Branch Nunley to David H. Standford his son in law a tract of land. 25 December 1844. (Pp. 468-469)

Francis G. Baker to Logan D. Ray. 1849. (P. 469)

DEED BOOK T

Swan Thompson, George A. Thompson, and James S. Thompson enters into an agreement in which the said Swan Thompson gives his two sons the tract of land on which he lives. 8 January 1850. (Pp. 470-471)

Stephen Barrett to James Barrett a tract of land. 8 January 1850. (Pp. 471-472)

Richard Barkley of Arkansas to Jeremiah Jamison a tract of land. 1850. (Pp. 472-473)

Richard Barkley to Jeremiah Jamison. 1850. (Pp. 473-475)

Nicholas Smith to Joseph H. Bogle 122 acres. 5 January 1847. (Pp. 475-476)

Coleman S. Sampson to John A. Smart a negro boy. 6 January 1849. (P. 476)

James S. Kemp to Nancy Thomas a tract of land on the Cumberland River. 15 January 1850. (Pp. 476-477)

John M. Crutchfield to William Hallum a tract of land. 26 January 1850. (Pp. 477-478)

J. B. Hughes to his son Lemuel H. Hughes 150 acres. 19 January 1850. (Pp. 478-479)

John L. Arundell to Jefferson Jeffreys 50 acres. 1850. (P. 479)

A. J. Vantrease to Elijah Scott a tract of land on Hickman's Creek. 26 December 1849. (P. 480)

William B. Tuggle to James Gill and Thomas Gill 103 acres. 20 January 1850. (Pp. 480-481)

Benjamin Graves to John Hiett 50 acres. 26 November 1821. (Pp. 481-482)

C. L. Pyran to Thomas Strother a tract of land. 1 February 1850. (Pp. 482-483)

Jacob Waggoner, George Waggoner, Mary Uhles, Darrell Waggoner, Nicholas Waggoner, William Waggoner, Solomon Wyatt and wife Sally, William Duke and wife Susan versus John Waggoner, Martha Davis, David Bass, Henry Milton Taylor and wife Elizabeth, all heirs of Mary Morris. (Pp. 483-484)

John H. Bedford to Hyram Lyles a tract of land on the Caney Fork. 22 October 1849. (Pp. 484-485)

Ellis Beasley to John Tunstall a tract of land. 29 March 1849. (Pp. 485-486)

William D. Hale to John Burford a tract of land. July 1850. (Pp. 486-487)

William M. Jordon and Elizabeth Jordon to Matilda Prowell a tract of land belonging to the estate of Mathew Harper. 24 January 1849. (Pp. 487-488)

DEED BOOK T

Clement McGinnis to Robert Warren a tract of land in the 16th District. 9 February 1850. (Pp. 488-489)

Presley Baley to William Craighead 93 acres. 3 February 1850. (P. 489)

Harriet Summersett to Gideon Gifford her interest in the estate of her husband Joseph Summersett. 11 February 1850. (P. 490)

John D. Bass to David McCall. 1 December 1849. (Pp. 490-493)

William W. Seay to John D. Bass 214 acres. 1 December 1849. (P. 493)

Robert Douglas to Mary Risan 80 acres. 31 January 1849. (P. 494)

William Brim to Joel Gregory a crop of tobacco. 11 February 1850. (P. 495)

William Duvall to W. W. Bailey a negro girl. 15 February 1850. (Pp. 495-496)

John S. Davis to Thomas Kitchen a tract of land on Mulherin's Creek. 23 January 1849. (P. 496)

Hopkins Richardson to William Massey 120 acres. 8 January 1838. (P. 497)

John McClarin to Charles McClarin a tract of land. 23 February 1850. (P. 498)

Robert Oldham to Joseph H. Nickson his interest in the estate of his grandfather Charles Nickson. 1 March 1850. (P. 499)

John Bridges to James B. Moores a tract of land. 22 February 1850. (Pp. 499-500)

B. B. Sullivan to Harbert H. Sullivan. 11 December 1849. (P. 501)

Adam Ferguson to Alfred M. Winkler a negro girl. 1850. (Pp. 501-502)

Frances Dowell to Benjamin M. Davis a tract of land on Hickman's Creek. 20 November 1849. (P. 502)

Mary B. Ward to Henry Dowdy a negro girl. 7 January 1850. (P. 503)

Richardson Roberts to Logan D. Key a tract of 50 acres. 4 March 1850. (Pp. 503-504)

William Farley to Logan D. Key a quit claim deed. 4 March 1850. (P. 504)

Frances Dowell to Wilson Turner a tract of land. 4 March 1850. (P. 505)

Mary M. Linnow to C. J. Linnow. 1850. (P. 505)

DEED BOOK T

Hansford A. Boulton to Robert W. Knight 91 acres. 19 February 1850. (P. 506)

Robert D. Hayley to Thomas Haley a tract of land. 4 March 1850. (Pp. 506-507)

Robert D. Hailey to Lucy Hailey and William D. Hailey 90 acres. 4 March 1850. (Pp. 507-508)

Thompson Mace to his son D. Mace a tract of 100 acres. 15 September 1849. (P. 509)

W. Y. Martin to John H. Ligon the tract of land where my father and mother once had a still house. William Martin is the father of the said W. Y. 4 January 1850. (Pp. 509-510)

Benjamin (Perry) to James High a tract of land. March 1849. (P. 510)

William D. Sullivan to William Bates his interest in the estate of Horace Sullivan. 17 November 1849. (P. 511)

John Denny and wife Narcissa Oliver, Luther B. Cheek and wife Susan, and Martha Cliver, heirs of Bluford Oliver, to B. Oliver and Rellis Oliver their interest in a tract of land. November 1849. (P. 512)

Jeremy Baird of Lawrence County, Arkansas appoints Jeremy P. Baird of the same place as his attorney. Said Jeremy P. takes the place of Andrew Baird. 20 December 1849. (Pp. 513-514)

Nathaniel W. Cage to Mosley Lipscomb a man slave. 22 January 1849. (P. 514)

William Baker to William B. Whitley a negro girl. 25 March 1850. (P. 514)

H. H. Sullivan to William Notes a tract of 280 acres. 8 March 1850. (P. 515)

William Bates to H. H. Sullivan 75 acres. 8 March 1850. (Pp. 515-516)

Joseph G. Pickett to William B. Campbell his interest in a house and lot in the town of Carthage. 27 March 1850. (Pp. 516-517)

M. S. Mann to Stephen Mann a negro woman. 25 February 1850. (P. 517)

Daniel Robertson to Campbell Crutchfield and Moses Reeves a negro woman. 19 February 1850. (Pp. 517-518)

John Smart to Frances Dowell a tract of land. 1 April 1850. (Pp. 518-519)

Robert and Anna H. Roberts to John M. Vance, James M. Vance, Matilda Vance, John T. Dawson, William H. Overstreet, and Ramsey Vance a tract of 191 acres. March 1850. (P.

DEED BOOK T

519)

Sanders Haley to William J. Beasley a tract of land on the Cumberland River. 29 March 1850. (P. 520)

Charles S. Tate to William D. Tate a tract of land on the Cumberland River. 22 September 1849. (P. 521)

Thomas W. Page to Sanders Haley 200 acres. 10 February 1849. (P. 522)

Charles S. Tate and William D. Tate to Sanders Haley a tract of 20 acres. 22 September 1849. (P. 523)

Thomas Carman to William B. Perkins 20 acres. 1 April 1850. (P. 524)

James Boston and George Nash to James Taylor a tract of land on Peyton's Creek. 1850. (P. 525)

Robert Oldham to Joseph H. Nickson a tract of land belonging to his deceased father Samuel Oldham. 21 March 1850. (P. 526)

William Hallum to Hardy Calhoun a negro slave. April 1850. (P. 527)

Josiah Hallum to William Hallum 86 acres. 9 April 1850. (Pp. 527-528)

Jesse G. Frazer to Abram H. King a negro girl child. 8 April 1850. (Pp. 528-529)

Charles Neal and wife Mary Ann, children of Elias Dowell, to ( ) Palmer and Joel M. Weatherford a tract of land they received as grandchildren of Nehemiah Dowell. 28 February 1850. (Pp. 529-530)

R. D. Flippin appoints William M. Price as his attorney. 16 April 1850. (P. 531)

Henry Dowdy to John Payne a little negro girl. 7 May 1850. (P. 531)

The heirs of Miles F. West versus Ridley R. West and others. 1850. (Pp. 532-533)

Henry Dowdy to George Allen a tract of land. 7 May 1850. (P. 533)

Drury Cornwell to James A. King 63 acres. 19 October 1848. (P. 534)

Young Marley to Samuel M. Fite his interest in a tract of land in the town of Carthage. 8 May 1850. (P. 535)

Neal Patterson to ( ) Smith a tract of land. 6 May 1850. (Pp. 535-536)

James C. Sanders to Jonathan H. Smith 57 acres. 13 April 1850. (P. 536)

Daniel James to Paul L. Walker. 1850. (P. 537)

DEED BOOK T

Daniel James to Joel J. James a tract of land on Hickman's Creek. 18 April 1850. (Pp. 537-538)

Daniel James to Jeremiah Agee 22 acres. 14 May 1850. (P. 538)

Daniel James to Jeremiah Agee 41 acres. 1 February 1850. (P. 539)

Thomas C. Overton to Archibald W. Overton a tract of land. 1 February 1850. (Pp. 539-540)

Archibald W. Overton and Mary G. Overton his wife to Thomas C. Overton a tract of land. 1 February 1841. (P. 541)

Andrew G. Pickett to John Payne a negro child. 27 May 1850. (P. 542)

Benjamin Wilbourn to Washington Payne 20½ acres. 6 October 1849. (Pp. 542-543)

Lucy Kerby, James Kerby, Sally Young, John Talbot and wife Lucy versus Aletha Hester, Puss Hester, and Robert Hester, heirs of Robert Hester. 1850. (Pp. 543-544)

Mathew Harper to Solomon Smallen the dower of Lucy Kerby which I purchased. 28 May 1850. (P. 545)

William P. Hughes to James Newbell a tract of land. 8 March 1845. (Pp. 545-546)

Edmund Rucks of Dallas County, Arkansas appoints his brother Benjamin Rucks as his agent. 1 April 1850. (Pp. 546-547)

America D. Boulton to John ( ) 30 acres. May 1850. (P. 547)

Asa Brinkle and wife Mary Ann to ( ) Green 50 acres. 3 January 1850. (P. 548)

Robert Massey to Isaac A. Massey his interest in the estate of Sims and Sarah Massey. 24 July 1849. (P. 548)

John Meador to James Climer 30 acres. 28 September 1849. (P. 549)

Thomas Noles to James D. Day a tract of land on Dixon's Creek. 18 February 1850. (Pp. 549-550)

Nancy Upton to her daughter Lucy Gwaltney a tract of land on Hickman's Creek. 9 May 1850. (P. 550)

Nathaniel W. Parrott to John McGee two acres. 4 May 1850. (P. 551)

Lucian B. Sullivan, administrator of Horace N. Sullivan, to David H. Farmer a tract of land. 13 April 1849. (P. 552)

W. and R. Alexander to Thomas J. Noles a tract of land on Dixon's Creek. 13 February 1850. (Pp. 552-553)

DEED BOOK T

Bassel G. Carman to James Climer a tract of land on Goose Creek. 20 August 1849. (Pp. 553-554)

William B. Rutherford to Willis Woodman 60 acres. 18 December 1849. (Pp. 554-555)

James Boulton to Vincent Thompson 180 acres. 1850. (P. 555)

Andrew McClellan to Robert D. Allison a tract of land belonging to the heirs of Robert and Pheby Anderson. 21 August 1848. (P. 556)

Robert D. Allison to Sewel L. Heflin 100 acres. 23 February 1849. (Pp. 556-557)

William Parkhurst to Miles West 25 acres. 14 April 1846. (P. 557)

Cain Stafford to Robert Marshall a tract of land on Goose Creek. 15 December 1842. (P. 558)

George N. Williams to D. A. Tyree a tract of land. 14 October 1849. (P. 559)

William Young to Richard ( ) a tract of land. May 1850. (Pp. 559-560)

J. W. Martin to Daniel Huddleston his interest in the estate of Thomas Martin. 19 June 1850. (P. 560)

Elizabeth Chambers, H. M. Carman and wife Lethe, Samuel Chambers, Robert Hodges and wife Jane, Franklin Chambers, Elizabeth Chambers, Jr., William Chambers, and Mary Chambers to John Chambers their interest in the tract of land on which Elijah Banks now lives. 12 November 1845. (P. 561)

William Hallum certification. 19 January 1850. (P. 562)

Adam Ferguson to Henry Haynie a negro girl. 20 June 1850. (Pp. 562-563)

John McGinnis to Kinchen D. Exum 108 acres. 11 February 1850. (P. 563)

Benjamin L. H. Mathews to Rufus Perry his interest in the estate of his father in law Thomas Martin and in the estate of his brother in law James Martin. 21 June 1850. (P. 564)

W. M. Bains relinquishment. 6 July 1850. (P. 564)

James Parris, L. B. Allison and wife Sarah, F. M. Smart and wife Nancy, all heirs of James Parris, Sr. to Jeremiah H. Baird a tract of land. 2 March 1850. (P. 565)

Adam Ferguson to Thomas Carman a negro girl. June 1850. (P. 566)

Henderson Haley to William W. Anderson a tract of land. 12 April 1850. (Pp. 566-567)

DEED BOOK T

The heirs of William Chambers to Daniel Taylor a tract of land. March 1844. (P. 568)

Adam Ferguson to John Chambers a negro woman. 20 July 1850. (P. 569)

Joseph Cooksey to Benjamin Cooksey a tract of land. 12 June 1850. (P. 569)

James Shelton to Benjamin Cooksey 31 acres. 23 May 1850. (P. 570)

Joseph Cooksey to Benjamin Cooksey his interest in two tracts of land. 2 July 1850. (Pp. 570-571)

W. L. Alexander, Richard C. Alexander, and Romulus Wright to Romulus Wright. 22 May 1850. (P. 571)

John D. Day to James B. Guffey a negro girl. 21 July 1846. (P. 572)

William Tunstall to James P. Wilson one half acre. 29 June 1850. (Pp. 572-573)

E. P. Haley to Benjamin Cooksey 15 acres. 1850. (P. 573)

Harris Grissim to N. B. Anderson 50 acres. 10 September 1846. (Pp. 573-574)

William Duvall and William Farley to William Parks a negro man. 4 June 1849. (P. 574)

Jesse G. Frazer to James B. Moores a tract of land. 6 April 1850. (P. 574)

William Crosslin to William Massey 50 acres. 21 March 1850. (Pp. 575-576)

James Young to his two sons, Oliver F. Young and James H. Young, 300 acres. 20 June 1850. (Pp. 576-577)

Jeremiah Baird of Lawrence County, Arkansas to Lewis Hall a tract of land. 25 February 1850. (P. 577)

H. B. Clark to R. W. Mann 150 acres. 8 August 1848. (P. 579)

James M. Shepherd of Jackson County to Jeremiah (Belk) 50 acres. 6 October 1847. (P. 580)

James Tuggle to Marmaduke Mason a tract of land on Mulherin's Creek. 12 June 1850. (P. 581)

William Baker to U. R. Bradford 175 acres. 22 July 1850. (Pp. 581-582)

The executor of Stephen Kelly, to John T. Stokes 600 acres. 11 October 1849. (Pp. 582-583)

William Cartwright to James C. Williams a tract of land. 25 September 1846. (Pp. 583-584)

James C. Williams to James Russell. 1850. (P. 584)

DEED BOOK T

Ellis Kemp to John Lawrence 15 acres. 1850. (P. 585)

Ellis B. Kemp to James Kerby a tract of land on Defeated Creek. 6 January 1846. (P. 586)

James C. Williams to John Ballard 87 acres. 1850. (P. 587)

Dandridge A. Witt to I. E. and W. W. Belcher 23 acres. 22 July 1850. (P. 588)

Washington Meacham to John Dickens a tract of land. 15 July 1850. (P. 589)

John McGinnis, Martha McGinnis, and Martha Exum to Kinchen D. Exum their interest in the estate of Joseph Exum. 19 June 1850. (Pp. 589-590)

Tilman B. Flippen versus Mariah Wilson. 1850. (Pp. 590-591)

William M. Gregory to William L. Smith 50 acres. 1850. (Pp. 591-592)

James Jenkins to Archibald Jenkins 25 acres. 4 March 1845. (P. 592)

J. S. Reece to James Barry, administrator of Jane Hoskins, for the benefit of Elizabeth F. Reece and her children. 25 July 1850. (Pp. 592-593)

Martin Whitten to David Smith ten acres. 24 July 1850. (P. 593)

Henry Williams to George N. Williams a tract of land on Plunkett's Creek. 30 January 1850. (P. 594)

Lewis Hall to R. G. Davis a negro man. 16 January 1847. (P. 595)

John S. Reece to Isaac R. Moore 113 acres. 30 October 1849. (Pp. 595-596)

Jeremiah Jamison to John H. Burford. 1849. (P. 596)

Archibald Scruggs to Martin Whitten ten acres. 14 March 1846. (P. 596)

Matlock Roberts to Rufus Perry. July 1850. (P. 597)

Articles of agreement between John Harper and Samuel (Becker). 1850. (Pp. 597-598)

James W. Bransford to H. M. Carman 120 acres. 27 September 1849. (Pp. 598-599)

Daniel A. Smith to Johnson Dillehay 25 acres. 1850. (Pp. 599-600)

James Rollings versus Larkin Corley. 1850. (Pp. 600-604)

William Strother to Rufus Perry 100 acres. 19 June 1850. (P. 604)

DEED BOOK T

Thomas J. Noles to Cain Stafford a tract of land. 11 February 1850. (Pp. 604-605)

A. D. Exum to Robin Hays 100 acres. 15 July 1850. (P. 605)

John Barbee to James Craig a tract of land. 9 May 1850. (P. 606)

James Reed of Rutherford County to Flemming Merrit a tract of land. 19 July 1834. (Pp. 606-607)

James Reed to Edward Lawrence a tract of land. 19 July 1834. (Pp. 607-608)

Daniel A. Smith to William M. Gregory 50 acres. 15 November 1848. (Pp. 608-609)

James Gill, executor of John Gill, to Frances P. Gill 140 acres. 23 December 1848. (P. 609)

Vaughan & Tunstall to Levi C. Winkler a tract of land on Peyton's Creek. 6 September 1849. (P. 610)

John Russell, Sr. to David Russell 12 acres. 29 July 1850. (Pp. 610-611)

Sheriff John Bridges to Willis Dunn. 13 December 1848. (Pp. 611-612)

Thomas Stewart to Robert Barton a tract of land. 3 November 1848. (P. 612)

Ellis B. Kemp to John Sneed 230 acres. 6 August 1850. (P. 613)

R. W. Mann to Henry B. Clark 25 acres. 14 April 1849. (P. 614)

William L. Alexander to Archibald Debow one half acre. 3 July 1850. (Pp. 614-615)

Joseph C. Cowan to Robert W. Mann 180 acres. 1 November 1846. (P. 615)

Marmaduke Mason to Diggs W. Thomas a tract of land on Mulherin's Creek. 11 July 1850. (P. 616)

Isaac Webb to Frances B. (   ) 390 acres. 14 April 1850. (P. 617)

William C. Norris, Nancy Norris, Delia Stephenson, William M. Reeves, and Eliza P. Reeves to Ellis Beasley a tract of land in the town of Rome. 1 April 1850. (P. 618)

John House to the Phillipi Schoolhouse a tract of land on Mulherin's Creek. 7 August 1850. (P. 619)

H. H. Kemp appoints Ellis B. Kemp as his attorney. 17 April 1850. (Pp. 619-620)

H. H. Kemp to Ellis B. Kemp. (P. 620)

DEED BOOK T

John Arundell to Stephen Mann 139 acres. 29 December 1848. (P. 621)

Thomas Lancaster to Henry Stans and Charles Stans 42½ acres. 4 November 1847. (P. 622)

James G. Wyatt to James Ballard 50 acres. 30 August 1849. (Pp. 622-623)

Asa Russell to George Boston 30 acres. 25 April 1844. (P. 623)

John L. Cowan and wife Almira, John F. Vance, James M. Vance, John M. Vance, Matilda Vance, William Overstreet to Benjamin J. Vaden 120 acres. 16 August 1850. (P. 624)

John L. Cowan and others to William H. Overstreet a tract of land. 16 August 1850. (P. 625)

John L. Cowan and others to Matilda Vance 23 acres. 16 August 1850. (P. 626)

John L. Cowan and others to James M. Vance 73 acres. 16 August 1850. (P. 627)

James Kerby to Braxton Butler a tract of land on Defeated Creek. 19 August 1850. (P. 628)

Jacob Roberts to William B. Campbell 75 acres. 24 August 1850. (Pp. 629-630)

Van H. Allen to Americus D. Boulton a tract of land. 19 August 1850. (P. 630)

Americus D. Boulton to Joseph Allen of New Orleans a tract of land. 24 August 1850. (P. 631)

William B. Dillon to James S. Bradley. 29 August 1850. (P. 632)

John J. Barnett to Armstead Moore a tract of land. 23 March 1850. (P. 633)

James S. Kemp to Ellis B. Kemp a tract of land in the 2nd District. 30 August 1850. (Pp. 633-634)

John Hauk to James Hawkins his claims in the estate of Willis Hawkins. 29 August 1850. (Pp. 634-635)

Ellis Beasley to William M. Price and Jefferson Link a tract of land. 10 August 1850. (P. 636)

Elijah Butts, Mary Butts, and Thomas W. Wooten to Jacob Waggoner a tract of land on the Cumberland River. 27 August 1850. (Pp. 637-638)

John Harris to Rufus Perry a crop of tobacco. 2 September 1850. (P. 638)

Richard Boze to Rufus Perry a crop of tobacco. 15 March 1850. (Pp. 638-639)

Eliza Payne and James Rowland bind themselves to each other. 21 November 1846. (P. 639)

DEED BOOK T

James P. King to William H. Allen a tract of land. 29 August 1850. (P. 640)

Henry B. Clark to William Marlow 15 acres. 6 October 1847. (P. 641)

Stephen Mann to S. B. Hughes 30 acres. 2 September 1850. (Pp. 641-642)

Hopkins Richardson to Henry Wilmore a tract of land on Debow's Creek. 25 December 1841. (Pp. 642-643)

John Kelly to Rufus Perry a crop of tobacco. 3 September 1850. (P. 643)

John B. Hughes to his son Lemuel H. Hughes a tract of land. 15 September 1849. (Pp. 643-644)

Jesse G. Frazer to Abram H. King a tract of land in the town of Carthage. 6 April 1850. (P. 644)

Charles Reece to D&C West a crop of tobacco. 9 September 1850. (P. 645)

William Duvall to Henry W. Hart a crop of tobacco. 10 September 1850. (Pp. 645-646)

William Collom to Timothy Walton 22 acres. 6 September 1850. (P. 646)

Robert Donalson and wife Susan, Hannah Manley, William Gaston, Hugh Gaston, and Susan Gaston court case. 1846. (Pp. 647-660)

John Harris to W. Lowe 149 acres. 14 September 1850. (P. 660)

Richard Jones to Samuel W. Barrott a tract of 115 acres. 18 September 1850. (P. 661)

William T. Hall to R. Averett a crop of tobacco. 15 September 1850. (P. 662)

John H. Sanders to E. T. Seay a crop of tobacco. 14 September 1850. (P. 662)

Henry Rutland to J. B. Rutland. 10 December 1849. (P. 663)

Robert L. Lynch to John McClarin a tract of land belonging to him as an heir of Mary Lynch. 20 September 1850. (P. 664)

J. J. Holladay and William Holladay to D&C West a crop of tobacco. 21 September 1850. (P. 665)

Evin J. Williams and Harriet Williams to Mahaley Whitley during her life and then to James Wiley and Temperance, Lacy Ann, and Elizabeth Whitley their interest in the estate of Josiah Whitley. September 1850. (Pp. 665-666)

William Kelly to John Dice 22¼ acres. 29 March 1850. (P. 666)

DEED BOOK T

William Haynie to Thomas C. Taylor a tract of land on Peyton's Creek. 30 September 1850. (Pp. 667-668)

Elijah Cornwell to William Belcher and the other trustees a tract of land in the 2nd District for a meeting-house. 20 November 1849. (P. 668)

William M. Payne to Rufus Perry a crop of tobacco. 25 September 1850. (P. 669)

James M. Thomas to D&C West a crop of tobacco. 25 September 1850. (P. 669)

Jesse Martin to ( ) ( ) a crop of tobacco. 25 September 1850. (P. 670)

James ( ) to Rufus Perry a crop of tobacco. 25 September 1850. (P. 670)

Jonathan H. Smith to William H. Tyree 57 acres. 26 September 1850. (P. 671)

Elias Barbee to Evin J. Williams 130 acres. 6 September 1850. (P. 672)

Henry Goad to John S. Cowan a tract of 36 acres. 20 September 1850. (P. 673)

Joel Bates & John Bates to Stephen R. Sampson a crop of tobacco. 25 September 1850. (Pp. 673-674)

Benton Kemp to D&C West a crop of tobacco. 25 September 1850. (P. 674)

James Barnett to Henry Williams a tract of land on Plunkett's Creek. 24 September 1850. (Pp. 674-675)

James Craig and Hiram M. Craig to James Mofield 65 acres. 28 September 1850. (Pp. 675-676)

Caleb Stafford of Obion County, Tennessee to John Perier a tract of land. 11 June 1849. (Pp. 676-677)

William H. Allen to Richard Holland ten acres. 1849. (P. 677)

James J. Malone to A. G. Donoho 365 acres. 1 January 1849. (P. 678)

E. R. Thompson to William Brittain a tract of land. 20 February 1847. (P. 679)

George C. Allen to William W. Carter five acres. 1850. (Pp. 679-680)

David Warford to John Washer a tract of land. 4 September 1848. (Pp. 680-681)

William M. Payne to James Haynie. 7 October 1850. (Pp. 681-682)

Jacob Roberts to Logan D. Key six acres. 1 October 1850. (P. 682)

DEED BOOK T

David Black to James C. Sanders the negroes which belonged to my mother. 13 April 1850. (Pp. 682-683)

Andrew Williby to Ligon & Sampson a crop of tobacco. 7 October 1850. (P. 683)

William Reece to B. M. Richardson. 9 October 1850. (Pp. 683-684)

David Rawley to John McClelin a crop of tobacco. 8 October 1850. (Pp. 684-685)

John Shoulders to D&C West a crop of tobacco. 19 September 1850. (P. 685)

Mathew Harper to D&C West a crop of tobacco. 8 October 1850. (P. 685)

B. S. Cardwell to John W. Huddleston. 10 October 1850. (P. 686)

William Young to Edwin Kitrell 281 acres. September 1850. (Pp. 686-687)

John Bowman to Lemuel Skelton a tract of 33 acres. 15 October 1850. (Pp. 687-688)

Yancy Blackwell to E. P. Gifford nine acres. 24 October 1850. (P. 688)

Yancy Blackwell to E. P. Gifford four acres. 24 October 1850. (P. 689)

George W. Rose to William Grissam 100 acres. 29 July 1850. (P. 690)

B. E. Warren to William Grissam a tract of land on Fall Creek. 16 October 1850. (Pp. 690-691)

John R. James versus the heirs of John Gwaltney. 1850. (Pp. 691-692)

The heirs of Mary Lynch to M. E. Corley. 1850. (P. 693)

Jason Winchester to Jacob Null a tract of land. 22 June 1844. (Pp. 694-695)

B. B. Uhles to John McClarin a crop of corn. 25 September 1850. (P. 695)

B. R. Noles to Yancy Blackwell four acres. 23 February 1850. (Pp. 696-697)

Enoch Gann to Robert Gann his interest in the estate of his father James Cunningham. 1850. (Pp. 697-698)

Ridley R. Teague to John L. Powell 17½ acres. 13 October 1850. (P. 698)

Daniel Allen to Burton Allen 100 acres. 25 August 1840. (P. 699)

Ellis B. Kemp to Asa Kemp. 1850. (P. 700)

DEED BOOK T

Mary E. Crastic of Weakley County, Tennessee appoints Barney Lane as her attorney. 7 June 1850. (P. 701)

Mary E. Crastic to Leroy H. Cage the land of Sherrod Crockett. 4 November 1850. (Pp. 701-702)

The heirs of John Harris, to wit, Widow Susan Harris, Margaret Harris, Thomas Lindner and wife Mary, and Archibald Harris versus Dolly Ann Harris, Samuel Harris, William B. Harris. 1850. 1850. (Pp. 702-703)

Mary E. Crastic, Joseph Crastic, and Barney Lane versus Judith H. Crastic. 1850. (Pp. 703-704)

Elizabeth Buckley to John C. Casley a tract of land on the Cumberland River. 24 July 1848. (Pp. 705-706)

Mary W. Cage to James McMurtry a tract of land. 4 November 1850. (P. 706)

B. E. Warren to Isaac Swan 100 acres. 28 October 1850. (P. 706)

Joel B. Falks to James A. Thomas his interest in the estate of his father Joel Fulks. 22 ( ) 1850. (Pp. 706-707)

Thomas Shoulders to Betsy Gregory 32 acres. 1 November 1850. (Pp. 707-708)

Robert Gann to Tilman B. Flippin a tract of land that belonged to James Cunningham. 1850. (P. 708)

William H. Grisham, administrator of Harris Grisham, to N. B. Anderson 50 acres. 21 October 1850. (Pp. 708-709)

M. L. Uhls to Henry Perkins a crop of tobacco. 15 April 1850. (P. 709)

Isaac Lynch to Rufus Perry a crop of tobacco. October 1850. (P. 710)

Frances Kerby and Samuel Harris to Charles Pyram a tract of land on Goose Creek. November 1850. (Pp. 710-711)

James Rucks of Washington County, Mississippi to Prudence R. Hubbard his interest in the tract of land owned by Josiah Rucks deceased. 26 January 1850. (P. 711)

James Barrett to Frances Hobbs. 11 October 1850. (P. 711)

George Walker to Susan Moss a tract of land on Dixon's Creek. 9 December 1848. (Pp. 712-713)

William Lynch to Rufus Perry a crop of tobacco. 9 November 1850. (P. 713)

Moses Loy to Wright & Alexander. 28 October 1850. (Pp. 714-715)

Division to Valentine Banks. 1850. (P. 715)

DEED BOOK T

Elizabeth Sloan to Josiah Sloan 91 acres. 8 February 1848. (P. 716)

Woodson Hubbard, Richard Hubbard, John C. Hughes, Martha (Dunn), Pleasant Rose and wife Sally, David Moseley, Nancy Moseley, Lent Boulton and wife Eliza, Simon Hughes, William Hughes, George P. Simmons and wife Sarah A., Josiah R. Hubbard, William Hubbard, Elizabeth Hubbard, and Thomas Hubbard, all heirs of Sally Hubbard. 1850. (Pp. 717-718)

Lot Hazard to Thomas D. Seaton 51 acres. 4 November 1850. (P. 718)

William Glasgow to Leman Hale a tract of land. 11 September 1812. (P. 719)

Francis Duffy from Sheriff John Bailey. 12 February 1848. (P. 720)

Milton Brockett to Martin W. Sloan a tract of land on Turkey Creek. 18 October 1848. (Pp. 720-721)

Gideon Gifford to T. P. G. Gifford six acres. 20 November 1850. (Pp. 721-722)

Franklin Rollings to Frances Parker his interest in a tract of land he is to receive at the death of Elizabeth Gifford. 25 October 1850. (P. 722)

Jonathan Bailey of Wilson County to Moses Caster 206 acres. 19 November 1850. (P. 723)

Jonathan Bailey to Moses Caster a tract of land. 6 November 1850. (P. 724)

Elijah W. Hale to William H. Hale his interest in the estate of Leman Hale. 23 June 1831. (P. 725)

Andrew Harris and Mathew A. Harris to William Hale his interest in the estate of Leman Hail. 4 November 1850. (P. 726)

William Dillon to James W. Martin some personal property. November 1850. (Pp. 727-728)

Winney Martin to Andrew Carter 130 acres. 12 November 1850. (Pp. 728-729)

Samuel C. Debow to George H. Bandy 158 acres. 15 November 1850. (P. 729)

Thomas Malone, Vincent McIntire, and Thomas ( ) to Thomas L. Finley 72½ acres. 25 August 1849. (P. 730)

Thomas L. Finley to Thomas J. Finley 72½ acres. 1850. (Pp. 730-731)

Eliza Scott to Abel and John Hunt. 26 December 1849. (Pp. 731-732)

Whaley Newby to George F. Carpenter a tract of land on Round Lick Creek. 10 May 1848. (Pp. 732-733)

DEED BOOK T

Stephen (Hickman) to Thomas Fisher 100 acres. 22 November 1850. (Pp. 733-734)

John S. Winkler to Arthur Winkler his interest in the estate of his mother Perlina Winkler who has a life estate in the property of Ephraim Winkler. 25 July 1848. (Pp. 734-735)

Thomas Fisher to Stephen Hickman 50 acres. 22 November 1850. (P. 735)

George Whitlock to James N. Boon two acres. 23 June 1849. (P. 736)

Samuel Burdine to David McCall a tract of land in the town of Rome. Bounded: Methodist Episcopal Church. 6 April 1849. (Pp. 736-737)

S. B. Grissim to Thomas W. Page her dower. 29 November 1850. (Pp. 737-738)

John Beckman to Henry B. McDonald a tract of land. 20 January 1848. (Pp. 738-739)

John Russell to Thomas Russell 160 acres. 1 August 1842. (Pp. 739-740)

Frances Cunningham to Robert Gann his interest in the estate of his father James Cunningham. 29 November 1850. (P. 740)

Lucy W. Allen to John S. Rowls two tracts of land. 2 November 1849. (P. 741)

John Lancaster to Russell & Marchbanks. 24 August 1842. (P. 742)

Isaac Moores to Edward Lawrence a tract of land on Brush Creek. 14 May 1838. (Pp. 742-743)

Jesse B. Andrews to C. W. Andrews a negro slave. 26 July 1850. (P. 744)

Edwin Kitrell to J. E. and W. W. Belcher three acres. 3 October 1849. (Pp. 744-745)

Edward E. Cage to James Bradley his interest in the estate of his father P. W. Cage. 21 December 1850. (P. 746)

John Sneed to Ellis B. Kemp a tract of land. 1 November 1850. (P. 747)

Isaac Bradley to Thomas Snoddy, Sr. a tract of land. 2 December 1850. (P. 748)

J. J. Hibbitt to Mosley Lipscomb 76 acres. 12 January 1850. (P. 749)

Lemuel H. Hughes to Simon Hughes 150 acres. 25 November 1850. (P. 750)

L. J. Squires to Mathew H. Ward. 1850. (P. 751)

DEED BOOK T

David C. Bradley, Edward Bradley, Frances Bradley, William A. Herod and wife Judith, Charles McClarin and wife Nancy, William Bradley, Henry B. Haynie and wife Sarah, Thomas Bradley, Mary Bradley, and Elizabeth Bradley, heirs of John Bradley. 1850. (P. 752)

William Winchester to Joseph Mitchell 30 acres. 14 October 1850. (P. 753)

(Page 754 is blank)

William Winchester to Coleman Helmes a tract of 65 acres. 14 October 1850. (P. 755)

(Page 756 is blank)

Lemuel H. Hughes to his wife Mary Ann Hughes a negro man. 25 November 1850. (P. 757)

Jesse G. Frazer to James B. Moores. 6 April 1850. (P. 758)

DEED BOOK U

George C. Gifford to George H. Burnley 40 acres. 15 November 1850. (P. 1)

John Robinson and wife Sarah B. to George B. Martin their interest in the estate of Thomas Martin. 16 November 1850. (P. 2)

William Shoemake certification. 1850. (Pp. 2-3)

John R. Rollings to W. W. Carter a negro man. 3 January 1851. (P. 3)

William Sloan to Britton M. Richardson 270 acres. 31 December 1850. (Pp. 3-4)

Stephen Hickman to his mother Silvy Hickman. 15 January 1851. (Pp. 4-5)

David Burford to Calvin Brewer a tract of 95 acres. 28 December 1850. (P. 5)

Allen L. Bains to Brice M. Bains his interest in a tract of land belonging to George Bains. 30 December 1850. (P. 6)

John H. Bedford to D. Stanford a slave. 24 December 1850. (P. 7)

Benjamin J. Armstrong to Martin W. Armstrong his interest in the estate of his father John B. Armstrong. 11 January 1845. (P. 7)

Jeremiah Jamison to David W. Hance 343½ acres belonging to the heirs of Hugh Gaston. 1 January 1851. (Pp. 8-9)

John Maggart to David Harville a tract of land. Bounded: Jane Maggart. 13 March 1848. (P. 9)

Joseph Bowman to James W. Grissam a tract of land. 30 December 1850. (P. 10)

Green Wright to William Cullum a slave. 3 January 185?. (P. 11)

W. Y. Walker to Leroy Bradley a woman slave. 9 November 1850. (P. 11)

Wilson Boulton to Bridges and others. 30 December 1850. (P. 12)

James H. Butler to Benjamin J. Vaden a crop of tobacco. Said Butler is indebted to the estate of Patrick Hubbard of which Polly Hubbard executed. 1851. (Pp. 12-13)

Andrew G. Pickett to Edward B. Haynie a mulatto girl. 7 January 1851. (P. 13)

The heirs of James Cunningham to Robert Gann. 1851. (P. 14)

Robert Gann to Henry D. Wilson 75 acres. 22 January 1851. (P. 15)

DEED BOOK U

Joseph H. Baker to Susan Baker a tract of land belonging to the estate of George Baker. 3 January 1849. (P. 16)

Robert Gann to Harvy D. Wilson 150 acres. 23 January 1851. (P. 17)

Elizabeth Chambers to Charles H. Tunstall a man slave. 6 January 1851. (P. 18)

Jefferson Link to John H. Bates three negroes. 1 January 1851. (P. 18)

Adam Ferguson to Joseph Bowman several negroes. 8 January 1851. (Pp. 19-20)

John Brim to Adam C. Perkins 50 acres. 24 August 1840. (P. 21)

Thomas B. Durham and Jeptha Durham to John Buckner two and one half acres. 24 October 1850. (Pp. 21-22)

Adam C. Perkins to Richard J. Brown a tract of land on Peyton's Creek. 6 January 1851. (Pp. 22-23)

Stephen Mann, administrator of John Harper, to Samuel Bickers 40 acres. 4 January 1851. (P. 23)

Gion Gregory and wife Amanda to Thomas Key their interest in the estate of Thomas Gregory which they are to receive at the death of Elizabeth Gregory. 8 January 1851. (P. 24)

John H. Bates to Jefferson Link 195 acres. 1 January 1851. (P. 25)

William Gregory, Sr. to James L. Gregory 100 acres. 3 January 1851. (P. 26)

Leighton Philips to Thomas Hines 120 acres. 14 October 1850. (P. 27)

Albert H. Ross to Samuel M. Fite his interest in a tract of land in the town of Carthage. 9 January 1851. (P. 28)

Boling D. High to Rufus Perry some slaves. 14 January 1851. (Pp. 28-29)

John McMurry to Skelton T. Harris of Sumner County a negro woman. 2 July 1849. (P. 29)

Charles Powell, Malinda Powell, Benjamin Mathews, Martha Mathews, George Powell, and Rebecca Powell to William J. Martin their interest in the estate of Thomas Martin. 15 November 1850. (P. 30)

William B. Campbell to Stephen Mann a negro girl. 14 January 1851. (P. 31)

Henry Williams to his daughter Susan Mary Harris, now the wife of Ewing R. Harris, some slaves. 17 January 1851. (P. 32)

DEED BOOK U

Mary B. Ward, James L. Thompson and wife Tabitha, A. M. Ward, and B. C. Ward to John Rowls a tract of land on the Cumberland River. 2 January 1851. (Pp. 33-34)

William B. Campbell to Henry Hackett two tracts of land. 25 January 1851. (Pp. 35-36)

William Duvall to Charles McClarin some personal property. 30 January 1851. (Pp. 36-37)

John McKinnis of Simpson County, Kentucky to Brice H. Piper a tract of land on Peyton's Creek. 7 March 1849. (Pp. 37-38)

Britton M. Richardson to Eli Gammon 40 acres. 30 January 1851. (Pp. 38-39)

Ewing R. Harris to Evin J. Williams. 3 February 1851. (P. 39)

Mathew Harper to John W. Bowen a tract of land on the Caney Fork. 3 February 1851. (Pp. 39-40)

Jason R. Sloan, administrator of Sampson Sloan, to John Evans 134 acres. 9 October 1850. (Pp. 40-41)

Isham Beasley to his grandson Edward Andrew Metcalf a negro girl. 12 February 1851. (P. 41)

John Evans to James T. Sutton 134 acres. 1851. (P. 41)

Joel J. James to John C. Sanders 62 acres. 11 January 1851. (Pp. 42-43)

Neal Patterson to John Evans a tract of land in the 6th District. 14 September 1849. (P. 44)

Eli Gammon to Britton M. Richardson 54½ acres. 30 January 1851. (P. 45)

Caleb Pate of Louisiana appoints Anthony William Pate his attorney in settling the estate of Stephen Pate. 9 January 1850. (P. 46)

Peyton Pate of Louisiana appoints Anthony William Pate of Louisiana as his attorney in settling the estate of Stephen Pate. 4 January 1851. (P. 47)

Samuel S. Bailiff versus Green Woods, Harriet Woods, Sarah Elizabeth Woods, Nancy Woods, and Lucy Ann Woods. 1851. (Pp. 48-49)

Catherine Ramsey to William A. Smith 97 acres. 27 October 1848. (P. 49)

Archibald Allen and wife Sarah versus Elizabeth Booker and Mary Booker. 8 February 1851. (Pp. 50-51)

John F. Jones of Madderson County, Mississippi to Mary Ann Payear his sister a tract of land. 9 January 1851. (Pp. 51-52)

DEED BOOK U

Herald D. Marchbanks, Russell Marchbanks, and Thomas C. Marchbanks to Valvery S. Stephen 27½ acres. 5 September 1848. (Pp. 52-53)

John Hallum, executor of William Hallum, to William A. Herrod a tract of land in the town of Carthage. 19 December 1844. (P. 54)

Nelson Thornton to Sampson McClelin a tract of land. 10 February 1851. (Pp. 55-56)

David G. Shepherd to Isaac Massey 100 acres. February 1851. (Pp. 56-57)

Solomon Baker to Vaden & Lee a negro woman. 11 February 1851. (P. 57)

Washington L. McDonald to Henry B. McDonald his interest in the estate of his uncle James B. Crowder. 25 October 1849. (Pp. 57-58)

J. H. McDonald to Henry B. McDonald his interest in the estate of James B. Crowder of Carroll County, Mississippi. Said J. H. McDonald is one of the children of Mary McDonald who was a sister of James B. Crowder. 26 September 1846. (P. 58)

William Coffee and Polly Coffee to Henry B. McDonald their interest in the estate of Joshua Congo. Other heirs: Elisha Congo, William Congo, and John Congo, Joshua Coffee and wife Delilah, Jackson Wallace and wife Nancy. 30 October 1844. (Pp. 59-60)

Isham Beasley to his son William H. Beasley a negro girl. 12 February 1851. (Pp. 60-61)

Isham Beasley to Jere Belk a tract of land on the Cumberland River. 7 February 1851. (P. 61)

Adam Ferguson to David McCall a negro boy slave. 11 January 1851. (P. 62)

Avin Ward to W. Ward a tract of land on Mulherin's Creek. 26 February 1851. (Pp. 62-64)

William Alford to Franklin B. Pierce his power of attorney. February 1851. (P. 64)

Henderson P. Williams to James Piper a negro boy. 27 February 1851. (P. 65)

Winny Martin and Any Martin to Hensley Smith four acres. 12 March 1850. (Pp. 65-66)

Ramsey Vance to Bedford L. Herring a tract of land. 22 September 1849. (Pp. 66-67)

John S. Reece and wife Elizabeth F. and John S. Reece, administrator of Thomas C. Hoskins and James Barry, administrator of Jane Hoskins and William Hoskins minor. 1851. (Pp. 67-68)

DEED BOOK U

Charles R. Blair to James T. High a tract of land on the Cumberland River. 3 March 1851. (Pp. 68-69)

B. F. Ballenger to Johnson Underwood two slaves. 13 February 1851. (P. 69)

Gregory Moore to Jorden Kilzer 14 acres. 1 March 1849. (P. 70)

Dixon Brown to Robert Brown his interest in his father's estate. 8 March 1857. (P. 71)

William Dawson to William McKinney a tract of land on the Cumberland River. 5 March 1851. (Pp. 71-72)

Nathaniel Macon and wife Elizabeth to William Moore 186 acres. 31 December 1850. (Pp. 72-73)

Adam Ferguson to Joseph Bowman a tract of land. 19 March 1851. (Pp. 73-76)

Elizabeth Gifford to her son Edmond P. G. Gifford 100 acres. Mentions Joseph Gifford and J. C. Gifford. 27 March 1851. (Pp. 76-77)

Andrew Harris and Martha A. Harris to William H. Haile a tract of land on which Leamon Haile resided at the time of his death. Said Martha A. was a daughter of the said Leamon Haile. 4 November 1850. (Pp. 77-78)

D. W. Humphrey appoints Gideon Gifford as his attorney. to receive the estate of his father Charles Humphrey. 9 April 1851. (Pp. 78-79)

B. F. Ballenger to Robert Espey a negro boy. 17 April 1851. (P. 79)

David McCall to Adam Ferguson a negro boy. 24 March 1851. (P. 80)

Daniel K. Kelly and P. N. Kelly to William P. Kelly and George P. Kelly a tract of land. 18 February 1850. (Pp. 80-81)

Adam Ferguson to Joseph Bowman a negro boy. 24 March 1851. (Pp. 81-83)

Nathaniel W. Cage to Bias Russell a tract of land. 1 January 1851. (Pp. 83-84)

John Rowls to D. H. and W. N. Suit a tract of land. 17 January 1851. (P. 84)

Jesse T. Hollis to Isaac Jones six acres. 3 March 1849. (P. 85)

S. M. Coffee to John Lamberson his interest in the estate of David Coffee he is to receive at the death of Scythia Coffee. 24 March 1851. (P. 86)

John Rawls to Edmond Harrison 77 acres. 13 February 1851. (Pp. 86-87)

DEED BOOK U

D. H. and W. N. Suit to Henry Page a tract of land in the 12th District. 24 March 1851. (Pp. 87-88)

Lewis Hall to Benjamin Avant 150 acres. 1 October 1850. (Pp. 88-89)

Giles Williams heirs to Jeremiah Coggin a tract of land. Heirs: Elizabeth Williams, Rachael F. Nixon, Louisa H. Nixon, and Semantha J. Nixon. 11 April 1851. (Pp. 89-90)

J. B. Jones, Daniel Jones, and John Stuart to Samuel L. Bailiff a tract of land for a school building in the 15th District. 16 August 1851. (P. 90)

Robert Oldham and wife Rhoda to James Piper, Jr. their interest in the estate of their father Samuel Piper. 25 January 1851. (Pp. 91-92)

Smith Gregory to Joseph N. Gregory and James N. Gregory 160 acres. 9 May 1848. (P. 93)

Joseph N. Gregory and William Gregory to Archibald Jenkins 100 acres. 31 August 1850. (P. 94)

Moses Reeves versus B. B. Uhles, James Hogan, William Hogan, Hoden W. (   ) and wife Elizabeth (   ). 1851. (Pp. 94-97)

John Page to Clinton Hooks a tract of land in the 12th District. 2 August 1850. (P. 98)

Clinton Hooks to Bryan Ward a tract of land on Douglas' Creek. 15 February 1851. (Pp. 98-99)

Ellis B. Kemp to John H. Davis 143 acres. (Pp. 99-100)

Barton Allen to George Waggoner a tract of land on Mulherin's Creek. 29 March 1851. (Pp. 100-101)

Daniel McCachern to Benjamin S. Enoch 144 acres. 31 March 1851. (Pp. 101-102)

B. E. Warren to Anderson Woods 50 acres. 11 November 1850. (Pp. 102-103)

B. F. Thomas to J. W. Johnson a negro man slave. 4 March 1851. (P. 103)

Orville Green to James T. High a tract of land on the Caney Fork. 31 March 1851. (P. 104)

Benjamin Enoch to Robert Enoch a tract of land. 20 February 1847. (Pp. 104-105)

James Eaton to James N. Eaton 50 acres for love and affection. 29 December 1849. (Pp. 105-106)

John Trousdale to W. W. Bailey a tract of land. 30 December 1849. (Pp. 106-109)

Alfred M. Winkler to Daniel Taylor a tract of land on Peyton's Creek. 19 March 1850. (Pp. 110-111)

DEED BOOK U

W. W. Seay and John H. Bedford to James A. Crutcher a tract of land in the town of Rome. 15 December 1850. (P. 111)

George W. Bradley and Phebe C. Cary to Leroy H. Cage a tract of 33 acres. 26 March 1850. (P. 112)

A. M. Debow to J. D. Bennett a tract of land on Goose Creek. 23 March 1851. (Pp. 113-114)

Thompson Mace to Thomas Shoulders 131¼ acres. 27 July 1848. (Pp. 114-115)

Christian N. Nash to William L. Smith his interest in the estate of George R. Nash. 8 February 1851. (Pp. 115-116)

William W. Wills to John Dedman eight acres. 3 January 1851. (P. 116)

John Page to Peter Hackett a tract of land on the Cumberland River. 11 April 1851. (P. 117)

Christian Boston to James Corley a tract of land on Peyton's Creek. 23 November 1849. (P. 118)

Edward R. Wills to William W. Wills his interest in a tract of land he bought from his brother Stephen R. Wills and whereon James Wills resided. 9 April 1851. (Pp. 118-119)

William W. Wills to Bethel Dedman 27 acres. 3 January 1851. (P. 120)

Division of land between M. L. Alexander of one part and William Alford and Mary Ann Pearyear of the other part. 12 April 1851. (Pp. 120-122)

David Burford to his son Robert A. Burford a tract of land on Dixon's Creek. 25 July 1849. (P. 123)

John H. Ammonett and Jacob Ammonett to Moses Preston 160 acres. 3 October 1850. (P. 124)

W. M. Price, executor of M. ( ), to H. A. Massey a negro man. 15 January 1851. (P. 125)

Paul Walker to Bethel and William D. Agee a tract of land on Hickman's Creek. 7 October 1850. (Pp. 125-126)

James A. Smith to Frederick Starnes a tract of seven and one half acres. 15 April 1851. (Pp. 126-127)

Mary Elizabeth Oliver to Banks Oliver, Killes Oliver, and Warner Oliver 122 acres. 28 January 1851. (Pp. 127-128)

The minor heirs of John Baysinger, to wit, Catherine Baysinger and Holden D. Baysinger to John Dedman 108 acres. 1851. (Pp. 128-129)

Jesse Smith and Margret M. Smith to Archibald F. Wilkerson. 23 April 1851. (P. 129)

DEED BOOK U

Frances Dowell to David Fry his interest in the estate of Tucker Woodson, purchased of Elijah Beden and wife Loucinda, James Preston and wife Isabella. 22 February 1850. (P. 130)

Jonathan Hart and wife Elizabeth to David Fry 133 acres. 21 March 1851. (Pp. 130-131)

W. Lambeth to John Palmer a negro girl. 15 April 1849. (P. 132)

James T. Sutton to Barnett Cornwell 20 acres. April 1851. (Pp. 132-133)

S. A. Sloan to William K. Sloan 60 acres. 17 January 1837. (P. 133)

William K. Sloan to M. W. Sloan his interest in a tract of land. 13 December 1844. (P. 134)

John Dedman to Bethel Dedman 110 acres. 27 August 1849. (P. 135)

Andrew Carter to Jane Carter, Samuel Hinds and wife Melissa, William B. Carter, John Carter, Sarah Morgan, Jesse Carter Daniel Temple and wife Milly, William Grisham and wife Maria, Elizabeth Carter, Mary Ann Carter, Samuel Carter, (Eissa) Carter, and Andrew Carter a tract of land. 18 April 1851. (Pp. 135-136)

James Williams to William P. Arnett 20 acres. 8 November 1849. (Pp. 136-137)

William P. Arnett to John G. Anderson 70 acres. 25 October 1850. (Pp. 137-138)

Elizabeth Banks of Williamson County to Maderson C. Banks of Robinson County and Thomas Banks of Williamson County her sons the tract of land left her by her husband Thomas Banks. 20 June 1850. (P. 138)

Thomas Banks to Thomas W. Spivy a tract of land. 20 June 1850. (P. 139)

Maderson C. Banks to Thomas W. Spivy a tract of land on Peyton's Creek. 20 June 1850. (P. 140)

Thomas W. Spivey of Williamson County to Sophia Miller a tract of land. 23 November 1850. (Pp. 141-142)

The administrator of Joel Cheatham decree. 1851. (Pp. 142-144)

William Parkhurst and wife Rebecca to William S. Smith their interest in the estate of John Russell, Sr. 15 May 1851. (P. 145)

Adam Ferguson to Timothy H. Williams a tract of land in the town of Carthage. 20 May 1851. (Pp. 146-148)

D. B. Allen to George C. Allen a negro woman. 30 January 1851. (P. 148)

DEED BOOK U

William Uhls to James B. Bradley 68½ acres. 21 May 1851. (Pp. 149-150)

Moses S. Woodmore to William C. Johnson 53 acres. 20 February 1851. (Pp. 150-151)

Samuel Hunter and Samuel Sullivan sale. 1846. (P. 151)

John Fisher and Ailsey his wife, Emily Reynolds, daughter of Granville Reynolds, James W. Reynolds, son of Washington Reynolds, James B. Reynolds, William W. Reynolds, Noble Reynolds, Malvina Reynolds, widow of Washington Reynolds, S. Reynolds, and Clinton Reynolds, heirs of James Reynolds. 1849. (Pp. 152-153)

Nathaniel Corley to William H. Christian 120 acres. 7 June 1851. (P. 154)

Samuel Fitzpatrick to James G. Wyett a tract of land on the Cumberland River. 15 June 1848. (Pp. 155-156)

Edwin Kitrell to W. W. Belcher two acres. 30 May 1851. (P. 157)

John Woodson to David Fry 136 acres. 20 October 1849. (P. 158)

David McCall to Johnson Underwood a half acre. 2 May 1851. (Pp. 158-159)

Stephen M. Jones to William M. Bell one fourth acre. 1851. (Pp. 159-160)

Alfred Catron to George W. Catron a town lot in the town of Rome. 1851. (P. 161)

Alfred Catron to George W. Catron one fourth acre. 4 June 1851. (P. 162)

J. C. Naley to Anderson Paschale and Calvin Pope his interest in the estate of William Naley. 11 April 1851. (Pp. 162-163)

Isaac Moore to John F. Goodner and James Goodner 65 acres. 4 April 1851. (Pp. 163-164)

Procession of the lands of Nancy Tarver. 19 June 1851. (P. 164)

Benjamin J. Vaden to Samuel Maze 11½ acres. 7 July 1851. (P. 165)

D. B. Allen to George C. Allen a negro boy. 4 July 1851. (P. 166)

John Reeves to David A. Tyre 61 acres. 7 July 1851. (Pp. 166-167)

Samuel Maze to James T. High 61½ acres. 8 July 1851. (Pp. 167-168)

Samuel Burdine to John McCall. 1851. (Pp. 168-169)

DEED BOOK U

Seay Bedford to W. W. Seay a tract of land in the town of Rome. 29 September 1847. (Pp. 169-170)

Thadeous F. Green to Samuel Maze a tract of land on Snow Creek. 26 July 1850. (P. 170)

Thomas Boulton to William Hallum. 14 July 1851. (P. 171)

James Trousdale, administrator of Ira Trousdale, petitions the court to sell a tract of land. 17 July 1851. (Pp. 171-172)

David Palmer to Jorden Filzer a tract of land on Mulherin's Creek. 12 July 1851. (Pp. 172-173)

David Palmer to William A. Harris a tract of land. 12 July 1851. (Pp. 173-174)

David Palmer to Gregory Moore 118 acres. 12 July 1851. (Pp. 174-175)

Alexander Stubblefield to Jacob Ellen five acres. 21 June 1851. (Pp. 175-176)

John H. Bedford and wife Elizabeth and Thomas A. Metcalf and Fanny Metcalf, minors. 24 July 1851. (Pp. 176-177)

Burton J. Ferrell bound to John Cunditt. 30 August 1843. (Pp. 177-178)

Stephen Mann and Ramsey Vance to William Hearn of Wilson County a negro woman. 11 August 1851. (P. 178)

Adam Ferguson to Joseph Bowman some slaves. 30 July 1851. (Pp. 179-181)

Davidson Draper to Mathew Johnson nine acres. 30 July 1851. (P. 182)

John A. Sloan to David White 50 acres. 19 November 1849. (Pp. 182-183)

John H. Bedford to William Douglas 100 acres. 31 May 1851. (Pp. 183-184)

Olive Dickerson to Jacob Eller a tract of land. 12 June 1851. (Pp. 184-185)

E. P. G. Gifford to Jacob Towson a tract of land on Goose Creek. 26 April 1851. (Pp. 185-186)

E. P. G. Gifford to Joseph L. Carter a tract of land on Goose Creek. 8 July 1851. (Pp. 186-187)

E. P. Gifford and Gideon Gifford to Jacob Towson a tract of land. 26 April 1851. (Pp. 187-188)

Michael Shoemake to Robert Glover 21½ acres. 24 November 1847. (P. 188)

Samuel Fitzpatrick to Robert (Glover) 45 acres. 17

DEED BOOK U

August 1851. (P. 189)

B. J. Vaden to Davidson Draper two acres. 30 July 1851. (P. 190)

John Sneed to Jonathan Kemp a tract of land on Defeated Creek. 24 February 1851. (Pp. 190-191)

Agnes F. Green to Samuel Mays 50 acres. 12 April 1851. (Pp. 191-192)

William J. Hale to William Moore his interest in the suit W. J. Hale against W. W. Bailey. 29 July 1851. (P. 192)

William Hall to Richard Averett a crop of tobacco. 30 July 1851. (P. 193)

John A. Sloan to William Uhls 67 acres. 4 February 1848. (Pp. 193-194)

Richard ( ) appoints James B. Moore as his attorney. 1 February 1851. (Pp. 194-195)

Willis Cornwell to C. J. ( ) a slave. 1 December 1848. (P. 196)

Colbert Porter to Henry Piper his interest in a tract of land formerly owned by Alexander Piper, the father of the said Henry Piper. 4 August 1851. (P. 196)

James M. Spain to Absolum Spain 101 acres. 1 March 1851. (P. 197)

Elizabeth Bellar to David Smith ten acres. 4 August 1851. (P. 198)

William Manning to Willis McClanahan and John Manning. 11 August 1851. (Pp. 198-199)

Lettice Mann to Stephen Mann her life estate. 9 July 1851. (P. 200)

Martisha Mann to Stephen Mann her interest in the property she is to receive at the death of Lettice Mann. 13 August 1851. (P. 200)

Fred R. Bailey and wife Rebecca to Stephen Mann his interest in the land to be received at the death of Lettice Mann. 9 July 1851. (P. 201)

Frederick R. Bailey and John H. Mann and Robert W. Mann bound to Stephen Mann. 13 July 1851. (Pp. 201-202)

A. P. Taylor to Coleman Samson a crop of tobacco. 15 August 1851. (Pp. 202-203)

James C. Sanders to Henry B. McDonald 29 acres. 30 November 1847. (Pp. 203-204)

Richard McConnell to Henry B. McDonald a tract of land. 4 August 1851. (P. 205)

James Jones versus Hugh Bradley. 1851. (Pp. 206-208)

DEED BOOK U

John Ballard versus Martin W. Sloan, Samuel T. Coker, James R. Wallace, Lake Ford, Samuel Ford. 18 August 1851. (Pp. 208-209)

Johnson Underwood to Barton Underwood a tract of land on Round Lick Creek. 25 August 1851. (Pp. 209-210)

Larkin Corley to Mathew Denney 21 acres. 3 January 1851. (Pp. 210-211)

Mathew Denney to William Manning 21 acres. 5 August 1851. (Pp. 211-212)

Daniel Smith, administrator of Bry Gregory, versus William Parkhurst, George Boston, and A. A. Brevard. 1851. (Pp. 212-213)

Joel L. Gregory to Abel Gregory a tract of land. 26 August 1851. (Pp. 213-214)

Sheriff John Bridges to Frances Duffey. 29 August 1851. (Pp. 214-215)

Thomas W. Page, administrator of John S. Page, versus Louisa W. Williams, Nancy, Louisa, and Mary A. Page, heirs of the said deceased. 1851. (Pp. 215-216)

William Thomas to William Holliday a crop of tobacco. 1 September 1851. (P. 217)

Andrew Williby to S. R. Samson a crop of tobacco. 1 September 1851. (P. 218)

Nathan H. Grubbs to Joseph Bowman a crop of tobacco. 1 September 1851. (Pp. 218-219)

William Farley to Henry B. McDonald a town lot in the town of Carthage. 1 September 1851. (P. 220)

H. W. Marley to James M. Shepherd a negro woman. 8 September 1851. (Pp. 220-221)

Ephraim Cheek to William H. Cheek 83 acres. 28 August 1850. (P. 221)

John Bates and Joel Bates to S. R. Samson a crop of tobacco. 4 September 1851. (P. 222)

James F. Cooper to William Jones a crop of tobacco. 4 September 1851. (P. 222)

Samuel R. Goss and Abram Davis to Henry D. Goss a crop of tobacco. 4 September 1851. (P. 223)

John Kelly to Rufus Perry a crop of tobacco. 2 September 1851. (P. 224)

Enoch Gann to Alfred L. Bains a crop of tobacco. September 1851. (Pp. 224-225)

William Duvall to John McClain a tract of land. 6 September 1851. (Pp. 225-226)

John Shoulders to Crain & Bridgewater. 1851. (P. 227)

DEED BOOK U

William Dillon to James W. Martin some livestock. 8 September 1851. (Pp. 227-228)

J. B. Lewis to Richard Averett a crop of tobacco. 15 September 1851. (P. 229)

Creed H. Pankey to C. W. West a crop of tobacco. 8 September 1851. (Pp. 229-230)

John Morris to Joel W. J. C. Minton a tract of 36½ acres. 19 September 1851. (Pp. 230-231)

John Morris to Andrew J. Minton 46 acres. 19 September 1851. (Pp. 231-232)

James T. Butler to Rufus Perry a crop of tobacco. 9 September 1851. (P. 232)

Joseph Birdwell to Rufus Perry. September 1851. (P. 233)

James M. Thomas to William T. Thomas a crop of tobacco. 19 September 1851. (P. 234)

William Parkhurst to Crain & Bridgewater. 30 August 1851. (P. 235)

James L. Bridges, executor of Joseph Bridges, versus Barnett Bridges, Willis Bridges, Smith Bridges, John Bridges, John Wooten and wife Martha, Elizabeth Denton, Thomas Bridges, Joseph J. Bridges, Isadella Bridges, and Martha Tunstall, 1851. (Pp. 235-236)

William H. Tyree to Jonathan H. Smith a tract of land on the Cumberland River. 23 September 1851. (P. 236)

William R. Costello to J. West. 13 September 1851. (P. 237)

John Hughes to John B. Hughes 260 acres. 11 February 1820. (Pp. 238-239)

Burrel Robinson to William Overstreet a crop of tobacco. 15 September 1851. (P. 239)

George W. Beasley to James Beasley a tract of land. 15 September 1851. (P. 240)

John Martin to Rufus Perry a crop of tobacco. 13 September 1851. (P. 241)

William P. Anderson to Overton B. Anderson a tract of land on Hurricane Creek. 1 February 1848. (Pp. 241-242)

E. R. Harris to O. J. Williams a crop of corn. 16 September 1851. (Pp. 242-243)

William and John Edens to Crain & Bridgewater a crop of tobacco. 17 September 1851. (P. 243)

Samuel Burdine to George W. Catron one fourth of an acre. 14 February 1851. (P. 244)

Samuel Burdine to George W. Catron. 1851. (P. 245)

DEED BOOK U

Leroy Bradley and Harriet B. Bradley to James Bradley her interest in the estate of her father P. W. Cage. 19 September 1851. (Pp. 246-247)

James W. Cage to James Bradley his interest in the estate of P. W. Cage. 18 September 1851. (P. 247)

Moses Reeves to Campbell Crutchfield a negro slave. 2 April 1851. (P. 248)

STATE OF TENNESSEE to Armstead Moore 50 acres. 4 December 1828. (Pp. 248-249)

Agnes Williams to Jeremiah Coggin her dower. 22 September 1851. (Pp. 249-250)

Sarry Huddleston of Cullin County, Texas appoints Asberry Cartwright to represent her in settling the estate of Patan and Martha Huddleston. 20 July 1851. (P. 250)

David Harris to John Owen a crop of tobacco. 11 September 1851. (Pp. 250-251)

Thomas Boulton and others to John Owen a crop of tobacco. 18 September 1851. (P. 251)

Jacob White and Wiley White to John Owen a crop of tobacco. 1 March 1851. (P. 252)

Jackson Ross to Thomas Key a crop of tobacco. 24 September 1851. (P. 252)

W. M. Bradford and John Hall to Harrison Bennett a tract of land on Mulherin's Creek. 31 July 1851. (P. 253)

Adam Ferguson to Andrew McClain some livestock. 26 September 1851. (Pp. 254-256)

John Perrin to Joseph L. Carter a tract of 30 acres. 23 September 1851. (P. 257)

Martha Flowers to Joshua Kent 96 acres. 14 June 1851. (Pp. 258-259)

Lawrence Thompson to Adam Stafford a tract of land on Goose Creek. 28 November 1838. (P. 259)

William Reece to Charles J. Coker a crop of tobacco. 27 September 1851. (P. 260)

James R. Robinson to Henry Strother a crop of tobacco. 1 October 1851. (P. 261)

W. M. Payne to John McClarin a crop of tobacco. 27 September 1851. (P. 261)

David G. (Hughes) of Hot Springs County, Arkansas appoints his brother in law, Edmund Rucks, as his attorney in settling the estate of Tarlton Hughes. 17 September 1851. (P. 262)

Harrison Bennett to Daniel Hart 100 acres. 4 October 1851. (P. 263)

DEED BOOK U

Harrison Bennett to Lewis J. Parker 100 acres. 27 March 1851. (P. 264)

George W. Bradley to Leroy H. Cage a cow and calf. 2 October 1851. (Pp. 265-266)

Van Allen to George Allen. 6 January 1849. (P. 267)

Randolph Sandlin to Allen Jones three acres. 1 October 1851. (Pp. 267-268)

Early Orange to Francis M. Orange his interest in 37 acres. Bounded: Widow Holly Ward. 14 October 1851. (Pp. 268-269)

William Sloan to Jason R. Sloan 100 acres. 1 February 1848. (Pp. 269-270)

Henry ( ) to Wilson Y. Martin a crop of tobacco. 3 October 1851. (Pp. 270-271)

William Dillard to William Lancaster 50 acres. 20 November 1850. (P. 271)

A. S. Parker appoints William ( ) as his attorney in settling the estate of his half brother James F. Willingson. July 1851. (P. 272)

Jere Jamison to James F. Warf a tract of land on Dry Creek. 30 September 1841. (Pp. 272-273)

Martin McMurry to John B. Beal 258 acres. 21 January 1851. (Pp. 273-274)

Sabry Minton to A. J. Minton her right of dower to 46 acres. 30 September 1851. Witnesses: John S. Mason and James Minton. 30 September 1851. (Pp. 274-275)

Russell Marchbanks and Thomas C. Marchbanks to Thomas A. Lancaster several tracts of land. 15 September 1851. (Pp. 275-276)

Lewis R. Vance, Mary Ann McNichol, and Margret Vance, all of Jackson County, to Jacob Null a tract of land. 26 May 1851. (P. 277)

James R. Toncy versus Rice M. Ballow and Lorenzo D. Ballow, administrators of Leonard Ballow. 1843. (Pp. 278-279)

William R. Taylor to Stephen R. Samson a crop of tobacco. 11 October 1851. (P. 279)

Nathaniel Bomer of Dekalb County to James R. Bomer his interest in the estate of his father William J. Bomer. 1 February 1848. (P. 280)

Daniel Hart and wife Mary to David Fry 133 acres. 21 March 1851. (P. 281)

William Young, administrator of William T. Bennett, and the widow Kitty C. Bennett, versus James Lacke and wife Elizabeth, James D. Bennett, William M. Bennett, Benjamin M. Bennett, William Terry, Mary Terry, Kitty A. Terry, Sarah G.

DEED BOOK U

Terry, and William T. Bennett, Jr. 1851. (Pp. 281-283)

John Hesson of Saline County, Arkansas appoints James Anderson as his attorney to settle the estate of M. Hesson. 1851. (Pp. 283-284)

George Lynch to John D. Owen a crop of tobacco. 19 September 1851. (P. 284)

Alfred Butler to Sampson McClelin a crop of tobacco. 21 October 1851. (P. 285)

Ira Shoulders to Crain & Bridgewater a crop of tobacco. 15 April. (P. 286)

Benjamin Mathews to Rufus Perry a crop of tobacco. 25 October 1851. (P. 286)

Edward H. Sloan appoints John L. Sloan as his attorney in settling the estate of Edward Settle. 3 November 1851. (P. 287)

Mathew Smith to William C. and B. F. Brockett ten acres. 3 November 1851. (Pp. 287-288)

Robert Warren to B. J. Vaden. 1 November 1851. (Pp. 288-289)

E. R. Smith to Hezekiah Love and S. P. W. Maxwell 60 acres. 28 October 1851. (Pp. 289-290)

William Winchester to R. E. Smith 60 acres. 27 October 1851. (Pp. 290-291)

Hardy Calhoun to Braddoc Beasley a negro woman. 1851. (Pp. 291-292)

John Dice to William Tunstall the land he inherited from Thomas Dice. 4 October 1851. (P. 292)

Frederick J. Tubb, William Tubb, John L. Tubb, William Hall, and Elizabeth A. Hall, all of Izard County, Arkansas to George W. Decker a tract of land in the 15th District. 6 January 1849. (P. 293)

John Russell to Miles W. Austin 48 acres. 28 September 1850. (P. 294)

William Winchester to R. E. Smith 60 acres. 27 October 1851. (Pp. 290-291)

Loderick Vaden to Blake B. Thackston 12 acres. 24 October 1851. (P. 295)

Jesse H. Baird to Josiah Baird, Jr. 158 acres. 6 October 1851. (P. 296)

R. Flowers appoints Joel S. Flowers as his attorney to sell some slaves. 3 October 1851. (P. 297)

Bethel B. Bradley and wife Mary, Olive Mormon and wife Cely to William T. Martin their interest in the estate of Thomas Martin. 17 November 1851. (Pp. 297-298)

DEED BOOK U

John H. Flowers to Catherine Sary by Alfred Sary a town lot in the town of Rome. 6 January 1851. (Pp. 297-298)

Silas C. Cornwell to Pleasant Cornwell his interest in the estate of Frances Cornwell. 1851. (Pp. 298-299)

J. H. Newbell to Nancy Penn, daughter of Thomas Penn, a gray mare for love and affection. 30 September 1851. (P. 299)

William Lynch to John D. Owen a crop of tobacco. 5 October 1851. (P. 300)

Joel J. Holliday to Rufus Perry a crop of tobacco. 20 November 1851. (P. 300)

John Page to his granddaughter Eliza M. Donnell a negro girl. 6 October 1851. (P. 301)

W. W. Bailey to Joseph G. Pickett two tracts of land. 24 November 1851. (Pp. 301-302)

Charles Rittenberry to Richard G. Rittenberry a tract of land in the 10th District. 6 September 1851. (Pp. 303-304)

Richard Johnston to John D. Owen a crop of tobacco. 1 March 1851. (P. 304)

Mary Chandler and Thomas Bridges to Joshua Wilson 70 acres. 14 December 1849. (P. 304)

Horace Lawson to Archibald Parker eight acres. 8 April 1850. (P. 305)

Martha F. Harman, Jessie C. Nichols, Henry B. Nichols, Jasper C. Nichols of Illinois appoint Newton Jackson as their attorney in settling the estate of Bird Nichols. 31 October 1851. (Pp. 305-306)

The heirs of Peyton Huddleston, to wit, Thomas L. Draper, Mary Law, Martha Russell, Elizabeth Draper, Robert Huddleston, James Russell, A. Cartwright, James Law, and Joseph Huddleston enter into an agreement. 25 November 1851. (Pp. 307-309)

Albert G. Hallum to John McClarin a crop of tobacco. 29 November 1851. (P. 309)

John Lipscomb to Tandy P. D. Hall one acre. 19 August 1851. (P. 310)

Robert Warren to J. M. Nichols $38\frac{1}{4}$ acres. 29 September 1851. (Pp. 310-311)

Christopher C. Ford to Joseph B. Allison 83 acres. 28 November 1851. (Pp. 311-312)

William Reeves to O. H. Bruce a tract of land in the town of Rome. 23 July 1851. (Pp. 312-313)

DEED BOOK U

Alfred Sary and wife Catherine to Caroline Ballenger a town lot in the town of Rome. 1 December 1851. (P. 313)

Stephen Mann to Robert Hodges a negro girl. 5 December 1851. (P. 314)

Robert L. Hodges to Stephen Mann a negro woman. 5 December 1851. (P. 314)

James Wammack to Charles R. Blair a crop of tobacco. 10 September 1851. (P. 315)

Matlock Roberts to Rufus Perry a crop of tobacco. 6 December 1851. (P. 315)

George R. Nash, administrator of William Choffur, to Abel Smith 224 acres. 1850. (Pp. 315-316)

Charles Powell to D&C West a crop of tobacco. 3 December 1851. (P. 317)

Levi G. Smith to Henderson P. Williams 150 acres. 6 December 1851. (Pp. 317-318)

Charles Pigg to William Agee a tract of land on Mulherin's Creek. 6 December 1851. (P. 318)

John H. Bedford and wife Elizabeth A. to W. W. Seay their interest in the estate of Thomas Allen. 6 October 1851. (P. 319)

Solomon Debow to Lawrence Thompson 14 acres. 15 December 1851. (Pp. 320-321)

Mathew Harper to Stokard W. Coffee his interest in the estate of Mathew Harper which he is to receive at the death of Sarah Harper. Said Mathew has previously purchased the shares of William Harper, Henry Harper, Solomon T. Williams and wife Mahulda. 13 December 1851. (P. 321)

Henry Sadler to Benjamin Wooten a tract of land on Ward's Creek. 10 December 1851. (P. 322)

Elizabeth Bransford to Lipscomb P. McMurry 14 acres. 4 December 1851. (P. 323)

Richard Hodges to his sons David P. Hodges and Robert L. Hodges 178 acres. 20 December 1851. (P. 324)

Robert L. Hodges to David P. Hodges the tract of land he is to receive at the deaths of Richard Hodges and wife Delila. 20 December 1851. (P. 325)

Adam Ferguson to Timothy H. Williams. 23 October 1851. (Pp. 326-327)

Edwin Mathis to Thomas W. Arundell a crop of tobacco. 24 September 1851. (P. 327)

Samuel McClelin to Samuel Russell a tract of land on Buffalo Creek. 23 September 1851. (Pp. 327-328)

Samuel McClelin to James T. McClelin a tract of land on Buffalo Creek. 23 September 1851. (Pp. 328-329)

DEED BOOK U

Edward Wilson to Stewart Montgomery 55 acres. 23 May 1849. (Pp. 329-330)

Polly Nunley and William A. Nunley to H. B. Haynie a negro boy. 19 September 1851. (P. 330)

Russell and Thomas C. Marchbanks to George Fisher 250 acres. 18 March 1851. (P. 331)

Winny Mitchell to Robert J. F. Mitchell her son 30 acres which he is to keep for her daughter Elizabeth Mitchell. 6 October 1851. (P. 332)

William Uhls to Wilson Y. Martin six or seven acres. 26 September 1851. (P. 333)

Elijah Wheeler to Wiley Thomas 615 acres. 2 August 1851. (P. 334)

Trayley N. Violet to Richard Parker a tract of land. 8 September 1851. (Pp. 334-335)

William W. Jones to John H. Newbell 56 acres. 24 October 1851. (Pp. 335-336)

William Winchester to James P. (Stell) 80 acres. August 1851. (P. 337)

Robert Barton to Clem McKinney a tract of land on Snow Creek. 12 August 1850. (Pp. 337-338)

Gideon Gifford to Allen Jones a tract of land on Goose Creek. 24 January 1850. (P. 338)

Jason R. Sloan, administrator of S. A. Sloan, to William R. Sloan a tract of 60 acres. 21 October 1851. (P. 339)

Harvey D. Wilson to C. J. Williams 85 acres. 10 November 1851. (P. 340)

Thomas Snoddy, Sr. to Thomas Snoddy, Jr. a tract of land. 22 November 1851. (P. 341)

Joseph H. Durham to William Moreland 91 acres. 30 December 1846. (P. 342)

George Allen of Jackson County and Darcus Anderson to Robert Warren a tract of land on Snow Creek. 6 September 1851. (P. 343)

Frederick Starnes to John Starnes 45 acres. 24 November 1851. (Pp. 343-344)

John Starnes to William Braswell 45 acres. 25 November 1851. (Pp. 343-344)

William F. and A. W. Allen to Daniel Richardson a tract of land on Snow Creek. 3 September 1851. (Pp. 344-345)

B. A. James and E. A. James to William F. Dowell a tract of land belonging to the estate of Willis Dowell. 19 November 1851. (Pp. 345-346)

DEED BOOK U

Frances Dowell to William Pigg 475 acres. 4 November 1851. (Pp. 346-347)

Henry Wilmore to Thomas Shoulders a tract of land on Peyton's Creek. November 18__. (Pp. 347-348)

Priscilla Warren to Leonard H. Cardwell her interest in the estate of John Warren. 21 December 1851. (P. 349)

Leonard H. Cardwell to Robert R. Williams 380 acres. 1 January 1852. (P. 350)

George C. Allen to David Sanders a negro woman. 27 January 1851. (P. 351)

Christian Austin to James Rossell six acres. 31 May 1851. (Pp. 351-352)

Frances Boulton and Lent Boulton to Horace Oliver their interest in a negro slave. 5 January 1851. (P. 352)

Levi Austin to Philip Austin 81 acres. 10 August 1850. (Pp. 352-353)

James ( ) to Thomas Stovall. 1 January 1852. (Pp. 353-354)

Joseph Payne to William L. Alexander a negro woman. 23 December 1851. (P. 352)

W. S. Alexander to W. W. Cunningham one acre. 3 June 1851. (P. 353)

N. L. Barren to David C. Sanders all his drugs, medicine, surgical instruments, etc. 10 January 1852. (P. 356)

William Hallum to Thomas Boulton. 12 January 1852. (P. 357)

Thomas Boulton to Horace Oliver his interest in a negro boy. 12 January 1852. (P. 357)

The heirs of William T. Bennett file suit. 1851. (Pp. 358-360)

Daniel C. Davis to John G. (Park) a tract of land on Buffalo Creek. 16 October 1851. (Pp. 360-361)

David F. Wamack to Albert H. Ross a negro woman. 12 January 1852. (P. 361)

William Brim to Hambleton Nickson a crop of tobacco. 12 January 1852. (P. 362)

Bedford Haddock to John McClarin a crop of tobacco. 19 January 1852. (Pp. 363-364)

Nathaniel T. Bomar to Sanders. 20 January 1852. (Pp. 364-365)

Nathan Jared of Jackson County to John Johnson a tract of land on the Caney Fork. 19 February 1850. (Pp. 365-366)

DEED BOOK U

Charles Durey, executor of John Durey, Sr. to Wilborn Driver. 28 March 1849. (Pp. 366-367)

Thomas T. Dias to Warren Walker his interest in the estate of his grandfather Thomas Dias. 8 June 1849. (P. 367)

Lawrence Thompson to George H. Burnley 118 acres. 1851. (P. 368)

Lawrence Thompson to M. S. Woodmore 200 acres. February 1851. (P. 369)

L. J. Squires to Mathew H. Ward a negro man. 18 September 1851. (Pp. 370-371)

William Crosslin to Benjamin Crosslin a negro girl. 17 January 1852. (P. 371)

Hugh H. Bradley to Thomas Carman a negro woman. 5 January 1852. (P. 371)

William L. Booker to William B. Allen 50 acres. 25 February 1872. (Pp. 372-373)

Fleming Merritt to Lewis Pendleton a tract of land on Brush Creek. 15 July 1850. (Pp. 373-374)

John C. Lenon and Nancy Lemmon of Jefferson County, Illinois to Owen J. Lemmon their interest in a tract of land on Turkey Creek. 17 May 1851. (Pp. 374-375)

C. S. Tate to Joseph Dickerson a negro girl. 7 February 1852. (P. 375)

M. G. Ward to William M. Price a man slave. 5 December 1851. (P. 376)

Henry B. McDonald to John J. Burnett. 10 February 1852. (Pp. 376-377)

Anne Sullivan to Harbert H. Sullivan a tract of land on Smith's Fork. 10 July 1851. (Pp. 377-378)

P. Gold to James W. Stewart a tract of land on the Caney Fork. 5 January 1852. (Pp. 378-379)

R. H. Crank to William Kerby a negro boy. 11 February 1851. (P. 379)

Coleman Hallum to Jacob Null 65 acres. 6 January 1852. (Pp. 379-380)

William B. Allen to George Walker 50 acres. 24 January 1849. (Pp. 380-381)

Mary Lankford to John Lamberson 125 acres. 22 December 1846. (Pp. 381-382)

George Thomason and Catherine Thomason to John Jones three acres. 10 January 1848. (Pp. 382-383)

Cynthia Hiett to John Hiett, Jr. 1852. (Pp. 383-384)

DEED BOOK U

William B. Davis to Stephen Nolin 80 acres. 16 February 1852. (Pp. 384-385)

Stephen Nolin to M. W. Lack 54 acres. 24 February 1852. (Pp. 385-386)

Lewis McFarlin to his daughter Eliza Jane, wife of John Elliott, some negro slaves. 23 August 1851. (Pp. 386-387)

David Burford to James B. Duffey a tract of land. 1 January 1849. (Pp. 387-388)

A. Ferguson to his wife Hester Ann a negro girl. 1 March 1852. (P. 388)

Daniel Huddleston to Richard Mormon a tract of 40 acres. November 1851. (P. 389)

Campbell Crutchfield to John Bray 20 acres. 23 February 1852. (P. 390)

John Bray to Thomas J. Slaughter one acre. 13 March 1852. (P. 391)

Elijah Morris and wife Martha, George Coatney and wife Sarah, Elisha Coatney, Thomas Coatney, Moses F. Coatney, Sarah J. Coatney, children of Mary Coatney versus Moses Atwood and Newton Atwood. 1847. (Pp. 392-394)

harvey D. Wilson and Robert Gann to John H. Bates. 11 September 1851. (Pp. 394-395)

Anderson Williams to Bethwell B. Bradley a tract of land. 14 May 1850. (Pp. 395-396)

George Baker to Charles Patey 78 acres. 28 March 1849. (Pp. 396-397)

Ellis B. Kemp of Macon County to James Young of Jackson County. 7 November 1851. (Pp. 397-398)

W. W. Cunningham to W. S. Alexander one acre. 3 March 1852. (Pp. 398-399)

Evin J. ( ) to George W. (Hudson) the tract of land on which his mother Sarah Hudson resides. 14 April 1852. (Pp. 399-400)

James Wammack to Henry Dillard some livestock. 27 March 1852. (P. 400)

Calvin Brewer to William M. Price 100 acres. 8 November 1848. (P. 401)

Clement McKinney to J. M. and J. Nichols 15 acres. 2 January 1852. (P. 402)

W. W. Bailey to Pleasant Gold one half of a negro woman. 23 March 1852. (P. 403)

Jesse Hail to P. W. Presley a tract of land on Wolf Creek. 4 December 1851. (Pp. 403-404)

DEED BOOK U

John Roe to Joseph Payne a tract of land in the town of Rome. 26 February 1852. (Pp. 404-405)

D. K. Timberlake to John Armstead 23¼ acres. 2 March 1852. (Pp. 405-406)

John Roe to Joseph Payne a tract of land in the town of Rome. 13 March 1852. (Pp. 406-407)

Robert McHood to George Petty and wife Eliza and her children 30 acres. 28 March 185?. (P. 407)

Henry B. Clark and Robert Brown to William F. and W. Allen 105 acres. 31 December 1846. (Pp. 408-409)

Sheriff John Bridges to Samuel Allison a tract of land. 3 April 1852. (Pp. 409-410)

E. J. Hudson to Jesse Hollis a tract of land on Brush Creek. 6 April 1852. (P. 411)

E. J. Hudson to Jesse Hollis nine acres. 6 April 1852. (P. 412)

John H. Davis to Harrison West 50 acres. 3 April 1852. (P. 413)

Joel B. Fulks to Edmund Jones ten acres. 27 April 1852. (P. 414)

Albert Arington to Willis Wilson 86 acres. 12 September 1851. (P. 415)

Thomas Arington to Edmon Wilson 40 acres. 5 September 1850. (P. 416)

Isaac H. Davis to Robert G. Davis 50 acres. 10 January 1839. (Pp. 416-417)

Thomas Tunstall to Yancy Clardy 50 acres. 24 September 1852. (Pp. 418-419)

James Tunstall to C. W. Mahan 36 acres. 14 September 1850. (P. 419)

Thomas Tunstall to William Beasley 148½ acres. 27 September 1850. (P. 420)

Thomas Hines to William G. Lemon 53 acres. 4 November 1851. (P. 421)

William H. Jones to William Exum 175 acres. 2 August 1847. (P. 422)

K. D. Exum to Rolin Keays 100 acres. 6 March 1852. (P. 423)

Milton Cleveland, Mary Bransford, Joseph Cleveland, Susan Piper, Harriet Gregory, Carline Stafford, Robert E. Cleveland, Alexander Cleveland, William J. Cleveland, Hazzard Cleveland, Martha Cleveland, Joel M. Cleveland, Nancy Richardson, Matilda Taylor, Susan Cleveland, Laticia Smith, W. N. Cleveland, William Taylor, heirs of William Cleveland. (Pp. 423-424)

DEED BOOK U

Robert Oldham to Joseph Bowman his interest in the estate of his father Samuel Oldham. 4 January 1852. (P. 425)

Alexander Allison, Andrew Allison, and Robert P. Allison appoint James B. Moores as their attorney. 16 October 1851. (Pp. 426-427)

Lydia Jenkins and Arthur Jenkins appoint Samuel T. Vaden as their attorney in settling the estate of Lambeth D. Grissom by Peter Grissom, executor. 24 May 1852. (Pp. 427-428)

Henry B. McDonald to Abraham Parker a negro slave. 6 February 1852. (P. 428)

Mathew Nichols to Abraham Parker his interest in the estate of his father Jessie Nichols. Mentions sister Phebe Parker and brother James Nichols. 14 February 1852. (P. 429)

D. B. Allen to Alfred W. Williams a tract of land on Horseshoe Bend on the Cumberland River. 24 May 1852. (Pp. 429-430)

William Leman to L. H. Cardwell and William B. Young 53 acres. 3 May 1852. (Pp. 430-431)

Robert R. Williams to Alfred W. Williams 380 acres. 25 May 1852. (Pp. 431-432)

Romulus C. Wright to Ellis Beasley 300 acres. 6 December 1851. (P. 433)

S. W. Coffee and Minerva Coffee to John ( ) their interest in the estate of Mathew Harper. 13 December 1851. (P. 434)

Henry B. Kelly to Thomas Lancaster his interest in the estate of his father Spencer Kelly. 17 January 1852. (Pp. 435-436)

Bird Moore of Hickman County to Samuel B. Moore of the same county his interest in the estate of Armstead Moore. 29 September 1851. (Pp. 436-437)

Joseph H. Durham to William F. Allen. 19 November 1845. (P. 438)

John B. Norris and Alexander Posey and wife Nancy of Wilson County to Jonathan Lamb 96 acres. 26 January 1852. (Pp. 439-440)

Tilman Norris and wife Mary Ann, John E. Warder and wife Eveline of Barren County, Kentucky to Jonathan Lamb their interest in the estate of George Norris. 28 November 1851. (Pp. 440-441)

Ellis Beasley to Johnson Underwood a town lot. 8 June 1852. (Pp. 442-443)

DEED BOOK U

Leonard J. Cardwell to William Robinson 90 acres. 1852. (Pp. 443-445)

James N. Boon to James Larner 57 acres. 24 October 1850. (P. 445)

Thomas Wooten to Thomas Crutchfield 59 acres. 9 June 1852. (Pp. 445-446)

Michael Shoemake to James D. Shoemake a tract of land on Hurricane Creek. August 1851. (Pp. 446-447)

Michael Shoemake to Miles W. Shoemake a tract of land on Hurricane Creek. 14 August 1851. (Pp. 447-448)

James D. Shoemake to Miles W. Shoemake 50 acres. 10 March 1852. (Pp. 448-449)

Michael Shoemake to Patrick A. Shoemake 109 acres. 14 August 1851. (Pp. 449-450)

Alexander Allison and others to Jesse G. Frazer six acres. 19 February 1852. (Pp. 450-451)

Evan J. Williams and Harriet Williams to Marmaduke Mason their interest in the estate of Josiah Whitley. 28 June 1852. (Pp. 451-452)

Ira B. Cowen to John Hughes $322\frac{1}{4}$ acres. 1 July 1852. (P. 452)

Chafin McCormack to John McClarin & Brother a crop of tobacco. 28 June 1852. (P. 453)

P. A. Thomason, Mary A. D. Thomason, Thomas C. Marchbanks, and Josephine Marchbanks to William Bates and David Malone their interest in the estate of H. N. Sullivan. 6 July 1849. (Pp. 453-454)

Thomas A. Lancaster to Jefferson Roland 140 acres. 10 June 1852. (P. 455)

Thomas A. Lancaster to A. W. Betty 47 acres. 10 June 1852. (P. 456)

Ephraim Cheek to James H. Davis 150 acres. November 1851. (Pp. 456-457)

Leonidas D. Hogg to David Hogg a tract of land. 30 September 1851. (Pp. 457-458)

Matilda Prowell to William Craighead a tract of land on Mulherin's Creek. 22 November 1851. (Pp. 456-457)

Leonidas D. Hogg to David Hogg 50 acres. 30 September 1851. (Pp. 457-458)

Matilda Prowell to William Craighead a tract of land on Mulherin's Creek. 25 December 1851. (Pp. 458-459)

Orville Green to Robert Denton 46 acres. 11 January 1851. (Pp. 459-460)

DEED BOOK U

Joseph Jones to Leonard H. Cardwell 80 acres. 11 December 1851. (P. 461)

Joseph Derickson to Robert H. Cato one acre. 23 September 1850. (P. 462)

James D. Shoemake to Charles R. Blair 15 acres. 20 December 1851. (P. 463)

Alexander Allison and others to Timothy H. Williams one acre. 14 July 1852. (P. 464)

Timothy H. Williams to William W. Ward a tract of land. 17 July 1852. (Pp. 465-467)

Joel S. Flowers to John S. Rowls 104 acres. 13 March 1851. (Pp. 467-468)

William Shields to L. D. Hogg a negro man. 20 July 1853. (P. 468)

William Dillard to Lewis Ferguson 150 acres. 7 February 1852. (P. 469)

Samuel Allison to James Cheek a tract of land. 27 July 1852. (Pp. 469-470)

Burrel Robinson and Martha P. Robinson to Jesse Robinson their interest in the estate of John Cardwell. 2 July 1852. (P. 471)

Humphrey Smithwick to James P. Garrell a tract of land on Dixon's Creek. 26 July 1852. (Pp. 471-472)

Alfred M. Winkler to John S. Winkler 34 acres. 17 April 1851. (Pp. 473-474)

John Turner to Robert Denton a negro girl. 20 June 1844. (P. 474)

James Martin to John G. Martin the tract of land where I now live. 28 June 1852. (Pp. 475-476)

Oliver F. Young to James Young of Jackson County 300 acres. 2 February 1852. (Pp. 476-477)

Jesse Patey to John Webb a tract of land. 9 March 1852. (Pp. 477-478)

Gideon Gifford to A. P. Whitesides a tract of land on Goose Creek. 21 October 1851. (Pp. 478-479)

John S. Cornwell to Drury Cronwell a man slave. 2 January 1850. (P. 480)

L. Pope to Robert W. Pope a tract of land. 15 July 1852. (Pp. 480-481)

R. W. Knight and Timothy W. Mann to George C. Mann 91 acres. 7 January 1852. (Pp. 481-482)

Green Wright to his daughter Harriet Richardson a negro woman. 15 March 1852. (P. 482)

DEED BOOK U

Russell and Thomas C. Marchbanks to Yancy (Waldon) 74½ acres. 12 September 1851. (Pp. 482-483)

William F. Hughes versus Harriet T. Rucks. 1852. (Pp. (Pp. 483-485)

The heirs of P. W. Cage to Thompson Mace a tract of land. 1852. (Pp. 485-486)

Samuel C. Bridgewater, Wilson Y. Martin and wife Mary B., Walter C. Allen and wife Nancy, Richard A. Bridgewater, Thomas Cryer and wife Emily, Lucy J. Bridgewater, and Elizabeth Johnson versus Thomas Phelps and wife Ann, Chesley W. Bridgewater, and John C. Bridgewater. 1852. (Pp. 486-488)

Sampson Sloan to Wiley Kemp a tract of land on Peyton's Creek. 14 September 1836. (Pp. 488-489)

C. W. Bridgewater to R. A. Bridgewater a negro woman. 3 May 1852. (P. 489)

John J. Smith to Vincent Thompson some negro slaves. 3 May 1852. (P. 490)

Henry B. McDonald to Vincent Thompson some slaves. 1 January 1849. (Pp. 490-491)

Edwin R. Mathews to Leonard H. Cardwell a crop of tobacco. 28 July 1833. (Pp. 491-492)

Ellis Beasley to Gabriel Beasley a tract of land. 14 October 1851. (Pp. 492-493)

Ellis Beasley to William H. Grissam a tract of land on the Cumberland River. 14 October 1851. (Pp. 493-494)

Ellis Beasley to Henderson Haley a tract of land. 14 October 1851. (Pp. 494-495)

William Shoemake to Blake B. Thaxton two acres. 10 December 1844. (Pp. 495-496)

Martha Fulks to James A. Thomas her dower. May 1852. (Pp. 496-497)

Johnson Underwood to William Denny, Sr. a tract of land. 3 May 1851. (Pp. 497-498)

Jason R. Sloan, administrator of S. A. Sloan, to ( ) ( ). 14 June 1852. (Pp. 498-499)

John Hudson to Barrett Cornwell a tract of land on Peyton's Creek. 1 August 1852. (Pp. 499-500)

John Webb and wife Mary to John D. Owen a tract of land. 2 August 1852. (Pp. 500-501)

Asa Brindley to Robert Warren a crop of tobacco. 4 May 1852. (Pp. 501-502)

Thomas Owen to T. B. Flippin a tract of 17½ acres. 5 May 1852. (Pp. 502-503)

DEED BOOK U

Alexander B. Kinney to George Dillard all his mercantile books. 10 August 1852. (Pp. 503-504)

Thomas J. Stratton to Samuel Burdine a tract of 457 acres. 28 April 1852. (Pp. 505-506)

William M. Price to James L. Thompson a tract of land. 5 January 1852. (P. 506)

John Campsey to John Owen 107 acres. 15 June 1852. (P. 507)

Miles W. Shoemake to Charles R. Blair 30 acres. 3 August 1852. (P. 508)

James S. Bradley to Robert A. Burford 2560 acres. 11 August 1852. (Pp. 509-511)

John J. Barnett to W. W. Ward a boy slave. 11 August 1852. (Pp. 511-512)

John Merritt to William Garner of Dekalb County a tract of land. 21 August 1844. (Pp. 512-513)

Mathew Harper to W. W. Ward a tract of land. 14 August 1852. (Pp. 513-514)

Ezekiel Parkhurst to Joseph Bowman a tract of 100 acres. 14 August 1852. (Pp. 514-515)

Bartley Beal to Henry M. Gregory a tract of land on Peyton's Creek. 25 May 1852. (P. 516)

William Holleman and wife Mary to James Sadler their interest in the estate of Andrew Clark. 7 August 1852. (Pp. 516-517)

William J. Hall to Richard Averett a crop of tobacco. 20 August 1852. (P. 518)

James Grissom to Josiah Baird a tract of land on Hickman's Creek. 31 December 1830. (Pp. 518-519)

Elijah Toney to his daughter Elizabeth A. Cornwell. 29 August 1848. (P. 520)

Charles Tunstall to David Stanford a tract of land. 23 August 1852. (Pp. 521-522)

Thomas A. Clark and wife Emily appoint David C. Hodges as their attorney in settling the estate of Jesse Nichols, Sr. 29 March 1852. (Pp. 522-523)

Henry V. Nichols of Franklin County, Missouri appoints David Hodges as his attorney. March 1852. (P. 524)

Henry V. Nichols, Thomas A. Clark and wife Emily to Abraham Parker a negro woman. 24 August 1852. (P. 525)

Sheriff Samuel Allison to Willis Cornwell. 1852. (Pp. 525-527)

Samuel Burdine to William Reeves. 1852. (Pp. 527-528)

DEED BOOK U

Alexander Allison and others to William Reeves a tract of land in the town of Carthage. 23 August 1852. (Pp. 528-529)

David Nichols to Joel Minton a gray horse. 1852. (P. 529)

Amzi P. Hall to Daniel Hunt 100 acres. 28 April 1853. (P. 530)

Widow Jane Harper, John Borum and wife Emily, James Williams and wife Meddy, Sarah Wood, Josiah Harper, Jr. versus Elizabeth Harper, Franklin Harper, Thomas Harper, Martha Harper, Paul Harper, John Harper, Timothy Harper, James Harper, and Josiah Harper. 1852. (Pp. 531-532)

John Roe to Samuel Bickers a town lot in the town of Rome. 12 April 1852. (Pp. 532-533)

John Minton to Muholda Minton. 1852. (Pp. 533-534)

Stephen W. Martin to his niece Elizabeth Jane Driver and her husband Burrel Driver three slaves. 6 September 1852. (P. 535)

William M. Payne to Daniel Smith a crop of tobacco. 20 August 1852. (P. 536)

W. W. Bailey and others to David Fray a tract of land. 1852. (Pp. 536-540)

William Foutch, Sr. to William Foutch, Jr. 121 acres. 30 December 1851. (Pp. 540-541)

William Foutch, Jr. to James R. Cheek 121 acres. 30 December 1851. (Pp. 541-542)

Philip Austin to Barrett Cornwell eight acres. 4 September 1852. (Pp. 542-543)

Samuel W. Garrett and William J. Payne to William Reese 215 acres. 30 August 1852. (P. 543)

Andrew Williams to James Eaton a tract of land. 17 October 1849. (Pp. 544-545)

James Eaton to Andrew Williams a tract of land. 17 January 1852. (Pp. 545-546)

James Eaton to James N. Eaton 22½ acres. 23 July 1852. (Pp. 546-547)

Chaffin Cardwell to John McClarin & Brother a crop of tobacco. 11 September 1852. (P. 547)

Campbell Crutchfield to Richard Bray a tract of land. 11 November 1841. (P. 548)

N. B. Anderson to C. S. Tate 50 acres. 15 September 1852. (P. 549)

Samuel Bickers to Samuel A. Owen 40 acres. 15 September 1852. (P. 550)

DEED BOOK U

James M. Blackwell to Archibald Debow three slaves. 23 June 1851. (P. 550)

Hardy Calhoun to William Edens 75 acres. 5 August 1852. (P. 551)

William Edens to Crain & Bridgewater 75 acres. 3 August 1852. (P. 552)

William B. Lack to John McClarin a crop of tobacco. 21 September 1852. (P. 553)

Robert W. Mann to B. B. Uhles a tract of land on Snow Creek. 29 August 1851. (Pp. 553-554)

J. B. Tinis to Richard Averett a crop of tobacco. 20 September 1852. (P. 554)

Robert Smith to William L. Smith 50 acres. 26 December 1847. (P. 555)

John W. Austin to William L. Smith his interest in the estate of Levi Austin. 30 January 1852. (P. 556)

Cthial Serls to George W. Lamb a tract of land. 5 October 1850. (P. 557)

Thomas J. Jenkins to Drury Cornwell a crop of tobacco. 6 October 1850. (Pp. 558-559)

Zary Dillard, widow, and Peggy, Matthew, et al, the heirs of Elisha Dillard file suit. 1852. (Pp. 559-560)

Wesley Kemp of Jackson County to James C. Williams 86 acres. 28 November 1852. (Pp. 560-561)

Samson Anderson and wife Rachel to James Sadler their interest in the estate of Andrew Clark. 14 August 1852. (Pp. 561-562)

John Kemp to William P. Cornwell 80 acres. 3 September 1852. (Pp. 562-563)

David Dias, James Dias, James T. Merryman and wife Elizabeth, Ezekiel Parkhurst and wife Polly, Lovick Dias, Thomas Dias, Robert Dias, and Lewis Dias versus Edy B. Dias, Margret Dias, Ruth J. Dias, Josiah Dias, Lovick Dias, Jr., Thomas Dias, Jr., David W. Dias, and Martha J. Dias, heirs of Thomas Dias, Sr. 1852. (Pp. 564-567)

Jesse B. Andrews to James Oakley 176 acres. 29 September 1852. (P. 568)

William T. Hackett to Peter Hackett, Sr. a tract of land. 1852. (Pp. 568-569)

Stockard W. Coffee, executor of Joel Coffee versus Patsey E. Coffee, Alfred Coffee, Stockard Coffee, Isham Coffee, Darthula Coffee, Matilda Coffee, Franklin Coffee, and Taylor Coffee. 1852. (Pp. 569-571)

John Simmons to Thomas Woodmore. 1852. (Pp. 571-572)

DEED BOOK U

John Page to John B. Morris a tract of land. 8 June 1852. (Pp. 572-573)

George R. Dillard to William Dillard 120 acres. 18 August 1852. (Pp. 573-574)

Miles W. Shoemake to Charles R. Blair a tract of land on Hurricane Creek. October 1852. (Pp. 574-576)

Silas J. Granade and wife Ann to William L. Smith their interest in the estate of Levi Austin. 1852. (Pp. 576-577)

P. Clay to Asa Kemp a tract of land in the 5th District. 17 November 1851. (Pp. 577-578)

P. Gold to James W. Stuart his interest in a tract of land. 25 September 1852. (Pp. 578-579)

Winslow Carter to Frances Dowell. 4 October 1852. (Pp. 579-580)

B. B. Smith to James W. Washburn his interest in the estate of his father Jacob Smith. Also to receive his share in the estate of Lucy Wakefield who was the daughter of William Phelps. 10 September 1852. (P. 580)

James H. Davis to James Turner 44 acres. 2 October 1852. (P. 581)

George Lynch to Robert Warren a crop of tobacco. 4 October 1852. (P. 582)

John Johnson to Martha B. Smith a tract of land. 20 January 1851. (Pp. 582-583)

James B. McMurtry to Humphrey Smithwick the tract of land the said James B. bought from Mary Cage, widow of P. W. Cage. 13 August 1852. (P. 584)

William Duvall to Lemuel Skelton a crop of tobacco. 5 October 1852. (Pp. 584-585)

The heirs of Thomas Dias decree. 1851. (Pp. 586-589)

William Lynch to Henry Perkins a crop of tobacco. 11 October 1852. (P. 589)

Charles Smith to William L. Smith. 8 October 1852. (Pp. 589-590)

William Hallum certification. 1852. (P. 591)

Charles Powell to D&C West a crop of tobacco. 20 October 1852. (P. 591)

John Page to Thomas W. Page and Norvell A. Page of Obion County. 1852. (Pp. 591-592)

Ridley R. West to Claborn W. West a tract of land on Defeated Creek. 20 October 1852. (P. 593)

DEED BOOK U

Sheriff John Bridges to Adkins W. Timberlake a tract of land belonging to the heirs of Patrick Hubbard with the exception of Mary Shoemake, formerly Mary Hubbard. 4 June 1851. (Pp. 594-595)

Martha Durham and ( ) Durham appoint William Dawson as their attorney to settle the estate of Peter Grissom. 22 October 1852. (Pp. 595-596)

Alfred Butler to Robert A. Holliday a crop of tobacco. 22 October 1852. (Pp. 596-597)

Leonard H. Cardwell to Thomas Snoddy, Sr. and Joshua Snoddy 100 acres. 26 October 1852. (Pp. 597-598)

David Dodd and wife Elizabeth of Wilson County to Jacob H. Boston a tract of land on Dixon's Creek. 2 March 1852. (Pp. 598-599)

Evin J. Williams to R. Enox 130 acres. 27 September 1842. (Pp. 599-600)

Benjamin Crosslin to Overton B. Anderson 100 acres. 19 October 1852. (Pp. 600-601)

Jason R. Sloan to Wiley Kemp. 1852. (Pp. 601-602)

James C. Sanders to Jefferson Bowman 67 acres. 18 June 1852. (Pp. 602-603)

George W. Davis to John J. Smith several articles. 3 November 1852. (P. 603)

Henry B. McDonald to David C. Sanders and Quinton C. Sanders a town lot. 30 October 1852. (P. 604)

William Reese to Britton M. Richardson a crop of tobacco. 5 November 1842. (Pp. 604-605)

Joshua Wilson to Edmund Wilson 24 acres. 16 September 1851. (Pp. 605-606)

John Roe to William Douglas a tract of land. 15 November 1852. (Pp. 606-607)

William Douglas to Joshua Wilson 150 acres. 15 November 1852. (Pp. 607-608)

NAME INDEX

Abby, Frances 16
Abel, James 57
Acock, Thomas 91
Acuff, Joseph 51
Acuff, Joseph S. 102
Adams, Aaron L. 70
Adams, Aaron S. 102
Adams, Abraham 36
Adams, Allen 25,38
Adams, Elijah 74,75,76
Adams, Frances 11,36,53,60
Adams, Hiram C. 17
Adams, Jackson 191
Adams, James 36
Adams, John 70,75
Adams, John A. 17,75,99,110
Adams, Joseph 75
Adams, Leroy P. 17,71,75,99,104
Adams, Lewis 25
Adams, N. M. 166
Adams, Nathan M. 90
Adams, Nathaniel M. 58
Adams, Nathaniel W. 68
Adams, Patsy 191
Adams, Robert 8,38
Adams, Wesley M. 76
Adams, Wilson 191
Adamson, Joseph 1
Adamson, Samuel 77
Adcock, James 98
Adcock, Joseph 153
Agee, Bethel 262
Agee, Daniel 206
Agee, Daniel B. 160
Agee, Ephraim 56,138,154
Agee, Jeremiah 160,200,243
Agee, Jonathan 56,160,206
Agee, Jonathan W. 56
Agee, William 160,273
Agee, William D. 262
Ahart, George W. 134,183,199
Alexander, Anderson 47,95
Alexander, D. F. 44
Alexander, Daniel 44,69,197
Alexander, Daniel F. 47
Alexander, Easther W. 44
Alexander, Esther 44
Alexander, James 201
Alexander, M. B. 69

Alexander, M. L. 262
Alexander, Madison 44
Alexander, Madison B. 43,45,47
Alexander, R. 243
Alexander, Richard 120,121,122,191,245
Alexander, Robert 44,95
Alexander, W. 243
Alexander, W. L. 245
Alexander, W. S. 275,277
Alexander, William 3,8,38,120,121,122,126,176,191,192
Alexander, William L. 48,111,127,147,247,275
Alexander, William L., Jr. 199
Alexander, William L., Sr. 199
Alexander, William R. 95
Alford, William 158,259,262
Algood, Joel 229
Allen, A. W. 274
Allen, Alethia 222
Allen, Alletha 189,223
Allen, Archibald 154,258
Allen, Archibald V. 214,229
Allen, Armstrong W. 228
Allen, Barton 261
Allen, Burton 7,251
Allen, Charles 25
Allen, D. B. 263,264,279
Allen, Daniel 70,85,152,251
Allen, Elizabeth 211
Allen, G. C. 189
Allen, George 220,242,270,274
Allen, George C. 189,238,250,263,264,275
Allen, George E. 202
Allen, Grant 31,127,199,202
Allen, Hannah 229
Allen, James 168,205,221
Allen, James G. 189
Allen, James T. 209
Allen, Joe W. 38
Allen, John 211
Allen, Joseph 135,168,248
Allen, Joseph W. 37,68,115,135,179,189,216
Allen, Lucy A. 209
Allen, Lucy W. 163,254
Allen, Martha 211
Allen, Mary 211
Allen, Nancy 111,282
Allen, Robert 67,68,101,113,159,168,171,189
Allen, Robert, Jr. 9,29

Allen, Robert, Sr. 238
Allen, Sarah 258
Allen, Thomas 37,111,273
Allen, Van 270
Allen, Van H. 216,248
Allen, W. 278
Allen, W. H. 238
Allen, Walter C. 282
Allen, William 7,16,20,51,
  66,83,85,111,173
Allen, William B. 154,276
Allen, William F. 148,168,
  274,278,279
Allen, William H. 249,250
Allen, William R. 69
Allgood, Joel 219
Allison, Alexander 279,
  280,281,284
Allison, Andrew 42,43,52,
  132,153,171,189,279
Allison, James 35
Allison, Joseph 35,114,117
Allison, Joseph B. 272
Allison, L. B. 244
Allison, Lewis 4,114,117,
  145
Allison, R. D. 85,95,104,
  105,188
Allison, Robert D. 128,
  157,244
Allison, Robert P. 279
Allison, Samuel 114,135,
  145,150,175,192,202,203,
  211,213,223,233,238,278,
  281,283
Allison, Sarah 244
Allison, Stephen 225
Allison, Thomas 33
Allman, Willis 70
Alsup, G. M. 93
Alsup, H. H. 93
Alsup, Hiram H. 94
Alsup, S. J. 93
Alues, Zachariah 7
Alvis, Thomas G. 223
Ammonett, Jacob 262
Ammonett, John H. 238,262
Ammonette, Jacob 98,135,
  186
Ammonette, James H. 186
Ammonette, John H. 186
Anderson, Darcus 274
Anderson, Drury 48
Anderson, Edward 106
Anderson, James 25,28,271

Anderson, John 234,235
Anderson, John G. 166,177,263
Anderson, Johnson 28,37,165,
  178,193,204
Anderson, Margaret 194
Anderson, Matthew 37,53,87,168
Anderson, N. B. 245,284
Anderson, Overton B. 70,268,287
Anderson, P. 111,114
Anderson, Pheby 244
Anderson, Poley 103
Anderson, Polly 27
Anderson, Rachel 285
Anderson, Robert 244
Anderson, Samson 285
Anderson, Theby 195
Anderson, William 70
Anderson, William P. 268
Anderson, William W. 107,244
Andrews, C. W. 254
Andrews, Drury 4,6,19,32,48
Andrews, James 19
Andrews, Jesse B. 132,254,285
Andrews, John 92
Andrews, John A. 171
Andrews, Mary 110
Andrews, Samuel 110,123,235
Andrews, William 92
Andrews, William F. 65,150
Anthony, Hannah 86
Anthony, Josiah 86,176
Anthony, Samuel 86
Apple, Alisha 222
Apple, Anthony 118,135,146
Apple, Daniel 222
Apple, David 151,160
Apple, Elizabeth J. 155
Apple, George 192
Apple, Madison D. 118
Apple, Milton 186
Apple, Oliver 151
Archer, Ann W. 137,156,165
Archer, Harriet F. 157
Archer, William 91,137,156,157,
  165
Arington, Albert 278
Arington, Thomas 214,278
Armstead, Amanda T. 161
Armstead, James 236
Armstead, John 23,48,234,278
Armstead, John H. 161,175
Armstead, Martha 124
Armstead, Mary F. 161
Armstead, Nancy 21,48
Armstead, Samuel A. 175

Armstead, William 124
Armsted, Jesse M. 16,111
Armstrong, B. 155
Armstrong, Benjamin J. 256
Armstrong, J. W. 155,212
Armstrong, James M. 93
Armstrong, John B. 5,131,
   181,212,256
Armstrong, Joseph W. 181,
   212
Armstrong, Martin 60
Armstrong, Martin W. 136,
   256
Armstrong, Nancy 5
Armstrong, Nancy M. 136,
   158
Armstrong, Robert 154
Armstrong, Thomas T. 131
Arnett, William 177,237
Arnett, William P. 263
Arnold, Daniel 75
Arnold, James 99
Arnold, Joseph 18,40
Arrington, Albert 172
Arundel, Benjamin 103
Arundell, Benjamin 29,58,
   165,167,168,217
Arundell, John 248
Arundell, John L. 221,239
Arundell, Thomas W. 273
Arvin, Drury 14
Asbury, Kelly 85
Ashley, William 19,47,
   51,56,81,85,123
Ashlock, Gilbert 179
Ashlock, Nancy 179
Asken, James 21
Asken, Phebe 21
Askew, Malinda 80
Askew, Thomas 80
Askew, Thomas B. 35,38,44,
   91,154
Askew, William 35,38
Askin, Thomas 29,32
Askin, Thomas D. 28
Askin, William 28,32
Askins, Adison 161
Askins, Presley 64,69,93,
   100,109,121,148
Atkinson, John W. 106
Atwood, Edwin 51,71,96,
   170,198,218
Atwood, Elizabeth 219
Atwood, Moses 277
Atwood, Newton 277

Austin, Christian 67,68,275
Austin, John W. 285
Austin, Larkin K. 11
Austin, Levi 275,285,286
Austin, Miles W. 271
Austin, Philip 275,284
Austin, Solomon 91,162,197
Austin, Stephen 226
Austin, Susan 197
Austin, William 91,162
Avant, Benjamin 261
Averett, E. C. 194
Averett, R. 249
Averett, Richard 188,266,268,
   283,285
Avrett, C. E. 188
Bailey, Fred R. 266
Bailey, Frederick R. 266
Bailey, Henry 218
Bailey, John 162,163,164,169,170,
   176,184,187,198,200,203,204,
   217,218,220,226,253
Bailey, Johnson 137,202
Bailey, Jonathan 65,95,117,137,
   193,209,230,253
Bailey, Rebecca 266
Bailey, W. W. 55,65,67,68,73,84,
   86,88,90,93,94,95,96,99,101,
   105,114,115,124,125,127,132,
   139,141,144,146,149,151,152,
   159,160,169,171,184,185,193,
   195,198,199,202,203,219,240,
   261,266,272,277,284
Bailey, Wiatt 84
Bailey, Wiatt W. 12,25,61
Bailey, William 7,31
Bailey, Wyatt W. 59
Bailiff, Samuel 141,211,261
Bailiff, Samuel S. 258
Bailiff, Thomas 115,181,192,193,
   200,202
Bailiff, William 34
Baines, A. S. 104
Bains, A. L. 78,116,162,170
Bains, A. S. 108,109,174,181,189
Bains, Alfred L. 267
Bains, Allen L. 256
Bains, B. M. 89,180,189
Bains, Brice M. 256
Bains, Elizabeth 189
Bains, George 189,256
Bains, Mary M. 189
Bains, Samuel 189
Bains, W. M. 244
Bains, William 189

Baird, Andrew 241
Baird, Brice M. 109
Baird, J. H. 218
Baird, Jeremiah 245
Baird, Jeremiah H. 244
Baird, Jeremy 241
Baird, Jeremy P. 241
Baird, Jesse H. 271
Baird, Josiah 14,26,209,
  218,283
Baird, Josiah, Jr. 218,
  236,271
Baird, Josiah, Sr. 236
Baird, Reuben 67
Baker, A. J. 178
Baker, Andrew J. 107,133
Baker, C. 224
Baker, F. G. 202,226
Baker, Frances 193
Baker, Frances G. 238
Baker, George 73,134,184,
  214,257,277
Baker, Jacob 118,122
Baker, James 224
Baker, John 12,37,143,
  155,224
Baker, Jonathan 26
Baker, Joseph H. 257
Baker, Louisa 12
Baker, Marinda 12
Baker, Mary 12
Baker, Morgan H. 224
Baker, S. 192
Baker, Sally 12,40
Baker, Samuel 78
Baker, Solomon 62,259
Baker, Susan 257
Baker, Thomas M. 224
Baker, William 91,125,
  151,197,212,241,245
Baley, Presley 240
Baliff, Thomas 6
Ball, Elijah 235
Ballad, John 114,139
Ballard, Elizabeth 147
Ballard, James 124,233,
  248
Ballard, John 24,35,55,
  77,114,145,147,156,
  174,246,267
Ballard, John W. 205
Ballard, William 214,216
Ballenger, B. F. 260
Ballenger, Benjamin 227,
  228

Ballenger, Caroline 273
Ballenger, James 228
Ballenger, Thomas 227,228
Ballenger, William 59,101,104
Ballew, Ann 153
Ballew, Anthony M. 108
Ballew, Chesley 153
Ballew, James L. 153
Ballew, James M. 56,77,92,153
Ballew, L. D. 123
Ballew, Leonard 108,121,123
Ballew, Martha A. 153
Ballew, Mary E. 153
Ballew, William J. 123
Ballinger, Elizabeth F. 190
Ballinger, Franklin 190
Ballinger, Harris B. 190
Ballinger Heirs 208
Ballinger, James 190
Ballinger, Meredith 190
Ballinger, Peter 190
Ballinger, Thomas 190,218
Ballow, Leonard 221,270
Ballow, Lorenzo 221,270
Ballow, Rice M. 270
Bandy, George H. 253
Bandy, Richard 102
Bandy, Thomas 66,82,123
Banks, Elijah 70,89,144,201,244
Banks, Elijah S. 10
Banks, Elijah, Sr. 182
Banks, Elizabeth 263
Banks, Elizabeth L. 238
Banks, Emerelda 229
Banks, Ermehilda 238
Banks, Jane 70,201
Banks, Maderson C. 263
Banks, Thomas 263
Banks, Valentine 252
Barbee, Elias 213,250
Barbee, John 46,138,216,247
Barbee, Joseph 216
Barbee, Joseph, Sr. 216
Barkley, Richard 239
Barksdale, Harriet 200,201
Barksdale, Hickerson 128,200,
  201,210,217,223
Barnet, James 62
Barnett, James 13,44,80,182,188,
  190,208,211,222,250
Barnett, John J. 215,248,283
Barnett, Lemuel 170
Barnett, Mary 222
Barnett, Thomas 100
Barnett, Thomas R. 234

Barren, N. L. 275
Barret, James 199
Barret, Stephen 199
Barrett, James 73,107,157,228,239,252
Barrett, Stephen 239
Barrot, James 61
Barrott, James 190
Barrott, Nancy 190
Barrott, Samuel W. 249
Barrow, R. 114
Barrow, Reason 3,8,141
Barrow, William 38
Barry, James 80,82,246,259
Barton, Hugh B. 19
Barton, Isaac 209
Barton, John 19,41,55,63
Barton, Robert 215,247,274
Barton, Samuel 13,41,63
Bass, David 239
Bass, John D. 240
Bates, Isaac 67,69,83,103,115,172,174,192
Bates, Israel 18
Bates, James 99,192
Bates, Joel 191,218,232,250,267
Bates, John 218,232,250,267
Bates, John H. 158,216,218,229,230,235,257,277
Bates, William 115,172,192,202,206,230,232,241,280
Baugh, Instance 231
Baugh, William 233
Baughman, Christopher 125
Baughman, John 73
Baysinger, Catherine 262
Baysinger, Holden D. 262
Baysinger, John 262
Beal, Bartley 283
Beal, John B. 270
Beasley, Braddock 26,91,167,191,195,271
Beasley, Ellis 17,20,33,35,36,54,79,182,223,224,239,247,248,279,282
Beasley, Gabriel 282
Beasley, George W. 268
Beasley, H. F. 230

Beasley, Henry 36,68,158,166,171,177,182,183,191,192
Beasley, Isham 4,19,20,21,24,112,144,165,173,221,258,259
Beasley, Isham, Jr. 21
Beasley, Isum 14
Beasley, James 268
Beasley, James E. 25
Beasley, Jesse 97,205
Beasley, Johnson 115
Beasley, Jordan 159,177
Beasley, Major A. 89,92,152,177,189
Beasley, Mary A. 195
Beasley, Robert 38
Beasley, Shelby C. 62
Beasley, Walter A. 192
Beasley, William 278
Beasley, William H. 38,221,259
Beasley, William J. 242
Beasley, William P. 93
Beck, Phillymon 93
Beck, William 16,79
Becker, Samuel 246
Beckman, Christopher 23
Beckman, John 130,148,187,192,204,254
Beckman, Nancy 23
Beckwith, James 101,131
Beckwith, John 127
Beckwith, Rachael 101
Beden, Elijah 263
Beden, Lucinda 263
Bedford, Elizabeth 265
Bedford, Elizabeth A. 237,273
Bedford, John H. 16,162,176,180,181,206,212,237,239,256,262,265,273
Bedford, Seay 265
Belcher, I. E. 246
Belcher, J. E. 254
Belcher, Jacob 175
Belcher, N. G. 202
Belcher, S. E. 2
Belcher, Thomas 55,68,115,154
Belcher, W. W. 246,254,264
Belcher, William 68,250
Belfor, Andrew 211
Belfor, Henry 211
Belfor, Mary 211
Belk, Jere 259
Belk, Jeremiah 245
Bell, Ervin 7
Bell, John 10,167,190
Bell, Robert D. 160,173

Bell, Samuel 55,201,238
Bell, William M. 264
Bell, William W. 230
Bellah, Moses 232
Bellar, Elizabeth 266
Bellew, Rice M. 6
Beloat, James, Sr. 2
Bennett, Benjamin M. 270
Bennett, H. D. 205
Bennett, H. G. 173
Bennett, Harrison 234, 269,270
Bennett, J. D. 262
Bennett, James D. 187, 216,270
Bennett, Kitty C. 270
Bennett, William 23
Bennett, William J. 12, 13,116,214
Bennett, William M. 270
Bennett, William T. 89, 166,219,225,270,275
Bennett, William T., Jr. 271
Benson, Frances 15
Benson, John R. 61,78
Benton, Albert 89
Berry, James 234
Betty, A. W. 280
Betty, Alfred M. 21
Betty, George 24
Betty, George W. 24
Betty, Mary J. 24
Betty, Permelia 24
Betty, Polly 24
Betty, W. S. 28
Betty, William R. 42,85, 86,88,114,117,184,229
Bias, Isaac A. 216
Bickers, Samuel 257,284
Bigelow, L. 3
Bigs, Richard 227
Binion, Francis 75
Binion, Martin 48
Birchett, James 10
Birdwell, Joseph 268
Bishop, James 186
Bishop, Joseph 90,116,161
Bishop, Thomas 7
Bishop, Thomas B. 31,34
Black, David 193,197,251
Black, Elizabeth 154,197
Black, John 10,32,37,38, 39,42,44,58
Black, Robert 197

Black, Samuel 122,191
Black, Thomas 1,46,47
Black, Thomas J. 59,85,92,197
Black, William 152,197
Blackfan, Jesse 105
Blackwell, Elizabeth 119,121, 122,139,140
Blackwell, James 31
Blackwell, James M. 92,119,140, 285
Blackwell, James W. 229
Blackwell, John 140
Blackwell, Yance 82
Blackwell, Yancy 170,184,251
Blair, Charles 208
Blair, Charles R. 35,57,166,260, 273,281,283,286
Blankenship, Barnet 58,102
Blankenship, David 102
Blankenship, Hezekiah 101
Blankenship, Jesse M. 58
Blankenship, Joel 103
Blankenship, John 58,101
Blankenship, Rhoda 101
Blare, Charles R. 207
Blew, David 172
Block, John 8
Blount, John G., Jr. 105
Blount, John G., Sr. 105
Bockman, Mariah 137
Bogle, Joseph H. 239
Bohannon, Darcus 66
Boley, Presley 133,177
Bolton, Charles 29,59,60,61,81
Bolton, Charles J. 52
Bolton, Cinderella 59
Bolton, Elizabeth 106
Bolton, Estell 59,81
Bolton, James 61
Bolton, Lent 60
Bolton, Lorenzo D. 108
Bolton, Louisa 81
Bolton, Lousa 59
Bolton, Lucretia 59,81
Bolton, W. 214
Bolton, Wilson 87,114,226,230
Bomar, Elijah 113
Bomar, Nathaniel T. 275
Bomar, William 82
Bomar, William J. 161
Bomer, Elijah 106
Bomer, James R. 270
Bomer, Nathaniel 270
Bomer, William J. 270
Bond, G. 73

Bond, J. D. 73
Booker, Elizabeth 258
Booker, Mary 258
Booker, William L. 276
Boon, James N. 254,280
Boose, James 113
Boothe, Manerva 67
Boothe, Robert 67
Borum, Emily 284
Borum, John 284
Boston, Andrew 19
Boston, Christian 191, 193,262
Boston, George 52,74,120, 170,220,248,267
Boston, Jacob H. 287
Boston, James 193,228,242
Boston, John 205
Boulton, America D. 243
Boulton, Americus D. 248
Boulton, Charles 114,136, 153,210
Boulton, Charles, Sr. 153
Boulton, Eliza 253
Boulton, Elizabeth 211
Boulton, Frances 211,275
Boulton, Hansford 215,241
Boulton, James 40,143,150, 153,224,244
Boulton, Lent 32,122,130, 133,142,148,153,211,253, 275
Boulton, Martha 210
Boulton, Mary 211
Boulton, Thomas 211,265, 269,275
Boulton, Wilson 79,153, 170,223,224,227,256
Bowen, Grant A. 127
Bowen, John H. 127,161,184
Bowen, John W. 108,228, 231,258
Bowin, Grant 145
Bowman, James 220
Bowman, Jefferson 234,287
Bowman, Jefferson C. 213
Bowman, Jefferson E. 235
Bowman, John 251
Bowman, Joseph 10,131,152, 166,174,177,191,220,256, 260,265,267,279,283
Bowman, Rachel 158,191,220
Bowman, Robert 1,10,45,105, 133,158
Boyers, Robert M. 77

Boze, Elizabeth 33,136,182
Boze, James 134,135,158,220
Boze, Richard 248
Braden, Johnson M. 200
Braden, Thomas 200
Bradford, D. M. 150
Bradford, John H. 142
Bradford, Joseph 9
Bradford, U. R. 245
Bradford, V. R. 191,193
Bradford, Vincent R. 36,67,87, 124
Bradford, W. M. 269
Bradley, Bethel B. 271
Bradley, Bethwell B. 277
Bradley, C. S. 94
Bradley, Charles 215
Bradley, David C. 255
Bradley, Edward 214,255
Bradley, Elizabeth 142,255
Bradley, Frances 255
Bradley, George 215
Bradley, George W. 262,270
Bradley, Harriet B. 269
Bradley, Hugh 26,266
Bradley, Hugh H. 22,42,110,125, 276
Bradley, Isaac 35,56,128,152,254
Bradley, James 4,25,33,98,120, 142,172,229,254,269
Bradley, James B. 264
Bradley, James C. 138
Bradley, James S. 214,248,283
Bradley, John 29,229,255
Bradley, John D. 142,148,162
Bradley, Judith 215
Bradley, Leroy 166,256,269
Bradley, Rebecca 166
Bradley, Mary 255,271
Bradley, Robert 47,79,94,125, 128,138
Bradley, Samuel 114
Bradley, Thomas 11,255
Bradley, William 255
Brame, John 35
Brandon, John 72
Brandon, John, Sr. 54
Brandon, William 131
Brandon, William, Jr. 12
Bransford, Elizabeth 273
Bransford, Gideon H. 10
Bransford, James W. 28,119,121, 123,143,212,222,246
Bransford, John 88,222
Bransford, John F. 91

Bransford, Lindley M. 88
Bransford, Lindsley M. 222
Bransford, Mary 278
Bransford, Mary C. 222
Bransford, Nancy 222
Bransford, Richard 27, 212,238
Bransford, Richard H. 222
Bransford, Richard R. 28, 170
Bransford, William 222,235
Bransford, William C. 2
Braswell, Bennett 96
Braswell, John 117,209
Braswell, Reuben 104,129, 133,134,169
Braswell, Richard 117
Braswell, Robert 116,141
Braswell, William 274
Bratton, Anderson 54
Bratton, Charles J. 53,54
Bratton, David 7,66,68
Bratton, William 53
Brauner, Jeremiah 29
Brawner, Henry 37,38
Bray, John 277
Bray, Richard 284
Bray, Thomas 69,86
Breeden, Elijah 218
Breeden, Lucinda 218
Brent, Samuel 121
Brevard, A. A. 267
Brevard, Alfred A. 9,19, 41,44,92,147,201
Brevard, Cyrus W. 2,8,23, 41,105,147
Brevard, John C. 44,221
Brewer, Calvin 256,277
Brickhouse, Tully 102
Bridges, Allen J. 2,42,118
Bridges, Barnett 268
Bridges, Isadella 268
Bridges, James L. 268
Bridges, John 42,54,125, 168,169,186,198,222,225, 228,232,234,237,240,247, 267,268,278,287
Bridges, Joseph 74,148,268
Bridges, Joseph J. 123,268
Bridges, Milly 42
Bridges, Smith 268
Bridges, Stephen 2
Bridges, Thomas 124,135, 214,268,272
Bridges, Thomas B. 204

Bridges, Willis 268
Bridgewater, Ann 213
Bridgewater, C. W. 282
Bridgewater, Chesley 41,87,115, 123,213,282
Bridgewater, John C. 282
Bridgewater, Lucy J. 282
Bridgewater, R. A. 200,282
Bridgewater, Richard A. 282
Bridgewater, S. C. 141,230
Bridgewater, Samuel C. 125,200, 226,282
Brien, John 61
Brien, John S. 30,184
Brien, Manson 184
Brien, R. G. 23
Bright, Nancy 78
Bright, Rowland 78
Brim, James H. 90
Brim, Joel 126
Brien, John 257
Brim, William 240,275
Brindley, Asa 282
Brinkle, Asa 243
Brinkle, Mary A. 243
Brittain, William 250
Britton, Abraham 142,176
Britton, James 176
Britton, Nathan 48
Britton, Nathaniel 89
Britton, Richard 48,50,86,142, 176
Britton, Susannah 86
Brockett, B. F. 271
Brockett, Benjamin F. 158
Brockett, M. 184
Brockett, M. Y. 186
Brockett, Milton 166,253
Brockett, William C. 158,271
Brooks, C. D. 164
Brooks, Charles 179
Brooks, Charles D. 165
Brooks, Henry 208
Brooks, Mary A. 179
Broom, Elizabeth 112
Broom, William 112
Brown, Dixon 260
Brown, James 45,82,186
Brown, John W. 108
Brown, Joseph 91
Brown, Nelson 134
Brown, Richard 22,30
Brown, Richard J. 257
Brown, Robert 260,278
Brown, Samuel 133

Brown, Valentine H. 27
Brown, William F. 83
Browning, T. P. 114
Browning, William H. 183
Bruce, Mary 231
Bruce, Milton 231
Bruce, O. H. 272
Bruer, Calvin 151
Bryan, John S. 228
Bryan, Manson 228
Bryan, R. G. 48
Bryant, Allen 58
Bryant, Edmund P. 58
Bryant, Howell H. 125
Bryant, R. G. 40,58,108,
  110
Bryant, Rhodeham G. 17
Buckley, Elizabeth 180,
  252
Buckman, Christopher 19
Buckman, Henry 19
Buckner, John 6,21,28,
  57,108,138,187,257
Buckner, John T. 53
Buckner, Margaret 108
Buie, Daniel 19,77,153,
  231
Bundy, Rebecca 60
Bundy, Thomas 60
Bundy, William 60
Burdine, John B. 142
Burdine, N. B. 114,133,
  147,174,205,217
Burdine, Nathan B. 155
Burdine, S. 67
Burdine, Samuel 2,20,48,
  67,79,82,93,113,131,
  142,147,154,157,198,
  217,231,254,264,268,283
Burford, B. W. 78
Burford, Benjamin 76
Burford, Benjamin W. 20,23
Burford, David 30,31,33,
  38,44,51,92,98,104,131,
  133,135,170,173,197,198,
  201,204,206,209,219,256,
  262,277
Burford, John 239
Burford, John H. 4,49,106,
  186,209,246
Burford, John P. 237
Burford, Robert A. 262,283
Burford, William 202,205
Burk, Joseph 73
Burk, William 6

Burks, H. C. 200
Burks, Henry C. 192
Burnett, Elizabeth 12,20
Burnett, J. J. 227
Burnett, John 85
Burnett, John J. 87,94,151,226,
  232,234,276
Burnett, Thomas R. 119
Burnley, George H. 256,276
Burns, A. S. 180
Burns, Gregory 62
Burns, Gregory D. 121,176
Burns, John G. 27,28
Burns, Moses 126
Burris, Jacob 66
Burris, Martin H. 28,43,66
Burris, Susannah 66
Burris, William 42
Burris, William T. 43
Burrow, John 100
Burrow, William 38,47,55,66,68,
  69
Burrus, Jacob 174
Burrus, Martin 52
Burrus, Martin H. 42
Burrus, William T. 42
Burton, A. J. 25,39
Burton, Albert 22,40
Burton, Albert G. 145
Burton, Charles F. 140
Burton, David W. 35
Burton, Elizabeth 22
Burton, H. B. 25
Burton, Hugh B. 39
Burton, Jabez 57,78,140,157,177,
  178,180,195
Burton, Jacob H. 40
Burton, Jubal 78,140
Burton, Landon 215
Burton, Robert 40,50,112,192
Burton, Robert G. 140
Burton, Stephen D. 155
Burton, William A. 145
Bush, Ivy 175
Bush, Jeremiah 32
Bush, John 76
Bush, Joseph 73,215
Bush, Mary 76
Bush, William 212
Butler, Alfred 271,287
Butler, Braxton 248
Butler, James H. 256
Butler, James T. 268
Butler, Lydia 189
Butler, Richard 113,200

Butler, Thomas 189
Butter, Anney 87
Butts, Eli 20,113
Butts, Elijah 248
Butts, Joseph 5
Butts, Mary 146,213,248
Butts, Sally 146
Butts, Wilson 10,12
Cage, Edward E. 254
Cage, Elizabeth 202
Cage, James W. 226,269
Cage, Leroy H. 104,123,
  199,252,262,270
Cage, Mary 286
Cage, Mary W. 252
Cage, Nathaniel W. 236,
  241,260
Cage, P. W. 30,41,62,82,
  123,184,214,229,254,
  269,282,286
Cage, Palemon W. 84
Cage, Palimore W. 41
Cage, Pleneon W. 226
Cage, Poleman W. 120,128,
  134
Cage, Thomas D. 237
Cage, Wilson 30,69,76,
  78,99,110,132
Caleb, Pate 258
Caley, John 221
Calhoun, Hardy 74,230,
  242,271,285
Cameron, Joseph 95
Campbell, Fanny I. 141
Campbell, George 212
Campbell, George H. 63,
  106,142
Campbell, Hugh 106
Campbell, James S. 106
Campbell, Joseph 100
Campbell, Michael 73
Campbell, Sarah 77
Campbell, Susan 180
Campbell, William B. 141,
  159,179,182,185,202,
  238,241,248,257,258
Campbell, William G. 73
Campsey, John 159,175,283
Canada, Stephen 142
Canaday, David 14,133
Canaday, Stephen 203
Cannon, Elijah 34
Cannon, Newton 88
Cannon, Tilman 151
Caplinger, Andrew 122

Caplinger, John 115,131,141
Caplinger, Samuel 1,9,21,88,
  94,99,109,115,116,122,160,
  173,177,179
Caplinger, Solomon 66,117
Carditt, J. B. 19
Cardwell, A. P. 215
Cardwell, Alben P. 129,232
Cardwell, Alvan 228
Cardwell, Anderson 76
Cardwell, B. S. 185,215,218,223,
  224,230,232,233,235,251
Cardwell, Buckner 118,128
Cardwell, Buckner A. 45
Cardwell, Buckner J. 163
Cardwell, Chaffin 284
Cardwell, Daniel 163
Cardwell, John 281
Cardwell, L. H. 81,103,224,279
Cardwell, Leonard 45,46,227
Cardwell, Leonard H. 26,40,61,
  85,98,174,191,232,235,275,
  281,282,287
Cardwell, Leonard J. 152,280
Cardwell, Micajah 15,121
Cardwell, Pamelia 228
Cardwell, Thomas D. 56
Cardwell, Varnel L. 129
Cardwell, William 121
Cardwell, William T. 131
Carlie, William 25,27,201
Carlisle, Hannah 229
Carlisle, Wesley 229
Carman, Aletha 201
Carman, Bassil G. 180,244
Carman, Caleb 25,81,82,92,110,
  113,123,132,153,158,188,198,
  204,238
Carman, Elijah 62,81,132
Carman, Elizabeth 153
Carman, Frances 158
Carman, H. H. 186
Carman, H. M. 244,246
Carman, Hopewell 61
Carman, Lethe 244
Carman, Moses 59
Carman, Rusia 158
Carman, Susannah 82
Carman, Thomas 68,80,82,89,108,
  110,114,123,132,139,158,181,
  182,188,194,197,242,244,276
Carmicle, Abraham 87
Carmon, Caleb 22
Carpenter, Ann 148
Carpenter, George F. 221,236,

237,253
Carr, Henry M. 65
Carr, James D. 44
Carr, James R. 65
Carr, Jesse D. 16,43
Carter, Andrew 253,263
Carter, Charlotte 36
Carter, Edward 189
Carter, Eissa 263
Carter, Elijah 170
Carter, Eliza A. 179
Carter, Elizabeth 263
Carter, George M. 41,53
Carter, Henry D. 171
Carter, J. B. 20
Carter, Jane 217,263
Carter, Jesse 253
Carter, John 28,36,263
Carter, John L. 10
Carter, John S. 1,161
Carter, John T. 217
Carter, Joseph 149
Carter, Joseph L. 32,33, 40,54,56,57,60,62,80, 221,269
Carter, Joseph S. 105,108, 113
Carter, L. 76
Carter, Lavinia 189
Carter, Littleton H. 62, 105
Carter, Mary A. 263
Carter, Mathew 150,177,193
Carter, Price 80
Carter, Prier 80,110
Carter, W. W. 256
Carter, William 15,68,93, 179
Carter, William B. 6,23
Carter, William S. 18,29, 40
Carter, William W. 250
Carter, Winslow 286
Cartwright, A. 272
Cartwright, Asberry 40,77, 269
Cartwright, James 88,89, 128
Cartwright, Joseph 4
Cartwright, Lorenzo D. 71, 141
Cartwright, Oliver 128,178
Cartwright, Polly 214
Cartwright, Rachael 200
Cartwright, Richardson C. 89,156

Cartwright, Thaxton 200,204
Cartwright, Thomas 40,77
Cartwright, William 89,158,245
Caruthers, Abraham 66,92,95, 97,103,131,151,160,217,236
Caruthers, Elizabeth 54
Caruthers, J. J. 132
Caruthers, Joseph 69
Caruthers, Josiah 35,50,88
Caruthers, Josiah J. 69,70,100
Caruthers, Mary 195
Caruthers, R. C. 149
Caruthers, Robert L. 59,99,165, 171
Caruthers, Sally 59,132
Caruthers, Samuel 54
Caruthers, Sarah S. 80
Carver, Cornelius 52
Carver, Edward 223
Carver, John 145,223
Carver, John, Jr. 42
Carver, Joseph 52
Carver, William 52,77
Cary, A. 15
Cary, Ann E. 4,15
Cary, Beverly 4
Cary, Mary J. 4,15
Cary, Milton 4,15
Cary, Phebe C. 4,15,262
Casey, Samuel 55
Casley, John O. 252
Cassity, Ensley 54
Cassity, T. D. 209
Cassity, Thomas 53,54
Cassity, Thomas D. 135,151
Cassity, William 45
Caster, Moses 253
Cates, John B. 45
Cato, Robert H. 107,281
Catron, Alfred 225,230,264
Catron, G. W. 181
Catron, George W. 170,176,264, 268
Catron, O. P. 170
Cawthon, James 124
Cawthorn, James 166
Cawthorn, Parthenia 166
Cempsey, John 136
Chamberlain, James M. 52
Chamberlain, William 39,42
Chambers, Benjamin F. 201
Chambers, Elizabeth 201,244,257
Chambers, Elizabeth, Jr. 244
Chambers, Franklin 244
Chambers, James 23,70,144,224
Chambers, John 70,244,245

Chambers, John C. 123,238
Chambers, Mary 201,244
Chambers, Richard 144,208, 229
Chambers, Samuel 171,201, 244
Chambers, Samuel B. 174
Chambers, William 201, 244,245
Champ, James 184
Champ, Mary 184
Chandler, Eliza G. 198
Chandler, Hugh L. 198
Chandler, James 198
Chandler, Mary 272
Chandler, Parks 76,144, 152,153,198
Chandler, S. B. 101
Chandler, Samuel B. 15
Chandler, William 198
Chandler, William E. 78
Chandler, Winston 108
Chapman, A. J. 153
Chapman, Amos 106
Chapman, Frances 153
Cheatham, Edmund E. 50, 116
Cheatham, Joel 263
Cheek, Ephraim 161,199, 226,267,280
Cheek, James 281
Cheek, James R. 284
Cheek, Luther 227,241
Cheek, Susan 241
Cheek, William H. 267
Childrop, Mitchell 15
Chism, John A. 197
Chism, Sarah 197
Chisom, John A. 94
Chisom, Sarah 94
Chitwood, Charles 71
Chitwood, Daniel 71
Chitwood, Pleasant 6,71, 94
Chitwood, Richard 43
Choffer, William 273
Christer, Thornton 147
Christian, William H. 264
Christie, Thornton 218
Chuck, William H. 87
Circy, William 144
Claiborn, Daniel D. 79
Claiborn, John 79
Claiborne, Adam F. 96
Claiborne, Thomas 129

Clarada, Drury 158
Claraday, Drury D. 180
Clardy, Benjamin 4
Clardy, Drury 87
Clardy, John C. 53
Clardy, Yancy 278
Clardy, Yancy F. 231
Clark, Alfred 180,193
Clark, Amanda 222
Clark, Andrew 70,222,283,285
Clark, Eason B. 222
Clark, Emily 229,283
Clark, H. B. 245
Clark, Henry 196
Clark, Henry B. 94,159,197,229, 247,249,278
Clark, James 191
Clark, Joseph M. 164
Clark, L. 60
Clark, Pamelia 143
Clark, Roland 11,88
Clark, Rowland 129
Clark, Susan 217
Clark, Thomas 229
Clark, Thomas A. 283
Clay, Marthy 227
Clay, P. 286
Clay, Paul 227
Clement, Charlott 31
Clemmons, James 39
Clemmons, Sarah 162
Clemmons, Thomas 126
Clemmons, William 162
Clenden, Aletha 228
Clenden, Henry W. 228
Cleveland, Alexander 278
Cleveland, Alphema 35
Cleveland, Hazzard 278
Cleveland, Jacob M. 108
Cleveland, Joel M. 278
Cleveland, Joseph 278
Cleveland, Martha 278
Cleveland, Milton 278
Cleveland, Nancy 167
Cleveland, Patsy 44,238
Cleveland, Robert E. 55,278
Cleveland, Susan 278
Cleveland, W. N. 278
Cleveland, William 3,26,35,44, 108,134,167,173,278
Cleveland, William J. 278
Clevelin, Joel M. 211
Cliborn, C. 5
Cliburn, Daniel 14
Cliburn, George 65

Cliburn, John 14,79,102
Cliburn, John M. 51
Cliburn, Meredith 75
Cliburn, O. 76
Cliburn, William F. 102
Clifton, William 226
Climer, James 108,120,
    129,177,190,243,244
Climer, Thomas 160,167
Climire, James 192
Coaley, Cresay 196
Coatney, Elijah 277
Coatney, George 277
Coatney, Mary 277
Coatney, Moses F. 277
Coatney, Sarah 277
Coatney, Sarah J. 277
Coatney, Thomas 277
Cochran, David 92,98,112,
    154,229,260
Cochran, John 6,87,101,
    112,114,126,136,154,
    225,229
Cockerham, Franklin 211
Cockerham, Henry 211
Cockerham, J. G. 211
Cockerham, Thomas 142,211
Coffee, Alfred 285
Coffee, Darthula 285
Coffee, Delilah 259
Coffee, Franklin 285
Coffee, Isham 285
Coffee, Joel 126,128,
    149,158,163,175,187,
    196,201,206,285
Coffee, Joshua 175,202,259
Coffee, Joshua M. 54
Coffee, Matilda 285
Coffee, Minerva 279
Coffee, Patsey E. 285
Coffee, Polly 259
Coffee, S. M. 260
Coffee, S. W. 279
Coffee, Scythia 260
Coffee, Stockard 285
Coffee, Stockard W. 223,
    237,273,285
Coffee, Taylor 285
Coffee, William 118,175,
    259
Coggin, Jeremiah 88,112,
    135,184,231,261,269
Coggin, Loyd P. 179
Coggin, William 87
Coggin, Willis 65,97,217

Coggins, Jeremiah 229
Coggins, Willis 143
Coker, C. J. 62,189
Coker, Charles 29,44,75,221
Coker, Charles J. 269
Coker, Charles T. 189
Coker, George 78
Coker, Margaret 84
Coker, Samuel F. 182
Coker, Samuel T. 56,84,183,187,
    197,213,217,267
Coker, Warren 78
Colbert, Elijah 67
Cole, Angeline M. 97
Cole, Charles 26,171
Cole, J. F. 26
Cole, Jackson F. 63,71,76
Cole, Samuel F. 63,71,76
Cole, William C. 129
Coleman, Ann 140
Coleman, Jesse 99
Coleman, John J. 99,139,186
Coleman, L. B. 201
Coleman, Little B. 93,99,188,212
Coleman, Littleberry 72,203
Coleman, Nancy 94
Coleman, Nelly 99
Coleman, Philadelphia 72
Coleman, Samuel P. 140
Coleman, Sarah C. 99
Coleman, Thomas 98
Coleman, Wiatt 33
Coleman, William C. 112
Coley, Frances 47,95
Collie, William 10
Collier, Joseph 16
Collom, J. H. 150
Collom, James 110
Collom, John 110,150
Collom, William 193,203,249
Collum, John 48
Compton, Margaret 216
Compton, William 71
Condett, John 149
Conditt, Fielden 21
Conditt, Fielding 86,193
Conditt, J. B. 23
Conditt, J. M. 113
Conditt, James B. 152,178,191
Conditt, John 23,174,190
Conduitte, Fielden 80
Conger, John 25,56,76,106,179
Conger, Joshua 179
Congo, Elisha 259
Congo, John 98,113,117,140,259

Congo, Joshua 259
Congo, Malinda 98
Congo, William 259
Cook, Amanda 198
Cook, Calvin 101,103
Cook, David 141,171
Cook, Harris 112
Cook, Henry M. 46,112
Cook, James 5,112
Cook, Sion 58
Cook, William 1
Cook, William A. 198
Cook, William M. 181
Cooker, Warren P. 60
Cooksey, Benjamin 211,222,
   245
Cooksey, Ephraim 211
Cooksey, Hiram C. 222
Cooksey, Gilly 211,222
Cooksey, James B. 118
Cooksey, John 211
Cooksey, Joseph 245
Cooksey, Lilley 222
Cooper, James F. 267
Cooper, John 16,22,90,111,
   124
Corder, Azakiah 117
Corder, Azariah 147
Corder, Ezariah 216
Corder, Ezekiel 116
Corder, Zachinah 21,104
Corley, E. T. 89
Corley, Edmund 55,197
Corley, Edward A. 230
Corley, Elizabeth 83
Corley, Elviry 83
Corley, James 262
Corley, John 35,113,168,
   198,238
Corley, Larkin 83,97,107,
   246,267
Corley, M. E. 251
Corley, Mary 83
Corley, Matthew 41,170,197
Corley, Nancy 35,83
Corley, Nathaniel 264
Corley, William 41,107
Corley, William A. 12,17,
   29,38,172
Corley, William O. 230
Cornick, Elizabeth W. 28
Cornick, Horatio 28
Cornwell, Alfred 148
Cornwell, Allen 30,31,52
Cornwell, Barnet 140
Cornwell, Barnett 216,263

Cornwell, Barrett 282,284
Cornwell, Drewry 195
Cornwell, Drury 37,42,43,137,
   242,281,285
Cornwell, Elijah 250
Cornwell, Elizabeth 149,229
Cornwell, Elizabeth A. 283
Cornwell, Frances 272
Cornwell, Henry 24
Cornwell, Henry M. 118,132
Cornwell, Jesse 19
Cornwell, John L. 169
Cornwell, John S. 79,281
Cornwell, John Y. 74,78,86
Cornwell, Larkin 118
Cornwell, P. F. 133,153
Cornwell, Pleasant 229,273
Cornwell, Pleasant F. 149
Cornwell, S. C. 110
Cornwell, Silas C. 27,105,121,
   129,136,140,145,153,223,272
Cornwell, William P. 285
Cornwell, William T. 16,53,110
Cornwell, Willis 226,266,283
Corten, Robert 111
Cosby, Elizabeth 111
Cosby, John C. 47,53,111,189
Cosby, Thomas W. 111
Cosby, William H. 111
Costello, John B. 162
Costello, William R. 268
Cothran, Drury A. 92
Cothran, James 131
Cothran, John 90
Cothran, Robert 92
Cothran, Lambert M. 57,90
Couch, John 15
Cowan, Almira 248
Cowan, I. H. 226
Cowan, Ira B. 155,157,185,187
Cowan, John L. 248
Cowan, John S. 250
Cowan, Joseph 192
Cowan, Joseph C. 247
Cowan, Josephus 200
Cowen, Ira B. 151,280
Cowen, Josephus 83
Cowen, Josephus C. 16
Cowen, Mathew 137
Cowley, Lucy 228
Cowley, William D. 228
Craig, H. M. 220
Craig, Hiram M. 83,123,232,250
Craig, James 83,123,130,138,
   247,250
Craig, Jane 138

Craig, John 138
Craig, John, Sr. 130,138
Craig, Joseph 130,138
Craig, Moses 185,220
Craighead, Peter 119
Craighead, Robert 10,74
Craighead, William 177, 240,280
Crain, H. S. 233
Crank, R. H. 276
Crank, William B. 159,191
Crastic, Joseph 252
Crastic, Judith H. 252
Crastic, Mary E. 252
Crawford, Rawley 70,79
Creacy, George 39
Creacy, William 39
Creal, A. R. 224
Creal, Elijah 176,195
Creasy, Jesse S. 72
Creel, Elijah 116
Crenshaw, D. A. 1
Crenshaw, David A. 28
Crofford, Rolley 118
Crosslin, Benjamin 276,287
Crosslin, William 1,22,45, 245,276
Crosslin, Wright W. 13,22
Crostick, Sharard 33
Crowder, James B. 151,196, 236,259
Crowder, Joanna 231
Crowder, Joannah 223
Crowder, John 70
Crowell, Allen 140,193, 195,231
Crowell, Benjamin 101,106
Crowell, Elijah W. 233
Crowell, Even A. 214
Crowell, Mitchel M. 214
Crutcher, Ferebee C. 215
Crutcher, James A. 215,262
Crutchfield, Campbell 31, 34,124,187,231,241,269, 277,284
Crutchfield, John M. 239
Crutchfield, Thomas 280
Cryer, Emily 282
Cryer, Thomas 282
Culbreath, Amanda E. 17
Culbreath, Hezekiah 17
Culbreath, James 89
Culbreath, James H. 17
Culbreath, John 17,18,56, 74,106,124,133,145
Culbreath, Nancy A. 17

Culbreath, Roseta 17
Culbreath, Rosetta 133
Cullom, William 160,165,169
Cullum, William 256
Culwell, Ruth 83
Cummins, Allison G. 191
Cunningham, Frances 254
Cunningham, James 46,65,66,67, 69,171,177,184,194,222,238, 251,252,254,256
Cunningham, Jesse 222
Cunningham, John H. 171
Cunningham, Nancy 238
Cunningham, Samuel 177
Cunningham, Sarah 210
Cunningham, W. W. 275,277
Cunningham, William 145,150,151
Cunningham, William W. 156,174, 177,178,182,191
Curlee, James 230
Dale, Isaac A. 35
Dale, Thomas 35
Dale, William 7
Dalton, B. S. 5
Dalton, Booker 6,42
Dalton, Booker L. 69
Dalton, Booker S. 147,165,195
Dalton, Calvin 153
Dalton, R. C. 143,195
Dalton, Robert 194
Danby, Darthula C. 196
Dannon, Mary W. 198
Darnell, Charles 90
Daugherty, Edward 35
Daugherty, George 31,130
Daugherty, J. W. 229
Daugherty, John W. 223
Davenport, John G. 46,224
Davenport, Joseph 13,18,21
Davenport, Sally 224
Davidson, Josiah 97
Davis, A. R. 96
Davis, Abram 267
Davis, Alfred 37,107
Davis, Alfred R. 83
Davis, B. C. 226
Davis, Basil 138
Davis, Benjamin 33
Davis, Benjamin C. 72,173,192, 231
Davis, Benjamin M. 240
Davis, Daniel C. 275
Davis, David 15,36,166,219
Davis, Delila 81,214
Davis, E. C. 5,30,31
Davis, Eli 33

Davis, Elijah C. 3,25
Davis, Elijah W. 77,81
Davis, Ely 4
Davis, George W. 287
Davis, Gilbert 199
Davis, Hannah 138
Davis, Hannah M. 95
Davis, Henry H. 41
Davis, Isaac 6
Davis, Isaac H. 4,11,51,
  52,54,195,278
Davis, James H. 280,286
Davis, John 81,88,193
Davis, John H. 223,225,
  234,237,261,278
Davis, John S. 223,240
Davis, Martha 239
Davis, Martin 198
Davis, Matthew 60,77,140
Davis, Nelson 107
Davis, Perlina 41
Davis, R. G. 246
Davis, Robert G. 278
Davis, Sarah 198
Davis, William 96
Davis, William B. 277
Davis, William J. 166,210
Dawson, Cowan W. 200
Dawson, Harriet 213
Dawson, Henry 213
Dawson, Isaac 213
Dawson, James 213
Dawson, John 32,63,108,
  213
Dawson, John T. 241
Dawson, Nancy 213
Dawson, Olive 169,202
Dawson, Stephen 213
Dawson, William 32,108,
  158,222,260,287
Day, Franklin B. 4,7,8,
  25,46,69
Day, Henry D. 181
Day, Henry L. 7,8,14,30,
  54,69,73,89,120,121,
  123,150,164,177,203
Day, Henry S. 104,190
Day, James D. 243
Day, John D. 34,91,119,
  245
Day, Philip T. 34,46,104,
  121,160
Day, Phillip T. 14,19,25
Day, Thomas B. 19,25,37,
  39

Dean, Thomas 148
Debow, A. M. 262
Debow, Archibald 131,161,210,
  247,285
Debow, Archibald M. 99,127,145,
  172,183,186
Debow, Bird 109
Debow, Elizabeth 54
Debow, James R. 131
Debow, John A. 3,10,32,49,54,
  144,146,158
Debow, Nancy G. 183
Debow, Sam C. 131
Debow, Samuel C. 253
Debow, Solomon 32,54,97,161,273
Debow, Stephen 8
Decker, Frederick 6,7,58,104
Decker, George W. 108,271
Decker, Richard B. 108
Decker, Summer 178
Decker, Summers 94,108,110
Dedman, Bethel 262,263
Dedman, John 66,204,262,263
Dedman, John, Jr. 235
Dedman, John, Sr. 235
Dedman, Jonathan 55
Dedmon, Jonathan 95
Degernett, John M. 101
Dejarnette, John M. 80
Denney, Benjamin 132,226
Denney, Charles 98
Denney, Charles C. 134
Denney, Mathew 267
Denney, William 132,134
Dennis, William 49
Denny, Benjamin 7,35
Denny, Eveline 234
Denny, John 241
Denny, John, Sr. 38
Denny, Narcissa O. 241
Denny, William 24,47,48,62,63,
  147,165,182,198,208,217
Denny, William, Sr. 282
Denny, Willie 118
Denny, Willis 191
Denton, D. M. 162
Denton, David 36,90,115
Denton, Drury 9
Denton, Drury W. 36,37
Denton, Elizabeth 268
Denton, James 106
Denton, James W. 216
Denton, Robert 90,115,280,281
Depres, James 3
Derickson, Joseph 281

Dew, Samuel 205
Dewhit, Samuel 6,43
Dias, David 285
Dias, David W. 285
Dias, Edy B. 285
Dias, James 285
Dias, John 210
Dias, Josiah 285
Dias, Lewis 285
Dias, Lovet 73
Dias, Lovick 285
Dias, Lovick, Jr. 285
Dias, Lovitt 89
Dias, Margret 285
Dias, Martha J. 285
Dias, Robert 285
Dias, Ruth J. 285
Dias, Thomas 43,44,210,
  276,285,286
Dias, Thomas, Jr. 285
Dias, Thomas, Sr. 285
Dias, Thomas T. 276
Dice, John 249,271
Dice, Silas 193
Dice, Thomas 271
Dickens, Bryant 231
Dickens, Caroline 41
Dickens, Dickerson 217
Dickens, Hiram 31
Dickens, James W. 219
Dickens, Jeremiah 74,88,
  231
Dickens, John 13,22,74,
  165,246
Dickens, Joseph 89
Dickens, Joseph C. 27,134
Dickens, Rebecca 231
Dickens, William 13,41
Dickerson, James R. 217
Dickerson, Joseph 276
Dickerson, Lawson 167
Dickerson, Olive 265
Dickerson, Samuel 175
Dickins, William 217
Dickson, Jeremiah 201
Dies, David 11,22,70
Dies, Thomas 44,225
Dill, James M. 52
Dill, Phiomon C. 23
Dill, William 23
Dillaha, Joanna 109
Dillard, Ala 235
Dillard, Alessander 1,8
Dillard, Alex 105
Dillard, Alexander 56,74,
  77,83,106,125,126,132,
  136,181,184,202,203
Dillard, Candis 48
Dillard, Daniel 45,98,158
Dillard, Elisha 74,93,98,111,124,
  141,158,219,285
Dillard, Frances 57
Dillard, G. G. 190,191,195
Dillard, Gabriel 14,62
Dillard, George 23,283
Dillard, George R. 1,112,286
Dillard, Helen 238
Dillard, Henry 277
Dillard, John L. 48,238
Dillard, Joseph 57,231
Dillard, Matthew 285
Dillard, Peggy 285
Dillard, William 8,98,228,235,
  270,281,286
Dillard, William H. 172
Dillard, Zary 285
Dillehay, Alexander 56,219
Dillehay, Alexander R. 121,127
Dillehay, Barnet T. 121
Dillehay, Barnett 208
Dillehay, Barnett T. 217
Dillehay, Edmond 206
Dillehay, Harriet 214
Dillehay, Johnson 246
Dillehay, Margaret 84,219
Dillehay, T. 206
Dillon, Elizabeth J. 101
Dillon, Isaac 70
Dillon, James 101
Dillon, Jane G. 101
Dillon, Nathan 27,75
Dillon, Polly 70
Dillon, Thomas 101
Dillon, Thomas L. 61
Dillon, William 63,82,112,181,
  184,188,253,268
Dillon, William B. 22,50,61,65,
  101,150,248
Dirickson, David S. 97
Dirickson, Joseph 97,104
Dixon, Dan C. 1
Dixon, Don C. 79
Dixon, Henry 94,96,108,159
Dixon, Jeremiah 75
Dixon, Martha 94,96,108
Dixon, Tilmon 31
Dixon, William 7,15
Dobbins, Hannah 27
Dobbins, James 6
Dodd, David 287
Dodd, Elizabeth 287
Donalson, Robert 249

Donalson, Susan 249
Donelson, Jacob D. 132
Donelson, Robert 217
Donelson, Susan 217
Donelson, William 132
Donnell, Eliza M. 272
Donoho, A. G. 250
Donoho, Charles 49
Donoho, D. B. 48,89
Donoho, E. C. 6,31,35
Donoho, Golman 128
Donoho, H. L. 30,35
Donoho, James C. 44
Donoho, James M. 44
Donoho, Jane 48
Donoho, John 65,99,105
Donoho, M. L. 30
Donoho, Marcus 147
Donoho, Marcus L. 2,198
Donoho, Marquis L. 31,50
Donoho, Patience 35
Donoho, Wilson 99
Dornwell, Eliza 97
Dortch, James 197
Doss, Stewart 229
Dotson, John 71
Dotson, Thomas 71,72
Douglas, J. C. 210
Douglas, Martha 143
Douglas, Robert 223,240
Douglas, Stephen H. 84
Douglas, William 265,287
Douglass, Benjamin L. 45
Douglass, Martha 22,85
Douglass, Nancy 21,48
Douglass, Robert 21,48
Douglass, Robert J. 85
Douglass, Stephen H. 85, 90,95,101
Dowdy, Henry 183,233,240, 242
Dowdy, John 227
Dowell, Elias 145,167, 173,242
Dowell, Elisha 173
Dowell, Frances 98,118, 147,157,162,173,164,185, 187,195,218,221,233,240, 241,263,275,286
Dowell, James 173
Dowell, John 173
Dowell, Nancy 116
Dowell, Nehemiah 155,242
Dowell, Presley 173
Dowell, R. 151
Dowell, Robert 155,167, 173,205,215
Dowell, William 173
Dowell, William F. 274
Dowell, Willis 98,162,184,185, 196,274
Drake, E. B. 135
Draper, Andrew 209
Draper, Brice M. 22,27,118,149, 169
Draper, Davidson 1,43,62,130, 139,164,165,265,266
Draper, Edward 22
Draper, Edward B. 78,118,149,169
Draper, Elizabeth 272
Draper, James W. 221
Draper, Melton 22
Draper, Milton 118
Draper, Philip 192
Draper, Thomas I. 145,164,272
Draper, William 1,216
Driver, Burrell 284
Driver, Dempsey 103,108
Driver, Didama 80
Driver, Elizabeth 103,284
Driver, Jesse 103,109
Driver, Joel 46,194
Driver, Labon 80
Driver, Saban 107
Driver, Thomas 238
Driver, Wilborn 276
Drury, John 13,52,70
Duffee, F. 200
Duffee, James B. 186
Duffee, John C. 14
Duffy, F. 40,42
Duffy, Frances 15,16,17,18,19,20, 30,36,40,52,53,74,80,86,89,98, 105,115,129,150,253,267
Duffy, J. C. 29,79
Duffy, James 89,106,122,142,143
Duffy, James B. 277
Duffy, John C. 15,16,17,18,19,20, 30,40,42,52
Duffy, M. 15,16,22,29,37,38,39, 56,57,220
Duffy, P. 15,16,22,29,37,38,39, 56,57,151,165,179
Duke, Micajah 130
Duke, Richard 130
Duke, Susan 239
Duke, William 239
Duncan, Edwin 24,35
Duncan, Flemin W. 35
Duncan, George A. 35
Duncan, George M. 33,50,51
Duncan, John 21,49,67,128

Duncan, Marshall 143
Duncan, Marshall B. 42,88, 99,154,176,180
Duncan, Nancy 8
Duncan, William 25,35,53
Duncan, William S. 8
Dunkan, Calfornia 180
Dunkan, M. B. 180
Dunlop, Margaret 25
Dunn, Martin 253
Dunn, Willis 247
Dupriest, John B. 24,27
Durey, Charles 276
Durey, John, Sr. 276
Durham, Jane 90,121
Durham, Jephtha 79,80,121, 257
Durham, Joseph H. 11,47, 66,159,274,279
Durham, Martha 287
Durham, N. 66,90
Durham, Nepthali 13,26
Durham, Thomas 203
Durham, Thomas A. 69,70, 131,132,136
Durham, Thomas B. 79,80, 121,257
Durkee, Asabel H. 65
Durkee, Mary E. 65
Duvall, Charles 235
Duvall, William 150,169, 183,187,208,212,226, 228,229,230,235,236, 240,245,249,258,267, 286
Dycus, Suleny 38
Dyer, Benjamin F. 29
Dyer, James S. 159,216
Dyer, Joel 3,14
Dyson, Mark 54,123,130, 139
Early, John 56
Early, Stephen 56
Early, Stephen D. 86
Earp, Asa 17
Earps, James 130
Easley, John 216
Easley, Stephen D. 14,86
East, Ezekiel 72,103
East, Synthia 103
Eastes, James M. 141
Eastes, John M. 140
Eastes, Moses 60,65,66
Eatherly, John R. 75
Eaton, James 2,3,66,82, 100,134,261,284
Eaton, James M. 261,284
Eden, William 147,177
Edens, John 268
Edens, William 126,268,285
Edmundson, J. K. 88
Edmundson, John K. 88
Edmundson, Matilda G. 88
Elison, James 66
Elison, Joseph 66
Ellen, Jacob 265
Eller, Jacob 265
Elliott, Eliza J. 277
Elliott, John 277
Ellis, Amos 221
Ellis, Isham 25
Ellis, James 23,94
Ellis, John 69
Ellis, Thomas L. 72
Ellis, William P. 94
Ellison, Nancy 138,221
Ellison, Sam 200
Ellison, Stephen 221,232
Elms, Thomas S. 186
Elston, Eliel 199
Elston, Martha 199
Enoch, Benjamin 261
Enoch, Benjamin S. 261
Enoch, John 49
Enoch, Robert 261
Enock, John 181
Enose, John 11
Enox, R. 287
Epperson, Ananias 59
Epperson, Annania 47
Epperson, Anthony 26,27,47,48,59
Epperson, Essex 27
Epperson, Excum 103
Epperson, Peter 48,102
Epperson, Silas 26
Ervin, Eleaster 180
Ervin, Elum A. 109,185
Ervin, Richard 109
Erwin, Easter 12
Erwin, Elizabeth A. 145
Erwin, Franklin 131
Erwin, John P. 12
Erwin, Nancy 131
Erwin, Richard 145
Erwin, Tennessee 183
Escum, William 4,96
Espey, Robert 260
Estates, G. W. 71
Estates, Fanny 71
Estes, Edmund 55,100,123

Estes, James M. 183
Estes, John W. 76,175
Estes, P. W. 206
Eurlow, Abraham 42
Evans, Abner 144
Evans, Dicy 202
Evans, Ezekiel 32,124
Evans, James 4
Evans, John 159,258
Evans, John T. 202
Evans, Lucy 144
Evans, Nancy A. 202
Evans, Nathan 1,3
Evans, Philip 202
Evans, Sarah 24
Evans, William D. 6,66,
 68,101
Evans, William P. 214
Everet, David 90
Everett, J. 233
Everett, Martin 193
Everett, Martin J. 150
Everett, William 49,50
Evetts, David 148,167,192
Evetts, James 12,26
Evetts, Joseph 212
Evetts, Moses 28,110,212
Evetts, Samuel 19,150,165
Evins, William P. 216
Evitts, Samuel 76
Ewing, Alfred 16,45,113,
 130,140
Ewing, E. S. 225
Ewing, Eveline L. 168
Ewing, Oscar S. 162
Exum, D. 227
Exum, Jackey A. 228
Exum, John 209
Exum, Joseph 189,227,246
Exum, K. D. 247,278
Exum, Kinchen D. 244,246
Exum, M. W. 227
Exum, Martha 246
Exum, Mathew 228
Exum, T. D. 189
Exum, William 14,129,134,
 171,234,278
Fagg, James 4
Fagg, Lidia 97
Fagg, Robert 97
Fairstair, Nancy 32
Fairstair, William L. 32
Fairstair, William S. 13
Falks, Joel B. 252
Fanner, Littleberry 234

Fare, J. L. 65
Fare, Jonathan 65
Farguhar, Elizabeth 85
Farley, Emily 11
Farley, John 11
Farley, Mary 11
Farley, Raleigh 11
Farley, Richard E. 104
Farley, William 11,138,167,179,
 206,225,240,245,267
Farmer, D. H. 190
Farmer, John 22,73,93,176,185
Farmer, John A. 36,51,58,103,
 118,128
Farmer, Stephen A. 100,148,225
Featherstone, Charles 179
Featherstone, E. 119,126
Featherstone, Edward 180
Featherstone, Edwin 145
Featherstone, Mary 122
Featherstone, Phebe A. 122
Fedlock, Richard 91
Felton, Thomas 1,133
Fentress, Cynthia 22
Fentress, James 11,22
Ferguhar, Elizabeth 82
Ferguson, A. 113,277
Ferguson, Adam 6,49,94,108,140,
 159,161,173,211,235,240,244,
 245,257,259,260,263,265,269,
 273
Ferguson, Alexander 28,35,58,96
Ferguson, Dixon 23,69
Ferguson, Elinas 139,140
Ferguson, Hester A. 277
Ferguson, Hugh 11
Ferguson, Lewis 195,281
Ferguson, Lynus 113
Ferguson, Patrick 6,49
Ferrell, Burchett F. 59,67
Ferrell, Burton G. 59,139,149,
 167,189
Ferrell, Burton J. 265
Ferrell, George 218
Ferrell, Theodrick 15,59
Ferrell, Thomas 167
Ferrell, William 124,155
Fields, Mathew 203
Fields, Rufus 203
Fields, Sarah 132,202,203
Finch, Celia 144
Finch, William 118,121,144
Finley, Britain B. 90
Finley, Dan C. 1
Finley, Thomas J. 253

Finley, Thomas L. 253
Fisher, Ailsey 264
Fisher, Cornelius 100,198
Fisher, George 274
Fisher, James 160
Fisher, James H. 71
Fisher, John 203,264
Fisher, Rebecca 160
Fisher, Thomas 160,222, 254
Fisher, Thomas, Jr. 123
Fisher, Thomas, Sr. 160
Fitch, Peter 21,52
Fitchpatrick, Samuel 167
Fite, Jacob 1
Fite, John 145
Fite, Leonard B. 138
Fite, Moses 1
Fite, Sam 140,204
Fite, Samuel M. 192,226, 242,257
Fitts, Mary 20
Fitts, Tanday W. 177
Fitts, Woodson 2,68
Fitzpatrick, Samuel 146, 188,236,264,265
Fitzpatrick, Sarah 236
Fiveash, William 24,168, 199
Fleaman, John 29
Fleman, John 105
Flippin, A. B. 116
Flippin, Abner A. 46,78, 107
Flippin, Araminta 227
Flippin, Armstead 94
Flippin, Armstead B. 96
Flippin, Frances 94,96,108
Flippin, George F. 225
Flippin, H. D. 181,218
Flippin, H. G. 116
Flippin, Henry 96
Flippin, Henry D. 178
Flippin, J. B. 116,204
Flippin, R. G. 218,242
Flippin, T. A. 74
Flippin, T. B. 232,282
Flippin, Thomas A. 147,214
Flippin, Tilman 49,227
Flippin, Tilman B. 96,181, 188,246,252
Floid, William 200,205,231
Flowers, George C. 162,164
Flowers, Joel S. 162,163, 203,224,271,281

Flowers, John H. 163,272
Flowers, Martha 219,269
Flowers, R. 271
Flowers, Rolfe K. 163,172,224
Flowers, William 58,66,69,124, 162,163,172
Flowers, William L. 163
Flowers, William, Sr. 4,67,162, 163,164
Floyd, William 2,205
Foley, Bossee 56
Ford, Andrew G. 8,29
Ford, Andrew J. 51
Ford, C. C. 91,107,108,109,110, 124,133,134,151,166,204,205
Ford, Charles R. 144
Ford, Christopher 51
Ford, Christopher C. 135,159, 272
Ford, Ferdinand 122,140
Ford, Harrison J. 107
Ford, Hiram C. 100,107,115,197
Ford, J. L. 202
Ford, James G. 36,133,138,161, 162
Ford, Lake 267
Ford, Luke 43,113,126
Ford, Martha 162
Ford, Martha J. 156
Ford, Mary A. 135
Ford, Milton 188
Ford, Moses 33
Ford, Moses G. 111
Ford, Nancy H. 156
Ford, Samuel 126,171,267
Ford, Sarah P. 156
Ford, Susanah 111
Ford, W. L. 136
Ford, Walter L. 148
Foster, Alfred H. 162
Foster, Nancy 162
Foster, Sinah 26
Fouch, Elijah 48
Fouch, M. 48
Foust, Peter 79
Foutch, David 198
Foutch, Elijah 198
Foutch, John 198
Foutch, Levi 199,237
Foutch, William 32,198
Foutch, William, Jr. 284
Foutch, William, Sr. 284
Fowler, Jacob 9
Franklin, Henry 13,81,218
Franklin, Joel 83

Franklin, John 13,81,150, 218
Franklin, Lewis 150,152, 153,179
Franklin, Louis 218
Franklin, Mary A. 218
Franklin, Sally, Sr. 218
Franklin, William R. 150
Fray, David 284
Frazer, Ebenezer M. 183
Frazer, J. G. 218
Frazer, Jesse 206
Frazer, Jesse G. 167,242, 245,249,255,280
Frazer, Robert 41
Frazier, Jesse G. 225,226
Freeland, James 125
Freeland, Jeremiah 112, 120,125
Freeman, James 17
Freeman, James, Sr. 29,36
Freeman, Martin 23,47
Freeman, Moses B. 15,33, 34,55,81,132,143
Freeman, Richard 17,29,36
Freeman, Walter 143
Frohauk, Thomas A. 178
Frohock, Sarah A. 190
Frohock, Thomas A. 12,190, 212,218,231
Fry, D. 226
Fry, David 138,231,237, 263,264,270
Fry, Jacob 138
Fulks, Archibald 23,54, 63,92
Fulks, Elijah 169
Fulks, J. 23
Fulks, Joel 252
Fulks, Joel B. 278
Fulks, Martha 23,137,153, 173,282
Fulks, Nancy 23
Fuller, Jesse 65,97
Furguson, Archibald P. 11
Furlong, Luther 180
Furlong, Mary J. 185
Furlong, Samuel 19,25,80
Furlong, T. J. 163
Fuston, Samuel 157
Gains, James F. 11
Galbreath, D. F. 92,103
Galbreath, David F. 92,102
Galbreath, Franklin 102
Games, William 25,26

Gammon, Eli 82,117,145,150,161, 170,183,258
Gammon, Elijah 39,158
Gammon, Frances 158
Gammon, James A. 80
Gammon, Jeremiah 12,77,127
Gammon, John 37
Gammon, John B. 82,119,132,158
Gammon, John H. 29,106,127
Gammon, John L. 93
Gammon, Levi 53
Gammon, Rusia 158
Gann, Enoch 251,267
Gann, Enock 177,184,194,213
Gann, George 116,227
Gann, John 50,82,94
Gann, Lewis M. 101
Gann, Robert 184,210,222,227, 238,251,252,254,256,257,277
Gann, William 116,227
Garner, John 82
Garner, Peregrine C. 43
Garner, Thomas 82
Garner, William 9,77,283
Garrell, James P. 281
Garrett, James P. 236
Garrett, Rubin 72
Garrett, Samuel W. 284
Garrett, Stephen 40,102
Garrett, W. A. 215
Garrett, William 153,221
Garrett, William D. 26,43,102, 103,121,156,236
Garrison, Benjamin 30
Garrison, James 27,124
Garrison, Levi 67
Garrison, Obadiah M. 1
Garrot, William 215
Garrott, Josiah 56
Garrott, Stephen 56
Garrott, William 61
Gaston, Alexander F. 155,158
Gaston, Hugh 249,256
Gaston, Susan 249
Gaston, William 155,158,249
Gays, Nathan 54
Gentry, J. D. 23,65
George, Presley 138
Gibbs, A. 76
Gibbs, A. W. 107
Gibbs, Archibald 91,149
Gibbs, Gilbert 69
Gibbs, Gilbert B. 59
Gibbs, John 129
Gibbs, Thomas 12

Gibbs, Thomas W. 158
Gibson, James 50
Gibson, James W. 15
Gifford, Barnett 92
Gifford, C. P. 194
Gifford, E. P. 163,208,
  215,227,251,253,265
Gifford, Edmond P. 260
Gifford, Elizabeth 253,260
Gifford, G. C. 160,163
Gifford, George 44,70
Gifford, George C. 31,33,
  63,123,138,150,164,211,
  256
Gifford, Gideon 25,27,38,
  47,80,92,122,170,183,210,
  215,235,240,253,260,265,
  274,281
Gifford, Gideon, Sr. 99
Gifford, J. C. 260
Gifford, Jabez 32,66,76
Gifford, Jabus 92
Gifford, John 76
Gifford, Joseph 62,66,73,
  194,260
Gifford, Joseph F. 22
Gifford, L. 205
Gifford, Malinda 160
Gifford, P. G. 160
Gifford, Richard G. 90,150
Gill, Carolina 72
Gill, Frances P. 247
Gill, Jacob 72
Gill, James 7,121,126,144,
  177,192,239,247
Gill, John 247
Gill, Thomas 239
Gillespie, Ann 213
Gillespie, William 213
Gillham, Elenor C. 129
Gillham, Elizabeth 129
Gillham, Matilda 129
Gilliham, Clement 105
Gilliham, William 105,215
Gillum, Liza 170,171
Gipson, James W. 78
Gipson, T. C. 142
Givan, William 35
Glascock, Spencer 164
Glasgow, James 235
Glasgow, John 235
Glasgow, Rebecca 235
Glasgow, William 253
Gleaves, William F. 8
Glen, Daniel 222

Glen, Mary 222
Glenn, Mary 2
Glover, Charlotte 231
Glover, Daniel 2,32
Glover, Edward 66
Glover, George W. 231
Glover, Henry W. 59,60,100
Glover, Robert 43,62,139,165,
  265
Glover, Robert C. 1
Glover, Robert J. 164
Glover, Washington 36,46,146
Gloves, William F. 15
Goad, Abraham 186
Goad, Coleman D. 141
Goad, George 8
Goad, Henry 53,130,162,164,250
Goad, Isham 228
Goad, Joshua 11,222
Goad, Noel 84
Goad, Polly 187
Goad, Stephen 140,150,165,222,
  228,230
Goad, Susan 230
Goad, Susannah 228
Goad, William 184
Goff, Andrew 68
Gold, Josiah 195
Gold, P. 276,286
Gold, Pleasant 82,87,137,175,197,
  199,211,214,218,226,277
Gomer, John 129
Goodall, Charles 17,142
Goodall, David 1,55
Goodall, David L., Jr. 115
Goodall, David, Sr. 115
Goodall, Frances 201
Goodall, G. 146
Goodall, Harriett 16
Goodall, Harrison 201
Goodall, I. D. 236
Goodall, Isaac 16
Goodall, Z. G. 55,164
Goodloe, A. J. 1
Goodner, Cyrus 14,19,22
Goodner, Jacob 19
Goodner, James 264
Goodner, John 29,41,88
Goodner, John F. 264
Gordon, F. H. 156
Gordon, Frances 40
Gordon, Frances H. 9,78,123,127,
  128,200,237
Gordon, Francis H. 31,81
Gordon, James G. 20

Gordon, John 7,20,51,
   65,71,81,85,124,136,
   193,205,212,231
Gordon, Sarah 212
Gordon, Uel S. 128
Gordon, William M. 86
Goss, Eliza 17
Goss, Hardy 165
Goss, Henry D. 217,267
Goss, John D. 218
Goss, Joseph 90
Goss, Nathan 54,70,72,77
Goss, Samuel 193
Goss, Samuel R. 174,220,
   267
Gowan, William D. 66
Gowen, William D. 28
Graff, Samuel 30
Granade, Ann 286
Granade, Silas J. 286
Grandstaff, James 221
Grandstaff, John 6
Grandstaff, Nicholas 165
Grandstaff, William 199,
   200
Grant, Edwin C. 110,131
Grant, Mary 3,35
Grant, Mary V. 36
Grant, William 178
Graves, Beaman 30
Graves, Benjamin 239
Graves, Beverly 98
Graves, Judy 98
Gray, Fielding 136,144
Gray, Fielding W. 144
Gray, George W. 174
Gray, Jacob 174
Gray, Jesse 1,18
Gray, James S. 144
Gray, Joseph 53
Gray, Joseph M. 144
Gray, Julia A. 144
Gray, William 174
Green, Agnes F. 266
Green, Andrew 7
Green, James 9,107,185
Green, James H. 30
Green, Orville 33,93,138,
   144,153,168,178,189,
   198,208,217,228,261,280
Green, Thadeous F. 265
Green, William 35
Greenwood, James C. 75,
   126
Greer, Andrew 1,88,90,104,
   114,130
Greer, Archibald O. 1
Greer, E. H. 130,133
Greer, Elihu H. 135,154
Greer, Jane B. 104
Greer, Joseph A. 130
Greer, Sarah S. 7
Gregory, Abel 172,202,267
Gregory, Amanda 257
Gregory, B. J. 149
Gregory, Bethel 177
Gregory, Bethel J. 190
Gregory, Betsy 252
Gregory, Bry 38,82,84,91,267
Gregory, Elizabeth 81,82,175,257
Gregory, George 134,173
Gregory, Gion 257
Gregory, Godfrey 8,29,57,58,82,
   85,99,117
Gregory, Harriet 278
Gregory, Henry M. 283
Gregory, James D. 131,257
Gregory, James N. 261
Gregory, Jane 217
Gregory, Joel 125,140,191,195,
   208,231,232,240
Gregory, Joel L. 267
Gregory, John 111
Gregory, Joseph 26,134
Gregory, Joseph B. 144,156,168
Gregory, Joseph N. 261
Gregory, Major 111
Gregory, Smith 37,67,91,173,186,
   261
Gregory, Thomas 44,71,78,108,
   111,134,138,165,166,178,179,
   197,226
Gregory, Thomas D. 168
Gregory, Thomas, Jr. 108,134
Gregory, Uel 3,81
Gregory, Uriah 128,218
Gregory, William 14,78,89,146,
   166,177,191,261
Gregory, William J. 127
Gregory, William M. 246,247
Gregory, William R. 191
Gregory, William, Sr. 257
Gresham, Davis 45
Gresham, Harris 178
Gresham, Joseph 117,118,130,131,
   139,156,162,164
Gresham, William 212
Grief, Joseph 53
Griffin, James 14
Griffin, Stephen 74,77

Griffith, David 1
Griffith, Jonathan 1
Grigg, Branch 17,40,41,58
Grigg, Peter 17,41
Grisal, Asa 80
Grisal, Franky 80
Grisham, Harris 252
Grisham, James W. 116
Grisham, Joseph 14,31,52, 83
Grisham, L. D. 174
Grisham, Maria 263
Grisham, Peter 90
Grisham, William 263
Grisham, William H. 252
Grissam, James W. 256
Grissam, William 251
Grissam, William H. 282
Grissim, Harris 245
Grissim, James W. 83,92, 108,168
Grissim, S. B. 254
Grissim, William H. 92
Grissom, James 48,49,283
Grissom, James W. 88
Grissom, Lambeth D. 279
Grissom, Peter 279,287
Grissom, Thomas B. 199
Grissom, Thomas C. 194
Grissum, James W. 79,109
Gross, John 70
Grubbs, Nathan H. 267
Guffey, James B. 245
Gullick, J. B. 208
Gullick, John B. 80,173, 218,220,226
Gullick, Jonathan H. 173
Gunn, James 111
Gunn, Jehu 71
Gunn, John 17
Gunn, Lewis 111
Gunn, Mary 111
Gunn, Samuel 111
Guthery, Carter 73
Guthrey, Carter 14,17,19
Guthrie, Joseph 42,99
Guthrie, Polly 42,99
Gwaltney, Ann 209
Gwaltney, Dawson 211
Gwaltney, Elias 141
Gwaltney, John 8,29,57,85, 87,171,251
Gwaltney, John, Jr. 85,114, 172
Gwaltney, John, Sr. 95

Gwaltney, Laura 174
Gwaltney, Leodicy 141
Gwaltney, Lucy 243
Gwaltney, Lucy G. 195
Gwaltney, Polly 141
Gwaltney, Solomon 141
Gwaltney, Thomas 95,229
Gyger, Larkin 191
Gyger, Nancy 191
Hackett, Henry 258
Hackett, Peter 69,262
Hackett, Peter, Sr. 285
Hackett, William T. 285
Haddock, Bedford 275
Haden, Joseph 26,48,98
Hadley, Joshua 5
Haggerty, John 101
Haggerty, Ogden 101
Hail, Elijah 24,29
Hail, Eliza J. 225,237
Hail, Jesse 277
Hail, Leman 253
Hail, William 134,135,215
Hail, William D. 225
Haile, Leamon 260
Haile, William H. 260
Hailey, John 228
Hailey, Lucy 241
Hailey, Robert D. 241
Hailey, William D. 241
Haines, William 136
Hale, Elijah 4,42
Hale, Elijah W. 134,253
Hale, Eliza J. 238
Hale, Ezekiel 178
Hale, Jesse 215
Hale, John 1,208
Hale, Leman 253
Hale, Linton 234
Hale, Nancy 208
Hale, Sterling 225
Hale, Thomas 12
Hale, W. J. 266
Hale, William 155
Hale, William D. 211,237,238,239
Hale, William H. 253
Hale, William J. 266
Hale, William P. 203
Haley, E. P. 222,245
Haley, Elizabeth 162
Haley, Henderson 14,18,195,244, 282
Haley, John 58,117,167,185,229
Haley, Oliver 226
Haley, Robert 77,123

Haley, Sanders 242
Haley, Thomas 34,77,116,
   159,230,241
Hall, Adam 165
Hall, Amzi P. 284
Hall, Clabourn 37,85,185
Hall, David 66,96,118
Hall, Elizabeth A. 271
Hall, Faleena 181
Hall, G. H. 21
Hall, Henry 66
Hall, James 100
Hall, John 66,96,120,196,
   269
Hall, John W. 122,147
Hall, Lewis 82,107,162,
   195,196,245,246,261
Hall, M. P. 187
Hall, Malinda 16,154,180,
   187
Hall, Manerva 21
Hall, Nathan 41,120
Hall, P. D. 117
Hall, Pleasant 54
Hall, R. P. 119
Hall, Richard B. 180
Hall, Richard T. 180
Hall, T. P. 181
Hall, Tandy 117
Hall, Tandy P. 156,272
Hall, Thomas 180,181
Hall, Thomas M. 54,180
Hall, Thomas T. 54
Hall, William 26,55,163,
   179,180,187,271
Hall, William A. 227
Hall, William J. 283
Hall, William T. 180,249
Hall, Williamson 154
Hall, Williamson T. 117
Hallady, Allen 74
Hallmontoller, Anthony 60
Hallum, Albert G. 272
Hallum, Andrew 40,50
Hallum, Coleman 276
Hallum, Elizabeth 162
Hallum, Henry 11,33
Hallum, John 29,76,115,
   150,259
Hallum, John L. 63
Hallum, Josiah 109,133,
   160,174,218,236,242
Hallum, Mary 204
Hallum, Priscilla 162
Hallum, Rachel 160

Hallum, Richard 204
Hallum, Sarah 162
Hallum, Sarah W. 63
Hallum, W. R. 13
Hallum, W. V. 160,171
Hallum, William 168,239,242,244,
   259,265,275,286
Hallum, William V. 225
Halmantoller, Anthony 173
Halmantoller, Michael 177,209
Halmontoller, Anthony 60
Hamilton, George 2,37
Hamilton, James K. 37
Hamilton, John C. 63
Hamilton, Patrick 50
Hamilton, Polly 68
Hammack, Brice W. 86
Hammack, Daniel 86,121
Hammack, Elijah H. 126
Hammack, James D. 121
Hammack, James M. 86
Hammack, Joseph T. 86
Hammack, L. A. 166
Hammack, Lemuel A. 28,66,86,121,
   164
Hammack, Leonard A. 57
Hammack, Martin 86
Hammack, Mary 57,121,126
Hammack, Patsy 86
Hammack, Samuel A. 126
Hammack, Talliferro 76,102,103
Hammack, William H. 86
Hammock, Talifaro 15
Hance, David W. 256
Hanes, Austin L. 102
Hanes, Austin S. 103
Hanes, Fountain 75,102
Hanes, John D. 151
Hankins, Timothy 188
Hankins, William 144
Hannah, Edny 181
Hannah, Patterson 181
Hanson, Josiah W. 220
Hard, Jesse 3
Hardcastle, John 98
Hardee, Thomas L. 149
Hardie, Thomas L. 21,91
Hardwick, Frances B. 110
Hardy, Thomas L. 3,63
Hargis, Dennis 22,28,36,56,74,
   80,89
Hargis, Howel 21
Hargis, Howel H. 39,103
Hargis, J. B. 110
Hargis, Jackson W. 80

Hargis, L. D. 57
Hargis, Lionel 36
Hargis, S. D. 110
Hargis, William 80
Hargis, William C. 70
Harkreader, Jane E. 104
Harkreader, Sylvester 104
Harkreader, Sylvester H. 178
Harley, John 191
Harlin, Isaac 100
Harlin, James 72
Harlin, John 72
Harman, Martha F. 272
Harmon, Bazzle 222
Harper, Alfred 13,114,129,142
Harper, Benjamin 161,176
Harper, Elizabeth 284
Harper, Franklin 284
Harper, Grogan 86,219
Harper, Henry 110,273
Harper, James 63,190,219
Harper, Jane 284
Harper, John 50,155,171,176,246,257,284
Harper, Josiah 284
Harper, Josiah, Jr. 284
Harper, Martha 284
Harper, Mary 184
Harper, Mathew 145,184,205,208,212,219,220,225,229,233,239,243,251,258,273,279,283
Harper, Mathew, Sr. 145
Harper, Matthew 13,114,115,142,174
Harper, Nancy 201
Harper, Paul 284
Harper, Robert 63,155,175,201
Harper, Sarah 145,205,273
Harper, Shelton 131
Harper, Thomas 155,158,176,284
Harper, Timothy 284
Harper, William 145,273
Harring, Lewis 201
Harris, Andrew 253,260
Harris, Archibald 252
Harris, Armstead G. 187
Harris, Austin L. 74
Harris, B. W. 199
Harris, Baxton 212
Harris, Burrell 59
Harris, Burton 209
Harris, David 162,170,193,218,269
Harris, Dawson B. 234
Harris, Dolly A. 252
Harris, E. R. 268
Harris, Emanuel 19,123,153
Harris, Ewing R. 257,258
Harris, F. L. 142
Harris, F. S. 13
Harris, Fergus S. 170
Harris, Fleming 153
Harris, Fountain 76
Harris, H. 198
Harris, Hannah 76
Harris, Jane 153
Harris, John 140,235,248,249,252
Harris, Joseph H. 235
Harris, Margaret 252
Harris, Martha 153
Harris, Martha A. 260
Harris, Mary 153,173
Harris, Mathew A. 253
Harris, Nicy 123,196
Harris, P. H. 198
Harris, Rachel 138
Harris, S. T. 231
Harris, Samuel 252
Harris, Skelton T. 257
Harris, Susan 252
Harris, Susan M. 257
Harris, Thomas E. 153,171
Harris, Turner 140
Harris, W. W. 138
Harris, William 57,135
Harris, William A. 265
Harris, William B. 252
Harris, William C. 74,75
Harris, William W. 178
Harrison, E. 7,12,225
Harrison, Edmund 109,237,260
Harrison, Edward 138
Harrison, James 20,61,62,67,75,77,83
Harrison, Samuel 197
Hart, Daniel 269,270
Hart, Elizabeth 263
Hart, H. W. 225
Hart, Henry 224
Hart, Henry W. 160,211,249
Hart, James 224
Hart, Jonathan 263
Hart, Mary 270
Hart, Patsy 224
Hart, William 31,45,71,113,142,154,159,160,179,184,236

Harvel, Allen 177
Harvel, John 231
Harvel, John D. 167
Harvel, Lewis 88
Harvel, Martha 231
Harvey, James 235
Harvey, Thomas 42
Harvey, Wesley 8,14,15
Harvey, William 73
Harville, David 256
Harville, Lewis 74
Harwood, Francis G. 72
Haskel, Peter 26
Hastey, William 134
Hatchett, Elizabeth 108
Hatchett, Isaac 108
Hatchett, Mary 108
Hatchett, Thomas 108
Hauk, John 248
Haw, John 94
Hawkins, Betsy 92
Hawkins, Charlotte 156
Hawkins, James 248
Hawkins, John 92
Hawkins, Joshua 88,89,111
Hawkins, Meredith 97,108,
  114,162
Hawkins, Robert 122
Hawkins, Willis 248
Hayes, Reuben 189
Hayley, Robert D. 241
Haynes, Cary 188
Haynes, David 141
Haynes, James 120,139
Haynes, John D. 132
Haynes, Milton 177
Haynes, Richard 26
Haynes, Rufus 164
Haynes, Stephen 10,88,127
Haynes, Thomas 164
Haynes, William 151
Haynie, Edward B. 103,256
Haynie, Elijah 9,185
Haynie, H. B. 216,274
Haynie, Henry 244
Haynie, Henry B. 143,255
Haynie, James 141,156,
  224,250
Haynie, Milton 149,159,
  161,182,191
Haynie, Nancy 224
Haynie, Sarah 255
Haynie, William 224,250
Hays, Peter 3
Hays, R. G. 170

Hays, Reuben 181,189
Hays, Robert 114,173,203
Hays, Robin 100,247
Hazard, C. M. 1
Hazard, J. R. 14,141
Hazard, John R., Jr. 124
Hazard, John, Sr. 124,141
Hazard, Lot 1,6,23,83,90,101,118,
  119,125,171,187,188,190,202,
  208,211,212,217,228,233,253
Hazard, Nathan E. 141
Hazard, Susannah 160
Hazard, Tabitha 118,119
Hazard, Tabitha D. 150
Hearn, John 84
Hearn, William 265
Heath, John 60
Heflin, Hawkins 45,136,169,181,
  208,211,220
Heflin, S. F. 225
Heflin, Sewel L. 244
Helmes, Coleman 255
Helmontoller, Anthony 23
Helmontoller, Harriett 161
Helmontoller, Nancy 23
Helms, Archibald 41
Henderson, John 19,97
Hendrix, John 33
Henry, Stephen 28
Hensley, Benjamin 179
Hensley, John T. 222
Henson, Alex 129
Herod, Judith 255
Herod, Peter 14,110,111,168
Herod, William A. 180,255
Heron, Arthur 2
Herring, Bedford L. 130,259
Herring, William 185
Herrod, James 5,203
Herrod, James M. 234
Herrod, John 44
Herrod, Mary A. 5
Herrod, Will A. 74
Herrod, William 5,192
Herrod, William A. 137,150,259
Herron, Arthur 71
Hesson, Andrew 72
Hesson, John 271
Hesson, W. 271
Hester, Aletha 243
Hester, Avery 54,183,196
Hester, Garland 169
Hester, James 10,46
Hester, John 10,91
Hester, Pauline 10

Hester, Puss 243
Hester, Robert 243
hester, Sarah 10
Hester, Christopher 228
Hewitt, Isaac 74
Hibbitt, J. J. 254
Hibbitt, John J. 122,126
Hibbitt, Joseph F. 63,148
Hibbitts, D. C. 88
Hibbitts, David C. 96,112
Hickman, Mary A. 188
Hickman, Silvy 256
Hickman, Stephen 160,173, 254,256
Hickman, Thomas 7,60,82
Hickman, William 173
Hicks, Henry 165
Hicks, John 93
Hicks, Yeatman 106,127
Hiett, Cynthia 276
Hiett, John 47,119,239
Hiett, John, Jr. 276
High, Bolen D. 147
High, Boling D. 180,257
High, James 50,90,189, 213,214,241
High, James T. 260,261, 264
High, John 122
High, Martha 180
High, Mitchell 167
High, Samuel 36,236
High, Winston 39
Highers, David 131,182,213
Highers, Dixon 213
Highers, George 131,182,185
Highers, Henry 117
Highers, John 205
Highers, Josiah 131,182,213
Highers, Judiah 213
Highers, Mary 213
Highers, Nancy 213
Highers, Tennessee 213
Highers, Thomas 61,117
Hill, Samuel 59
Hinds, Melissa 263
Hinds, Samuel 263
Hindsley, John L. 152
Hines, Gabriel 62,78,86
Hines, Thomas 257,276
Hinsley, John 193
Hinsley, John S. 173
Hinsley, John T. 200
Hinton, Judith 142,154
Hinton, Reuben 179,214

Hire, Lewis 27,51
Hobbs, Frances 252
Hodges, David 196,202,229,283
Hodges, David P. 273
Hodges, Delila 273
Hodges, Elizabeth 5
Hodges, Hannah 166
Hodges, Jane 244
Hodges, June 201
Hodges, Richard 159,273
Hodges, Robert 5,59,60,201,223, 244,273
Hodges, Robert L. 273
Hodges, William 7
Hodges, William R. 137
Hodges, Willis 166
Hogan, A. S. 85
Hogan, Anthony 105,136,228
Hogan, Arthur L. 7,16
Hogan, Arthur S. 44
Hogan, Bailey P. 105,228
Hogan, Benjamin R. 105,228
Hogan, James 61,105,261
Hogan, James E. 228
Hogan, Martha 105
Hogan, Martha J. 228
Hogan, Thomas B. 228
Hogan, Thomas J. 105
Hogan, William 61,261
Hogan, William B. 16
Hogg, Cynthia 146,167,217
Hogg, D. 163
Hogg, David 67,91,169,213,280
Hogg, Harvey 80
Hogg, L. D. 213,281
Hogg, Leonidas D. 38,56,91,280
Hogg, Malvina V. 188
Hogg, R. L. 79,99
Hogg, Shelby 53
Holeman, John 169
Holeman, Mary 169
Holladay, Allen 11,62,236
Holladay, J. J. 249
Holladay, Joel 11,74
Holladay, Robert 65,99,100
Holladay, William 249
Holland, Anthony 237
Holland, Britton 100
Holland, Drewry 206
Holland, Drury 40,90,159,161,172
Holland, Elbert 39
Holland, Elbert G. 52,95,105
Holland, Emeline 206
Holland, Harvey H. 45
Holland, James 206,222

Holland, John 30,62,206
Holland, Matilda 206
Holland, Milton 206
Holland, Nancy 222
Holland, Richard 206,250
Holland, Stephen 24,70,206
Holland, William 206
Holleman, Joel 78
Holleman, Mary 283
Holleman, William 283
Holliday, Allen 89,110
Holliday, Joel J. 272
Holliday, Robert 33
Holliday, Robert A. 233,287
Holliday, William 267
Hollis, Jesse 278
Hollis, Jesse T. 215,220, 260
Holloman, Joel 10
Holly, John 219
Holmes, Joseph 14,26,176
Holt, Giles 77,78,100
Holt, Mary 77,78
Honeycut, David 177
Hooker, John 4,25,125,127, 131,206
Hooker, Sarah 131
Hooker, Thomas 131,206
Hooker, Walker 201,207
Hooker, William 206
Hooks, Clinton 40,261
Hopkins, John 219,235
Hoppel, Mary 191
Hord, James 87
Hord, Jesse 87,136
Horn, Samuel W. 82
Horton, John J. 99
Hoskins, Jane 246,259
Hoskins, Thomas C. 259
Hoskins, William 259
House, Agnes 174,175
House, John 247
House, Meret 174,175
House, William 174
Howard, Samuel P. 6,9,13, 16,21,28,29,31,33,43, 46,47,49,56,91,132,150, 157,168,187,210,225,226, 227
Howard, Thomas 161
Howell, Charles 233
Howell, Eason 54,73,82
Howell, Josiah 39,41,42,59, 70
Howell, Sarah 70

Howell, Sophia 233
Hubbard, David C. 145
Hubbard, Elizabeth 152,253
Hubbard, Frances 57
Hubbard, George 187
Hubbard, George W. 145
Hubbard, Jacob 145,157,163,187
Hubbard, John 152,227
Hubbard, John W. 145
Hubbard, Josiah R. 253
Hubbard, Judas 57
Hubbard, Mary 287
Hubbard, O. B. 5,14,63,96,129, 151
Hubbard, Obadiah B. 90
Hubbard, Obediah 51
Hubbard, Patrick 1,24,25,49,57, 94,123,161,166,213,217,220, 256,287
Hubbard, Polly 256
Hubbard, Prudence R. 252
Hubbard, Richard 227,253
Hubbard, Sally 106,152,187,227, 253
Hubbard, T. J. 197
Hubbard, Thomas 253
Hubbard, Thomas J. 2,16,152,181, 237
Hubbard, W. C. 187
Hubbard, William 253
Hubbard, William B. 50
Hubbard, William C. 96,154,155, 156,172
Hubbard, William H. 145
Hubbard, Woodson 237,253
Huddleston, Amelia 206
Huddleston, Daniel 78,109,155, 196,203,204,244,277
Huddleston, Draper 8
Huddleston, James 206
Huddleston, John W. 251
Huddleston, Joseph 272
Huddleston, Martha 269
Huddleston, Paton 269
Huddleston, Peyton 272
Huddleston, Robert 272
Huddleston, Sarah 206
Huddleston, Sarry 269
Huddleston, Thomas 32
Hudson, E. J. 278
Hudson, Evin J. 277
Hudson, George W. 277
Hudson, John 49,282
Hudson, Sarah 277
Hudson, William 71

Huff, Peter 80
Huggins, Reuben 100
Hughes, Benjamin F. 209, 219
Hughes, David G. 269
Hughes, Edwin M. 156
Hughes, F. B. 72
Hughes, Gedeliah 152
Hughes, George 197
Hughes, George W. 62
Hughes, Gidaliad 141
Hughes, Gideliah 72,120, 198
Hughes, Gideon 220
Hughes, Isa 72
Hughes, J. B. 156,227,239
Hughes, Jesse 72,219
Hughes, Jesse P. 72
Hughes, John 72,236,268, 280
Hughes, John A. 11
Hughes, John B. 21,135, 145,156,169,186,204, 249,268
Hughes, John C. 253
Hughes, John J. 117,138, 200,237
Hughes, John P. 124,125, 127,171,198
Hughes, John, Sr. 21
Hughes, John W. 104,122, 124,125,141,168,182
Hughes, L. B. 210
Hughes, Leander 72,191, 192
Hughes, Lemuel H. 239,249, 254,255
Hughes, Leonard 72,233
Hughes, Leonard F. 82,101
Hughes, Little B. 27,46, 96,98
Hughes, Littleberry 15,72
Hughes, Lydia 163
Hughes, M. L. 216
Hughes, Mary A. 255
Hughes, Nancy 72
Hughes, Obadiah 72
Hughes, Powell 72
Hughes, R. D. 143
Hughes, Richard P. 101,113, 117,151
Hughes, Robert D. 142,181
Hughes, Robert L. 97
Hughes, S. B. 249
Hughes, S. P. 148

Hughes, Sally 72
Hughes, Samuel 11,55,72
Hughes, Samuel D. 89
Hughes, Simon 253,254
Hughes, Simon P. 143
Hughes, Simon P. 1,12,14,36,57, 62,71,88,117,141,143
Hughes, Tarlton 44,269
Hughes, Thomas 72
Hughes, Virginia 124
Hughes, Wade 72
Hughes, William 72,253
Hughes, William F. 172,282
Hughes, William L. 202
Hughes, William P. 26,82,96,102, 104,107,117,118,124,127,137, 151,168,170,182,243
Hughs, J. B. 156
Humphrey, Charles 260
Humphrey, D. W. 260
Hunt, Abel 205,253
Hunt, Daniel 284
Hunt, David 170,171
Hunt, J. H. 1
Hunt, John 253
Hunt, Mary C. 119
Hunter, Henry 231
Hunter, John T. 173
Hunter, Samuel 120,143,154,231, 264
Hunter, Thomas 59
Hunter, William 154
Hutchinson, Thomas D. 50,58
Hutchinson, William 50,58
Hutchison, William 26,27
Hutson, P. 46
Hutson, William 46
Hyett, John 120
Hyette, John 119
Hylten, Sterling 13
Hylton, Elijah 58,84,136
Hynes, Gabriel 55
Irby, Joseph 114
Irwin, E. 176
Irwin, W. H. 118
Isom, Arthur 71
Isom, Eleanor D. 71
Ivanson, Elizabeth 137
Jackson, Andrew 132
Jackson, Caleb 198
Jackson, Calvin 104
Jackson, Calvin W. 90
Jackson, Jane B. 90,104
Jackson, Thomas 5,28
Jackson, William 227

Jackson, William H. 96
Jaden, John N. 228
James, Alexander 40,43,178
James, B. A. 274
James, Bartlett 41,176,
   187,200,217,220
James, Bartlett, Jr. 63,
   86,95,117
James, Bartlett, Sr. 69,
   86,138,172,176,178
James, Benjamin 187
James, Daniel 41,42,197,
   212,242,243
James, E. A. 274
James, Edmund 137,186
James, J. R. 117,187,199,
   204
James, James R. 209
James, Joel J. 243,258
James, John 224
James, John R. 35,91,116,
   119,122,126,128,141,
   151,157,176,203,251
James, Richard 225
James, William 224
Jamison, Jere 270
Jamison, Jeremiah 115,135,
   137,151,154,166,172,180,
   186,203,204,206,226,239,
   246-256
Jared, John 70,228
Jared, Nathan 275
Jeffres, Joseph W. 96
Jeffrey, Jefferson 170
Jeffreys, Jefferson 221,239
Jeffreys, Osbourn 198
Jenkins, Archibald 246,261
Jenkins, Arthur 279
Jenkins, Eliza H. 11
Jenkins, George 122
Jenkins, Henry 232
Jenkins, James 36,75,100,
   102,246
Jenkins, Jefferson 135
Jenkins, Joseph 11,102
Jenkins, Lydia 279
Jenkins, Obediah 173,186
Jenkins, Thomas J. 285
Jenkins, W. H. 118
Jent, A. 58
Jent, Elizabeth 103
Jent, Thomas 103,109
Jente, Thomas 108
Johns, Benjamin 176
Johns, Bennet S. 126

Johns, Bennett 138,141
Johns, Elias 126,141,176
Johns, Isaac 45
Johns, William 90
Johnson, Asa 27
Johnson, B. 214
Johnson, D. M. 161,182
Johnson, Davidson 189
Johnson, Drucilla 211
Johnson, Duncan 160,176
Johnson, Dunkin 196
Johnson, Elizabeth 282
Johnson, H. H. 8,16,18
Johnson, Hiram H. 10,17,24
Johnson, J. W. 261
Johnson, Jacob L. 39
Johnson, Jacob S. 2,73
Johnson, James 210,229
Johnson, Jane 24
Johnson, Jesse 12
Johnson, John 2,19,21,24,72,136,
   137,154,187,203,223,229,275,
   286
Johnson, John A. 24,46,87
Johnson, John L. 61
Johnson, John S. 47,79,100
Johnson, Joseph 75
Johnson, Martha 47
Johnson, Mathew 265
Johnson, Oscar D. 197
Johnson, Othiel 154
Johnson, Patsy 24,46,143
Johnson, Permelia 24
Johnson, Reuben 9
Johnson, Samuel 19,47
Johnson, Stephen 7
Johnson, Thomas D. 56
Johnson, William 13,47,180,183
Johnson, William B. 197,198
Johnson, William C. 264
Johnston, John B. 45
Johnston, Mary 154
Johnston, Oliver 154
Johnston, Oscar 154
Johnston, Owel 154
Jones, Alexander 235
Jones, Allen 270
Jones, B. J. 88
Jones, Benjamin 18,40,44,140
Jones, Benjamin F. 48,62,134,
   148,151,208
Jones, Benjamin J. 51,61,85
Jones, Charles 31
Jones, Charles T. 31
Jones, Clabourn 91

Jones, Daniel 233,261
Jones, David 5,42
Jones, Edmund 278
Jones, Elizabeth 189
Jones, Frederick 105,147, 154,217
Jones, George W. 185
Jones, Guilford 18,39,44, 49,78
Jones, H. C. 131,136
Jones, Hardy 1,39,41
Jones, Henry 69
Jones, Henry C. 15,51,98, 113,125,127,138
Jones, Henry H. 1
Jones, Isaac 3,233,260
Jones, J. B. 261
Jones, Jacob 27
Jones, James 11,28,67,237, 266
Jones, James C. 70
Jones, James H. 1
Jones, James R. 184
Jones, Jefferson 118,125, 132,134,199,161,166
Jones, Jesse 99,154
Jones, John 111,151,237
Jones, John F. 258
Jones, John J. 164
Jones, John L. 153
Jones, John S. 31
Jones, Joseph 105,228,281
Jones, Joseph, Jr. 54
Jones, Joseph, Sr. 131, 132,171
Jones, Lemuel A. 151
Jones, Leonard 27
Jones, Lewis 51
Jones, Mary 21
Jones, Nancy 185
Jones, Richard 132,171,203, 249
Jones, Ruth 22,25,106,188
Jones, Sally 228
Jones, Samuel 26
Jones, Simeon 100
Jones, Simon 2,55
Jones, Stephen M. 79,118, 162,169,196,230,264
Jones, Thomas 68,140
Jones, Thomas A. 201
Jones, Thomas B. 111
Jones, Thomas J. 38,150,191
Jones, W. E. 1,135
Jones, Wesley W. 32

Jones, Wiley 88
Jones, William 21,44,90,108,109, 111,136,138,162,235,267
Jones, William E. 96,150,156, 178,188,190,197,206,226,237, 238
Jones, William H. 55,107,134, 152,189,278
Jones, William J. 168,201
Jones, William W. 81,98,141,161, 274
Jones, Willis 22,50
Jones, Young B. 195
Jordan, I. N. 216
Jordon, Elizabeth 239
Jordon, William M. 239
Jovance, Andrew W. 194
Jovance, John 79
Jovance, Mary 79
Jovann, Andrew W. 82
Jovann, John 82
Kearby, Austin 17
Kearby, Franklin 42
Kearby, James 44,113
Kearby, Jesse B. 32
Kearby, Samuel 17
Kearby, William 44
Kearley, James 143,212
Kearley, James F. 97
Kearley, William 143
Kearly, Richard 88
Keays, Rolin 278
Kelley, John 172
Kelly, Daniel K. 260
Kelly, George P. 260
Kelly, Henry B. 279
Kelly, John 200,232,249,267
Kelly, Lewis 77
Kelly, P. N. 260
Kelly, Reuben 200
Kelly, Spencer 77,94,155,279
Kelly, Stephen 245
Kelly, William 22,249
Kelly, William P. 260
Kelzer, Jordan 113
Kemp, Alfred M. 131,143
Kemp, Alsey 54
Kemp, Asa 235,251,286
Kemp, Auls 55
Kemp, Benton 250
Kemp, Beverly S. 216,217
Kemp, E. 54
Kemp, Elizabeth 228
Kemp, Ellis 123,132,143,146,228, 246

Kemp, Ellis B. 164,216,
  218,223,230,232,246,
  247,251,254,261,277
Kemp, H. H. 247
Kemp, Harriet M. 216
Kemp, Henry 163,216
Kemp, Henry D. 146,196
Kemp, Henry H. 216
Kemp, James S. 78,233,239
Kemp, Jenks 146,216
Kemp, John 128,228,285
Kemp, Jonathan 266
Kemp, Judith 228
Kemp, Larkin 216
Kemp, Leonidas 216
Kemp, Lorey S. 216
Kemp, Lucresy 144
Kemp, Lucretia 165
Kemp, Molly 228
Kemp, Richard 28,116
Kemp, Ruth E. 216
Kemp, Sampson D. 216
Kemp, W. W. 216
Kemp, Wesley 285
Kemp, Wiley 282,287
Kemp, William 228,232
Kenney, Alexander 198
Kenney, Peggy 198
Kenny, Robert 78
Kent, Joshua 269
Kerble, James 176
Kerby, Austin 231
Kerby, Daniel 45
Kerby, Frances 29,169,
  188,252
Kerby, James 164,243,246,
  248
Kerby, Jesse B. 4,81
Kerby, John 143,158,194
Kerby, Lucy 243
Kerby, Nathan 80
Kerby, Sarah A. 215
Kerby, William 35,159,190,
  231,276
Kerley, James 231
Kerley, James, Sr. 144
Kerr, James R. 65,115,144
Kettle, Micajah 1
Key, Logan D. 240,250
Key, Solomon 14
Key, Thomas 257,269
Killard, G. G. 230
Kilzer, Jordan 100,206
Kilzer, Jorden 260,265
King, A. H. 18,198,201,
  202,227
King, Abraham 193
King, Abraham H. 3,35,49,118,225
King, Abram H. 206,225,242,249
King, James 233
King, James A. 99,147,242
King, James P. 249
King, Samuel 147
King, William 14
Kinney, Alexander B. 283
Kinney, Robert 50
Kirby, Ann 112
Kirby, John 42
Kirby, Nathaniel 112
Kirby, Richard 54
Kirby, William 145
Kitchen, Thomas 221,240
Kitrel, William H. 152
Kitrell, Catherine 219
Kitrell, Edwin 119,191,206,215,
  219,220,251,254,264
Kitrell, Fielding 185,218
Kitrell, Isaac 57,116,119,172,
  191,206,221
Kitrell, Isham 79,185,214
Kitrell, John F. 119
Kitrell, William 221
Kittle, John 144,177
Kittle, Micajah 26,152,153
Kittle, William H. 152
Kittrell, Isham 76
Knight, Ellis E. 59,220
Knight, Henry 72,85
Knight, Henry M. 59,203
Knight, John 3,59,60,72,85
Knight, John C. 152
Knight, R. W. 281
Knight, Robert W. 90
Knight, Sarah H. 109
Knight, Thomas 109
Knight, Thomas L. 3,59
Knight, Tiloadson 199
Knight, William 72,85
Knight, William M. 59,105,232
Knight, Woodson 198
Knotts, Levi 90
Knowles, Thomas J. 190
Kyle, B. 157,166
Kyle, Barkley 157
Kyle, Bartlett 163,185
Kyle, Elizabeth 188
Kyle, Nelson 63,156
Kyle, Nelson F. 118,159
Kyle, William 11,41,63,84,112
Kyle, William B. 131,169

Kyle, Wilson F. 161
Lack, Abner 9
Lack, H. W. 217
Lack, Obediah 109
Lack, William 12
Lack, William B. 285
Lacke, Elizabeth 270
Lacke, James 270
Lake, D. L. 19
Lake, Daniel T. 59,63, 188,210
Lamb, George W. 31,51, 285
Lamb, Jonathan 279
Lamberson, Conrood 179
Lamberson, Editha 206, 230
Lamberson, John 94,118, 175,260,276
Lamberson, Leonard 179
Lamberson, Richard 206, 230
Lambert, Warner 224
Lambeth, W. 263
Lambeth, Warren 236
Lancaster, Clarissa 108
Lancaster, Dabney 2
Lancaster, Jesse 1,94
Lancaster, Jesse S. 98
Lancaster, John 8,25,67, 94,104,108,109,110,126, 128,155,254
Lancaster, John, Sr. 35, 126,128
Lancaster, Rhoda 109
Lancaster, Robert 100
Lancaster, Samuel 232
Lancaster, Samuel T. 103
Lancaster, Thomas 248,279
Lancaster, Thomas A. 3,42, 48,58,73,75,77,94,98, 100,126,140,155,167,227, 231,270,280
Lancaster, Thomas, Jr. 148
Lancaster, William 126,155, 216,270
Lancaster, William A. 125, 155
Land, Burrell R. 173
Lane, Barney 252
Lane, David M. 5
Lane, Emily 114
Lane, Granville 114
Lane, Mary A. 5
Lankaster, Samuel 97

Lankford, Mary 276
Lapley, Robert A. 222,223
Larner, James 280
Latiner, Robert 72
Lauderdale, John W. 63
Law, Damacis 43
Law, Damaris 137
Law, Darcus 43
Law, E. P. 188
Law, Elizabeth 43,137
Law, Henry 37,43
Law, James 272
Law, Jesse 43
Law, John 43,132,133,137,138,155
Law, Joseph 27,38,75
Law, Mary 272
Law, Nancy 43,137
Law, Rebecca 43,137
Law, Samuel 51
Law, William 43
Lawrence, Edward 170,247,254
Lawrence, Frances 220
Lawrence, John 246
Lawrence, R. R. 231
Lawrence, Samuel 27,51,102,111
Lawrence, William 51,205,220
Lawrence, William P. 3
Lawson, Frances 162
Lawson, Horace 195
Lawson, John 71
Lawson, Moses 227,237
Lay, Bennett 57
Lay, Berrel 57
Lay, Burrel 69
Lea, Barnet, Jr. 43
Lea, Thomas J. 202
League, Dabner M. 126
League, Riley 81
Leath, Freeman 149,190
Leath, Nancy 138
Leath, Thomas 18,53
Leath, William L. 138
Leatherwood, A. M. 69
Ledbetter, Charles 229
Ledbetter, Ira 24,88
Ledbetter, Rufus 11
Lee, Abraham 176
Lee, Abraham C. 189
Lee, T. J. 125
Leftwick, Wamon 29
Leman, William 279
Lemmon, Nancy 276
Lemmon, Owen J. 276
Lemon, William G. 278
Lenon, John C. 276

Lester, Elijah 93
Lewis, J. B. 268
Lewis, John B. 25
Lewis, Lucrecy 201
Lewis, Lucretia 175
Lewis, Randolph 175,201
Liggin, Sarah 71
Ligon, Drucilla 213
Ligon, Jane 163
Ligon, John H. 88,106,121,
 129,241
Ligon, Sarah 2,106
Ligon, Thomas P. 196
Ligon, W. W. 196
Ligon, William C. 196
Ligon, Willis 106
Lite, Stephen B. 62
Lindner, Mary 252
Lindner, Thomas 252
Lindsey, Archibald 178
Lindsey, Rhoda 178
Lindsey, Robert 35,66
Lindsey, Susanah 201
Link, Jefferson 161,248,
 257
Linnow, C. J. 240
Linnow, Mary M. 240
Linsebaugh, James 105
Linsley, Aron G. 207
Linsley, Lafayette 207
Linsley, Susan 207
Linville, Emily 8
Linville, Henry 8
Linville, Moses 75,89,127
Linville, William 8,9,25
Lipscomb, John 8,104,119,
 182
Lipscomb, Mosby 119,182
Lipscomb, Moses 78
Lipscomb, Mosley 241,254
Lipscomb, Sarah 8
Lishy, Jacob 110
Lishy, Louis C. 110
Litchford, John 46,119,
 162,167,194
Litchford, Thomas 143,167
Litchford, William 119,143,
 162,167,181,236,238
Little, Benjamin 147
Little, William 159
Lock, Robert 13
Long, Charles S. 192
Love, Charles J. 50
Love, H. 164
Love, Hezekiah 82,116,129,146,
 149,271
Love, Ruth 83
Lovelady, Thomas 21,22
Lovelady, V. R. 15
Lovelady, Vincent R. 23
Lovick, George 16
Lovick, Phebe 16
Lowe, August H. 200
Lowe, E. P. 157,158,200,223
Lowe, Green B. 36,128
Lowe, W. 249
Loy, Moses 50,252
Loyd, Lemuel 183
Lucas, Joseph D. 5,188
Luckey, John 5,87
Lucky, John 31,41,53,62,63
Lyday, Jacob 23
Lyles, Hiram 239
Lyles, Stephen 41
Lynch, David 224
Lynch, George 271,286
Lynch, Isaac 107,196,252
Lynch, Mary 224,249,251
Lynch, Mathew 223
Lynch, Robert L. 249
Lynch, Sarah 224
Lynch, William 171,218,234,252,
 286
Lyon, Henry 5
Lyon, James 85
Lyon, John A. 128,131
McAlister, Drucilla 163
McAlister, William P. 151,217
McAllister, George 168
McAllister, William P. 168
McCabe, James H. 131
McCabe, John C. 148,149,150
McCachern, Daniel 261
McCall, Alexander 83,155
McCall, Arris 12
McCall, David 10,83,112,123,155,
 162,168,235,240,254,259,260,
 264
McCall, John 10,93,106,117,157,
 212,264
McCall, Joseph 10,83,87
McCall, Martin W. 231
McCall, Mary A. 10,83,155,158
McClain, Andrew 269
McClain, Jesse 171
McClain, Jesse S. 137
McClain, John 267
McClain, John T. 55

McClain, W. 185
McClain, William 5,55,63,
　124,157
McClanahan, James 147,
　152,153,176,177,179
McClanahan, Nancy P. 76
McClanahan, Philip 160
McClanahan, Philip F. 180
McClanahan, William A. 163
McClanahan, Willis 118,266
McClaran, John 183
McClard, Thomas 39,45,151
McClard, William 33,63
McClarin, Charles 139,201,
　240,255,258
McClarin, John 115,135,
　157,166,226,240,249,269,
　275,280,284,285
McClarin, Nancy 255
McClelan, Andrew 82,104
McClelan, Israel 112
McClelan, Sampson 125,126,
　132
McClelin, Andrew 16,60,61,
　62,117,192,236
McClelin, C. G. 174
McClelin, Hugh 62
McClelin, Israel 36,38,48
McClelin, John 251
McClelin, Sampson 76,147,
　148,164,166,167,175,177,
　178,184,187,193,195,203,
　204,216,232,234,259,271
McClelin, Samuel 18,219
McClelin, William 233
McClellan, Andrew 244
McClellin, Andrew 57,98
McClellin, James T. 273
McClellin, Martha 98
McClellin, Sampson 98
McClellin, Samuel 273
McClelon, Andrew 81
McClenan, Samuel 79
McClenon, Sampson 168,171
McConnell, James 16
McConnell, Richard 97,266
McCormack, Abraham 219
McCormack, Chaffin 10,53,
　280
McCormack, James 10
McCormack, John 10,53
McCormack, Judith 219
McCormack, William 82
McCormick, Judy 79

McCormick, Phebe 55
McCormick, William 36,79,112
McCulloc, James 215
McCullock, Charles 14,50
McCulloh, Jerusha 155
McDaniel, Henry S. 179
McDaniel, William 113
McDaniel, William F. 3,26
McDonald, H. B. 12,31,84,139,
　202,213
McDonald, Henry B. 2,30,33,50,
　73,76,91,99,109,125,127,149,
　181,196,197,211,212,217,238,
　254,259,266,267,276,279,282,
　287
McDonald, J. H. 259
McDonald, James G. 209,232
McDonald, John 4
McDonald, Mary 259
McDonald, Samuel B. 222
McDonald, Samuel H. 217
McDonald, Washington L. 259
McDonald, William 233
McDonald, Zebulon 230
McDougall, John 220
McDuffee, John 27
McDuffee, Neal 220
McDuffee, Neil 27
McDuffy, Eli 91
McEachern, Patrick 5
McEnturf, William 202
McFall, John 191
McFarlin, Lewis 277
McFearson, Joseph 154
McFearson, Nancy 154
McGaffee, Rachel 176
McGee, Elizabeth 27
McGee, Evaline 113
McGee, Evelina 27
McGee, George 27
McGee, George W. 27,113,212
McGee, Hiram 27,182
McGee, Hyram 113
McGee, Isaac 76
McGee, John 22,27,87,113,146,
　198,243
McGee, Joseph 182
McGee, Joseph C. 27,113
McGee, Mary 113
McGee, Nancy 113
McGee, William 76,89
McGinnis, Clement 240
McGinnis, John 140,234,244,246
McGinnis, Martha 246

McGinnis, Susannah 140
McGinnis, William 81,134
McGregor, Flower 67
McGuffee, John 176
McHill, Israel 105
McHood, Robert 23,278
McIntire, Vincent 253
McKee, Charles F. 238
McKee, James 18
McKee, John 175
McKee, Pinkney 152
McKee, Rebecca 229,238
McKenny, Clement 45
McKenny, Jourdan 45
McKiness, Daniel, Jr. 28
McKiness, Daniel, Sr. 28
McKiness, Thomas 28
McKinley, James 79,94
McKinney, Ann 90
McKinney, Clem 274
McKinney, Clement 47,97, 277
McKinney, Hugh 189
McKinney, John 111
McKinney, Jordan 109,215
McKinney, Martha 111
McKinney, Richard 90,128
McKinney, Wiley 47
McKinney, William 36,260
McKinnis, Andrew 236
McKinnis, Daniel 103
McKinnis, David 77
McKinnis, James D. 45,103
McKinnis, John 69,183,258
McKinnis, Margaret 69
McKinnis, Neill 16
McKinnis, Thomas 103
McKnight, James H. 224
McKnight, Miles 206
McMann, Jane 111,168
McMann, William W. 111,168
McMurry, Archibald D. 182
McMurry, Charles 25,32,39, 44,87,119,121,122,124, 125,139,178,222
McMurry, Elizabeth 182
McMurry, Fountain 222
McMurry, James 30,61,101, 143,164,180,222,238
McMurry, James G. 182
McMurry, Jane 143
McMurry, John 30,36,73, 75,101,122,194,231,257
McMurry, John M. 222
McMurry, Lipscomb P. 182,273
McMurry, Martin 54,125,143,144, 146,158,180,270
McMurry, S. D. 181
McMurry, Sally 182,222
McMurry, Samuel D. 120
McMurry, Sol 119
McMurry, Sollomon 194
McMurry, Solomon 30,119,120,125
McMurry, Thomas W. 182
McMurry, Vincent 182
McMurry, William 182
McMurtry, James 252
McMurtry, James B. 286
McNeely, John 42,99
McNeely, Robert 42,99
McNeill, Anny B. 48
McNeill, Archibald 19,48,88,104, 116,117,118,147,154
McNeill, G. B. 1
McNichol, Mary A. 270
McPherson, Joseph G. 142
McPherson, Lewis 206
McWhorter, Gabriel W. 98
McWhorter, Henry 86,102
Mace, D. 241
Mace, Thompson 37,65,78,87,103, 107,214,226,241,262,282
Macon, Elizabeth 31,113,260
Macon, Nathaniel 31,113,260
Madden, Greenberry 148
Madding, John 170
Maddux, Craven 18
Maddux, Elizabeth 18
Maddux, Thomas 18,104
Mading, B. W. 17,18,29,38
Mading, Banister W. 32
Mading, Bannaster W. 7,17
Mading, Thomas 8
Maggard, Jane 3,13,256
Maggart, John 57,133,157,179,180, 188,220,256
Mahan, C. W. 278
Malone, Amzi 148,210
Malone, Daniel 83
Malone, David 221,280
Malone, J. J. 210,214
Malone, Jackson 199
Malone, James 1,29,54,55,58,201, 205,210
Malone, James J. 148,151,250
Malone, Robert 57
Malone, Robert C. 148
Malone, Robert, Sr. 151

Malone, Stephen 116
Malone, Stephen W. 56,104,
    130
Malone, Thomas 88,201,209,
    229,233,253
Malone, William P. 181,196,
    198
Malone, Yancy A. 129
Manion, Ambrose 101
Mankin, Jeremiah 212
Manley, Hannah 249
Mann, Felix G. 223
Mann, Henry 70,73,104,109,
    125,127,128,144,149,158,
    160,163,206,220,223,230
Mann, John H. 266
Mann, John W. 6,70,73,97,
    130,197,210
Mann, Lettice 266
Mann, Lindsey 9,28
Mann, M. L. 241
Mann, Martisha 266
Mann, R. W. 133,245
Mann, Robert W. 118,124,
    130,143,148,151,166,192,
    206,247,266,285
Mann, Stephen 16,29,31,70,
    80,95,108,112,136,138,
    164,168,172,192,193,194,
    202,205,206,210,217,234,
    241,248,249,257,265,266,
    273
Mann, Timothy W. 281
Manning, John 266
Manning, William 266,267
Marchbanks, H. D. 23,46
Marchbanks, Herald D. 153,
    259
Marchbanks, Josephine 194,
    280
Marchbanks, Russell 23,
    128,155,259,270,274,282
Marchbanks, T. C. 155
Marchbanks, Thomas 23
Marchbanks, Thomas C. 128,
    153,179,194,259,270,274,
    280,282
Maricle, A. D. 137
Maricle, Alfred 66,137,187
Maricle, George 66,137,187
Maricle, George, Jr. 137
Maricle, Organ 137,187
Maricle, R. O. 66
Mark, Charles 7
Mark, Henry 7
Marks, Edith 42
Marks, John 164
Marley, Adam 157
Marley, Branch 156
Marley, H. W. 267
Marley, Hampton 157
Marley, Hampton W. 124
Marley, Josiah 157
Marley, Malvina 157
Marley, Marena O. 61
Marley, Newton 157
Marley, Robert 148,157,179,180,
    227
Marley, Susan C. 56
Marley, Young 157,187,238,242
Marlow, William 249
Marricle, George 15
Marsh, Charles 66
Marsh, Philip 66,71
Marsh, William 66
Marshall, Josiah 2,19,44,48,116,
    117,130,132,133,137,170,181,
    193,212
Marshall, Malina 145
Marshall, Robert 97,119,164,192,
    210,244
Marshall, Thomas 170,174,180,
    211,212
Martin, Anny 176,259
Martin, Brice F. 156
Martin, George B. 256
Martin, George W. 118,133
Martin, Henry 28
Martin, J. P. 138
Martin, J. W. 244
Martin, James 11,13,101,121,244,
    281
Martin, James W. 253,268
Martin, Jesse 233,250
Martin, John 24,56,268
Martin, John G. 11,13,281
Martin, Mary B. 282
Martin, Matthew M. 42
Martin, Price F. 53
Martin, Sally 8
Martin, Sarah S. 7
Martin, Stephen W. 101,236,284
Martin, Thomas 244,256,257,271
Martin, W. Y. 241
Martin, William 8,61,94,100,144,
    156,163,184,214,215,241
Martin, William J. 257
Martin, William, Jr. 50

Martin, William L. 7,86,
  106,117,138,221
Martin, William S. 94
Martin, William T. 271
Martin, Wilson 24
Martin, Wilson Y. 61,80,
  100,123,125,131,144,
  184,215,223,270,274,
  282
Martin, Winney 176,253,
  259
Mason, David 41
Mason, David G. 46,181,
  184
Mason, John 63,204,221
Mason, John L. 63
Mason, John S. 270
Mason, Marmaduke 136,142,
  157,187,211,220,245,
  247,280
Mason, William 221
Mason, William H. 63
Mason, William W. 234
Mason, Wyle 221
Massey, Henderson 166
Massey, Isaac 84,129,194,
  195,259
Massey, Isaac A. 104,243
Massey, Judith 215
Massey, Mary A. 134
Massey, Mary E. 142,166
Massey, Robert 243
Massey, Robert A. 104
Massey, Samuel 140
Massey, Sarah 243
Massey, Simms 125,243
Massey, William 6,97,142,
  166,215,240,245
Massie, Allen D. 74
Massie, Asa 74
Massie, John 74
Massie, Nancy 74
Massie, William 74
Mates, Wesley 2
Mathews, Allen 119,202
Mathews, Benjamin 149,257,
  271
Mathews, Benjamin L. 244
Mathews, Boaz 127
Mathews, Edwin R. 282
Mathews, Martha 257
Mathews, Peggy 117
Mathewson, James 95,108
Mathewson, Mary 108

Mathis, Edwin 273
Matlock, G. C. 139,180
Matlock, Gideon C. 137
Matlock, Thomas 126
Matthews, Alexander 68
Matthews, Allen 60,81,193,195,
  196,198,204
Matthews, Benjamin 19,40,55
Matthews, Clabourn 38
Matthews, Clibourn 57,180
Matthews, Elizabeth 198
Matthews, John 68
Matthews, Thomas 68
Maxey, Mildred 89,172
Maxwell, S. P. 271
Maxwell, Samuel P. 135,141
Mays, Samuel 266
Mayson, John 234
Maze, Samuel 264,265
Meacham, G. W. 178
Meacham, Jesse 6,37,109,178
Meacham, Washington 37,133,139,
  246
Meachum, Jesse 58,75
Meachum, Washington 1,88
Meader, Banister 48
Meader, Bannister 57
Meader, Bennet 57
Meader, Bennett 50
Meader, Ira 45
Meader, Job 27
Meader, Joel 27
Meader, John 45
Meader, John H. 45
Meader, Meredith 45,46,47
Meader, Pleasant C. 17
Meader, Wilson T. 3,12,50,58
Meaders, John 2
Meaders, Wilson 8
Meador, Anderson 70
Meador, Christopher 75
Meador, Ira 66,74,102
Meador, Jehu 51,66,102
Meador, Job 70,101
Meador, Joel 94,101,103
Meador, John 66,103,243
Meador, Jonas 75
Meador, Joseph 21
Meador, Lewis 71
Meador, Wilson T. 114
Meadow, Bennett 43
Meadow, Joseph 43
Meadows, William 129,150,170
Mentlo, Daniel W. 9

Mercer, Elbridge 113
Mercer, Eldridge 118
Mercer, J. M. 113
Mercer, James M. 118
Merrett, John 100
Merritt, Flemming 247,276
Merritt, John 137,283
Merryman, Elizabeth 285
Merryman, James T. 285
Merryman, John H. 110
Metcalf, Anthony H. 19
Metcalf, Edward A. 258
Metcalf, Fanny 265
Metcalf, Matilda 14,19
Metcalf, Thomas A. 265
Miller, Elijah 95,123
Miller, John 123
Miller, John L. 111,144
Miller, Martin 28,38,40, 65,143
Miller, Matilda 111,168
Miller, Nancy 111,168
Miller, Sophia 111,144, 263
Mills, James G. 133
Mills, John 132,133
Mills, Robert S. 161,169
Milton, James M. 215
Mingle, Isaac 69
Minion, John 200
Minion, Louisiana 200
Minton, A. J. 270
Minton, Andrew J. 268
Minton, James 270
Minton, Joel 284
Minton, Joel W. 268
Minton, John 7,164,189, 213,284
Minton, Muholda 284
Minton, Sabry 270
Minton, Thomas 229
Mires, George 201,220
Mires, White 230
Mitchell, Brite 186
Mitchell, David L. 67
Mitchell, Eliza J. 202
Mitchell, Elizabeth 274
Mitchell, F. E. 225
Mitchell, F. N. 29,169, 171
Mitchell, Frederick 3
Mitchell, Frederick N. 22, 44,46,51,143,179
Mitchell, Isaac 178

Mitchell, John 54,63,90,161
Mitchell, Joseph 59,74,188,230, 255
Mitchell, L. E. 234
Mitchell, Leroy E. 16,91,157, 172,225
Mitchell, Marcellus 5,7,73,202, 216
Mitchell, Martha 171
Mitchell, Mary 59
Mitchell, Phillip H. 178,179
Mitchell, Robert 188,216
Mitchell, Robert J. 274
Mitchell, Stanford 204
Mitchell, William N. 6
Mitchell, Winny 274
Mofield, James 250
Moles, James M. 97
Monday, Larkin 127
Monroe, David 163
Montgomery, Stewart 235,274
Mooningham, Henry B. 76,168
Mooningham, Matthew 67,118
Moore, A. 10,23,194
Moore, A., Jr. 96
Moore, Alexander 98
Moore, Armstead 22,98,110,147, 155,156,168,171,172,179,202, 213,216,226,236,248,269,279
Moore, Armstead, Jr. 97,110
Moore, Armsted 79,82,83
Moore, Benjamin 41
Moore, Benjamin F. 18
Moore, Bird 279
Moore, D. C. 8
Moore, Elijah 157,165,175
Moore, Elizabeth 31
Moore, Gregory 92,129,157,165, 174,176,212,260
Moore, Harriet F. 157,175
Moore, Henry S. 94
Moore, Isaac 4,28,32,53,264
Moore, Isaac R. 53,205,246
Moore, James B. 266
Moore, Jeremiah 105
Moore, John 9,92,113,124,185,192, 200,221
Moore, John A. 225
Moore, John H. 161
Moore, McCory 88
Moore, Martha 113
Moore, Matthew 73
Moore, Patrick 81
Moore, Robert 161

Moore, Samuel B. 279
Moore, Tabitha 161
Moore, Thomas 31
Moore, W. B. 8,22,23,189, 194
Moore, Will B. 20
Moore, William 79,113,175, 206,235,260,266
Moore, William B. 10,82, 110,115,117,133,147,168, 213
Moorehead, Henry G. 157
Moorehead, Marina 157
Moores, Elizabeth 135,136, 145,147,211,228,230
Moores, Henry L. 135,136, 145,147,148,187
Moores, Isaac 254
Moores, James B. 136,138, 139,140,148,217,225,240, 244,255,279
Moores, William 136,145, 147,230
Moorland, Jesse 214
Morehead, William T. 61
Moreland, Jesse 165
Moreland, Vincent 55
Moreland, William 274
Morgan, Alfred 76
Morgan, Amzi 52
Morgan, Caroline 185
Morgan, Henry 176,192,229
Morgan, Isaac 76
Morgan, James C. 214
Morgan, James W. 160,185
Morgan, John 139
Morgan, Joseph 27,37,81, 88,214
Morgan, M. 214
Morgan, Mary 27
Morgan, Sarah 263
Morgan, Thomas 37
Morgan, William H. 183
Morgan, William, Sr. 113
Morgan, Young 8
Mormon, Cely 271
Mormon, Olive 271
Mormon, Richard 277
Morris, Armstead G. 173
Morris, B. F. 4
Morris, Benjamin F. 17,31, 32
Morris, David 168
Morris, Eleanor 169

Morris, Elijah 277
Morris, Isaac 5,51,66
Morris, Isaac R. 96
Morris, J. B. 111
Morris, James B. 74,78,111,124
Morris, James, Jr. 125
Morris, James, Sr. 93,120
Morris, John 1,33,61,199,268
Morris, Joshua 3,66,96
Morris, Martha 277
Morris, Mary 239
Morris, Mathew W. 118,122,164, 169,175
Morris, Pleasant 125
Morris, William B. 228
Moseley, David 253
Moseley, Jonathan 85
Moseley, Nancy 253
Moses, Hiram 232
Moses, Joseph 45,80,89,130,150, 165,171,188,193
Moses, Josiah 27,34,45
Moss, Hugh 117,123,200,216
Moss, James W. 117,161
Moss, John 24
Moss, John A. 205,222
Moss, Joseph 117
Moss, Joseph G. 200
Moss, Samuel 222
Moss, Susan 226,252
Moss, Thomas 226
Moss, William P. 222
Motes, James M. 111,120
Motes, Wesley 16,20,23,109,111, 132,133
Mottley, B. T. 83,87,89,122
Muirhead, John 40
Mulherin, James 30
Mullinax, Sarah 1
Munday, William L. 183
Munford, Thomas J. 148
Mungle, Allen 180
Mungle, Isaac 50,68,99,158,160, 180
Mungle, John 68
Mungle, Nelly 180
Mungle, Sally 180
Mungle, Sarah 158
Murphree, James 87,112
Murphree, James L. 24,54,83,88
Murphree, James S. 4,12,165
Murray, Charles C. 166
Murray, Harriet 233
Murray, Randolph 9

Murry, Charles 35
Murry, Henry J. 6
Murry, Randolph 2,35
Murry, Samuel 233
Murry, Susannah 211
Myres, Isaac 107
Naley, J. C. 264
Naley, William 264
Nash, Christian N. 262
Nash, George 122,175,190, 242
Nash, George R. 230,262, 273
Nash, William 152
Nash, William D. 122,168, 190
Neal, Brittain J. 99
Neal, Britton 42
Neal, Charles 242
Neal, Elizabeth 42,99
Neal, Mary A. 242
Nealey, William 61
Neeley, William 141
Neil, Jacob 135
Nelson, Evan E. 95
Nelson, Holbrook 118
Nelson, James 74
Nelson, James M. 95
New, John 98
Newbell, Edmond 212
Newbell, George W. 212
Newbell, James 209,243
Newbell, James G. 209
Newbell, John H. 29,44,63, 80,85,86,99,103,115,119, 122,141,152,168,187,212, 274
Newbell, Stephen 195
Newbell, William 6,137
Newby, Henry 172
Newby, James 49
Newby, Roland W. 43,51,79, 121,141,173,192
Newby, Whaley 192,204,253
Newby, William 7,51,144, 192
Newel, Mathis 148
Newell, John A. 26
Newell, Mathis 130,166
Newhouse, John H. 118,125
Newhouse, John W. 123
Newman, Josiah 100,111
Newsom, A. B. 89,95
Newsom, Francis B. 232

Newsom, Nancy 227
Nichols, Beckman 57
Nichols, Bird 119
Nichols, David 284
Nichols, David H. 192
Nichols, H. 149
Nichols, H. V. 159,169
Nichols, Henry 128,148
Nichols, Henry V. 169,171,183, 283
Nichols, J. 277
Nichols, J. M. 277
Nichols, James 279
Nichols, Jesse 73,279,283
Nichols, Joel 194
Nichols, Joel M. 112
Nichols, John 60,148,152
Nichols, John B. 162,171
Nichols, John W. 128
Nichols, Lucy 119,149
Nichols, Mathew 279
Nichols, Mathew S. 73,193
Nichols, Matthew 15,16,69,70,81, 202
Nichols, Polly 81
Nichols, Richard 27
Nichols, Warren 112,159,194,217
Nichols, William 7
Nickson, Charles 240
Nickson, Hambleton 275
Nickson, John 165,167,183
Nickson, Joseph H. 240,242
Nickson, William 47
Niell, Jacob 80
Nixon, Charles 108
Nixon, Louisa H. 261
Nixon, Rachel F. 261
Nixon, Robert 86
Nixon, Samantha J. 261
Nolen, C. 60
Nolen, Charles 23,60
Nolen, Rebecca 23
Noles, B. R. 181
Noles, Levi 194
Noles, Thomas 243
Noles, Thomas J. 89,166,167,190, 243,247
Nolin, Stephen 277
Nollner, Ann L. 138
Nollner, John G. 116,138
Noolner, John 126
Noolner, John G. 126
Norris, George 90,116,279
Norris, J. B. 172

Norris, James 15,49,178, 220,224,238
Norris, John B. 104,235, 279,286
Norris, Mary A. 279
Norris, Nancy 224,247
Norris, Tilman 279
Norris, Tilmon 2
Norris, William C. 224,237, 238,247
Notes, William 241
Null, Jacob 47,87,164,230, 251,270,276
Nunley, Branch 10,180,238
Nunley, Polly 274
Nunley, William A. 274
Oakley, James 285
Oakley, William 133
Oats, David C. 165
O'Bannun, Milton 21
Oglesby, Clifton A. 93
Oglesby, Elijah 93
Oglesby, Henry 93
Oldham, George W. 96
Oldham, Rhoda 261
Oldham, Robert 240
Oldham, Samuel 87,138,242, 279
Oldham, William 232
Oldham, Willis 131,135
Oldham, Willis W. 135,138, 179
Oliver, B. 241
Oliver, Banks 262
Oliver, Bleuford 67
Oliver, Bluford 157,241
Oliver, Horace 5,12,223,275
Oliver, Killes 262
Oliver, Martha 241
Oliver, Mary E. 262
Oliver, Narcissa 241
Oliver, Rellis 241
Oliver, Warner 262
Oliver, William H. 95
Orange, Byrd 12,115
Orange, Early 270
Orange, Francis M. 270
Orange, Yearby 12,26,51
Orange, Zephaniah 116,121, 172,200
Organ, James 162
Organ, John 144
Organ, Rolly 162
Orwell, Benjamin 100

Overall, Elias 3
Overstreet, Henderson C. 203
Overstreet, Thomas 26,150,171
Overstreet, William 1,17,248, 268
Overstreet, William H. 241
Overton, A. W. 210
Overton, Archibald W. 92,129, 135,137,147,167,234,243
Overton, Mary G. 243
Overton, Thomas C. 243
Owen, Abner 81
Owen, B. R. 188,221
Owen, Benjamin R. 16,65
Owen, G. 50
Owen, Gronon 73
Owen, John 9,151,269,283
Owen, John D. 188,271,282
Owen, Mary A. 90
Owen, Samuel A. 284
Owen, Thomas 32,282
Owen, William 9,50,96,124
Owens, H. G. 36,123
Owens, J. T. 123
Owens, Thomas 6,92
Owens, William 27,32,36
Page, Cealia 24
Page, Elmore D. 127
Page, Henry 261
Page, John 21,24,25,127,161,196, 261,262,286
Page, John S. 7,124,174,183,267
Page, Louisa 267
Page, Mary A. 267
Page, Nancy 267
Page, Norvell A. 286
Page, Stephen 91
Page, Thomas W. 21,104,109,116, 120,137,155,159,177,189,236, 242,254,267,286
Palmer, Charlotte 57,81
Palmer, David 192,213,221,224, 237,265
Palmer, John 263
Palmer, John R. 76
Palmer, Thomas 26,189
Palmer, Woodson 57,81
Palmore, John R. 18
Pankey, Creed H. 268
Pankey, Elisa 228
Pankey, Sally 228
Pankey, Sarah 224,225,237
Pankey, Uria 132
Pankey, Uzzi 153,228,230

Pankey, Gilla 72
Paris, James 33,72
Paris, Julia A. 72
Park, John G. 1,7,36,37,
   59,275
Parker, A. S. 270
Parker, Abraham 51,279,283
Parker, Allen G. 81
Parker, Amanda F. 207
Parker, Archibald 38,39,40,
   47,67,77,81,92,93,106,122
Parker, Ellis 148
Parker, Frances 49,253
Parker, Francis 67,127
Parker, G. B. 92
Parker, Goolsberry 8,92,102,
   103
Parker, Hickman 51
Parker, Isaac A. 222
Parker, James 22
Parker, James D. 127
Parker, James G. 87,171
Parker, Jane 222
Parker, John 9,10,42,54,62,
   99
Parker, John C. 149,176
Parker, Jonathan 129,231
Parker, Joseph 37,103
Parker, Lewis J. 270
Parker, Phebe 279
Parker, Richard 274
Parker, Sarah 222
Parker, Vardaman 8
Parker, William 65,103
Parker, William M. 90
Parker, Womack 58
Parkhurst, David 52
Parkhurst, Ezekiel 49,56,
   283,285
Parkhurst, Polly 285
Parkhurst, Rebecca 263
Parkhurst, William 52,74,
   84,91,170,193,244,263,
   267,268
Parks, William 245
Parris, James 244
Parris, James, Sr. 244
Parris, Pleasant 236
Parris, Polly 141
Parris, William 182
Parrish, Booker 191
Parrot, Nathaniel 230
Parrott, Benjamin 6,7
Parrot, Elizabeth 113

Parrott, Mary 201
Parrott, Nathaniel W. 92,113,243
Parsons, Thomas 159
Parsons, William 159
Paschal, Anderson 22
Paschal, Andrew 22
Paschal, Samuel 22,36,157
Paschale, Anderson 264
Pate, Anthony W. 258
Pate, Booker 30,91
Pate, Hampton 30
Pate, Jubie E. 30
Pate, Peyton 258
Pate, Stephen 30,91,258
Patey, Charles 217,277
Patey, J. W. 143
Patey, Jesse 281
Patey, John W. 127
Patterson, Alex 159
Patterson, Amzi C. 4
Patterson, Bartlett 113,123
Patterson, Cynthia 233
Patterson, H. S. 212
Patterson, Horace H. 115
Patterson, Hugh 147,233
Patterson, James 100
Patterson, John C. 20
Patterson, Neal 242,258
Patterson, Neil 122,159
Patterson, Neill 66
Patterson, Rachel 20,69
Patterson, Robert 73
Patterson, S. F. 88,173
Patterson, Samuel F. 20,50,142
Patterson, William 6,20,22,23,69
Patton, J. E. 119,120
Patton, J. W. 120
Patton, John C. 119,120
Patton, Samuel F. 221
Paty, J. W. 2,131
Paty, John O. 16
Paty, John W. 25,78,116,175
Paty, Jonas 16
Paty, Nancy 16
Paty, Polly 16
Payear, Mary A. 258
Payne, Alfred 46,141
Payne, Andrew 3,9,12,21,37,43,149
Payne, Benjamin 16,42,164,237
Payne, E. 72
Payne, Eliza 248
Payne, Eliza J. 169
Payne, Esquire 67
Payne, Eunice G. 144

Payne, Eva 67
Payne, George 67,120
Payne, George W. 67
Payne, Greenwood 67
Payne, Isaac 168
Payne, Isaac N. 169
Payne, John 28,55,93,95,
  107,121,135,144,154,
  236,242,243
Payne, Joseph 55,144,275,
  278
Payne, July 67
Payne, Lacy 144
Payne, Larkin 42,95,181,
  196
Payne, Manerva 67
Payne, Martha 67
Payne, Mary 67
Payne, Spencer 67
Payne, Tennessee 67
Payne, W. M. 269
Payne, Washington 196,243
Payne, William 38,55,72,
  189,204,205
Payne, William J. 160,194,
  234,236,284
Payne, William M. 132,232,
  250,284
Payton, Ephraim 31
Payton, John 31
Pearce, Alfred 65,120
Pearce, Benjamin 65,120
Pearce, Elias 187
Pearce, Granville S. 120
Pearce, Isaac 80,120
Pearson, John B. 142
Pearson, Leonaita 142
Pearyear, Mary A. 262
Pendarvis, James 26,62,68,
  69
Pendarvis, William 130,173
Pendleton, Andrew J. 224
Pendleton, Lewis 165,276
Pendleton, Louis 234
Pendleton, Louisa 224
Penn, A. C. 47
Penn, A. G. 148
Penn, Abraham C. 28,29
Penn, Abraham G. 109
Penn, Agnes 125
Penn, Christopher C. 52,
  230
Penn, Creed 7,124,125,132,
  133,139,140,174

Penn, Pamela 133
Penn, Pamelia 50
Perier, John 250
Perkins, Abner 77
Perkins, Abner A. 182
Perkins, Abner C. 40,65
Perkins, Adam C. 28,35,77,190,
  191,257
Perkins, David 28
Perkins, David, Sr. 1
Perkins, Henry 139,234,252,286
Perkins, Sarah 106
Perkins, William B. 23,171,182,
  242
Perrin, John 269
Perry, Abraham 104
Perry, Benjamin 241
Perry, George W. 199
Perry, Rufus 137,150,152,167,168,
  186,218,219,231,232,233,235,
  236,244,246,248,249,250,252,
  257,267,268,271,273
Perry, Susan 183
Perry, Warren 183
Person, High 78
Person, William 135,146
Petross, Mathew 185
Petross, Matthew 86,101
Pettress, Matthew 31
Petty, Eliza 278
Petty, George 278
Petty, Stephen 113,122,136,179
Petty, William 8,104,115,117,
  127,179
Phelps, Ann 213,282
Phelps, Henry 95
Phelps, Thomas 6,17,28,30,31,53,
  213,282
Phelps, William 286
Phelson, William 210
Philips, C. 214
Philips, David 46,204,205
Philips, James 56,180,195,214
Philips, Leighton 257
Philips, N. 199
Philips, Nathan W. 138
Philips, Sinthia 103
Phillips, James 48,193
Phillips, Leighton 159
Phipps, William R. 160
Pickett, Andrew 31,56,71
Pickett, Andrew G. 157,161,162,
  172,176,180,181,183,186,195,
  200,202,206,218,243,256

Pickett, E. B. 182
Pickett, Edward B. 71,157
Pickett, Jonathan 31,71,
 157
Pickett, Joseph G. 71,
 157,213,241
Pierce, Alfred 48,128,158
Pierce, Benjamin 3,4,48,
 53,104,116,128,142,182
Pierce, Elizabeth H. 4
Pierce, F. B. 118
Pierce, Franklin B. 128,
 259
Pierce, George 4,128
Pierce, George B. 3,4
Pierce, Granville S. 128
Pierce, Isaac 104,128
Pierce, Washington G. 128
Pig, Charles L. 237
Pigg, Charles 273
Pigg, John 46
Pigg, Mary 53,56,87
Pigg, William 275
Pillow, Ann 67
Pillow, N. B. 219
Pinchum, John 156
Pinckley, John F. 110,111
Piper, Alexander 266
Piper, Allen 1,10,21,86,
 93,96,116,224,229,230
Piper, Benjamin 23,26,30,
 89,102,103
Piper, Brice H. 258
Piper, Henry 30,174,266
Piper, James 15,37,205,
 228,259
Piper, James, Jr. 261
Piper, John 74
Piper, Samuel 261
Piper, Susan 278
Pipkin, Alexander 49,72,
 107
Pipkin, Aley 108
Pipkin, Clemmy 71,72
Pipkin, Isaac 72,103
Pipkin, Jesse 71
Pipkin, Lewis 71
Pipkin, Samuel 103
Pipkin, Sena 72
Pipkins, Henry J. 175
Pistole, Alfred 206
Pistole, Betsy 206
Pistole, William 49
Plummer, Alia M. 231

Plummer, Thomas G. 231
Pope, Calvin 107,181,216,264
Pope, Elizabeth 216
Pope, Hizia 220
Pope, James 2
Pope, James H. 216
Pope, Jesse 216,220,234
Pope, John 216
Pope, John O. 123,160,190
Pope, L. 281
Pope, Nicey 216
Pope, Owen 20
Pope, Robert 180,193,199
Pope, Robert W. 281
Pope, Sewellen 216
Pope, Silas 216
Pope, Theoderick 216
Pope, William 46,142
Porter, Colbert 237,266
Porter, Colvert 205
Porter, James 52
Porter, Jemima 123
Porter, Peter 63,73,81,105,184
Porter, Thomas 10
Posey, Alexander 279
Posey, Nancy 279
Powel, Charles 144
Powel, Dempsey 4
Powel, Elijah 131
Powell, Charles 257,273,286
Powell, George 55,257
Powell, Jesse 58
Powell, John 75,171,183,232,234
Powell, John L. 14,58,136,251
Powell, Malinda 257
Powell, Rebecca 257
Presley, A. M. 151
Presley, P. W. 116,277
Presley, Pleasant W. 203,209
Presley, Valentine 47,101,214,230
Preston, Caleb 132
Preston, Isabella 218,263
Preston, James 218,263
Price, Benjamin H. 97
Price, T. D. 205
Price, Thomas D. 114
Price, W. M. 175,183,188,262
Price, W. W. 202
Price, William 158
Price, William M. 98,105,159,170,
 242,248,276,277,283
Pritchett, John 72
Prowell, David 109,129,170,184,
 185

Prowell, Matilda 184,212,
 237,239,280
Pruet, Joshua 199
Pruett, Elizabeth 61
Pruett, Holden W. 61
Pryor, Elizabeth 4
Pryor, Pleasant 135
Pugh, Carsey 42
Pugh, Delilah 63
Pugh, Frances 97
Pugh, Samuel 42,95,231,
 237
Pugh, Uriah 211,231
Pulley, William 108
Purnell, Noles 36
Purnell, Oscar 106
Purnell, Oscar F. 190
Pursley, C. 194
Pursley, David 68,69
Pursley, Elisha O. 100
Pursley, Ephraim 143
Pursley, H. L. 69
Pursley, Robert 68
Pursley, W. Y. 69
Pursley, William B. 68
Puryear, Pierce 117,127,
 128,129
Puryear, William 116
Pyram, C. L. 239
Pyram, Charles 252
Pyran, Charles T. 222
Pyran, David 222
Pyran, S. B. 222
Pyran, Tapley B. 210,222
Pyron, Charles 214
Pyron, Isaiah 121
Pyron, Tapley B. 214
Rafferty, William 40
Ragland, Delila 99
Ragland, James 63
Ragland, Reuben 99
Ragland, William 83,84,
 118,125,137,138,143,145
Ragland, William, Sr. 47
Ramsay, John 6
Ramsey, C. Y. 59
Ramsey, Catharine 84,85,
 219,258
Ramsey, Caty 72
Ramsey, William L. 156
Rankin, John 2
Rawley, Daniel 106,127,
 131
Rawley, David 251

Rawlings, Joseph 142
Rawlings, Leonaita 142
Rawlings, Margret E. 142
Rawlings, Sarah 108
Ray, George M. 114
Ray, James 42,238
Ray, Logan D. 238
Ray, Lydia 111,114
Reace, John 111
Read, Alfred 145,150,166,190
Read, Bird 89
Read, Caleb 28
Read, George 86,107,147,175
Read, George W. 197
Read, James 41,151
Read, John J. 14
Read, Mary 145
Read, Samuel 64,96,138,145
Read, William 170
Reasonover, George W. 20,23,65
Reasonover, J. E. 97
Reasonover, Jeremiah 228
Reasonover, Jeremiah E. 183,199
Reaves, Deana 186
Reaves, John 74
Reaves, Michael 12
Reaves, Moses 185,192
Reaves, William 63,84,186
Redman, John W. 28
Redman, Rhoda 93
Redman, Roda 69
Redman, Thomas 89
Redmon, John W. 16
Reece, Charles 249
Reece, Elizabeth F. 246,259
Reece, J. S. 246
Reece, Jeremiah 29
Reece, John 80,216
Reece, John S. 246,259
Reece, John, Sr. 223,234,238
Reece, Josiah 223
Reece, William 223,238,251,269
Reece, William B. 9,79
Reed, Alfred 204
Reed, George 15
Reed, James 247
Reed, Rena 74
Reed, Thomas 5
Rees, John, Sr. 82
Reese, James S. 205
Reese, William 190,284,287
Reeves, Eliza 224,237
Reeves, Eliza P. 247
Reeves, John 34,54,55,90,95,121,

161,177,181,200,213
Reeves, Moses 114,241,261, 269
Reeves, W. W. 237
Reeves, William 283,284
Reeves, William M. 247
Reeves, William W. 224
Reeves, Willis L. 175
Reid, James 104
Reynolds, Arthur E. 194
Reynolds, C. B. 233,236
Reynolds, Clinton 264
Reynolds, Clinton B. 153
Reynolds, Emily 264
Reynolds, Granville 264
Reynolds, James 123,153, 203,264
Reynolds, James B. 264
Reynolds, James W. 264
Reynolds, John 194
Reynolds, Malvina 264
Reynolds, Noble 264
Reynolds, S. 264
Reynolds, Washington 264
Reynolds, William W. 264
Rhodes, Henry 70
Rhodes, John N. 79
Rice, B. H. 85
Rice, William M. 77
Richards, Charles 12,130
Richardson, Alfred H. 167
Richardson, B. M. 251
Richardson, Barnard 126
Richardson, Bernard 24,76, 228
Richardson, Britton 37,109
Richardson, Britton M. 120, 231,235,236,256,258,287
Richardson, Daniel 274
Richardson, E. L. 54
Richardson, Edward 77
Richardson, Elijah L. 51, 53
Richardson, H. 3
Richardson, Harriet 281
Richardson, Hopkins 3,5, 107,120,121,154,240,249
Richardson, James 30
Richardson, James A. 222, 227,228
Richardson, James B. 39, 53,74
Richardson, John 81,89,98, 184

Richardson, John G. 122
Richardson, Josiah 120
Richardson, Mary 109
Richardson, Nancy 167,278
Richardson, Thomas 32
Richardson, Thomas S. 71
Richardson, William C. 120,231, 236
Richee, Lucy 30
Richee, Obediah S. 30
Riddle, David 73,79,114
Riggins, Lewis 33
Right, John 180
Right, John T. 170,197
Right, Stephen H. 219
Right, William P. 219
Rigsby, John 47,129,199,203
Rigsby, Right 47
Riley, William A. 1
Risan, Mary 240
Risen, Mary 223
Rison, James 196
Rison, Mary 196
Roach, James 88
Roark, Asa 58,72
Roark, Daniel 15
Roark, Elijah 58
Roark, Henry 104
Roark, John 39
Roark, Josiah 13,59
Roark, Levi 71,100
Roark, William 39,58,100,126
Robb, Hugh B. 77,175
Roberson, A. 42
Roberson, King 41
Roberson, Nathan 23
Roberson, Thomas 42
Roberson, William 73
Roberts, Anna H. 241
Roberts, Jacob 238,248,250
Roberts, James 153
Roberts, Jane 152
Roberts, Matlock 246,273
Roberts, Paschal 215
Roberts, Pleasant 112,169,196, 226
Roberts, Richardson 166,240
Roberts, Robert 241
Roberts, Thomas 15
Roberts, Zedoc B. 63
Roberts, Zodock B. 152
Robertson, Daniel 2,57,241
Robertson, David 2,208
Robertson, H. 3

Robertson, Hezekiah 3
Robertson, James C. 208
Robertson, John 102
Robertson, Martha 165
Robertson, Sarah 208
Robertson, William 37,165
Robinson, Alexander 197,203
Robinson, Alexander H. 194
Robinson, Alfred N. 193
Robinson, Allen 39
Robinson, Archery 29
Robinson, Augustine 211
Robinson, Augustus 63
Robinson, Brooks 49,99
Robinson, Burrel 268,281
Robinson, Daniel 92,112
Robinson, Elizabeth 32
Robinson, Guthridge L. 213
Robinson, Henry 121,148
Robinson, Higdon 100
Robinson, James 32
Robinson, James R. 269
Robinson, John 23,39,184,
    203,256
Robinson, Joseph 184
Robinson, Louisa 203
Robinson, M. 84
Robinson, Martha P. 281
Robinson, Morris 23
Robinson, Moses 194
Robinson, Nathan N. 62
Robinson, Rachel 211
Robinson, Sally 171
Robinson, Samuel N. 10
Robinson, Sarah B. 256
Robinson, Sarah C. 136
Robinson, Spearmon 144,215,
    219
Robinson, Stephen 18,63,
    76,126,135
Robinson, William 15,30,
    49,98,99,173,193,215,
    219,220,226,227,229,232,
    280
Robison, Daniel 174
Roddy, Emley 97
Roddy, Joseph 97
Roddy, Sally 97
Roddy, William 27,97
Rodgers, John H. 120,183,
    196,199,218
Rodgers, Thomas J. 154
Roe, Benjamin 9,90,109,128,
    160,178

Roe, Emily H. 90
Roe, Esther H. 90
Roe, Jacob W. 90,109,118,128
Roe, John 278,284,287
Roe, John, Jr. 79
Roe, Mary L. 90
Roe, Robert A. 90,118
Roe, Sarah B. 90
Roe, William 152
Roe, William C. 90,118,156,186,
    199
Rogers, Mary E. 65
Rogers, Warren 65
Roland, David 5
Roland, Jefferson 103,280
Roland, Stephen 2
Rolley, Daniel 237
Rollings, Franklin 253
Rollings, James 186,246
Rollings, John R. 256
Rollins, Enock 206
Rollins, James 68
Rollins, Jeremiah 219
Rollins, John R. 219
Rollins, Mary A. 219
Rolls, John S. 82
Rose, Ezekiel 162
Rose, George W. 162,251
Rose, John W. 162
Rose, Nancy 162
Rose, Parthena 162
Rose, Pleasant 162,227,253
Rose, Pleasant H. 162
Rose, Sally 253
Rose, Sally W. 162
Rose, Sary 227
Rose, William B. 68
Rose, William J. 162
Ross, A. H. 199,213
Ross, Albert H. 134,257,275
Ross, Jonathan 269
Ross, William 216
Rossell, James 275
Roulston, James G. 101
Roundtree, Mary A. 20
Roundtree, Turner 20
Rowland, David 16,59,100,162
Rowland, George 100,162,194
Rowland, James 17,29,178,186,
    194,234,248
Rowland, Jefferson 100,136,138,
    156,162,175,214,231
Rowland, John 234
Rowland, Malinda 16,181

Rowland, Martha 194
Rowland, Mary 204
Rowland, Robert 95,97,99, 115,162
Rowls, John 258,260
Rowls, John S. 254,281
Roy, James N. 107,129
Royster, George W. 135, 219,228
Rucks, Benjamin 30,33,96, 116,132,145,149,153,243
Rucks, C. 161
Rucks, Darthula 186
Rucks, Edmund 25,43,44, 96,153,172,198,243,269
Rucks, Harriet T. 282
Rucks, Howel 29
Rucks, Howel T. 43,145, 182,186
Rucks, James 4,96,252
Rucks, Josiah 33,153,252
Rucks, Warner F. 96
Russell, Asa 248
Russell, Bias 24,114,173, 260
Russell, Biaz 77
Russell, David 247
Russell, Elam 87,189
Russell, Elom 41
Russell, Elum 99
Russell, James 245
Russell, John 77,134,148, 200,254,271
Russell, John, Jr. 76
Russell, John, Sr. 76,247, 263
Russell, Robert A. 200
Russell, Samuel 273
Russell, Thomas 254
Rutherford, Margaret 119
Rutherford, Thomas 185
Rutherford, William 119
Rutherford, William B. 210
Rutland, Henry 231,249
Rutland, J. B. 249
Sadler, Elizabeth 48
Sadler, Fanny 231
Sadler, Halbert C. 87
Sadler, Henry 48,107,273
Sadler, James 283,285
Sadler, John 48,231
Sadler, John R. 220
Sadler, Philip 63,87
Sadler, Thomas 31,59,135

Sadler, William C. 87
Sampson, Coleman 73,88,104,213, 239
Sampson, Francis 23
Sampson, Johnson 122
Sampson, Letty 23
Sampson, Mary 209
Sampson, Stephen 213
Sampson, Stephen R. 217,250
Samson, Catherine 169
Samson, Coleman 266
Samson, Coleman S. 135,157
Samson, Johnson 101,112,139,149
Samson, S. R. 169,267
Samson, Stephen 101,118,122
Samson, Stephen R. 149,270
Sanders, D. C. 211,212,220
Sanders, Darthula A. 213
Sanders, David 275
Sanders, David C. 213,228,275,287
Sanders, Edith 42
Sanders, Eth 42
Sanders, Ethelbert 14,35,49
Sanders, H. C. 227
Sanders, J. C. 199,213
Sanders, James 14,51
Sanders, James B. 154
Sanders, James C. 60,84,136,154, 157,204,206,211,215,222,235, 242,251,266,287
Sanders, John C. 101,258
Sanders, John H. 249
Sanders, John L. 13,53
Sanders, John S. 106,151
Sanders, John W. 118
Sanders, Jourdan M. 14,35,49
Sanders, N. C. 118
Sanders, Quinton C. 287
Sanders, Romulus M. 14,35,49,50
Sandlin, Randolph 270
Sary, Alfred 273
Sary, Catherine 273
Saterfield, Evin R. 230
Saulman, Elijah 40
Saunders, David C. 91
Saunders, Fleming 127
Savage, John H. 152,228
Scoggins, George 106
Scoggins, George W. 17,106
Scoggins, James 106
Scoggins, Samuel 106
Scoggins, Sarah 106
Scoggins, William 106
Scott, Elijah 239

Scott, Eliza 253
Scruggs, A. 197
Scruggs, Archibald 98,105, 222,246
Scruggs, James A. 65,83, 86,114,120,159,224
Scudder, Matthias 2
Searcy, William 122,128,201
Searcy, William W. 160
Searls, Othaiel 145
Seaton, Thomas D. 253
Seay, Daniel 121,126,177, 184,201
Seay, E. T. 249
Seay, John 7
Seay, W. W. 262,265,273
Seay, William W. 16,142, 237,240
Self, Lucy 166,179,201
Ser, Abraham C. 145
Sercy, William 72
Serls, Othial 285
Settle, Edward 212,271
Settle, Emily 114
Settle, L. 91
Settle, Leroy B. 199
Settle, Leroy T. 114
Settle, Margery 114
Settle, S. 238
Settle, Strother 89,93,110
Settles, Strother 83
Shaw, Green W. 176
Shelton, James 10,15,59,66, 69,87,96,137,148,158,187, 189,245
Shelton, John 56
Shepherd, David G. 189,259
Shepherd, David L. 190
Shepherd, James M. 154,175, 190,245,267
Shepherd, John 84
Shields, William 188,281
Shines, Daniel Y. 16
Ship, Mecan 161
Shoemake, Jacob M. 9
Shoemake, James 75,152,167
Shoemake, James D. 280,281
Shoemake, Judas 57
Shoemake, Martin 9
Shoemake, Mary 287
Shoemake, Michael 57,62,165, 168,177,207,265,280
Shoemake, Miles W. 280,283, 286

Shoemake, Parker 9
Shoemake, Patrick A. 280
Shoemake, William 22,75,89,154, 169,256,282
Shoemake, William, Jr. 57
Shoemake, William, Sr. 57
Short, A. A. 26,79
Short, Alexander A. 9,12,40,43, 44,86,90
Short, J. B. 7,83
Short, Sally 86
Short, Thomas P. 40
Shoulders, Abner 75,203
Shoulders, Ira 271
Shoulders, James 189
Shoulders, John 165,197,202,205, 236,251,267
Shoulders, Malachi 30,57,184
Shoulders, Richard 191,203
Shoulders, Thomas 252,262,275
Shrum, C. L. 89
Shrum, John 53
Shutt, George H. 93
Shutt, Hannah 93
Shy, Andrew 139,174
Shy, Eli 129,139
Shy, James W. 139,174
Shy, Washington 129
Simmons, Andrew 52
Simmons, Christopher 47,94
Simmons, Edmund 62
Simmons, George P. 253
Simmons, Joel 39,48,49,92,102
Simmons, John 129,199,285
Simmons, Oran J. 165
Simmons, Robert 139
Simmons, Sarah A. 253
Simms, Elijah 3
Simon, David C. 103
Simon, William B. 103
Simon, William G. 103
Simpson, Effey 234
Simpson, John 108,194,234
Simpson, Mary 215
Simpson, Thomas 215
Sims, A. P. 132
Sims, Allen P. 132
Sims, Allen T. 199
Sims, Delana 139
Sims, Elizabeth 199
Sims, James 199
Sims, John 15
Sims, Reuben 17
Sitton, James M. 174

Sitton, Matilda 174
Sitton, William 174
Skelton, Duke 153
Skelton, Lemuel 251,286
Slate, John 24,40
Slate, Samuel, Jr. 23
Slate, Samuel, Sr. 23,24
Slaughter, Samuel G. 230
Slaughter, Thomas 201,216
Slaughter, Thomas J. 147, 277
Slaughter, William H. 224
Slinkard, William 41,157
Sloan, Agnes 93
Sloan, Archibald 56,62,83, 84,93,94,96,110,123,144, 156,162,168
Sloan, Archibald G. 56
Sloan, Edward H. 271
Sloan, Elias 49,56,112,135
Sloan, Elizabeth 84,111,253
Sloan, Elizabeth W. 219
Sloan, Green H. 45,46
Sloan, Hezekiah 5
Sloan, Hugh L. 62,83
Sloan, J. D. 206
Sloan, James D. 83,162
Sloan, Jason R. 84,168, 258,270,274,282,287
Sloan, John 37,60,84,168, 206
Sloan, John A. 56,83,84, 96,110,111,123,144,156, 182,219,235,265,266
Sloan, John L. 62,83,162, 212,271
Sloan, Josiah 84,109,253
Sloan, M. W. 75,78,86, 130,156,160,162,165, 174,226,263
Sloan, Martin W. 29,61,67, 93,94,97,111,123,130, 154,159,160,170,174,182, 194,219,220,253,267
Sloan, Mary 84,168
Sloan, Nancy 110
Sloan, S. A. 263,274,282
Sloan, Sam A. 159
Sloan, Sampson 67,159,258, 282
Sloan, Samuel H. 96
Sloan, William 93,94,214, 256,270
Sloan, William K. 263

Sloan, William R. 274
Slone, Jacob F. 208,210
Smallen, John 128,166,178
Smallen, Solomon 243
Smallin, Solomon 46,158
Smalling, John 150,205
Smalling, Solomon 22,23
Smart, F. M. 244
Smart, John 215,241
Smart, John A. 113,205,239
Smart, Nancy 244
Smart, W. D. 233,236
Smelledge, J. W. 62,161
Smith, Abel 273
Smith, Abner 56
Smith, Alben 228
Smith, Alfred 107
Smith, Alfred D. 178
Smith, Allen 76,91
Smith, Ann S. 45
Smith, B. B. 286
Smith, Benjamin B. 214
Smith, Charles 286
Smith, Charles E. 130
Smith, Charlotte 59,72,85
Smith, D. W. 195
Smith, Daniel 1,3,18,33,81,91, 103,119,173,202,206,233,236, 237,267,284
Smith, Daniel A. 246,247
Smith, David 111,140,157,189, 226,234,246,266
Smith, E. R. 271
Smith, Elijah 140,211
Smith, Fountain 211
Smith, George 139,140
Smith, Gideon 113
Smith, H. M. 211
Smith, Hensley 259
Smith, Isaac 51
Smith, J. B. 200
Smith, J. D. 153
Smith, J. H. 196
Smith, J. R. 126,133,135,136, 153,156
Smith, Jacob 286
Smith, James 45,230
Smith, James A. 262
Smith, James D. 24,45,71,84
Smith, James W. 9,24,151,217
Smith, Jane 81
Smith, Jeremiah 68,153,208,215
Smith, Jesse 62,262
Smith, Jessy 213

Smith, John 49
Smith, John G. 80,161
Smith, John J. 282,287
Smith, John R. 219
Smith, Jonathan 209
Smith, Jonathan H. 242,250, 268
Smith, Josiah R. 141,175
Smith, Larkin 173,187,211
Smith, Laticia 278
Smith, Levi G. 273
Smith, Margret M. 262
Smith, Martha 211
Smith, Martha B. 286
Smith, Martin 211
Smith, Mary 24,62
Smith, Matthew 87,271
Smith, Nancy 211
Smith, Nevels H. 176
Smith, Nicholas 115,116,239
Smith, Philip B. 198,211
Smith, Polly 197
Smith, Prudence 211
Smith, R. E. 271
Smith, Rebecca 176
Smith, Robert 139,195,285
Smith, Roland 197
Smith, Samuel 41
Smith, Sylvey 139
Smith, Thomas 20,37,57,187
Smith, Thomas H. 173
Smith, William 83,91,101, 130
Smith, William A. 214,258
Smith, William B. 230
Smith, William L. 149,246, 262,285,286
Smith, William S. 263
Smith, Winney 139
Smithage, J. W. 28
Smithwick, Humphrey 10,20, 281,286
Smithwick, Samuel 10,12,20
Smithwick, Thomas 120
Snead, John 46
Snead, William 36
Sneed, Jane 72
Sneed, John 72,247,254,266
Sneed, Thomas S. 12
Snider, Abraham 55
Snider, Brice 58
Snider, Julius 100
Snider, Price 98
Snider, William 9,10,11,14, 19,24,58,75,100
Snoddy, Joshua 287
Snoddy, Manerva 169
Snoddy, Thomas 20,122,124,125, 176,212
Snoddy, Thomas, Jr. 274
Snoddy, Thomas, Sr. 254,274,287
Snoddy, William 169,232
Solomon, Elijah 212
Spain, Absolum 266
Spain, James M. 266
Spain, James W. 202
Spears, Edward W. 200
Spears, William 43
Spencer, Henry 1
Spivy, Thomas W. 263
Spooner, Jacob K. 1,9
Spraggins, Leonidas 228
Springer, John 72
Springfield, Fanny 113
Springfield, Moses 113
Spurlock, Drury 3
Squires, John 147,158,187,216
Squires, L. J. 227,254,276
Squires, Levi 187,201,212,213, 217
Squires, Milly 201
Stafford, Adam 86,121,231,269
Stafford, Cain 125,244,247
Stafford, Caleb 250
Stafford, Cane 210
Stafford, Caroline 278
Stafford, John 7,22,39,42,46,81, 110,113,114,132,147,177,190, 194
Stafford, John, Sr. 40
Stafford, Stephen 30,46,125,144, 161,174,191
Stafford, Thomas 35,64,86
Stafford, William 177
Stalcup, George W. 73,78
Stalcup, William 37,186,198
Stalcup, William, Jr. 222
Stallings, H. H. 193
Stallings, John 10,90
Stamps, Mary 23
Stamps, Nathan 22,23
Standfield, Ashley 215,223
Standford, David H. 238
Stanford, D. 256
Stanford, David 4,15,172,205,283
Stanford, William 205
Stanford, William J. 172
Stanley, William 8

Stans, Charles 248
Stans, Henry 248
Stark, William 217
Starnes, Frederick 189, 262,274
Starnes, John 274
Starnes, Polly 189
Stell, James P. 274
Stephen, Valvery S. 259
Stephens, George 234
Stephens, H. L. 116
Stephens, Jane 3
Stephens, John 204
Stephens, Samuel 37,107
Stephenson, Delia 247
Stephenson, James W. 225
Stepp, Colly 184
Stepp, James W. 181
Stept, Joseph 32
Stevens, George 18,39,51
Stevens, James 171
Stevens, John 5,12,51,63, 67,124,136,164,171,174, 209,227
Stevenson, Delia 224,238
Stevenson, Joseph W. 238
Stevenson, Josiah 224
Steward, Elisha 23
Stewart, Donelson 130
Stewart, Edward 140
Stewart, James H. 276
Stewart, John 178
Stewart, Jordan 114,159
Stewart, Murdock 43
Stewart, Thomas 247
Stimson, Alexander W. 176
Stinson, Lawson 13
Stoke, Samuel 59
Stokes, J. T. 188
Stokes, John 104
Stokes, John T. 77,107,117, 152,167,245
Stokes, Jordan 97,162,214
Stokes, Jordan G. 24
Stokes, Sylvanus 24
Stokes, Thomas 24,32,126
Stokes, William 24
Stokes, William B. 77,107
Stone, Richard 12
Stone, Stephen 124
Stott, John S. 164
Stott, Rawleigh 164
Stott, Rawlings 219
Stoval, Peter 72

Stoval, Thomas 275
Stovall, Thomas T. 206
Strador, Lewis 123
Stratton, Amanda 43
Stratton, James 43
Stratton, Lewis 38
Stratton, Lucy J. 43
Stratton, Peter 43
Stratton, Robert 43
Stratton, Thomas J. 43,166,217, 283
Street, John 85
Strother, Henry 178,235,269
Strother, Judd 139,153,198
Strother, Thomas 239
Strother, William 68,122,173, 215,246
Stuart, Dallison 219
Stuart, Donalson 218
Stuart, James W. 286
Stuart, John 217,261
Stubblefield, Alexander 77,265
Stubblefield, Fleming 69,80,100, 183,186,188,201,208,221
Stubblefield, George 77
Stubblefield, John 99,172,201, 216,227
Stump, John 48
Stump, Nancy 48
Suit, D. H. 260,261
Suit, John 83
Suit, W. N. 260,261
Sulivant, Ira L. 35
Sulivant, Jordan 35
Sullivan, Abel J. 235
Sullivan, Ann 89,154,194,206, 232,276
Sullivan, Aram W. 108
Sullivan, B. B. 17,232,240
Sullivan, Daniel 75,94,108
Sullivan, Editha A. 194
Sullivan, H. H. 241
Sullivan, H. N. 280
Sullivan, Harbert 194,240
Sullivan, Halbert H. 276
Sullivan, Harris 194
Sullivan, Horace 232
Sullivan, Horace N. 230,243
Sullivan, Ira L. 62,91
Sullivan, Ira S. 107
Sullivan, Jourdan 62
Sullivan, June 194
Sullivan, Lucian B. 148,194,230, 232,243

Sullivan, Mary A. 194
Sullivan, Robert H. 232
Sullivan, Samuel 264
Sullivan, William 17,94,194
Sullivan, William D. 232, 241
Summersett, Harriet 52,240
Summersett, Joseph 40,41, 52,98,115,210,214,240
Summersett, William 30,179
Summersett, William W. 52
Sutton, George 12,77,78, 92,156
Sutton, James 53,78,88,156
Sutton, James T. 258,263
Sutton, Leroy 12,77
Swan, George L. 174
Swan, Isaac 252
Swan, James G. 174
Swan, Phillip 193,202
Sweatt, Edward 9
Sweatt, Edward C. 184
Sweatt, Sarah A. 184
Swindell, William H. 131
Sykes, Joshua 81,98,136
Sykes, Leodicia 174
Sykes, Leodicy 141
Sykes, Major L. 28,146
Sypert, Lawrence 160
Sypert, Stephen 50
Taite, Robert A. 109
Talbot, John 243
Talbot, Lucy 243
Talley, Benjamin 99
Talley, Ephraim 115
Tally, Benjamin 21
Tally, Charles N. 21
Tally, James 21
Tally, John F. 21
Tally, Leodosha 21
Tally, Patsy 2
Tarver, Benjamin 52
Tarver, Nancy 264
Tary, George 39
Tate, C. S. 276,284
Tate, Charles 162
Tate, Charles S. 186,242
Tate, Eliza 162
Tate, George W. 20,73
Tate, James 223
Tate, John 48,83,223
Tate, John V. 155
Tate, Robert 93
Tate, Robert A. 108
Tate, William D. 242
Taylor, A. L. 210
Taylor, A. P. 193,266
Taylor, Archibald 201
Taylor, Brazilla 92
Taylor, Brice M. 221
Taylor, Daniel 245,261
Taylor, Daniel L. 3,39
Taylor, David 116
Taylor, Endyman 4
Taylor, Ezekiel W. 61
Taylor, Henry M. 239
Taylor, Hezekiah 114,193,200
Taylor, James 11,65,184,210,242
Taylor, James A. 11,28
Taylor, James M. 229
Taylor, James W. 221
Taylor, John W. 200,201
Taylor, Joseph 92
Taylor, Joseph J. 210
Taylor, Mary 92
Taylor, Matilda 278
Taylor, Mildred 65
Taylor, Nancy 92
Taylor, Robert 210
Taylor, Robert L. 3,4,8,38,39, 56,68
Taylor, Tabitha 221
Taylor, Thomas 43,111
Taylor, Thomas E. 250
Taylor, Wildridge 140
Taylor, William 54,147,278
Taylor, William B. 68,103,130, 132,173,236
Taylor, William C. 65,140
Taylor, William R. 270
Teague, Dabney 46
Teague, Edmond 40
Teague, Edmund 46
Teague, Mary 46
Teague, Raleigh 46
Teague, Ridley R. 251
Telford, John 40
Temple, Daniel 263
Temple, Milly 263
Terry, G. W. 79
Terry, George W. 101,114
Terry, James 80,100
Terry, Kitty A. 270
Terry, Mary 270
Terry, Nathaniel 63,66,211,215
Terry, Sarah G. 271
Terry, Thomas 186
Terry, Thomas T. 186

Terry, William 270
Thackston, Blake B. 154, 169,271
Thackston, James 154
Thackston, Zadock B. 6
Thaxton, Blake B. 19,20, 282
Thaxton, James 45
Thaxton, Polly 24
Thomas, B. E. 261
Thomas, C. T. 71,85,105, 115,118,150
Thomas, Champion T. 26,65, 73,86
Thomas, Chesley B. 36
Thomas, D. W. 230
Thomas, Diggs W. 247
Thomas, Ferdinand 33
Thomas, Ferdinand P. 33
Thomas, Higgs W. 235
Thomas, James 86,122
Thomas, James A. 150,252, 282
Thomas, James M. 250,268
Thomas, Jefferson 11
Thomas, Joseph 114
Thomas, Nancy 239
Thomas, Wiley 274
Thomas, William 13,15,114, 137,144,162,196,237,267
Thomas, William T. 268
Thomason, Benjamin 12
Thomason, Catherine 139, 276
Thomason, David 8,65
Thomason, George 45,139, 276
Thomason, Mary A. 280
Thomason, P. A. 280
Thomason, Peter 41
Thomason, Pleasant 8
Thomason, Samuel 11,32
Thompson, Archibald 8,21, 144
Thompson, Charles 56,80, 83,92,143,149,189,197
Thompson, E. R. 250
Thompson, Elizabeth 8,21
Thompson, George 69,239
Thompson, Harriet 197
Thompson, James L. 258,283
Thompson, James S. 239
Thompson, Lawrence 7,8,18, 19,21,121,269,273,276

Thompson, Margaret 197
Thompson, Randel 82
Thompson, Ragen 82
Thompson, Regen 123
Thompson, Regin 30
Thompson, Resin 98
Thompson, Rezen 93,172
Thompson, Richard 82
Thompson, Rizen 219
Thompson, Robert 60
Thompson, Susan 56
Thompson, Swan 9,80,178,225,239
Thompson, Tabitha 258
Thompson, V. R. 129
Thompson, Vincent 197,235,244, 282
Thompson, William 68,82
Thorn, Augustine 160,238
Thornton, John 164
Thornton, Nelson 4,43,61,65,259
Thurman, Graves 12
Thurman, Nathaniel 94
Tibbs, John 4
Tillman, Larena 180
Tillman, William 179,180
Tilston, Lemuel 45
Timberlake, Adkin M. 213,287
Timberlake, D. K. 108,143,195, 234,278
Timberlake, David K. 25,95,106, 217
Timberlake, Elizabeth 152
Timberlake, David K. 185,205,237
Timberlake, James, Sr. 169
Timberlake, Jehu 122,123,148,152
Timberlake, John 95,130,233
Tinis, Ameliza 180
Tinis, J. B. 285
Tinis, John B. 180
Tinsley, Charlotte 233
Tinsley, Isaac 233
Tinsley, Samuel B. 191
Tipton, Mary 191
Tiree, Ann E. 180
Tiree, John 180
Toler, Henderson 33
Tolliver, Zachariah 90,104
Tomkins, J. R. 170
Tomkins, Mary 170
Toney, Elijah 18,39,43,49,93,115, 116,149,187,283
Toney, Elizabeth A. 96
Toney, Eveline 237
Toney, James R. 56,63,65,76,85,

86,92,96,98,115,120,133,
134,139,148,150,154,167,
169,185,191,192,270
Toney, John A. 96,115,157,
160,167,206
Tooley, Henry 198
Towler, Joel 11
Townsend, Joseph 72
Townsend, Mary 72
Towson, Jacob 52,201,210,
227,265
Towson, William 23
Towson, William C. 2,79,156
Tramel, Joshua 14
Trawick, Robert 77,185
Traywell, Henry 232
Traywick, Robert 114,139
Trigg, John H. 1,5
Trousdale, Ira 265
Trousdale, James 128,131,
148,152,183,185,265
Trousdale, John 83,106,108,
109,110,111,112,117,119,
124,126,130,137,139,148,
149,156,195,203,230,261
Trousdale, John, Jr. 33
Trousdale, John, Sr. 33
Trousdale, Martha 33
Trousdale, Nancy 33
Trousdale, Polly 152
Trousdale, Polly A. 186
Trousdale, William 152
Trousdale, William C. 148,
150
Tubb, A. 83
Tubb, Abraham 25,39
Tubb, Benjamin 80
Tubb, Benson 80
Tubb, Brien 55
Tubb, Elizabeth 80
Tubb, Frederick J. 271
Tubb, George 80
Tubb, Isaac 119
Tubb, James 25,67,69,83,
93,184
Tubb, Jephtha 80
Tubb, John 80,186
Tubb, John L. 271
Tubb, Malinda 108
Tubb, Mary 25
Tubb, Samuel 69
Tubb, William 67,80,271
Tubb, William L. 25
Tubbs, Abraham 18

Tuck, Edward B. 169,182,208
Tuck, John C. 67,95
Tuck, Philip H. 169
Tuck, Powell 81,97,107,134
Tucker, Jesse C. 226
Tucker, John 226
Tucker, Wesley W. 95
Tucker, William H. 231
Tuggle, H. B. 209
Tuggle, Henry 209
Tuggle, James 185,245
Tuggle, John H. 184
Tuggle, Martha J. 233
Tuggle, Thomas 184,201,233
Tuggle, William B. 239
Tunstal, Matthew J. 15
Tunstall, Charles 167,283
Tunstall, Charles H. 55,210,257
Tunstall, James 278
Tunstall, John 239
Tunstall, John M. 50
Tunstall, Martha 268
Tunstall, Matthew 8,13,18,165
Tunstall, Matthew J. 17
Tunstall, Thomas 124,126,128,
130,150,167,189,278
Tunstall, W. 205
Tunstall, William 52,184,188,189,
245,271
Turner, Benjamin 5,60
Turner, Berryman 68,117,147
Turner, Betsy 68
Turner, David 66,102
Turner, Elizabeth 193
Turner, Ely 152
Turner, Harriet T. 155,182
Turner, Henry 25
Turner, Hezekiah 58
Turner, James 199,286
Turner, John 5,59,68,121,170,178,
193,281
Turner, John J. 178
Turner, John L. 15
Turner, John S. 94
Turner, Jonas 148,166
Turner, Lewis 15,35
Turner, Nancy 68
Turner, Pleasant 193
Turner, Polly 68
Turner, Reuben 4,123,193
Turner, Robert 5,68
Turner, Robert B. 155
Turner, Robert H. 148
Turner, Samuel L. 15

Turner, Samuel S. 102
Turner, Sarah 193
Turner, Susannah 68
Turner, Talifero 138
Turner, Valerious 155
Turner, Vallirus B. 148
Turner, William 155,192
Turner, William B. 148,155, 193
Turner, William D. 21,38, 47,62,124,136,148,159
Turner, Wilson 26,172,240
Turney, Lemuel 3
Tyre, David A. 264
Tyree, D. A. 244
Tyree, David 48,101,103, 132,174
Tyree, David A. 157,177
Tyree, Elizabeth 174
Tyree, Sarah 174
Tyree, William 174
Tyree, William H. 250,268
Uhles, B. B. 85,87,251,261, 285
Uhles, Bartlett B. 87,88
Uhles, Frederick 73,133
Uhles, James 73,177,189
Uhles, Mary 239
Uhles, William 208
Uhls, B. B. 208
Uhls, Bartlett B. 7,29,42, 62
Uhls, Frederick 9,11,14
Uhls, Frederick J. 91,107
Uhls, Frederick, Sr. 117
Uhls, Frederick, T., Jr. 14
Uhls, Jacob 19,25,38
Uhls, James 8,56
Uhls, John B. 6,14,61
Uhls, M. L. 252
Uhls, Mary A. 208
Uhls, Michael 13,28
Uhls, Michael L. 7,52
Uhls, Nancy 97
Uhls, Richard 39,117
Uhls, William 3,11,15,264, 266,274
Underwood, Barton 267
Underwood, Burton 20
Underwood, Jackey A. 228
Underwood, Johnson 188,190, 260,264,267,279,282
Upton, Edward 141,158
Upton, James 185

Upton, Nancy 49,61,195,216,243
Vaden, B. J. 147,174,196,197, 266
Vaden, Benjamin 145,152
Vaden, Benjamin J. 53,65,117, 163,168,248,256,264
Vaden, James 23
Vaden, James H. 30,33,51,53,65, 120
Vaden, John 145,162
Vaden, John D. 163
Vaden, Loderick 97,99,132,143, 156,271
Vaden, Loderick, Sr. 153
Vaden, Lodwick 86
Vaden, Samuel 153,232
Vaden, Samuel T. 279
Vaden, William 59,60,176,186,236
Vance, James M. 241,248
Vance, John F. 130,248
Vance, John M. 241,248
Vance, Joseph 73
Vance, Lewis 204
Vance, Lewis R. 270
Vance, Margret 270
Vance, Matilda 241,248
Vance, Ramsey 173,241,259,265
Vandepool, Joseph 108
Vanderpool, John A. 93
Vanderpool, Joseph 129
Vantrease, A. J. 239
Vantrease, Andrew 197,229
Vantrease, Nicholas 200,206
Vaughan, Daniel 139
Vaughan, James H. 178,179,223
Vaughan, William 137
Vaughn, James H. 8,164
Vaughn, John S. 4
Vaughn, P. 65
Vaughn, Polly 70
Vaughn, William B. 137
Vincent, Elizabeth 138
Vincent, William 138
Violet, Trayley N. 274
Violet, Troylus 162
Wade, A. J. 115
Wade, P. M. 13,101
Wade, W. W. 32
Wade, Walker 41,55
Wade, William 12
Wadmore, James 8,41
Waggoner, Darrell 239
Waggoner, George 12,52,157,169, 239,261

Waggoner, Jacob 52,60,126,
    169,239,248
Waggoner, John 239
Waggoner, Nicholas 2,29,
    41,76,78,239
Waggoner, William 239
Wakefield, Booker 123,164
Wakefield, Henry, Jr. 97
Wakefield, Henry, Sr. 97
Wakefield, Lucy 286
Wakefield, Manerva 123
Wakefield, William 112
Waldon, Fielden 2,3
Waldon, Yancy 282
Waldrong, Jesse 61
Walker, Amanda 16
Walker, Denaris 115
Walker, Elijah 60
Walker, Elisha 10,80
Walker, Elizabeth 222
Walker, Frances 115
Walker, George 73,109,129,
    144,252,276
Walker, George W. 22,30,
    70,73,115,168,169,226
Walker, James 59
Walker, James R. 157
Walker, John 137,156,157,
    165,175
Walker, Mason 111,138,190,
    211,222
Walker, Nathaniel 21
Walker, Paul 262
Walker, Paul H. 209
Walker, Paul L. 197,242
Walker, Paul S. 174
Walker, Pleasant M. 36,39
Walker, Prudence 165,175
Walker, Samuel 9,55
Walker, Thomas 2,4,36,42,
    43
Walker, W. E. 16
Walker, W. Y. 256
Walker, Warren 191,276
Walker, William 22,60
Walker, Wilson 22,60
Walker, Wilson Y. 115
Wallace, Jackson 259
Wallace, James 171,221
Wallace, James R. 267
Wallace, Jefferson 29
Wallace, John 221
Wallace, Mary 221
Wallace, Nancy 259

Wallace, Robert 221
Wallace, Sarah 67
Wallace, Wade H. 65,67,217
Wallace, William C. 72
Wallas, Andrew 51
Wallis, Andrew 28,69
Wallis, Andrew W. 55
Wallis, Jackson 202
Wallis, Sarah 9,10
Wallis, Thomas M. 71,72
Wallis, William C. 72,111
Walton, Edward 48
Walton, George 48
Walton, James 5,11,50,55,83,84,
    85,92,96,204
Walton, Jesse 116
Walton, John 70
Walton, Timothy 5,11,32,44,52,
    84,85,87,92,141,149,150,159,
    160,170,187,204,249
Walton, Timothy, Jr. 18,125,149
Walton, Timothy, Sr. 149,158,167
Walton, William 85
Wamack, David F. 275
Wamack, James 65
Wammack, Alfred 208
Wammack, James 23,112,273,277
Ward, A. 36
Ward, A. M. 230,258
Ward, Aven 61
Ward, Avin 65,69,81,105,113,167,
    169,259
Ward, B. C. 258
Ward, Benjamin H. 129,130
Ward, Bryan 48,261
Ward, D. C. 10,13,19,22,23,30,
    32,49,171,194
Ward, David C. 92,93,123
Ward, Dicken 109
Ward, Dicking 1,36
Ward, Henry 48
Ward, Holly 270
Ward, John 105
Ward, M. G. 85
Ward, Martha 208
Ward, Mary B. 240,258
Ward, Mathew H. 189,227,254,276
Ward, Matthew 87
Ward, Meredith G. 196,223
Ward, N. 98,151,157,169,196
Ward, Nathan 99,134,140,167,169,
    190,208,213,226,228,234
Ward, S. 113
Ward, Sterling 151

Ward, W. 259
Ward, W. W. 283
Ward, William W. 281
Warder, Eveline 279
Warder, John E. 279
Wardrope, Reece 119,130
Wardrup, Reece 148
Warf, James F. 152,270
Warford, David 250
Warren, B. E. 40,58,251,
   252,261
Warren, Charlotte 78
Warren, Eth 84
Warren, Etheldred 53,92
Warren, John 53,85,98
Warren, John E. 53,92,98
Warren, Priscilla 81,275
Warren, Robert 81,85,97,
   192,215,235,240,271,274,
   282,286
Washburn, James W. 286
Washburn, W. W. 212
Washburn, William 205
Washer, Asa 202
Washer, Charles 198
Washer, John 210,250
Washer, Thomas 184
Washer, William 184
Waters, Mortimer 109
Waters, Mortimore 22,31,54
Waters, William 23,40,65,
   142
Watkins, Allen 217
Watkins, Allen S. 187
Watkins, N. W. 21
Watson, Cyrus 40,149,164,
   177
Watson, Joseph 50
Watson, Samuel 208
Watson, Thomas 209
Watts, John B. 145
Waugh, James W. 61
Waymouth, Joseph B. 187
Weatherford, Joel M. 242
Weatherford, Matilda 224
Weatherford, Thomas 9,114,
   185,224
Weaver, Joseph 89,104
Webb, Isaac 247
Webb, Jane 199
Webb, John 281,282
Webb, Mary 282
Webb, Ross 186,201,210
Webster, Peter 95

Weeks, Edith 42
West, Berry 41,109,208,214
West, C. W. 268
West, Claborn W. 286
West, Clabourn W. 227
West, Claiborn 214
West, Drewry A. 191,208,214,227,
   233
West, Drury A. 193
West, Edward 214
West, Ezekiel 57,190,214
West, Harrison 278
West, J. 268
West, James 176,214
West, Jesse 91
West, John 128
West, Margaret 91
West, Mary 68
West, Miles 21,46,101,111,133,
   134,156,193,214,244
West, Miles F. 176,227,231,242
West, Miles, Sr. 129
West, Patsy 59,72,85
West, Ridley R. 227,242,286
West, Robert 46,82,164,176,214,
   234
West, William 55,109,141,146,
   196,214
Wetherford, William B. 120
Wever, Walter 116
Whaley, Thomas 9
Wheeler, Elijah 13,51,274
Wheeler, James 121
Wheeler, James E. 53
Wheeler, John 50
Wheeler, Turman 36,51,121,132
Wheeler, Turner 81
White, Charles J. 50,85
White, David 265
White, Edward A. 71
White, George 14,65,68,102
White, Hiram 161
White, Hiram T. 185
White, Isaiah 201
White, Jacen 154
White, Jacob 129,162,197,219,
   235,269
White, James 110
White, Jesse 56,177
White, John 76,101,102,103
White, L. W. 71
White, Mary 161
White, Sam 161
White, Samuel T. 185

White, Uriah 99,101,102
White, Wiley 269
White, William 96
Whitesides, A. P. 281
Whitley, Elizabeth 249
Whitley, Excum 67
Whitley, Exum 97,167
Whitley, Jane 199
Whitley, Josiah 1,112,280
Whitley, Lacy 249
Whitley, Lucy 112
Whitley, Mahaley 249
Whitley, Taylor 34,36,140, 180
Whitley, Temperance 249
Whitley, W. B. 199
Whitley, Wiley 199
Whitley, William B. 43,151, 152,157,167,185,187,211, 218,220,241
Whitley, Willis 157
Whitlock, George 81,222, 231,254
Whitlock, Jeremiah 82
Whitlock, Sterling 33
Whitmore, Edwin 191
Whitson, James 24
Whitten, Martin 93,135, 139,197,222,224,246
Whitten, Robert 226
Wilborn, Thomas 106
Wilborn, Thomas, Sr. 106
Wilbourn, Benjamin 2,243
Wilbourn, Evans S. 32
Wilbourn, Gunnery 50,177
Wilbourn, John H. 2
Wilbourn, Lucy 122
Wilbourn, R. S. 122
Wilbourn, Thomas 50,121, 126,127
Wilburn, Evan S. 21
Wilburn, Thomas 21,91
Wilburn, William L. 71
Wilcott, John 156
Wilcut, John 186
Wildman, Jonah 75,79
Wildman, Josiah 70
Wiley, James 249
Wilkerson, Archibald F. 262
Wilkerson, Daniel 2,59,67, 197,220
Wilkerson, John M. 149
Wilkerson, Peter A. 20,81, 82,122,193,220

Wilkerson, Turner L. 22
Wilkinson, John M. 73
Wilkinson, Peter A. 53,72,73, 134,144
Wilkinson, Rachel 52
Wilkner, Alfred M. 172
Wilks, Martha 72
Wilks, Richard S. 72
Willeby, Isaac 32,118
Willeford, Hardy 92
Willeford, Jeremiah 97
Willeford, Nancy 92
Willeford, William 97
Williams, A. D. 55
Williams, Abel W. 233
Williams, Agnes 184,269
Williams, Alfred W. 279
Williams, Anderson 183,277
Williams, Andrew 34,284
Williams, Benjamin 236
Williams, Burton 201
Williams, C. J. 274
Williams, Charles 117,126
Williams, Charles E. 127,213
Williams, Elijah 12,57,79
Williams, Elizabeth 94,214,261
Williams, Evan 11,54
Williams, Evan J. 280
Williams, Evin J. 249,250,258, 287
Williams, George N. 198,208, 244,246
Williams, George W. 119
Williams, Giles 60,61,201,261
Williams, Harriet 249,280
Williams, Henderson P. 259,273
Williams, Henry 6,246,250,257
Williams, James 43,263,284
Williams, James C. 37,49,54,62, 77,112,123,134,164,183,231, 245,246,285
Williams, James M. 132,175,201
Williams, John 9,18,120,137,138, 172,178,200
Williams, Lewis 196
Williams, Louisa 267
Williams, Lucy 201
Williams, Mahulda 225,273
Williams, Mary C. 208
Williams, Matilda 82
Williams, Meddy 284
Williams, Nathaniel 117,126,127
Williams, Nathaniel A. 213
Williams, Nathaniel W. 228

Williams, O. J. 268
Williams, Patsy 216
Williams, Peter 82
Williams, Richard 17,71,124
Williams, Robert 2,139,155,
 166,167,168
Williams, Robert R. 275,279
Williams, Samuel 129
Williams, Samuel P. 106,220
Williams, Sarah 110,154,155
Williams, Sarah J. 160
Williams, Solomon 225,273
Williams, Thomas 82,89,106,
 151,160,181,191,216,230,
 236
Williams, Thomas P. 201
Williams, Timothy H. 226,
 263,273,281
Williams, W. T. 214
Williams, William 32,50
Williams, William B. 233
Williams, William F. 97
Williams, William M. 147
Williams, William T. 79,87,
 130,186,190
Williamson, Evan J. 150
Williamson, James 73
Williamson, Lidia 99
Williamson, Martin 74,91,
 151,166
Williamson, Thomas 99
Williaz, Margaret 3
Williaz, William 3
Williby, Andrew 251,267
Williford, Hardy 38
Willingham, Isaac 55,60
Willingham, Nancy 55,60
Willingson, James F. 270
Willis, Ann 112
Willis, Edward R. 235
Willis, Elizabeth 112
Willis, John 112
Willis, John A. 112
Willis, Stephen R. 183
Willis, William 30,151
Willis, William S. 32,50,
 122
Willman, Brantley 48
Willmore, Brantley 48
Wills, E. R. 234
Wills, Edward R. 177,262
Wills, James 262
Wills, Stephen R. 142,177,
 262

Wills, W. W. 234
Wills, William W. 262
Wilmore, Henry 249,275
Wilmot, John F. 56,85
Wilson, Allen G. 142
Wilson, Caleb 38,44
Wilson, Claborn 7
Wilson, Clabourn 44,60
Wilson, Clabran 130
Wilson, Edmon 278
Wilson, Edmund 287
Wilson, Edward 274
Wilson, Elijah 50,61
Wilson, Emsley 42
Wilson, Ewing 13
Wilson, George 106
Wilson, Harvey D. 236,257,274,
 277
Wilson, Henry D. 227,256
Wilson, James 47
Wilson, James H. 60,61,152
Wilson, James L. 13
Wilson, James P. 245
Wilson, John 6,14,19,38,40,44,
 112
Wilson, Joseph L. 13
Wilson, Joshua 287
Wilson, Margaret 13
Wilson, Mariah 246
Wilson, Mary G. 106
Wilson, Matilda 106
Wilson, S. G. 88
Wilson, Samuel H. 44,61
Wilson, Sarah G. 106
Wilson, Wallace 106
Wilson, Wallace G. 88
Wilson, William 44,112,185
Wilson, William G. 88
Wilson, Willis 185,278
Winchester, Andrew 209
Winchester, Jason 187,204,251
Winchester, Joseph 196
Winchester, William 204,255,271,
 274
Winfree, Allen C. 112,181
Winfree, Benjamin 181,182
Winfree, John T. 78
Winfrey, David F. 95,96
Winfrey, David T. 51,170
Winfrey, James 18
Winfrey, James M. 101,135,190
Winfrey, John T. 187
Wing, Alfred 113
Winkler, Alfred 229

Winkler, Alfred M. 15,66,
  110,134,240,261,281
Winkler, Arthur 254
Winkler, Ephraim 254
Winkler, John S. 254,281
Winkler, Levi C. 247
Winkler, Samuel 49,56
Winn, J. 72
Winn, James A. 215
Winn, Peter 72
Winn, Richard 72
Winn, Willis H. 72
Winston, N. C. 141,185
Winston, Nel 43
Winter, Sarah 16
Winter, Thack 16
Wiseman, Isaac 13,31,36,
  47,70
Wiseman, Peachy 31,70
Witcher, Daniel K. 27,59
Witcher, James 67
Withrow, Hampton T. 172
Witt, Dandridge A. 246
Wofford, Bartlett 198
Wofford, David 198
Wofford, Elijah 198
Wofford, Jane 198
Wofford, M. 198
Wofford, M. C. 198
Wofford, Mary 198
Wofford, Samuel 198
Wolf, James 224
Wood, Elihu 4,69,211
Wood, Elisha 211
Wood, Frances 195
Wood, George 234
Wood, James 90
Wood, Jefferson 160
Wood, Josiah 70,132
Wood, Martha 207
Wood, Mary H. 80,81,89
Wood, Patience 70,80,89,
  132
Wood, Sampson 212
Wood, Sarah 284
Wood, Selva 211
Wood, William 31,73,105,
  212
Woodcock, G. B. 106
Woodcock, Joseph 51
Woodcock, Mark 27
Woodcock, Mary 237
Woodcock, Wiley 77
Woodman, Willis 244

Woodmore, James 41,210
Woodmore, John 209
Woodmore, M. S. 276
Woodmore, Moses S. 41,209,210,
  264
Woodmore, Thomas 180,181,193,285
Woodridge, Kiziah 60
Woodruff, Moses 191
Woods, Anderson 261
Woods, Green 258
Woods, Harriet 258
Woods, Lucy A. 258
Woods, Nancy 258
Woods, Sarah E. 258
Woods, Squire 214
Woodson, John 264
Woodson, Obediah 152,237
Woodson, Obediah, Sr. 178
Woodson, Polly 42
Woodson, Thomas 178,226
Woodson, Tucker 42,218,219,263
Woolard, Wesly 209
Woolridge, Henry W. 90
Wooten, Benjamin 273
Wooten, James 19,30,63,69
Wooten, John 268
Wooten, Joseph 30
Wooten, Martha 268
Wooten, Thomas 109,280
Wooten, Thomas W. 104,211,216,
  248
Wooten, William 109
Wootten, James 6,7
Wootten, Joseph 6
Wootten, Thomas W. 26,28,144,
  157,158,178,229
Wootten, William 35
Worley, Elisha 63
Worley, Huldah 221,225,231
Worley, Joel 112,173
Worley, Joel L. 178
Worley, Mathew 225,231
Worley, Matthew 191,221
Worley, William 173
Worley, Zachariah 173,191,226
Worsham, Littleberry 146
Worsham, Robert 54
Worthy, A. 6
Wray, Gideon B. 170,183,209
Wright, E. A. 117,133,170
Wright, Ebenezer 101
Wright, Elijah A. 125,126,133,
  153
Wright, George 114,215

Wright, George T. 32,67,
 78,113,164,199,215
Wright, Green 16,35,58,
 179,207,231,256,281
Wright, Hubbard 29,69,115,
 197
Wright, James 196
Wright, Olivia 101
Wright, R. C. 215
Wright, Robert G. 62
Wright, Romulus 245
Wright, Romulus C. 279
Wyatt, Ezekiel 214
Wyatt, James G. 248
Wyatt, Sally 239
Wyatt, Solomon 239
Wyett, Frederick 188
Wyett, James 188
Wyett, James G. 264
Wynn, Peter 3
Yeargin, James 9
Yerger, Jacob 30
Yerger, Jacob S. 4
York, Custes W. 91
Young, A. D. 86
Young, A. L. 35
Young, Alanson 39
Young, Alonzo D. 86
Young, Haley 88
Young, Henry A. 35,64
Young, Jacob 9,10
Young, James 15,33,70,75,
 100,105,136,160,226,238,
 245,277,281
Young, James A. 188
Young, James H. 245
Young, Manson 25,39,99,
 100,207
Young, Oliver F. 237,245,
 281
Young, Patsy 35,86
Young, Sally 243
Young, T. L. 35
Young, Thomas 8
Young, W. B. 203
Young, Will 184
Young, William 6,12,27,84,
 94,104,108,138,150,152,
 166,179,193,195,198,199,
 210,219,227,233,237,244,
 251,270
Young, William B. 74,78,
 106,107,110,127,128,129,
130,131,137,140,189,199,279
Young, William M. 163
Zachary, Mary 76

MISCELLANEOUS INDEX

Bank of Tennessee 163,169,170,173,234
Barnet's Campground 80
Carthage Female Academy 225
Carthage Methodist Church 87
Defeated Creek Meeting House 49
Defeated Creek School House 49
Fifteenth District School 261
Hurricane Creek Campground 168
Hurricane Creek Methodist Church 165
Phillipi School House 247
Rome Methodist Church 254
Salem Cumberland Presbyterian Church 8
Second District Meeting House 250
Snow Creek Methodist Church 217

www.ingramcontent.com/pod-product-compliance
Lightning Source LLC
Chambersburg PA
CBHW020638300426
44112CB00007B/157